LITTLE, BROWN

LB

LARGE PRINT

For a preview of upcoming books and information about the author, visit JamesPatterson.com or find him on Facebook, Twitter, or Instagram.

THE
LAST DAYS
OF
JOHN LENNON

JAMES PATTERSON
WITH CASEY SHERMAN
AND DAVE WEDGE

(L)(B) LITTLE, BROWN AND COMPANY

LARGE PRINT EDITION

Little, Brown and Company
Hachette Book Group
1290 Avenue of the Americas, New York, NY 10104
littlebrown.com

First edition: December 2020

Little, Brown and Company is a division of Hachette Book Group, Inc. The Little, Brown name and logo are trademarks of Hachette Book Group, Inc.

The publisher is not responsible for websites (or their content) that are not owned by the publisher.

The Hachette Speakers Bureau provides a wide range of authors for speaking events. To find out more, go to hachettespeakersbureau.com or call (866) 376-6591.

ISBN 978-0-316-42906-1 (hc) / 978-0-316-42913-9 (large print)
Library of Congress Control Number: 2020945289

1 2020

LSC-C

Printed in the United States of America

On June 1, 1969, John Lennon gathered with some friends at a hotel in Toronto to record a song called "Give Peace a Chance."
"Sing along," he told the members of the chorus as he launched into the opening line, "Everybody's talking about..."
To this day, people are still talking—and singing—about John.
Thank you for your words...

Harry Benson
David Bowie
Bob Dylan
Dr. David Halleran
Mick Jagger
Billy Joel
Elton John
Ken Mansfield
Paul McCartney
Keith Richards
Geraldo Rivera

PROLOGUE

December 6, 1980

He sits in the airplane, inside a cloud of cigarette smoke. He opens his wallet and looks at the permit for his handgun. He was going to buy a .22 when the salesman steered him toward a .38.

Well, if you get a .22 and a burglar comes in, he's just going to laugh at you, the salesman said. *But if you have a .38 nobody's going to laugh at you. Just one shot with a .38 and you're going to bring him down.*

The safest way to transport the weapon, the Federal Aviation Administration told him over the phone, was to pack it, along with the ammo, inside a suitcase—which he did. The gun was purchased legally—personal protection, he told the salesman—in Hawaii.

The ammo is another matter. Hollow-points are

illegal in New York. If security decides to search his bag, he could be arrested.

It'll be fine, he keeps telling himself as he exits the plane. The biggest threat these days is skyjacking. He doesn't look like a terrorist.

He stands at the carousel inside LaGuardia, keeping an eye out for his bag while covertly watching the security people from behind the reddish-brown tinted lenses of his aviator-style eyeglasses.

No one is paying attention to him—a good sign. He picks up his suitcase.

No one comes running for him.

He heads for the exit.

No one comes looking for him.

The people he passes—business travelers and those who have come to the Big Apple to enjoy a few days of Christmas shopping—don't even acknowledge his presence. No eye contact, not a nod hello, nothing.

It's like I'm invisible.

And in a way, he is. He's been invisible his whole life. He's not remarkable in any way, which gives him a distinct tactical advantage. He can blend in anywhere, and he doesn't look threatening.

And I have to stay that way. I have to appear normal at all times.

Which means staying out of his head as much as possible.

His mind is a dangerous neighborhood.

He steps outside the airport, into the bright sunshine. The air is unseasonably warm. He drops his suitcase at the curb and, sweating and out of breath, hails a cab, his thoughts turning to the five bullets packed next to his gun. The FAA also told him that changes in air pressure could damage them.

He only needs one of them to work.

The five hollow-point Smith & Wesson +P cartridges are designed for maximum stopping power—and maximum damage. When one hits soft tissue, the tip mushrooms into a lethal miniature buzz saw that spins and bounces its way through the body, shredding tissue and organs.

One shot is more than enough to ensure John Lennon's death.

A yellow cab slides up next to him. He puts his suitcase in the trunk, then gets into the back seat. He gives the driver the address for the West Side YMCA, off Central Park West. It's only nine blocks away from his true destination.

He puts on his best smile and tells the cabbie, "I'm a recording engineer."

The taxi pulls away from the curb.

"I'm working with John Lennon and Paul McCartney."

The cabbie ignores him.

He glares at the back of the man's head. *If you only knew what I'm about to do, you would be paying attention to me. You wouldn't be treating me like some nowhere man.*

"Nowhere Man" is a song by his favorite group of all time, the Beatles. Well, they *used* to be his favorite, until they broke up. And he still hasn't forgiven John Lennon for saying that the Beatles were more popular than Jesus.

That was blasphemy.

The taxi gets in line with the bumper-to-bumper traffic heading into Manhattan. Everyone is rushing to Rockefeller Center. A sixty-five-foot Norway spruce has just been delivered, and electricians are working feverishly to prepare for the annual Christmas tree-lighting ceremony, which is only a few days away.

He takes out a bag of coke. Snorts a line off his fist.

The cabbie is now watching him in the rearview mirror.

"Want some?"

The driver shakes his head and returns his attention to the road.

The coke isn't working its magic. Instead of feeling a wave of intense pleasure, he's sweating and working himself into a rage, all of it aimed at Lennon.

"But I'd plug him anyway," he mutters. "Six shots through his fat, hairy belly."

He arrives at his destination. He pays his fare, and as he steps out of the cab, he imagines police swarming him, their weapons drawn, ready to arrest him. He sees himself locked inside a jail cell for the rest of his life.

The thought brings him comfort.

Peace.

He turns back to the driver. "I'm Mark Chapman. Remember my name if you hear it again."

CHAPTER 1

Isn't he a bit like you and me?
— "Nowhere Man"

Y ou'll like John," Paul McCartney's friend Ivan
Vaughan says. "He's a great fellow."

Paul knows John Lennon, but only by sight, really. John is older—almost seventeen—and the two have never spoken, even though they ride the same Allerton-to-Woolton bus to school.

Today John's singing with his band, the Quarry Men, at the St. Pete's Church fete, and fifteen-year-old Paul and Ivy have bicycled over to check them out. Well, Ivy's interested—Paul wants to check out the girls.

It's Saturday, July 6, 1957, and already hot when the Quarry Men take the outside stage.

John's wearing a "shortie"—a knee-length coat—over a checkered red-and-white shirt and black drainpipe jeans. He starts to cover the Del-Vikings' doo-wop tune "Come Go with Me." Paul has heard the American song only a handful of times, on the Decca Records show on Radio Luxembourg and playing in one of the record-shop booths.

Paul half listens and goes back to scouting the crowd. He's thinking about which girl to approach first when he hears John change the lyrics without skipping a beat. Paul knows a lot about the guitar, and he can't figure out what style John is playing as he breaks into a rockabilly cover of Gene Vincent's "Be-Bop-a-Lula." John dominates the stage. Owns it.

Which isn't much of a surprise. Everyone knows John Lennon is cocky and confident—and a local Ted, or Teddy Boy. Here in Liverpool, the Teds, with their long sideburns and oiled-up hair swept together in the back like a duck's arse, are hard, rebellious working-class men and boys who love getting into fights.

Paul follows Ivy inside the St. Peter's church hall, where the band's setting up to play another set. John is widely considered a hoodlum. He lives with his aunt instead of his mum. The talk around town is that John's father abandoned him, and now John's mum lives in sin with another man. They had two daughters out of wedlock.

The memory of Paul's own mother suddenly crowds his thoughts.

This past October, on the twenty-ninth, Mary McCartney went into the hospital. She didn't tell him or his brother, Mike, why. Then, two days later, on Halloween, she died—from breast cancer, Paul found out eventually. Eight months have passed, and the loss still pierces him.

And that's when he became consumed by music. As his brother puts it, "You lose a mother—and you find a guitar?"

If you can sing or play an instrument, Paul, you'll always be invited to the party, his dad, Jim, a jazz musician in his youth, tells him. Paul starts on the trumpet, but after hearing Elvis Presley and Lonnie Donegan, the so-called King of Skiffle, he takes the horn back to the Rushworth and Dreaper music shop and swaps it for a Zenith guitar.

The problem is he's left-handed, and guitars are made for right-handers. So he's learned to play the guitar in reverse—right hand working the fret board, shaping the chords, while strumming with his left.

Paul picks up one of the guitars in the hall and starts to play "Twenty Flight Rock"—a song Eddie Cochran performed in the movie *The Girl Can't Help It*—which he only learned a few days ago. It's an immensely tricky song to play, even more so if you're forced to play wrong-handed. But Paul's only ambition in life is to be like Elvis, so he puts a lot of swagger into his impromptu performance. John stands nearby, his eyes narrowed, almost slanted. It's the same look he had earlier while performing onstage, as though he were looking down on the crowd.

And now he's looking down on me. Thinks I'm just a fat schoolboy.

⁂

Paul finishes the song, then starts to tell John about how he works out his own lyrics: "Like I'm writing an essay or doing a crossword puzzle."

John nods, uninterested.

Paul goes over to a nearby piano. He sits and starts to play Jerry Lee Lewis's hit song "Whole Lotta Shakin' Goin' On." Paul really gets into the music, even pounding the keys like Jerry Lee does.

Paul feels John's arm on his shoulder. John leans over, contributing a deft right hand in the song's upper octaves. *He's drunk,* Paul realizes.

When they finish playing, John announces that it's time for the pub. Paul's heart thunders with excitement. *The coolest kid in Liverpool has just invited me.*

Bubbling beneath it is another feeling: apprehension. Every adult, including Paul's dad, says about John, *He'll get you into trouble, son.* John Lennon, with his intimidating glare and his sideburns and upturned collar. *You saw him rather than met him.*

Now that Paul has, he's sticking around.

CHAPTER 2

Won't you join together with the band?
—"Join Together"

John doesn't care that Paul is only fifteen. Musically, he's as serious as John is about rock 'n' roll. Paul's already composing songs and knows how to play the piano.

And he plays the guitar perfectly—*upside down.*

Should I ask Paul to join the band? What if he tries to take over? John ponders these questions as he stands on the cobblestones outside the Cavern Club, in central Liverpool, where the Quarry Men played their first gig. The club, located under a fruit and vegetable warehouse, is a well-known jazz venue. "We never get auditions because of the jazz bands," John says, but now jazz is on the way out, replaced by skiffle, a British version of jug-band music that the Quarry Men play.

But John's true love is American rock 'n' roll, and tonight he wants nothing more than to get onstage and bend the crowd's ears back with its raw rhythms. Except the Cavern Club doesn't allow that type of music. No place does.

Rock 'n' roll has had a bad reputation ever since the American film *Rock Around the Clock* came to Britain last year and waves of teenagers ripped up their cinema seats so they could dance to the title track, by Bill Haley and His Comets. Now the old guard is terrified of the music's destructive power. The BBC won't play it on radio or TV.

But rock 'n' roll isn't going away. Until just recently, the number-one song in the country was Elvis Presley's "All Shook Up." John first heard about Elvis from a schoolmate quoting a music magazine. *New Musical Express* featured this strangely named American singer who had women screaming and fainting when he sang "Heartbreak Hotel" and thrust his hips onstage.

John bought the record and rushed home with it. He lives with his aunt, Mimi Smith, not his mum, Mimi's sister Julia. At night, John gets underneath the bedcovers with his portable radio and turns the volume down low to listen to medium-wave Radio Luxembourg, which plays all the American rock 'n' roll hits.

Mimi does not approve of rock 'n' roll. She thinks people who listen to it are "low class" and wants him to stay focused on his schoolwork. Mimi doesn't know that he's formed a band, let alone that he has a gig tonight.

"A guitar's all right, John, but you'll never earn a living by it."

But John's sure she's wrong. "I wanted to write *Alice in Wonderland* and be Elvis Presley," he says, and as far as he's concerned, he can—and will—do both. A few days ago, he'd discovered that Mimi had yet again "cleaned" his room, tossing out all his drawings and poems. He was furious and didn't hold back: *You've thrown my fuckin' poetry out, and you'll regret it when I'm famous.*

John wonders what Mimi's reaction would be if she found out that the source of his forbidden Ted clothes is Julia, who loves Elvis just as much as he does. Julia, unlike puritan Mimi, has a record player and loves to sing and dance and toss about her gingery hair. She even bought him his first guitar, an acoustic Spanish flamenco-style model with steel strings that have cut painful grooves into his fingertips from his constant practicing.

By the time John meets up with his mates at the Cavern Club that evening, he's come to a decision about Paul McCartney. "It went through my head that I'd have to keep him in line," John later reveals. "But he was worth having." John seeks out a mutual friend, Pete Shotton, to extend the invitation.

A four-string guitar strapped around his shoulder, John stares out at the middle-aged audience. *God, they look stiff.* He turns to the band and cues them.

Rod Davis, the banjo player, sidles up next to him, frantic. "You can't *do* that," he says. "They'll eat you alive if you start playing rock 'n' roll in the Cavern!"

John ignores him and turns back to the crowd.

Let's give 'em a taste of the King.

John belts out Elvis Presley's "Don't Be Cruel." The Quarry Men follow.

The manager hears the chorus—*Don't be cruel to a heart that's true*—and rushes to the stage with a note.

Cut out the bloody rock 'n' roll.

John tosses the note aside and channels Jerry Lee Lewis and his new favorite, Buddy Holly and the Crickets, as he tears into another rock 'n' roll number from the American pop charts.

John invites Paul to play a gig with the Quarry Men at New Clubmoor Hall in Norris Green, the northern part of Liverpool—a good distance by bus from where they all live.

They open with "Guitar Boogie" by Arthur Smith and His Cracker-Jacks. The guitar solo is easy to play, a simple twelve-bar. But not only is this Paul's first time playing with the band, it's also his first guitar solo *ever*.

Onstage, John and Paul take turns singing. When one leads, the other harmonizes. John's strength is holding the lower key; Paul's voice is more suited for the higher range.

Paul starts his guitar solo.

His fingers won't move. It's like they're stuck to the fret board.

Paul fights his way through it until his round face is flushed. Wet.

After the show, everyone is looking at him, and he's frightened. Yet he's resolute on one point. "It wiped me out as a lead guitar player, that night," Paul says. "I never played lead again onstage."

John is in his bedroom, composing a poem on his portable typewriter, when he hears a knock on the back door, off the kitchen.

Mimi calls up the stairs: "John, your little friend's here."

She uses this patronizing tone with all his friends. "I thought John and Mimi had a very special relationship," Paul later says. "She would always be making fun of him and he never took it badly; he was always very fond of her, and she of him." Even though she "would take the mickey," Paul says, "I never minded it, in fact I think she quite liked me—out of a put-down I could glean the knowledge that she liked me."

Mimi thinks Paul is the one "taking the mickey out" of her with his posh accent. "I thought, 'He's a snake charmer all right,' John's little friend, Mr. Charming. I wasn't falling for it."

John enters the kitchen and finds Paul McCartney standing there, Mimi eyeing the guitar in Paul's hand and reminding them both to keep the noise down and not bother her student lodgers.

The University of Liverpool students Mimi takes in to supplement her widow's state pension don't interest John, though he's also earned a place at the Liverpool College of Art after a portfolio review of his cartoons and caricatures. *Maybe I can get a job drawing gorgeous girls for toothpaste posters* is his thought.

"We've got this song, Mimi, do you want to hear it?" John asks his aunt.

"Certainly not," Mimi scoffs. "Front porch, John Lennon, front porch."

John closes the door, telling Paul that he likes it out on the porch "as the echo of the guitars bounce[s] nicely off the glass and the tiles."

The moment Mimi leaves the house, they race upstairs and play Little Richard records. They both worship the singer from Macon, Georgia, and Paul can even mimic those trademark hollers and screams on "Tutti Frutti" and "Long Tall Sally."

But Elvis Presley is God, and they are his acolytes. They don't just play Elvis records—they also analyze them, trying to figure out the chord progressions, every single sound. All the rock songs they know are played with C, F, and G or G^7. They're determined to crack the chords to Elvis's "Blue Moon," but it's not until early winter that they discover that C, A minor, F, and G are the exact same chords Paul Anka used in his hit "Diana," recorded in 1957, when he was fifteen, the same age as Paul.

John's excitement is so fierce, so intense, that it's nearly blinding. It confirms what he's known all along: music is the reason he was put on this earth.

And he's going to do music with Paul McCartney.

CHAPTER 3

Help me get my feet back on the ground.
                                    —"Help!"

Paul walks home, still riding the high of finally cracking the chord progression for "Blue Moon." He prefers riding his bicycle, but he can't do that when he brings his guitar, since it doesn't have a case.

His father still has no idea he's hanging out with John Lennon, but it doesn't matter, really, whether his dad likes John. They're friends now. Musical brothers in arms.

John, of course, knows how Jim McCartney feels about him. John gives Paul some cleverly worded advice: *Face up to your dad! Tell him to fuck off!*

He's thinking about it.

Paul wishes he could find a way, some combination of words, to explain to his father just how *deep* John is. Not only in his passion for music but also in his art. That John composes poetry; that he could be a great writer.

Paul takes a shortcut via the Allerton Municipal Golf Course, which is closed for the season.

Paul is good at the guitar. And he's pretty good at singing. But playing *and* singing . . . that takes practice. And what a better place than the middle of an empty golf course?

Paul stops walking to listen. A couple of times, people have caught him, and when they do, he immediately stops playing and starts walking.

But right now, in the pitch black, he's pretty sure he's alone. He straps the guitar over his shoulder and, in his mind's eye, sees himself stepping onstage, in front of thousands of people. The crowd goes wild, clapping and screaming his name.

Paul steels himself. Summons his nerves.

He starts to play.

Sings.

The crowd roars in approval. The women are hysterical. Some have fainted.

Paul is getting into a good rhythm, singing at the top of his voice, when he hears someone behind him shout: *"Hey!"*

Paul stops playing.

Whips around and sees a man—a *policeman*—approaching him.

Oh, God, I'm going to get arrested for a breach of the peace.

"Was that you I heard playing the guitar?"

Paul considers lying, even though it's crystal clear he's been caught red-handed.

Even as his heart pounds, he decides to go with the truth.

"Yes, sir."

The policeman, tall and burly, towers over him. If he gets arrested, what will he tell his dad?

"Can you give me guitar lessons?" the man asks.

CHAPTER 4

I was so much older then
I'm younger than that now.
— "My Back Pages"

John and Paul's new project is to crack the intro to Buddy Holly's "That'll Be the Day."

They've been going at it for weeks.

The friends sit in chairs, practically toe to toe, and watch each other play guitar. It's like "holding a mirror up" between the left-handed Paul and the right-handed John.

John rarely goes to class. When he does, he's outspoken. Rebellious. Argumentative and stubborn.

"I was aggressive because I wanted to be popular," John later says. "I wanted to be the leader . . . I wanted everybody to do what I told them to do, to laugh at my jokes and let me be the boss."

At Liverpool College of Art, some classmates and teachers like him, though many despise him.

But *no one* ignores him.

Still, he is most in his element at the "eyeball to eyeball" sessions he and Paul undertake at Paul's empty home. Every weekday except Mondays, Paul cuts school at the Liverpool Institute High School for Boys, and they take the green double-decker 86 bus—sitting up top, outside, so they can smoke.

John finds the well-worn furniture, with its protruding springs hidden by cotton covers, comforting and warm—much more like his mum's than Mimi's more austere house. John takes a seat and removes his glasses from his pocket.

Paul is staring at him.

You never knew I wore glasses because I never wear them. When he started having vision problems, Mimi took John to the eye doctor. The other kindergartners ridiculed the thick lenses needed to correct his severe nearsightedness, though, and he still refuses to wear his glasses in public.

But he feels comfortable with Paul, who's like a younger brother. One who's insanely talented, ambitious, and determined.

They go at the chords over and over.

John works his guitar until he nails the intro.

To celebrate, Paul lights up his dad's spare pipe with a pinch of tobacco they find in the tea caddy.

John takes a puff and thinks, *Practically every Buddy Holly song is three chords. We should write our own.*

Though John ignored Paul the first time he talked about his songwriting techniques, now he's curious and draws him out.

Paul starts at the beginning. "I'd either sit down with a guitar or at the piano," he says, "and just look for melodies, chord shapes, musical phrases, some words, a thought just to get started with."

John wants in on this creative process, but it doesn't take long for him to discover that song-writing is hard.

Their first collaboration, "Too Bad About Sorrows," remains incomplete, as does their follow-up, "Just Fun." The next one they work on, "Because I Know You Love Me So," has a Buddy Holly feel to it. They've already worked out the harmony.

Paul turns to a fresh page in his notebook to start a new song. Up at the top, he writes, "Another Lennon-McCartney Original."

"I've got a mate who can play 'Raunchy,'" Paul says. Bill Justis's "Raunchy" is a recent hit from America and a tricky instrumental to cover. Being able to play it is a sign of a really good guitarist.

"Who?"

"George Harrison."

Right. Little George Harrison. John has met him, that small kid with a thick mop of hair who's still fourteen, eight months younger than Paul and a class below him at Liverpool Institute.

Still, Paul keeps talking his mate up. In addition to his rock-solid guitar skills, Paul tells John, Little George is *cool*. He even dresses cool—sometimes outrageously, to get a rise out of the adults. "Cocky" is the word Paul uses to describe him, approvingly.

But John isn't swayed from his opinion that "George was just too young."

"I didn't dig him on first sight," John says later. "George looked even younger than Paul, and Paul looked about ten with his baby face."

On February 6, 1958, the Quarry Men are playing Wilson Hall, sharing the bill with the Eddie Clayton Skiffle Group. (Clayton is the lead guitarist, backed by a drummer named Ringo Starr.)

After the show, John challenges George.

"John said if I could play like that, I could join them," George recalls.

Paul remains George's champion. "Go on, George, show him!"

George aces the audition. "I played 'Ranchee' [sic] for them, and he said I could join."

John agrees that George "knew more chords, a lot more, than we knew."

He's still a bit embarrassed to be seen with a fourteen-year-old, though. But he's even more appreciative of strength in numbers, calculating, "Now there were three of us."

CHAPTER 5

When I cannot sing my heart
I can only speak my mind...
—"Julia"

At a party celebrating Commonwealth Day, John and his band play on the back of a parked coal lorry. As he sings and plays, he sees three members of his family standing in the crowd.

His mum, Julia, and his younger half sisters—Julia, who shares Mum's name, and Jacqui—are the best kind of fans, singing along with him, shouting and screaming their praises. Julia acts more like a friend than his mother.

John still feels a bit like an outsider with them and Bobby Dykins, Julia's common-law husband, though he's comfortable enough at their house, on 1 Blomfield Road, to be there visiting on Tuesday, July 15, while Julia's off spending time with Mimi.

John is still waiting for Julia's return at nearly 10:00 p.m. With his sisters asleep upstairs, it's just John and Dykins when a knock comes at the door.

It's a policeman, who looks directly at John.

"Are you Julia Dykins's son?" the constable asks.

"Yes," John mumbles.

"I'm sorry to tell you your mother's dead."

———※———

Julia has been struck by a car while crossing Menlove Avenue to catch the bus home. Mimi went in the ambulance with her to Sefton General, and John and Bobby Dykins race over to the hospital, but when they arrive, John waits outside.

He can't bring himself to go in and say good-bye.

We'd caught up so much, me and Julia, John thinks. *We could communicate. We got on. She was great.*

The grief turns over to rage. *Fuck it, fuck it, fuck it. That's really fucked everything. I've no responsibilities to anyone now.*

———※———

Julia's funeral, at Allerton Cemetery, is real and yet not real.

The man who killed her was a student driver and off-duty policeman named Eric Clague, who is acquitted of all charges. The only punishment the man receives is a short suspension from duty.

When the verdict's read, Mimi looks at Clague and shouts, "Killer!"

John thinks of Julia, buried and all alone in the ground.

The awful finality shatters him.

Mother, you had me, but I never had you.

December 6, 1980

Mark checks in to the YMCA. The clerk might say he's a regular. He stayed here last month. He had flown in to kill Lennon.

The rooms are only $16.50 a night. He could afford to stay a while, scope out the Dakota.

The doorman at the apartment building didn't give his name, but Mark heard someone call him Jay. Jay is a Beatles fan, too. The man is also a liar. Last month, Jay told Mark that Mr. Lennon was "out of town." Then Mark saw Lennon and Yoko's picture on the front page of the *New York Times*.

That's when he went out to the movies and saw that stupid film, *Ordinary People*. Mark likes to think of himself as anything but ordinary, but then he had so closely identified with Timothy Hutton's character that he felt like making a confession, the way Hutton did to his psychiatrist.

Mark doesn't have a shrink, doesn't need one, so he did the next best thing: he went to a pay phone and called his wife. She's Japanese, like Yoko.

I'm coming home, he whispered. Then he looked around, making sure no one could overhear, and said the words out loud for the first time. *I came to New York to kill John Lennon.*

Come home, Gloria told him. *Come home.*

I'm coming home. Your love has saved me. I'm not going to do this.

Now Mark has no intention of returning home. This time he's committed to his goal. Lennon's death will prove to the world, once and for all, that the man is a phony. A liar and a sinner.

Gloria believes he has returned to New York to find himself, that he wants to write a children's book. She believes him—obeys him, grants his every desire. Gloria believes everything he tells her because she is a good Christian woman and does what she's told.

⁘

Safely tucked inside his YMCA room, with its single bed and black-and-white TV, Mark double-checks the lock on the door. Then he turns to his suitcase and removes the gun—a .38 caliber Charter Arms.

It's very similar to the snub-nosed Smith & Wesson handguns used by undercover police. The perfect weapon to use for assassination.

He knows how to handle a weapon. He put in plenty of hours on the range to get certified so that he could carry a .22 when he worked security. He knows how to get in a combat stance and how to sight a target.

Soon the world will know they're dealing with an expert killer.

There was a time when he preached against guns and violence. Lennon, ironically, was the inspiration for his awakening.

The Beatles are bigger than Jesus, Lennon boasted.

He took Jesus's side. Took shelter, too, in the spiritual laws of the Christian faith. Took up a life of purpose, starting at the Chapel Woods Presbyterian Church in Snellville, Georgia.

Guns, he told people, were evil. But he soon realized the error of his ways. Speaking is only a weak form of doing.

He had to do more, much more, than converting neighbors and leaving pamphlets in local restaurants. He took a job as a missionary with the YMCA's International Camp Counselor Program in Lebanon—until civil war broke out, brought him back home. In Lebanon he found even greater purpose as a first responder on the front lines of the wreckage of conflict.

The sights of Palestinian gunmen killing four people at a Christian church in East Beirut, militant leaders killing thirty Palestinian supporters on a bus, played on a permanent loop in his brain. As a counselor at a Vietnamese refugee camp, day after day he listened to stories of families being slaughtered and Vietnamese women being raped by American soldiers.

Or half listened, because he couldn't wait to speak his piece, set them on the right path. He taught them the ways of revenge—how to make themselves even stronger than their persecutors.

While he was sharing his strength, what was Lennon doing? Nothing. Living the life of a pampered celebrity inside the walls of the Dakota.

He told us to imagine no possessions. He's done the reverse. *There he is, with millions of dollars and yachts and farms and a country estate, laughing at people like me who had believed the lies and bought the records and built a big part of our lives around his music.*

Lennon's lyrics about peace and love—it's all bullshit. Lennon admitted as much in a recent article. All his work for peace—the bed-ins and concerts—were essentially put-ons. They were phony, fake, publicity-grabbing schemes.

A mirror hangs on a nearby wall. Mark stands in front of it, sees his double chin and his round, moon-shaped face. Sees the faint traces of a man who had once believed in Lennon and the Beatles and God and Jesus.

That person is dead. That person died last month, the day he quit his security job and signed out as "John Lennon."

Mark backs up until he can see his chest and torso. He slips the .38 into his jacket pocket, covers the gun with his hand.

Practices withdrawing the weapon and dropping into a combat stance. Does it again and again until he feels confident that he can remove the weapon in one smooth motion.

Now he takes in a deep breath and imagines himself standing outside the Dakota. He is Saint Peter the Apostle among the throng of Lennon disciples. They're all anxious to catch a glimpse of their false god, but only he has a testament to preach. With the Charter Arms as his witness.

In his mind, he sees a limousine pull up to the curb. Lennon gets out, alone, because he doesn't travel with bodyguards. He's a man of the people.

Lennon gives a quick wave, then dashes toward the Dakota's front entrance.

"Mr. Lennon?"

Mark imagines Lennon ignoring him. He'll make the man finally see. Mark swiftly removes the handgun, watches his reflection drop into a combat stance.

"Mr. Lennon."

This time, Lennon pays attention. He turns, sees the gun pointed at him, but it's too late.

Inside the room, Mark pulls the trigger. It clicks softly, because there's no ammo, but in his mind, he hears the gunshot go off. He sees Lennon collapse against the pavement. Lennon looks like he's about to say something—"I'm sorry," maybe, or "Please forgive me for my sins"—and Mark squeezes the trigger again.

And again.

Again.

All five shots.

It's over. Lennon is dead.

Mark loads the hollow-points given to him in Atlanta by his cop friend, Dana. *There's nothing more power-packed than these babies,* Dana had told him. Dana thinks Mark needs the ammo for protection on the dangerous streets of New York.

Dana had taken him into the woods for target practice and gave him some valuable pointers.

Mark's aim has improved considerably.

Lennon doesn't stand a chance.

Mark puts on his brimless Russian hat with its fake fur. He slips the .38 into his pocket and holds it.

The gun feels warm in his hands.

Mark smiles. Happy.

CHAPTER 6

There's something happening here.
— "For What It's Worth"

On May 5, 1960, John Lennon heads to Slater Street's Jacaranda Club, which has a jukebox and an Italian espresso machine. Coffee bars like this are popular teenage hangouts, and at night, downstairs in the former coal cellar, the Jacaranda has a members-only club for up-and-coming bands.

Now John finds Allan Williams standing behind the Jacaranda's counter. Williams, a tiny man with a black bushy beard, has suddenly become a key player in the Liverpool music scene.

"Allan," John says, "why don't you do something for us?"

Williams adjusts the black top hat he wears all the time, even in the summer.

"How do you mean 'us'? Who's *us*?"

"My group," John says. "The Beatles."

John's inspiration comes from the Crickets, Buddy Holly's band, as well as his love for wordplay. Changing the second *e* to an *a* gives "Beatles" a double meaning—both crawling things and rhythmic music.

John's heard that there's an audition with Billy Fury and tells Williams that he wants to be part of it.

Williams nods. "Sure. What's your group's lineup?"

John tells him about Paul and George and their new member, Stuart Sutcliffe, a fellow student from art college. Williams knows Stu as the student who painted the murals in the basement of the Jacaranda—but when Stu sells an abstract painting at Walker Art Gallery, John persuades him to use the windfall to purchase a Hofner 333 four-string bass. Stu doesn't know how to play it yet, but John's certain he'll learn.

Besides, Stu looks the part. He's a thin guy with a Vandyke beard who looks a lot like American actor James Dean. According to George, John wanted Stu in the band because he "looks so cool." He wears shades clipped on his eyeglasses.

"Who's the drummer?" Williams asks.

"We haven't got one," John admits.

"I'll try to find you one," Williams assures him. He delivers a fellow named Tommy Moore. Moore's married and old—almost twenty-nine—but promises to come to the audition on May 10, after his shift at the Garston Bottle Company factory.

They've upgraded their clothes—to black shirts and jeanslike trousers—and their equipment. George has a new guitar, a Futurama, and Paul purchased an Elpico amplifier. John's former guitar, a gift from his mother, broke into pieces after all the playing. Mimi refused to buy him another one ("If you want it," she told him, "prove it"), which forced him to get an actual *job,* laboring to construct the city's new water pumping station. His hands bled every day of the long, hot summer.

John bumps into Brian Casser, the lead singer of Cass and the Cassanovas. "What's your group called again?" Casser asks John.

"The Beatles."

Casser laughs at the unusual name. They go around and around until John settles on Long John and the Silver Beatles.

When their turn arrives, they play three songs—John taking lead in one, Paul taking lead in the second, the third an instrumental. Stu, who doesn't know the proper notes, plays with his back to music promoter Larry Parnes and the rest of the auditioners. It was Paul's suggestion—he called it "doing a moody," as if Stu, with his dark glasses, was too cool to be bothered.

Long John and the Silver Beatles fail the audition. The band needs a lot more practice.

⬚⬚⬚

Williams lets them use the Jacaranda cellar for rehearsals. George ties a microphone to a broomstick, and Cynthia Powell, John's girlfriend from art college, holds it up for whoever is singing.

One day, they have an audience—Rory Storm and his band the Hurricanes, with guitarist Johnny Guitar and drummer Ringo Starr, whose real name is Richard "Richy" Starkey.

"Why Ringo?" Cyn asks him.

He holds up a hand and says, "Because I wear three rings. That's what they called me at first—Rings." He tells Cyn the story behind each one. "This one's from me mum I got when I was sixteen, this one's an engagement ring from me girlfriend, and this one's me granddad's wedding ring I got when he died."

"He looked like a tough guy," George says after Ringo and his bandmates leave, "with that gray streak in his hair and half a gray eyebrow and that big nose."

John agrees. They all do.

CHAPTER 7

What can a poor boy do
'Cept to sing for a rock 'n' roll
band?

> — "Street Fighting Man"

The ballroom in Scotland's Alloa Town Hall is huge, beautiful—and packed. Larry Parnes has sent the Silver Beatles on a ten-day tour of Scotland as a backing band to Johnny Gentle. The group performs three songs, two of which are Elvis numbers—"Teddy Bear" and "Wear My Ring Around Your Neck"—and then the headliner makes his entrance. True to his name, he's quiet and relaxed. They play behind him for half an hour.

It's a disaster.

⦿⦿⦿

"We were crummy, horrible," George says as they're packing up their equipment. "An embarrassment."

George isn't wrong.

Worse, they find out that one of the local promoters called Parnes to complain: "They're a scruffy no-good group."

Johnny Gentle, though, seems okay. A ship's carpenter, he built his own guitar, and he can write songs. While they're in Inverness, he shows John and George an unfinished song of his, which "was fine up to the middle-eight."

John helps him with the lyrics.

Now the song *flows*.

"That's great," Johnny says, impressed. "I'm going to use it."

They've been promised £75 for the gig, and it hasn't come through. They sleep in the van; one night in a hayloft. It's a miserable week, but "a vital experience for us," Paul later says, "because after that we knew it was no breeze—you'd have to work hard and sort out where the money was coming from. It taught us a lot of lessons."

Ten days later, they arrive back home. John gets the results of his exams. Not only did he fail, he also got a "red letter" from the Liverpool College of Art that says, "Don't bother coming back next September."

Mimi is shattered. Her view of John's future is blacker than ever.

Paul, too, is facing pressure. His father wants him

to go get a job. Same with George, who lost his electrician apprenticeship when he left for Scotland.

"Well," Paul says when they all get together, in the early days of August, "what are we going to do?"

Allan Williams comes to them a week later, on August 11, 1960.

"Good news, lads. The Silver Beatles are going to play in Hamburg, Germany."

He sets one tough condition. "No drummer, no trip."

Paul has a solution. "What about the son of the owner of the Casbah Club?"

"Pete Best?" John asks.

Paul nods. "He's got his own drum kit."

Eighteen-year-old Pete is clearly a beginner, but "he could keep one beat going for long enough," says John.

CHAPTER 8

When I left my home and my
family
I was no more than a boy...
—"The Boxer"

They arrive in Hamburg's St. Pauli district around midnight, after traveling by ferry from Harwich to the Hook of Holland and then by van to Germany.

After signing contracts in German and English, they're shown to their dank, dismal living quarters behind the movie screen of the Bambi porno theater—"a pigsty...a run down fleapit"—across from the Indra Club, where they'll be working for Bruno Koschmider, a fiftysomething former circus performer who limps from a war injury.

"You're to play four and a half hours during the weeknights," Koschmider tells them through an interpreter. "You'll get three breaks, thirty minutes each. Weekends, you play six hours."

John feels the blood drain from his face. *The longest we've ever played is twenty minutes. Now we're being asked to play for up to six hours—for the next forty-eight nights?*

The Beatles take the small podium stage. It's eight o'clock on August 17, 1960. Twenty years earlier, Germany attacked Liverpool for the first time when Nazi planes dropped bombs on the docks.

Pete Best can't maintain an even tempo, but he's pretty good when he uses the pedal for the big bass drum. "We kept that big heavy four-in-a-bar going all night long," recalls George. The crowds start to swell along with the noise.

The Germans love it.

Night after night.

During their time at the Indra, the Beatles log 204 stage hours—or, if they were playing back home, 136 ninety-minute shows.

"Your voice began to hurt with the pain of singing," John recalls, not unhappily, of suffering what they called "Hamburg throat." To "keep it up for twelve hours at a time, we really had to hammer. We never would have developed as much if we'd stayed home."

By the time Allan Williams returns, in mid-October, he's amazed at how good they've become. "We were the best bloody band there was," John would reminisce about these early days. "There was nobody to touch us."

Whenever they're down and need a boost, John channels a clichéd cigar-chomping studio agent and, in a bad American accent, says, "Where are we going, fellers?"

They answer in their own awful American accents: "To the top, Johnny!"

"Where's that, fellers?"

"To the toppermost of the poppermost, Johnny!"

"*Riiiiight!*"

Bruno Koschmider offers them a new contract—October through the end of the year—at his bigger, more popular club, the Kaiserkeller, where they can split the weekend hours with another group.

"And who's this other band?" John asks.

"Rory Storm and the Hurricanes."

They're on par with Liverpool's top group.

CHAPTER 9

Man, I was mean but I'm changing my scene...
—"Getting Better"

Paul needs a new guitar. The one he's got now is breaking down from all the wear and tear. John has his eye on a Rickenbacker 325 with a natural blond finish and an American-made eighteen-watt Fender Deluxe.

Paul also thinks they need a new bassist. Stuart's playing has improved, but he doesn't take the music seriously. "Our band would be great," Paul says, "but with him on bass there was always something holding us back."

Paul's never really liked Stu, John knows, and it's not helped now by jealousy over Stu's stunningly gorgeous new photographer girlfriend, Astrid Kirchherr. Astrid and her friend Klaus Voormann, two young, arty Germans, have recently befriended the band. Truth be told, John's a bit peeved Astrid hasn't fallen in love with *him*.

Not that Paul's wrong about Stu. "The guy really couldn't play bass to save his life," says Tony Sheridan, a British rocker considered "the guv'nor" of the Hamburg scene. "He was 90 percent image, and the most you want is 50 percent because the other 50 percent must be a musical talent."

They didn't have to worry about Stu, though, as he's made it clear he plans on quitting the group. He's going to ask Astrid to marry him.

"Well, we've got to do something about Pete," Paul continues. "His drumming just isn't cutting it."

If only they could use Ringo.

They've been spending a lot of time with Ringo, the drummer for Rory Storm and the Hurricanes, drinking, getting to know him. The drummer George had thought "looked the nasty one" when they first met "turned out to be Ringo, the nicest of them all."

"We liked his style," John agrees, "but we'd only just got the other drummer so we couldn't do anything about it."

Instead, John tells the band that he's arranged a higher-paying gig—at the Top Ten Club.

Paul and George light up with excitement. The Top Ten is a *real* rock club, not a bar offering music—and it has a phenomenal sound system. They've visited it a few times and even played there with Tony Sheridan.

On November 28, Stu makes it official: he and Astrid have exchanged rings. They're engaged.

Bruno Koschmider calls them all into his office. He's gotten wind of John's Top Ten plan.

His interpreter does all the talking. "Sign this," he says, handing them each an agreement stating that the Beatles will not play any other Hamburg club in December.

John refuses, tossing the paper on the man's desk.

Concurrently, it seems, the German authorities have discovered that seventeen-year-old George is too young to qualify for a proper work permit, so he's being deported immediately. He stays up the whole night, teaching his guitar part to John. "I felt terrible," recalls George. "I had visions of our band staying on there with me stuck in Liverpool, and that would be it."

The rest of the Beatles grab their equipment and bring everything over to the Top Ten. As a parting gift, Paul and Pete hang a few condoms from nails on the walls of their rooms and try to light them on fire. It causes a bit of smoke damage on the concrete, but mainly just stinks up the place.

The next day, John, Paul, and Pete are arrested by the German *Polizei* for "attempted arson."

Stuart finds out what's going on and comes into the station to sign a statement written in German that says he didn't know about the fire. After some individual interrogations, the police let them all go—only for Paul and Pete to again be picked up by the police at the Top Ten Club the next morning, taken directly to the airport in handcuffs, handed their passports, and put on a plane—their first flight ever!—back to London. Stu stays behind with Astrid, but John follows on his own shortly after.

Slinking home this way, under such ignominious circumstances, doesn't inspire confidence in anyone.

Is this what I want to do? Is this it? John's left to wonder. *Should I continue doing this?* The Beatles, he's thinking, may be finished.

CHAPTER 10

So you wanna be a rock 'n' roll star?
—"So You Wanna Be a Rock 'n' Roll Star"

John's fears are premature.

Once George turns eighteen, at the end of February in 1961, he, Paul, John, and Pete all head back to Hamburg, performing at the Top Ten alongside higher-caliber acts like Tony Sheridan.

They even record seven songs with Sheridan that June under the name Tony Sheridan and the Beat Brothers. They include five covers that Sheridan sings—"My Bonnie," "The Saints," "Why," "Nobody's Child," and "Take Out Some Insurance"—plus the Tin Pan Alley standard "Ain't She Sweet," sung by John, and an instrumental, "Cry for a Shadow," cowritten by George and John. Aunt Mimi later would proudly play the "My Bonnie" single for her lodgers, viewing it as the first evidence that John might have a future in music.

With Stuart's defection from the band, Paul's been "lumbered" with playing the bass, but he refuses to take Stu's cast-off instrument and instead gets himself a left-handed Hofner 500/1. Klaus takes Stu's old bass instead.

It's progress... yet John can't escape the feeling of time passing. "I wasn't too keen on reaching twenty-one," he admits, feeling *I'm too old. I've missed the boat. You've got to be seventeen.* As he says later, "A lot of stars were kids, much younger than I was."

John continues to feel *I'm gonna make it,* but when and how remain elusive. He just knows they have *something.*

And he's not the only one who feels that way. The Beatles drew packed crowds in Hamburg, and their popularity only increases once they're back home. So much so that customers are coming into NEMS, the biggest and best record store in Liverpool, asking for the single of "My Bonnie" that the Beatles recorded with Sheridan.

At the Cavern, DJ and host Bob Wooler introduces the boys by the nicknames he's given them. "John Lennon, 'The Singing Rage!' Paul McCartney, 'The Rockin' Riot!' George Harrison, 'Sheik of Araby!' And Pete Best, 'The Bashful Beat!'"

John Lennon starts singing, standing with his legs spread wide apart—a stance Wooler privately refers to as John's trademark, that way "the girls up front would be looking up his legs, keeping a watch on the crotch."

After their set, Paul's dad, Jim McCartney, who works nearby, stops by to hand over groceries and instructions for preparing dinner to Paul while John tries to cadge a "ciggie" from a girl. Then he notices George talking to "some very posh rich feller" who's wearing a fancy suit and carrying a gold cigarette case. John heads toward them, but the man has disappeared by the time John gets there.

"Who's that?" John asks George.

"Mr. Epstein. He's the store manager at NEMS."

I thought he looked familiar. John spends a lot of time at NEMS buying records, especially obscure R&B.

Mr. Epstein comes back on several occasions and chats with the band. John is flattered by the attention, but why the interest? The Epsteins own NEMS, and twenty-seven-year-old Brian's got a big house on Queens Drive, drives a Ford Zodiac, and speaks like a member of the royal family—a skill no doubt acquired through his years spent at the Royal Academy of Dramatic Art.

When Brian invites them to come 'round NEMS on November 29, John's still suspicious. There are a lot of con men around, and he's not sure if Brian's one of them.

The boys, dressed in their leathers and cowboy

boots, arrive late—and a bit drunk, after having first spent some time at the Grapes pub.

John explains that they signed a six-page contract written in German, without the benefit of a translation, for Bert Kaempfert on June 19, 1961. As Paul will later say, "We signed all sorts of contracts when we were about eighteen, because we had no manager and we didn't know what we were doing."

"It seems to me with everything going on, someone ought to be looking after you." Brian asks how much the band earns.

"75p each per night," they reply. "That's above the normal rate at the Cavern."

Brian looks shocked. He genuinely feels them to be worth far more, later saying, "I hoped that even if I were not to run their affairs completely I could at least secure a decent rate for their performances."

When at a second meeting, on December 3, they begin discussing contract terms—Paul and Brian going back and forth about percentages; should it be ten, fifteen, or twenty?—it's clear that Paul isn't that keen on Brian. The most he'll concede is that Brian has "a good flair" and, like Paul, "is very into the look onstage."

As far as John is concerned, there's nothing to think over. Brian is clearly smart. He's wealthy and well read and has connections in London—all of which John likes.

But most important, Brian Epstein is a risk taker. Where Paul is not.

One time, John said to Paul, "Look, imagine you're like on a cliff top and you're thinking about diving off. Dive! Try it!" and Paul replied, "Like bloody hell I'm gonna dive. *You* dive and give us a shout and tell me how it is, and then if it's great I'll dive."

When John and Paul return to the table, they talk about the Cavern and the recordings they made with Tony Sheridan, including an original composition.

That takes Brian by surprise. "You write your own music?"

John nods and begins naming their Lennon-McCartney originals. "There's 'Like Dreamers Do,' and 'Hello Little Girl...'"

"And a rock-ballad called 'Love of the Loved,'" Paul adds.

Brian pauses, as if thinking over how to weigh their songwriting abilities against their demonstrated value as live performers. He looks the band over, praising their "star quality," before pronouncing, "You're going to be bigger than Elvis, you know."

John is astounded. Speechless. They all are. George will later say about this moment, "This is where Brian was good. He knew how to get it happening. We had felt cocky and certain but when Epstein said "You're going to be bigger than Elvis you know," we thought, 'Well, *how big do you have to be*? I mean, I doubt that.' That seemed outrageous, yet he did have the right attitude."

That shot of confidence is exactly what John's been looking for. They need someone like Brian to keep them in line. Truth is, he'll later admit, "We were in a daydream till he came along. We'd no idea what we were doing, or where we'd agreed to be."

John knows they can make it. The Beatles want to be the biggest.

And anyone can see that Brian has class, money, and connections in the music world.

Plus, he's from Liverpool. He's one of *them*.

"Right then, Brian," John says, deciding. "Manage us."

CHAPTER 11

Different strokes for different folks.
— "Everyday People"

On December 13, 1961, Brian Epstein invites Mike Smith, an A&R man at Decca, to the Cavern to see the Beatles play. Smith is impressed enough to schedule them to come to London on January 1, 1962.

The Beatles win the *Mersey Beat* magazine poll naming them Liverpool's top group, beating out Gerry and the Pacemakers and Rory Storm and the Hurricanes. For Christmas, Brian sends them each a gift—a traveling alarm clock. On the back of the business card he uses as a gift tag, he writes "My little bit to get you all on in time."

On December 27, the Beatles close out the year at the Cavern with "The Beatles' Christmas Party," but Pete Best is out sick.

They need a drummer, and the other three band members have a particular one in mind: Ringo.

When Ringo sits in, "it felt *complete*," George will later say. "It just really happened, it felt really good. And after the show we were all friends with Ringo and we liked him a lot and hung out with him, whereas Pete—he was like a loner. He would finish the gig and then he would go."

But Ringo joins Tony Sheridan's backing band in Hamburg, and Pete's still their drummer that first day of 1962.

Decca calls the studio recording a "commercial test." For the Beatles, it's the audition of their lives. The recordings they'd made in Germany were done in an auditorium connected to a high school. This is their first time in a real recording studio.

John and the others plug their guitars into the studio amps, and Pete sets up his kit behind a screen, but the sound levels will all be controlled by the men standing behind the glass, adjusting the controls, watching the four of them.

The red light goes on. The recording has started.

Here we go.

———⸘⸘———

"Look," Brian tells the boys back in Liverpool as they wait to hear from Decca. "If I get a huge offer, they won't take you in leather."

John says, "All right, I'll wear a suit—I'll wear a fucking *balloon* if somebody's going to pay me! I'm not in love with the leather *that* much."

Paul nods. It's time for a change. "It was a bit old-hat anyway, all wearing leather gear." But...are they selling out?

"I didn't really see it as selling out," George says. "I just saw it as playing a game: if it takes suits to get us on the television, and if we need to be on television to be able to promote ourselves, then we will put on suits. We would wear fancy dress, whatever it took to get the gigs."

"And while we're on the subject," Brian says, "if you really want to get into bigger places you have to stop eating onstage, stop swearing, stop smoking."

"We'll stop," John agrees. Onstage at least. "Brian was trying to clean our image up," John later explained. "Fucking hell! It was a choice of making it, or still eating chicken onstage. We respected his views."

On Monday, January 29, Brian takes the band to Beno Dorn, his tailor in Birkenhead, where the senior tailor *tsks* over the Beatles' insistence that "the lapels had to be narrow and they wanted their trousers *extremely* narrow." But the boys enjoy the whole experience enormously and leave the shopgirls swooning.

(The irony of John choosing—if unwillingly—to wear a suit and tie onstage delights Mimi. "Ha-ha, John Lennon, no more scruffs for you," she cackles.)

A week later, Brian heads to London to meet with Decca execs, alone. He is taken to the executive dining room, where he's greeted by Dick Rowe, the head of A&R, sales manager Steve Beecher-Stevens, and Arthur Kelland, one of his assistants. Having all these important men here is certainly a good sign, he assumes.

Not exactly.

Rowe speaks first. "Not to mince words, Mr. Epstein, we don't like your boys' sound. Groups of four guitarists are on the way out."

Brian is gutted, but he quickly recovers. "You must be out of your mind," he tells them. "These boys are going to explode. I am confident that one day they will be bigger than Elvis Presley." He shows the execs a copy of *Mersey Beat* with the headline that reads BEATLES TOP POLL!

"The boys won't go, Mr. Epstein. We know these things. You have a good record business in Liverpool. Stick to that."

The insult—and the condescending delivery—is all about London snobbery. Brian's sure of it.

He pushes back at them. Hard. He goes through a detailed list of why Decca is making a major mistake.

"How about this," Rowe says. "Do you know Tony Meehan?"

"The former drummer for the Shadows?"

"That's him. He's with Decca A&R now. He has firsthand experience of what the teenagers want."

Brian takes the meeting, but when he returns to his office on Saturday, February 10, he fires off a letter declining the offer of Mr. Meehan's producing services, boasting that "since I saw you last the Group have received an offer of a recording Contract from another Company."

This is an outright lie, but Brian is determined, with all his soul, to make Decca regret its decision.

Decca could have signed the boys for what it cost them to take me to lunch.

As Tony Meehan himself will say years later, "It was just a complete mess, as things generally are—a dreadful corporate blunder."

CHAPTER 12

Got to pay your dues if you wanna sing the
blues...
—"It Don't Come Easy"

The boys sit together at a pub, stunned by Decca's rejection.

"He'll be kicking himself," says Paul of Dick Rowe.

"I hope he kicks himself to death," says John.

"I think Decca expected us to be all polished," John later reflects. "We were just doing a demo. They should have seen our potential. I think a lot of halfwits were looking after it."

Then he delves into the music. "We didn't sound natural," he admits. The thirty-five-minute audition tape contains fifteen songs, and John can find fault on just about every single one: he sang like a crazed madman; Paul sounded like a woman. George, always the perfectionist, played well. But Pete's a painfully

54

average drummer. Plus, his stage presence is no presence at all. Pete never makes any eye contact, never smiles, just drums with his head down.

They haven't even bothered to tell Pete about the Decca rejection, as they are questioning his investment in the group.

"At least the BBC thinks we're good," George says. Brian's booked them to record in front of a live audience for a BBC radio program called *Here We Go* that will air them in a half-hour slot called "Teenager's Turn." It pays well and, even better, will reach millions of listeners.

The boys arrive dressed in their new mohair suits, bright white shirts, and thin ties. Their trousers are trim, and they're wearing Chelsea boots fitted with Cuban heels. Their hair is no longer slicked back with grease but clean and combed forward in a strange "mop-top" style. Astrid Kirchherr, Stuart's fiancée, gave Stu the haircut first, and George liked it so much he asks her to cut his hair, too. Paul and John are more skeptical. "John was always a little bit sarcastic," Astrid recalls, "so at first, even with the hairstyle, he couldn't stop laughing, but in the end he just joined in. That was John. That was typical." Which leaves only Pete still Brylcreemed, though Astrid points out, "Pete couldn't have the hairstyle anyway because he had curly hair."

Shocking new look aside, the Beatles are on their

best behavior. They play four songs—"Hello Little Girl," Chuck Berry's "Memphis," Roy Orbison's "Dream Baby (How Long Must I Dream)," and the Marvelettes' "Please Mr. Postman"—and win over the live audience of 250 young people, everyone cheering and clapping. As the band walks off, John feels happy, particularly with his singing on "Memphis" and their take on "Please Mr. Postman," which introduced the "Motown sound" to much of the British listening public. Last summer, Bob Wooler had declared in *Mersey Beat,* "The Beatles were the stuff that screams were made of." Tonight, when they finished their last song, nearly all the girls had indeed screamed.

"We should listen to the broadcast at my house," Pete suggests. They all agree, because the radiogram belonging to his mother, Mona, gets the best FM monophonic signals.

Their songs sound *great* on the radio.

The boys jump about the living room—even stoic Pete can't contain his excitement.

"We weren't just recording stars," Pete marvels, "but *radio* stars!"

CHAPTER 13

Life is very short...
> —"We Can Work It Out"

Brian Epstein is despondent. He confides in Bob Wooler about his struggles with the London agents, who are saying that "as the name Beatles doesn't mean anything they'll have to change it."

Wooler disagrees, not only because the band already has a large local following but also because there's power in a brief band name. He says, "When you put it on posters, the shorter the name the bigger the print."

John loses patience with Brian, lashing out that the manager is doing nothing and they're doing all the work, though he knows that's not true. After John cools down, he assures Brian that the band knows how hard he is working. "It was *Us against Them,*" John says later.

But it's hard to keep the faith when by March of 1962, every record label has turned down the Beatles.

"Bloody hell," Paul says. "What are we going to do?"

They keep playing.

They're off to Hamburg again for April and May. Brian's cleared their deportation troubles and has booked them at the Star-Club, Hamburg's top rock venue. The Beatles feel like real headliners now.

On April 10, 1962, John, Paul, and Pete fly from Manchester to Hamburg. The next day, the three return to the airport to meet Brian and George's flight. They're surprised to find Stu's fiancée, Astrid, and their German friend Klaus Voormann also in the arrivals terminal.

"Hello, where's Stu?" John asks.

Astrid answers, "Stu's dead, John."

<hr />

This news makes no sense to John. He starts "saying 'No, no, no!' and lashing out with his hands," Astrid recalls. Though in letters and during a recent trip home to Liverpool, Stu'd complained of debilitating headaches, he's only twenty-one. How can he be *dead*?

"Paul tried to be comforting; he put his arm around

me and said how sorry he was. Pete wept—he just sat there and cried his eyes out. John went into hysterics," Astrid says. "I remember him sitting on a bench, huddled over, and he was shaking, rocking backward and forward." But none of them really knows how to react.

"Not many of our contemporaries had died," Paul later reflects. "We were all too young. It was older people that died, so Stuart's dying was a real shock. And for me there was a little guilt tinged with it, because I'd not been his best friend at times."

It turns out that Stu's nasty headaches were signs he had a growing brain aneurysm, and he'd had a massive seizure and died of a cerebral hemorrhage just the day before.

Stuart's mother, Millie, is on the same plane with Brian and George, coming to claim her son. John and the boys remain in Hamburg while Millie accompanies Stu's body back home, but when Astrid returns from the funeral, she brings John and George over to her attic, where Stuart painted.

"Could you take a picture of me there?" John asks.

Astrid readies her camera. She takes photographs of him and George throughout the afternoon. Decades later, when she views them, she'll say John was "a little lonely feller," while nineteen-year-old George "had so much strength in his face, like he was saying to John 'I'll look after you.'"

"I looked up to Stu," John says, mourning his friend. "I depended on him to tell me the truth." He has long, long talks with Astrid about life, about relationships, about himself and Stuart, about their loss. "John used to say that Stuart was the second person to have left him," she recalls. "First his mummy left him, then Stuart. I think it was the root of his anger...that people he loved the most always left him." At the same time, though, John's very pragmatic.

"You have got to decide: either you die with Stuart or you go on living your life," John tells Astrid. "Be honest and decide. You can't just cry all the time, you've got to *get on*."

After all, that's what he's always done.

Yet his own grief manifests itself in other ways.

John drinks heavily and swallows "Prellies"— Preludin, German diet pills that act as stimulants— by the handful. "He'd take so many pills that he literally wouldn't be able to shut his eyes to go to sleep," Roy Young, a fellow musician in Hamburg, recalls. John appears onstage one night wearing a toilet seat around his head. Another night, he gets arrested and has to be bailed out. Though he writes often to his longtime girlfriend, Cynthia, there are plenty of other women to keep him occupied.

And humor is always his go-to defense. When the Beatles take the stage for the first time at the

Star-Club on Friday, April 13, just a couple of days after Stu's death, Klaus Voormann is in the audience. "John came onstage dressed like a cleaning-woman," he recalls. John does an over-the-top clown act, knocking over microphones and pretending to tidy up the other band members. "The people in the club were laughing—they didn't know Stuart had died. They didn't know Stuart. It gave me shivers to watch it, but this is what clowns do, bring humor to tragedy."

Voormann adds, "It was hilarious."

On May 9, 1962, George explodes into the room, wide-eyed, bursting at the seams with excitement and waving a telegram.

"We've got a record contract!"

CONGRATULATIONS BOYS EMI REQUEST RECORDING SESSION PLEASE REHEARSE NEW MATERIAL.

The boys fire off telegrams back to Brian:

[JOHN:] WHEN ARE WE GOING TO BE MILLIONAIRES
[PAUL:] PLEASE WIRE TEN THOUSAND POUND ADVANCE ROYALTIES

{GEORGE:} PLEASE ORDER FOUR NEW GUITARS

Most significant is the line "Please rehearse new material." Usually the record companies choose the material—but the Beatles are going to get to play their *own* songs.

After a lot of debate, Paul and John decide to revisit "Love Me Do," the best of their early songs. The first thing they do is rewrite it in the key of G, which gives the song a great bluesy sound, and John—influenced by a new song called "Hey! Baby"—incorporates a harmonica part they all like. Pete suggests adding a skip beat, a kind of fluctuation in tempo. It's a strange idea, but the result is solid. John and Paul accept it.

A week later, they've got two more new songs: "Ask Me Why" and "P.S. I Love You." By the time the Beatles return home, on Saturday, June 2, they've got three brand-new Lennon-McCartney songs for EMI's Parlophone label.

Their recording is in less than four days.

We've got a lot of work to do.

CHAPTER 14

It's only rock 'n' roll but I like it.
—"It's Only Rock 'n' Roll (But I Like It)"

After three days of feverish rehearsals, the Beatles set off for London on Tuesday, June 5, and on the late afternoon of June 6, they lug their road-worn equipment to Abbey Road and into EMI's huge Studio Two.

The studio had "great big white studio sight-screens, like at a cricket match, towering over you," Paul recalls, "and up this endless stairway was the control room. It was like *heaven,* where the great gods live, and we were down below. Oh God, the nerves."

He's hoping to keep the band's loosely guarded secret. "None of us really knows how to read or write music. The way we work it is like: just whistling. John will whistle at me, and I'll whistle back at him."

Today, the band will be recording four songs selected by Parlophone: "Besame Mucho" and three originals—"Love Me Do," "P.S. I Love You," and "Ask Me Why."

When the engineers, dressed in white lab coats, tell them it's time, everyone's nerves spike.

They all look at one another. *It's Us against Them. Liverpool against London.*

The red recording light goes on.

The man operating the tape machine is Chris Neal. He listens to the Beatles play a couple of songs, then looks to Norman Smith, the balance engineer, and says, "I'm not all that impressed."

Smith replies, "Oi, go down and pick up George from the canteen and see what he thinks of this."

George is George Martin, the head of Parlophone.

The label's publishing arm, Ardmore and Beechwood, is eager to obtain potentially lucrative song copyrights, so George makes the practical determination that he can turn this band into a profitable version of EMI superstars Cliff Richard and the Shadows. "That was how my mind was working at the beginning," he explains, "looking for the possibilities of one of them being the lead singer. When I met them, I soon realized that would never work."

George enters the control room and listens to the group play "Love Me Do."

Smith's concern is their rubbish equipment. "I got nothing out of the Beatles' equipment except for a load of noise, hum, and goodness-knows-what."

George is only nominally interested in pop, but as a classically trained musician himself, he quickly pinpoints the main issue with "Love Me Do": the arrangement.

The four young men from Liverpool stop playing and nearly stand at attention when they see a tall and dapper man in his thirties, wearing a black tie with a red horse motif, approach them. He introduces himself as George Martin, the head of Parlophone. George's crisp accent alone is enough to prove intimidating—as intended—though in truth he isn't upper class at all.

After they exchange hellos, Mr. Martin tells them he's got a few issues with "Love Me Do." For example, John can't both sing the title line *and* play the harmonica.

"Someone else has got to sing 'love me do' because you're going to have a song called Love Me *Waahhh*. So, Paul, will you sing 'love me do'?"

George Harrison puts aside his electric guitar and picks up an acoustic.

The producer returns to the control room.

The Beatles start "Love Me Do" from the beginning.

Paul's big moment arrives. *Everything stopped, no backing. The spotlight is going to be on me,* he thinks, leaning toward the microphone.

—⊗⊗⊗—

George Martin watches. Listens.

Paul McCartney's voice won't stop shaking.

Take after take after take.

"Well that was twenty minutes of torture," says Norman Smith with a sigh.

But the real problem is the subpar drumming.

"He's useless," producer Ron Richards says of Pete. "We've got to change this drummer."

George nods in agreement. "Tell them to come up to the control room."

The Beatles shuffle inside the small room and find places to stand. The space is tight, the air thick with a haze of cigarette smoke. The boys from Liverpool openly gawk at all the unfamiliar pieces of equipment.

George has them listen to the playback of the recordings. When it ends, the room is silent. Then Pete pipes up: "I think they're good."

George Martin shakes his head and delves into all the issues he's seeing and hearing.

"He was giving them a good talking to," engineer Ken Townsend remembers of George's lecture, but Smith recalls, "They didn't say a word back, not a word."

"Look," George finally says. "I've laid into you for quite a time, and you haven't responded. Is there anything you don't like?"

After an uncomfortably long pause, George Harrison drawls, "Well, for a start, I don't like your tie."

George Martin stiffens at the insult. The tension seems to draw on for hours...

And then the Beatles laugh.

George Martin does, too.

He hadn't been expecting comedy from the band, but next to classical music, comedy is what George Martin knows best. It's the icebreaker that saves what could have been a disaster.

The boys from Liverpool spend the next twenty minutes keeping the studio in absolute stitches. At least John, Paul, and George do—Pete, as usual, stays silent in the corner. By the time the Beatles leave, Norman Smith has to dry his tears of laughter. He turns to George Martin and says, "Phew! What do you think of that lot then?"

As George Martin would say later, "I did think they had enormous talent, but it wasn't their music, it was their charisma. When I was with them they gave me a sense of well-being, of being happy. The music was almost incidental."

If they have this effect on me, he thinks, *they are going to have that effect on their audiences.*

CHAPTER 15

You've got to hide your love away.
—"You've Got to Hide Your Love Away"

At home in Liverpool, the Beatles are preparing to face an audience of one. One of their own.

John, Paul, and George decide to tell Brian that he has to handle the uncomfortable job of firing Pete. As George will later admit, "Being unable to deal with the emotional side of that, we went to Brian Epstein and said, 'You're the manager, you do it.'"

Brian is upset by the news. "I think you should keep Pete," he says.

But the others felt they'd already given Pete enough of a chance. Another local drummer recalled encountering Paul and Pete huddled together at the Mandolin Club one afternoon in 1962, after a lunchtime session at the Cavern. "Paul was showing Pete the drum pattern he wanted on a particular song," the drummer remembered. "Pete tried to do it, but he didn't get it."

"It had got to the stage that Pete was holding us back," Paul later explains. "What were we gonna do—try and pretend he was a wonderful drummer? We knew he wasn't as good as what we wanted."

"Do you have someone in mind for his replacement?"

"Ringo," John says.

"He's rather loud," Brian says. "I don't want him."

"But *we* do." John lists the reasons why the Beatles want—*need*—Ringo. When Ringo is around, the Beatles feel like a full unit, both on and off the stage. And they know Ringo's interested. "We want Pete out and Ringo in."

Ringo, the three of them believe, is the key to making the band better.

On Thursday, August 16, 1962, a band meeting is called at the NEMS office. Only Brian and Pete attend. John and the others don't show up.

Though *Mersey Beat* later reports that Pete Best left the band "amicably," that's far from true. Pete had been in the Beatles for nearly two years, and to have been dismissed by Brian Epstein right when the band got its record deal . . . it cut *deep*.

"I knew the Beatles were gonna go places, I knew we were going to be a chart group—and to be kicked out on the verge of it actually happening upset me a great deal," Pete later tells an interviewer. "And the fact that they weren't at the dismissal hurt me a lot more. It was vicious and backhanded and I felt like putting a stone round my neck and jumping off the Pier Head."

On August 18, 1962, Ringo Starr lugs his drum kit into the Cavern for a two-hour rehearsal.

John is the first to notice how different Ringo looks. Not only has Ringo shaved off his beard, he's also restyled his hair to look like the rest of the band—something Pete never did.

John has always liked Ringo—has been, truthfully, a little bit in awe of him. Neither of them suffers fools, and both are quick and sharp with the tongue; and they both grew up with absent fathers. Both enjoy drinking and flirting and laughing, generally having a good time. Ringo hasn't had much formal schooling, yet he's very intelligent. Sharp.

John describes feeling a little intimidated by Ringo to a journalist. "To be so aware with so little education is rather unnerving to someone who's been to school since he was fucking two onwards."

The rehearsal goes amazingly well. They have great fun together.

And the chemistry is *perfect*.

"We were all very happy to have him," George will later say. "From that moment on, it gelled—the Beatles just went on to a different level."

Not all the fans see it that way.

Pete's a local favorite, and his firing is the talk of Liverpool's music scene. When the Beatles return to the Cavern on Sunday, the audience is buzzing with gossip—mainly theories that the rest of the band was jealous of Pete. As the Beatles take the stage, some people start shouting, "Pete Best forever, Ringo never!"

"The birds loved Pete," Ringo explains. "Me, I was just a skinny, bearded scruff. Brian didn't really want me either. He thought I didn't have the personality. And why get a bad-looking cat when you can get a good-looking one."

Brian declares himself "the most hated man in Liverpool."

Granada TV shows up three days later, for the band's lunchtime session at the Cavern. It's the first time the band will be on camera.

The Beatles give a rousing performance. The new foursome is tight and has great fun together. Unlike the surly Pete, Ringo smiles and laughs as he plays. The cameras capture the new Beatles in all their glory—despite, between takes, some fans shouting, "We want Pete!"

Pete, it turns out, *is* there.

In the audience.

Years later, in his autobiography, Pete reveals, "I sneaked in and sneaked out again."

The fans just need some time to warm up to Ringo, John thinks.

Besides, he doesn't have time to worry about how Pete's fans are taking the news.

He's getting married tomorrow.

"You're too young!"

Mimi's voice thunders and echoes inside her kitchen.

"Cyn is having a baby. We are getting married tomorrow; do you want to come?" John has just told her.

The following morning, John and his longtime girlfriend, Cynthia Powell, exchange their vows at the registrar's office, with Paul and George as witnesses and Brian as best man.

When they leave the building, it's pouring rain.

It's all so absurd that they burst out laughing.

CHAPTER 16

I can't do what ten people tell me to do...
— "(Sittin' on) The Dock of the Bay"

Brian hands John an acetate disc.

"What's this?" John asks.

"The song that will be your first record for EMI. You're going back in the studio Tuesday to record it. Mr. Martin believes it's going to be a number one song."

The Beatles come together at Brian's record store to listen. The song, "How Do You Do It," is pop treacle. They hate it.

Paul holds up the disc. "Well," he says, frustrated, "what are we going to do with *this*?"

They decide to rearrange it.

The Beatles resume their gigs at the Cavern, mixing in their own songs. On Monday, September 3, the day before their studio date in London, the band debuts a new song, John's "Please Please Me."

On Tuesday, September 4, 1962, at 2:00 p.m., the Beatles enter the Abbey Road studios once again. John feels a bit more relaxed than he did the first time—they all do, because they have a real drummer with them.

It's brilliant how this all worked out. I brought in Paul, Paul brought in George, and George brought in Ringo.

As they rehearse "Please Please Me," the head of Parlophone comes down from the control booth to address the group.

"You need to tone down the drumming," George Martin says, looking at Ringo.

A tense silence follows, and the producer cuts into it with further criticism.

"Double the speed," he says, and the song "might have something."

But the Beatles are there to record "How Do You Do It." Though they polish it in two takes, they still don't like the song.

"We want to record our own material," John says, "not some soft bit of fluff written by someone else."

George Martin accepts the challenge and extends one of his own. "I'll tell you what, John. When you write something as good as that song, I'll let you record it."

That seems to be the last word, but a few days later, back in Liverpool, Brian tells them Mr. Martin wants the Beatles back in the studio. " 'Love Me Do' will be the first Beatles single."

They couldn't have hoped for a better result. Now they just have to prove they were right.

George Martin isn't altogether wrong about "How Do You Do It," either—when Gerry and the Pace-makers record it a few months later, it goes straight to number 1.

CHAPTER 17

We all want to change the world.
—"Revolution"

On Friday, October 5, 1962, the day "Love Me Do" first goes on sale, John plays it for his aunt. "What do you think, Mimi?"

"If you think you are going to make your name with that, you've made a big mistake!" she tells him.

"Remember, I said I'd be famous," John says.

"What always worried me, John, was that you wouldn't be so much famous as notorious," Mimi shoots back.

Luckily for the Beatles, others are more enthusiastic.

"The whole of Liverpool went out and bought it, en masse," Ringo marvels proudly in later years. The Liverpool fans are loyal and numerous—they flock to the record stores in such huge numbers that the rumor mill immediately begins churning out theories that Brian personally bought ten thousand copies to artificially inflate sales.

"It sold so many in Liverpool the first two days—because they were all waiting for us to make it—that the dealers down in London thought there was a fiddle on," John recalls. "'That Mr. Epstein feller up there is cheating.' But he wasn't."

He *is* kicking his promotions into high gear, though. Parlophone isn't doing much in the way of publicity, so Brian picks up the slack, and "Love Me Do" sneaks into *Record Retailer*'s top fifty, at number 49.

Next he books the Beatles on a bill with one of their longtime idols: Little Richard.

Little Richard—though much more restrained in 1962 than he was in his fiery 1950s persona—leaves the Beatles starstruck. "We were almost paralyzed with devotion," says John. Conversely, though Little Richard finds John a bit crass, he deems both Paul and George "sweet."

And he's a bona fide fan of their music. "Man, those Beatles are fabulous!" Little Richard tells Alan Smith of the *New Musical Express*. "If I hadn't seen them I'd never have dreamed they were white. They have a real authentic Negro sound."

John has no idea that his band is the start of a music revolution.

The first Beach Boys album, *Surfin' Safari,* is released by EMI on the very same Friday that "Love Me Do" goes on sale, and across the ocean, in New York City, twenty-one-year-old Bob Dylan, whom *NME*'s weekly US columnist, Nat Hentoff, dubs "the most startling of all the American city folk singers," is playing Town Hall, on West 43rd Street.

Just a few months earlier, a young student from Iran named Fery Asgari revitalizes a basement music venue in west London called the Ealing Club by starting a weekly R&B night. The Ealing Club quickly becomes one of the hottest spots in London, with people lauding its R&B musicians, especially blues guitarists Alexis Korner and Cyril Davies. There, in April, Korner introduces young R&B fanatic Brian Jones to a nineteen-year-old student from the London School of Economics named Mick Jagger and Mick's friend Keith Richards. The rest is rock 'n' roll history. At the same time that the Beatles, the Beach Boys, and Dylan are debuting, Jones, Jagger, and Richards's newly formed band, the Rolling Stones, is playing its tenth gig down in Surrey.

"The Stones were playing little clubs in London—doing Chuck Berry songs and blues and things—and we thought we were totally unique animals, [that] there was no one like us," Mick Jagger says, reminiscing. "And then we heard there was a group from Liverpool. They had long hair, scruffy clothes and a record contract, and they had a record in the charts, with a bluesy harmonica on it, called 'Love Me Do'—when I heard the combination of all these things, I was almost sick."

The two bands frequent the same clubs. Mick Jagger sees the Beatles out one night in their matching suede coats.

"Fuckin' hell! I want one of those coats," he says. "I want a long coat like that, but to do that, I'll have to earn money."

With a record climbing the charts, the Beatles are on their way.

"Love Me Do" rises to number 46 in *Record Retailer*.

Then it goes to number 41.

And it keeps climbing.

"I was on my own at home this morning, and when I looked at the *NME* and saw we were in at 27 I was delirious," Paul later says. "'There it is! There we are!' I was *shaking*." Being on the charts is proof they've really made it. "Twenty-seven was the *height*."

Even when they return from another two-week gig back in Hamburg that Brian won't let them out of, "Love Me Do" remains at number 27 on the *NME* top thirty and is still moving up other charts. At the end of December, they head back to Germany again for their fifth—and final—Hamburg gig.

"We went in young boys," John later says about their time in Hamburg, "and came out old men."

⁂

The Beatles travel to London to meet with George Martin—and are stunned when the producer tells them, "I'm thinking we should make an album."

And not just any album. An album featuring *their* songs.

The concept of singer-songwriters is still almost unheard of among their contemporaries, but John and Paul grab the chance with both hands.

The question is, How will they determine credit? Anyone who gets credit will receive an additional—and with any luck, lucrative—future stream of income.

Paul asks, "Without wanting to be too mean to George, should three of us write or would it be better to keep it simple?"

John and Paul decide to keep it to the two of them and agree that they'll be a songwriting duo called "Lennon and McCartney." In a meeting with Brian, they lay out a plan. "Okay, what we'll do is we'll alternate it: Lennon and McCartney, McCartney and Lennon," based on contribution. But it's never put in writing, and the original credit order sticks. "I didn't mind," Paul claims. "It's a good logo, like Rodgers and Hammerstein. Hammerstein and Rodgers doesn't work."

Soon thereafter, George notices a shift in the band. "An attitude came over John and Paul of 'We're the grooves and you two just watch it,'" he'll say later.

On Monday, November 26, the Beatles head back into Studio Two to record "Please Please Me" and the B side, "Ask Me Why."

This time, there's no drama. Buoyed by the success of "Love Me Do," John and the boys feel relaxed. They have fun, and the chemistry they have onstage is with them in the studio.

"The thing I like about the Beatles is their great sense of humor—and their talent, naturally," George Martin tells journalist Alan Smith. "It's a real pleasure to work with them because they don't take themselves too seriously. They've got ability, but if they make mistakes they can joke about it. I think they'll go a long way in show business."

The Beatles record both singles in the allotted three-hour time frame, and the producer watches from the control room. As they wrap up, he presses the Talkback key, and his posh voice comes into the studio: "Gentlemen, you've just made your first number one record."

CHAPTER 18

I should have known better...
— "I Should Have Known Better"

The Beatles tour constantly throughout 1963. In January—as George Martin had rightly predicted—"Please Please Me" scores them the first of what will be twelve consecutive number-one songs.

On a single day in February, they record ten more songs to fill out their first studio LP, *Please Please Me*. The tunes are a mix of Lennon-McCartney originals and covers of their favorite American R&B songs, including "Twist and Shout," a hit the previous year by the Isley Brothers (later inducted into the Rock 'n' Roll Hall of Fame by Beatles admirer Little Richard).

John screams the lyrics of "Twist and Shout" with such raw intensity that everyone fears for his vocal cords. "I was always bitterly ashamed of it," he'll say later, "because I could sing it better than that. . . . You can hear that I'm just a frantic guy doing his best." Decades later, *Rolling Stone* magazine readers vote the Beatles' "Twist and Shout" the third-best vocal performance in rock history.

All four Beatles have aspirations to conquer the American charts. But there's one fact the boys can't escape: nearly every band from England has failed to make it there. The Beatles won't tour America until they've achieved a number-one hit, John vows, later saying of the American audience, "We knew we would wipe you out if we could just get a grip on you. We were new."

George, though, brings back some daunting intelligence after a September 1963 visit to Benton, Illinois, where his sister, Louise, lives. "They don't know us," he reports. "It's going to be hard."

But in England, it seems *everyone* knows them. When they return to Heathrow the following month after a tour of Sweden, the size of the crowds gathered to welcome them home astonishes even Ed Sullivan, whose eponymous variety show is among the most popular in America. Sullivan wagers that the excitement is translatable to the American market and invites the Beatles to appear on *The Ed Sullivan Show.*

In November, they'll play for royalty. Her Majesty Queen Elizabeth the Queen Mother asks the band to perform as part of a celebrity musical lineup that includes Marlene Dietrich and Burt Bacharach at her annual charity event. Her younger daughter, Princess Margaret, and Margaret's husband, Lord Snowdon, also attend (Queen Elizabeth, pregnant with Prince Edward, does not). John makes sure the glittering show at Prince of Wales Theatre, in London's West End, is unforgettable.

"For our last number," he announces from the stage with a mischievous grin, "I'd like to ask your help. The people in the cheaper seats, clap your hands. And the rest of you, if you'd just rattle your jewelry."

It is a cheeky thing to say (John originally told Brian he was going to ask the audience "to rattle their fucking jewelry"), but the audience is charmed.

"The Beatles are most intriguing," the Queen Mother pronounces, and the *Daily Mirror* exclaims, "How refreshing to see these rumbustious young Beatles take a middle-aged Royal Variety Performance by the scruff of their necks and have them beatling like teenagers."

The band closes out the year with a special supplement put out by the London *Evening Standard* declaring "1963...the Year of the Beatles." They also set a national milestone: their second album, *With the Beatles,* released November 22, 1963, the day President Kennedy is assassinated, is the first rock album in Britain to sell one million copies.

On January 13, 1964, the single "I Want to Hold Your Hand" is released in America.

The next day, the band flies to Paris for a three-week booking at the prestigious Olympia theater. They check into the George V hotel.

A French DJ sends over *The Freewheelin' Bob Dylan,* the folksinger's second album. "For three weeks in Paris, we didn't stop playing it," John says. "We all went potty about Dylan." He even has a leather cap identical to the one Dylan wears on the cover of his first album. "Everyone will think I copied it from him," John laments.

"Beat-les! Beat-les! Beat-les!" fans chorus outside the sold-out shows.

The British press, ever skeptical that Beatlemania is likely to spread across the Channel—or the Atlantic Ocean—gathers at the hotel on January 17, where news is breaking. After just three days on sale, the Beatles' new single has sold over 250,000 copies. Capitol Records telegrams Brian: "I Want to Hold Your Hand" is the number-one single in America.

According to road manager Mal Evans, the Beatles celebrate with their own brand of hijinks. "They always act this way when anything big happens—just a bunch of kids, jumping up and down with sheer delight. They felt this was the biggest thing that could have happened. And who could blame them."

Daily Express photographer Harry Benson witnesses

the scene. "One morning, the press is invited up to their room and Paul says, 'That was some pillow fight we had the other night,'" Benson recalls in a 2019 interview. "My eyes went up and I looked over at another photographer from the *Daily Mail* and I wondered if the bastard had picked up on it."

He hasn't. Benson is alone in his quest for the perfect shot.

"How about a pillow fight?" Benson asks the giddy band.

"John looks away, grabs a pillow and comes back hitting Paul in the back of the head," Benson recalls. "Now it's game on."

December 6, 1980

*S*ociety *means nothing to me, except as a tool to be used,* Mark tells himself as he leaves the YMCA. *People are things, objects for my pleasure.*

He can fool anyone.

Just like John Lennon fooled the world.

The Dakota is only a few blocks away. As he walks, he sees Lennon's face everywhere promoting his new release, *Double Fantasy.*

He locks eyes on the image all over newsstands, record stores, and billboards. *His target.*

It frightened him the first time he saw the Dakota, ringed by dozens of cast-iron black gargoyles, the creatures' jaws open, bodies and tails curled around the railings.

The more he studied the Gothic revival–style

building, gazing deeply into the gaslit entryway, the more his fear turned to excitement. By the time he'd crossed the street, he felt like Dorothy approaching the Emerald City in *The Wizard of Oz*.

As he draws closer, Mark sees three people gathered in front of the Dakota hoping to get a glimpse of Lennon—maybe even an autograph, if they're lucky.

He assesses the doorman, Jay, who's too friendly to be any threat. Now that Mark has made up his mind to kill Lennon, no one can stop him, really.

He notices a park bench across the street from the building. It's the perfect vantage point to look up at the seventh floor, where Lennon lives with Yoko, his second wife.

The shades and curtains are drawn, but Mark has no need to see inside. He has studied the details and photographs in a book about Lennon's life at the Dakota. Lennon, he knows, often prowls around at night and sleeps through the day, so he could be up right now serving lunch to his young son, Sean.

How can he get Lennon out of the apartment?

A bomb threat would do it. Mark has done it before, back in Honolulu, when from a pay phone he called one in to the Ilikai Hotel. He watched the evacuation proceed before him, the sight made even more beautiful by the knowledge that he was in total control. The only greater thrill he could imagine was shooting the people as they came out one by one.

But can he be sure that Lennon is even home?

Mark looks over at the knot of fans. Only two remain, both women.

He gets to his feet. As he crosses the street, hands in his pockets and gripping the gun, the piano intro to "Imagine" plays in his head.

"Imagine if John Lennon was dead," he sings under his breath. *"It's easy if you try..."*

CHAPTER 19

Climb in the back with your head in the clouds...
　　　—"Lucy in the Sky with Diamonds"

I n a way I'm sorry they've been so successful," Brian
Epstein—whom *The Observer* deems "a shrewd
young man who has caught the lightning"—
admits. "It's just that I'm kept so busy managing
their business affairs and I must share them with
everybody."

It's February 7, 1964, and the Beatles are
aboard Pam Am flight 101 for their first trip to
America. The flight's packed with journalists such
as twenty-two-year-old Maureen Cleave, from the
Evening Standard, and *Daily Express* photographer
Harry Benson.

Even though Cynthia Lennon isn't a Beatle, she's
one of the most famous passengers. Everyone in
Britain now knows about her and the baby, thanks to

the *Express*. The paper outed them last year with the headline BEATLE JOHN IS MARRIED.

Their son, John Charles Julian, was born April 8, 1963, in Liverpool. Though they call him Julian, he has three legacy names—the first for his father, the second for Cynthia's father, and finally for John's mother. John was on the road and didn't arrive at Sefton General Hospital until a week after his son was born. Brian volunteered to be Julian's godfather.

The revelation that John's a husband and father just as the band is peaking in popularity prompted some damage control. In a prepared response published by *Mirabelle* magazine in October, John spoke of his present life on the road with the band and his past experiences, including being raised by Mimi and the devastating loss of his mother. The story ended with a confession about his new wife: "I'd like to tell you more about her but I've this old-fashioned idea that marriage is a private thing, too precious to be discussed publicly. So forgive me and understand."

On board Pan Am flight 101, baby Julian is sleeping against his mother. Attuned to John's many moods (if not always the rationales behind them), Cyn puts her hand on his and asks, "What's on your mind?"

John flashes on a conversation he'd had with Sonny Freeman, the model wife of photographer Bob Freeman. Bob took the photo of the Beatles with their half-shaded faces for the cover of *With the Beatles* and its US counterpart, *Meet the Beatles,* released just two weeks earlier.

John has spent many late nights in the Freemans' wood-paneled apartment, "talking about things like life and death, the way you always do when you're young." He's also shared his premonition that he'd lead a life cut short by a gunshot.

"A bit nervous, is all," John says.

Though Beatlemania is in full swing back home, Capitol Records—EMI's US counterpart—had only begrudgingly taken the Beatles on, with the proviso that the label be the one to choose the songs for American albums. While it still stings that Capitol turned them down—repeatedly—there are signs that the label is taking the Beatles seriously by mounting a national promotional campaign. They print and distribute five million stickers announcing THE BEATLES ARE COMING and give every single disc jockey in the United States a stack of Beatles records to play.

Ahead of the American appearances, Capitol Records' press release had announced Lennon as a "determined twenty-three-year-old whose somewhat stern face gives the impression of an angry young man."

And now that face is staring back at his wife.

Cyn has brought along a stack of fan mail and reads aloud from the letter Sharon Flood of New York has written. "Perhaps you are not aware of this fact, but you are the first happy thing that has happened to us since the tragedy on November 22. You are the first spot of joy to come to a nation that is still very much in mourning, although the grief is personal and unpublicized."

The fan is referring to the assassination of President John F. Kennedy, on November 22, 1963 — not only the day EMI released *With the Beatles* in the UK but also the day Mike Wallace of the *CBS Morning News* gave the Beatles their American television debut. He aired a performance clip that was set to be rebroadcast by Walter Cronkite on the evening news — until the JFK tragedy struck and the clip was forgotten until December 10.

That was nearly two months ago.

On the transatlantic flight, Ringo struggles with the weight of the moment. As he later explains, "I felt as though there was a big octopus with tentacles that were dragging us down into New York."

Also on the flight is producer Phil Spector, who'd asked to catch a ride with the Beatles on the rationale that a jet carrying the British pop stars had to be crash-proof.

He's also a fan. "It's obvious that Paul McCartney and John Lennon may be the greatest rock and roll singers that we've ever had," Spector later tells *Rolling Stone*. "I mean there is a reason for the Beatles other than the fact that they're like Rodgers and Hart and Hammerstein, Gershwin and all of 'em. They are *great, great* singers. They can do anything with their voices."

John and Spector start talking about a new group that Spector has befriended back in London: the Rolling Stones.

John and the others met them last spring, on a Sunday night at a blues spot in suburban London called the Crawdaddy Club, where the Stones were the house band. The Beatles stopped by after taping the television music program *Thank Your Lucky Stars*. They were all impressed by the lead singer, Mike (soon to be known worldwide as "Mick") Jagger, while John was especially drawn to Brian Jones's technique on the harmonica.

The two groups started hanging out a lot together backstage, and when the Stones admitted they didn't have a follow-up to their debut single, a cover of Chuck Berry's "Come On" (which came and went), John offered them a Lennon-McCartney original—"I Wanna Be Your Man."

That night at the club, John relates, he and Paul "went off in the corner of the room and finished the song off while they were all just sitting there, talking. We came back and Mick and Keith said, 'Jesus, look at that. They just went over there and wrote it.'"

The Stones covered it, and their version of "I Wanna Be Your Man" reached number 13.

"That's when Mick and Keith decided they should write songs together themselves," John tells Spector.

Then Paul comes up the aisle with an important message from the pilot: "Tell the boys there's a big crowd waiting for them."

CHAPTER 20

How does it feel to be one of the beautiful people?
— "Baby, You're a Rich Man"

As Ed Sullivan predicted, the Beatles bring out the fans. More than four thousand of them are crowded into the arrivals terminal at the newly renamed John F. Kennedy International Airport, craning their necks to catch a glimpse of their idols.

CBS musical director Ray Bloch believes he's discovered the reason for the crush, and he's unimpressed. "The only thing that's different is the hair as far as I can see," he says. "I give them a year."

But the hair *is* important. "Won't be long before every group with long hair will be sought by American companies," *Cashbox* music magazine predicts.

As Dr. Joyce Brothers, writing on the front page of the *New York Journal-American* about "Why They Go Wild Over the Beatles," explains: "The Beatles display a few mannerisms which almost seem a shade on the feminine side, such as the tossing of their long manes of hair. . . . These are exactly the mannerisms which very young female fans (in the 10-to-14 age group) appear to go wildest over."

"They're so cute," June Clayton of Brooklyn tells the New York *Daily News*. "And Ringo's the cutest. Look at them comb their hair!"

But before they can take the stage at Broadway's Hammerstein Theater, the Beatles have to contend with the New York press corps.

"Do you wear wigs?" one of them asks.

John shuts down the attack on their signature look. "If we do they must be the only ones with real dandruff."

Although the boys from Liverpool don't wear wigs, everyone else seems to—not only does Ed Sullivan don a mop-top wig to introduce them on his show, but their airplane pilot also puts on a Beatles wig when they fly to Miami. Official promotional "Beatle Kits" (comprising an autographed photo, an I LIKE THE BEATLES button, and a wig) are even getting handed out.

Opinion makers seek to quantify what makes fans love the Beatles. Though it's no big mystery— England's *Daily Mirror* has already proclaimed, "You have to be a real sour square not to love the nutty, noisy, happy, handsome Beatles." Documentarians Albert and David Maysles capture every moment—from the Beatles' dazed emergence to screaming crowds waiting on the tarmac at JFK Airport to four limos carrying each individual band member to the Plaza Hotel, on Fifth Avenue, where they have rooms on the twelfth floor. The February 1964 footage for Granada TV is eventually released as the film *What's Happening! The Beatles in the USA.*

"The Americans will never understand it," Ringo later explains. "Now kids come to Liverpool and say, 'Oh, this is where *they* came from.' But for us, it was 'We're in America—where the music came from!' It was always about the music."

On February 10, at the Baroque Room in the Plaza, cameras flash as the band accepts two gold records—signifying one million copies sold apiece—for their album *Meet the Beatles* and their single "I Want to Hold Your Hand," which topped the American charts on February 1, just weeks after its December 26, 1963, rush release.

On Sunday, February 9, 1964, at 8:00 p.m., seventy-three million people—plus the 728 inside the theater—tune in to watch the Beatles perform live. An odd protester or two, including one young man holding a sign reading ALONZO TUSKE HATES THE BEATLES, contends with a robust police presence patrolling the streets.

The televised caption SORRY GIRLS, HE'S MARRIED

does little to calm the fervor of fans who decree by placard JOHN, DIVORCE CYNTHIA.

"Us guys had to play it kind of cool," recalls Joe Perry, who would go on to found and play guitar in the band Aerosmith, of his school-age self, "because the girls were so excited and were drawing little hearts on their notebooks—'I love Paul,' that kind of thing. But I think there was an unspoken thing with the guys that we all dug the Beatles, too. We just couldn't come right out and say it."

In Hicksville, Long Island, a musically inclined fourteen-year-old is also watching. "I remember noticing John that first time on the Sullivan show," Billy Joel later recalls. "He's standing there, looking around him as if to say, 'Is all this corny or what?'"

In the first of two musical segments, the Beatles sing "All My Loving" followed by the Peggy Lee ballad "Till There Was You." As John sings "She Loves You," a song he and Paul wrote while strumming their guitars on opposite beds at a hotel in Newcastle, England, he recalls that Paul's father, Jim, asked, "Couldn't you sing, 'She loves you, yes, yes, yes?' There's enough of these Americanisms around."

There is nothing proper about the way the fans—nearly three thousand of them—carry on a few days later, on February 12, at a pair of thirty-minute concerts at Carnegie Hall. "Shut up!" John shouts at the screaming masses, who were producing noise a local DJ describes as "the most piercing, uncomfortable sound I've ever heard."

It was like "that terrible screech the BMT Astoria train makes as it turns east near 59th Street and Seventh Avenue," remarks the *New York Herald Tribune*.

At their show in Washington, DC, the noise is so loud that journalist Michael Braun reports, "One of the policemen at the ringside removed two .38 caliber bullets from his belt and placed them in his ears."

The strain of their popularity is already starting to wear, even when it comes to making music.

Music journalist Larry Kane, who at age twenty-one is reporting for WFUN Miami, remembers, "They never did sound checks—usually there wasn't time. And modern musicians will look at the puny sound equipment they had and will be amazed. Some concerts had the music going out on the stadium public address system."

"No theater ever got it how we liked it," John says of the setup on the microphones. "They'd either be in the wrong position or not loud enough. They would just set it up as they would for amateur talent night. Perhaps we had a chip about them not taking our music seriously. It drove us mad."

The Beatles arrive in Miami, Florida, on February 16. Thirteen-year-old Lynn Henderson, a journalism student at Miami Springs Junior High, is wearing her construction-paper press badge when the band lands at Miami International Airport to a crowd of five thousand. She runs for the limousine, and the police give chase.

John Lennon sees Henderson's homemade badge and holds off the cops while he, Paul, and Ringo answer her interview questions. Then "John blew me a kiss and the window slid shut and they took off."

Henderson earns an A in class and so do the Beatles, whom Ed Sullivan introduces as "four of the nicest youngsters we've ever had on our stage."

The Beatles have never seen a palm tree before—or a policeman carrying a gun. But a staged press opportunity is already familiar.

"It was all part of being a Beatle, really," George says of the scene on February 18 at Miami Beach's 5th Street Gym, where twenty-two-year-old 1960 Olympic gold medalist boxer Cassius Clay is in training for an upcoming fight against world heavyweight champion Sonny Liston, and the Beatles are "just getting lugged around and thrust into rooms full of press men taking pictures and asking questions." Clay (later known as Muhammad Ali) "was quite cute" and goofed around with the band for a series of photographs. He delivers a taunt to his rival, the heavily favored thirty-one-year-old Liston, rhyming "When Liston reads about the Beatles visiting me / He'll get so mad, I'll knock him out in three!"

But Liston dismisses the gibes, sneering, "Are these motherfuckers what all the people are screaming about? My dog plays drums better than that kid with the big nose."

Liston is wrong about the Beatles and about his prospects against Clay. On February 25, Cassius Clay dethrones Sonny Liston, and the Beatles are back in the studio (taking a break that evening to celebrate George's twenty-first birthday), already hard at work recording for their next big project.

The Beatles are going to star in a film.

CHAPTER 21

So glad we made it.
— "Gimme Some Lovin'"

T he movie shoot is scheduled to take seven weeks. They're calling it *Beatlemania,* and the assumption is it'll be a cheap cookie-cutter teen flick designed to capitalize on the Beatles' massive success with that audience.

It's March of 1964, and "Can't Buy Me Love" (which Paul and John had written over the course of a few hours during a break in Miami) is the first British single to hit number 1 simultaneously in Britain and the United States. The record is certified gold even before its release, selling two million copies during its first week on sale.

The Beatles have the top five singles on the American charts.

John doesn't have high hopes for their film, which

chronicles the thirty-six hours leading up to a tele-vised concert—until he finds out that the director, Richard Lester, was responsible for bringing John's favorite zany radio comedy, *The Goon Show,* to televi-sion. The Beatles, John says, are "the extension of that rebellion." And the screenwriter, Alun Owen, was raised in Liverpool and wrote an acclaimed TV show about the city called *No Trams to Lime Street*—John cheekily noted that "Lime Street is a famous street in Liverpool where the whores used to be"—but more seriously, Owen "was famous for writing Liverpool dialogue."

"The trouble is, it's only us who can write for us," John laments. Still, with a director and screenwriter both as driven about filmmaking as John is about music, he readjusts his attitude.

But not about acting. It's "fucking stupid, isn't it?" he says to Dick Lester of his boredom with the strict shooting schedules, early morning calls, and endless waiting on set.

Lester quickly decides that little acting is required, choosing a black-and-white cinema verité style to capture the Beatles' humor, which is amplified by the bond among the four. "They had this great thing of gangs," the director later reflects, a sense of "us against the world."

Late in the filming, on set, Ringo is talking about their having yet another "hard day's night."

"What does that mean?" a young woman asks.

"It's a Ringoism," John explains, "said not to be funny, just said."

Ringo elaborates on his way with words. "I used to, while I was saying one thing, have another thing come into my brain and move down fast. Once when we were working all day and into the night, I came out thinking it was still day and said, 'It's been a hard day,' and looked round and noticing it was dark, '. . .'s night!'"

Dick Lester loves it, and during the film's final production stage, he tells John the movie title has changed from *Beatlemania* to *A Hard Day's Night*.

Which means John and Paul have to come up with a new title track.

It takes them twenty-four hours—with a little help from journalist Maureen Cleave.

In a taxi on the way to a recording session at Abbey Road, John shows her lyrics he had written on a fan's birthday card to Julian—"When I get home to you / I find my tiredness is through." Maureen balks at "tiredness" and, borrowing her pen, John changes the lines to: "When I get home to you / I find the things that you do / Will make me feel all right."

John takes full creative credit, saying that "I did practically every single with my voice except for "Love Me Do." Either my song, or my voice, or both"—though he acknowledges, "The only reason he [Paul] sang on 'A Hard Day's Night' was because I couldn't reach the notes."

But they can always deliver. Of the songwriting process, John says, "Sometimes we write together. Sometimes not. Some of them take four hours; some twenty minutes. Others have been known to take as long as three weeks."

"John needed Paul's attention to detail and persistence," says Cynthia. "Paul needed John's anarchic, lateral thinking."

Before the film even premieres, the Beatles perform songs from the sound track on their first world tour, which takes them as far as Australia. On June 11, Australian television—in operation only since 1956—makes the Beatles' arrival in Sydney live news.

The response delights Derek Taylor, press manager for the 1964 world tour, but it doesn't surprise him. Taylor met the band in May of 1963 as a reporter for the *Daily Express* covering a show at the Odeon Cinema in Manchester. "I'm obsessed with them," he says during the Australian tour. "Isn't everybody?"

"Each time we'd arrive at an airport," Taylor recalls, "it was as if de Gaulle had landed, or better yet, the Messiah. The routes were lined solid, cripples threw away their sticks, sick people rushed up to the car as if a touch from one of the boys would make them well again, old women stood watching with their grandchildren and as we'd pass by I could see the look on their faces. It was as if some savior had arrived."

John has brought along a personal savior on the world tour—Aunt Mimi. Despite their early antagonisms, "I owe her a lot," he says. "She practically brought me up single-handed after my mother died. A wonderful woman."

And one who was kept separate from tour antics. "There were lots of girls who were very keen to party with anybody from the tour," recalls Noel Tresider, keyboardist with Melbourne supporting act the Phantoms, but John takes the music as seriously as ever. When issues with the sound equipment in Wellington, New Zealand, can't be resolved, he threatens to cancel the remaining concerts. The shows go on until days before the film opens.

On July 6, the Beatles are back in England and join Princess Margaret, Lord Snowdon, and the Rolling Stones for the premiere of *A Hard Day's Night* at the London Pavilion. The movie opens to fantastic reviews—and record profits. The studio makes $5.8 million in six weeks against a $500,000 expenditure; the film later earns two 1965 Academy Award nominations, for best original screenplay and best music (for George Martin's score, not the Beatles' songs).

The film holds up as both a promotional piece and a legitimate work of art—a surrealist mock documentary–slash–Marx Brothers film that show-cases the Liverpudlian musicians' charisma and wit.

"No attempt has been made," *Variety* writes, "to build the Beatles up as Oliviers; they are at their best when the pic has a misleading air of off-the-cuff spontaneity."

But how do they rate back home in Liverpool, where John and the others have heard that the local fans have soured on the Beatles? The Cavern, where they haven't performed since August of 1963, has reportedly written them off. "That's Liddypool for you," grouses Paul.

In the four days between the London and Liverpool film premieres, near terror sets in. Fans, John says, "only like people when they're on the way up." Friends of the band "kept coming down to London," Ringo recalls, "saying, 'You're finished in Liverpool.'"

Yet lining the familiar streets surrounding the Odeon Cinema at home are fans, thousands and thousands of them, hoping to catch a glimpse of the four young men whose home-grown brand of fame and music are still very much celebrated.

John declares *A Hard Day's Night* "not as good as James Bond," though with the London premiere of *Goldfinger* due in September, he stands an even chance with Sean Connery for delivering on the third Bond film's tagline: "Everything he touches turns to excitement!"

CHAPTER 22

We can climb so high
I never want to die.
—"Born to Be Wild"

That August, the Beatles head back to America. They perform twenty-six shows across the United States and Canada.

The tour is intense.

Insane.

The fans are obsessed. Girls like fifteen-year-old Sandi Stewart do anything they can to sneak into hotels to meet the Beatles. Reflecting back, Sandi said of her favorite Beatle, John, "He seemed so intelligent and witty. His body was very sexy. He became the one I loved passionately," she says. "When absolutely nothing else in my life was good, I'd go to my room and have the Beatles, especially my darling John. They all furnished something I desperately needed."

"George is the handsomest and he's loving it all," states Maureen Cleave (again on tour with the band for London's *Evening Standard*) in a piece for the *San Francisco Examiner* headlined HOW THE FRENZIED, FURRY BEATLES TOOK OVER ENGLAND. An American fan swoons, "George has got sexy eyelashes. He's got sexy eyelashes!"

John breaks down the band's appeal. "We reckoned we could make it because there were four of us. None of us would've made it alone, because Paul wasn't quite strong enough, I didn't have enough girl-appeal, George was too quiet, and Ringo was the drummer. But we thought that everyone would be able to dig at least one of us, and that's how it turned out."

During performances, audience members toss objects at them, especially candies. Initially, the gesture is meant as a tribute to George, who was quoted in an article as professing a love of sweets, but by 1963 he replies to a fan letter and specifically asks it to stop.

"We don't like Jelly Babies, or Fruit Gums for that matter, so think how we feel standing on the stage trying to dodge the stuff, before you throw some more at us. Couldn't you eat them yourself, besides it is dangerous. I was hit in the eye once with a boiled sweet, and it's not funny!"

But instead the behavior only escalates. "They

hurt," Ringo says of being pelted with hard candies and objects like flashbulbs and hair curlers. "They just felt like hailstones."

John, who refuses to wear his heavy horn-rimmed glasses onstage—"Mustn't spoil the image," he says—has even had contact lenses painfully knocked out after flying offerings hit him in the face.

"You feel a clonk on the back of the head," John says, "and you look and it's a shoe. Then once one comes they all start thinking, 'Shoes: that'll attract their attention. If they get a shoe on the head, they're bound to look over here.'"

Beatlemania has intensified to a level that the group's press man, Brian Sommerville, deems "entirely out of control."

Photographer David Magnus, who travels with the band, illustrates the phenomenon. "I had been in one of the back dressing rooms, and one of the female studio staff put her hand on my shoulder and said, 'I must touch you—you've been in the same room as the Beatles.'"

"What happened to us in the States was just like Britain," Ringo says, "only ten times bigger, so I suppose it wasn't like Britain at all."

It was, John later says, "madness from morning to night with not one moment's peace."

America in 1964 is a vastly different place from England. Though John and Cyn are used to encountering some "really weird characters" outside their London flat, they seem more annoying than dangerous. But in America, where armed police are around and a popular president was recently gunned down, things feel more ominous. John wonders if someone out there in the mob of screaming fans is harboring dark thoughts.

He's not being paranoid. Right before their shows in Dallas and Las Vegas, the band is told that someone phoned in a bomb threat. Yet when John is performing, the stage is his sanctuary. "I feel safe as long as I'm plugged in," he tells a reporter. "I don't feel as though they'll get me."

The Beatles travel with an entourage, including British and American reporters. To pass the time on flights, the boys play poker and Monopoly. Art Schreiber, senior correspondent for the Westinghouse Broadcasting Company, says "John always got really involved and excited. He always stood up to throw the dice."

But Schreiber also picks up on a darker current in John, one that director Richard Lester had observed on the set of *A Hard Day's Night.* "I noticed this quality he had of standing outside every situation and noting the vulnerabilities of everyone, including myself," Lester remarks. "He was always watching."

"What really surprised me was what a helluva lot John already knew about this country,"

Schreiber—whose longtime beat was politics, not entertainment—later says about Lennon. "The thing he couldn't understand was the violence...the murder of Kennedy, the police brutality against innocent marchers in the South, the guns he saw being carried everywhere. I could see the soul of an activist building up in him."

An activist, yes—but not a diplomat. John especially chafed at expectations that the group appear on behalf of charitable causes. "I always hated all the social things," John says. "All the horrible events and presentations we had to go to. All false." At a cocktail party at the British embassy in DC, he became irate over the imperious way the diplomats acted. "These people have no bloody manners," he groused.

On August 23, 1964, they play the Hollywood Bowl. Months before, advance tickets had sold out in less than four hours. The amphitheater, with its white shell-shaped roof, dates to the golden age of Hollywood and is one of America's most important live-music venues.

John approves of it, noting, "We could be heard in a place like the Hollywood Bowl, even though the crowd was wild: good acoustics."

Crowd noise is a very real obstacle for George Martin, who is recording the concert (unreleased until 1977) for Capitol Records. Dealing with the screams from thousands of Beatles fans was like "putting a microphone at the tail end of a 747 jet," Martin says.

Ringo develops his own technique. "I just had to hang on to the backbeat all the time to keep everybody together" over the screams. "I used to have to follow their three bums wiggling to see where we were in the song."

But while they enjoyed this time in California—"I fell in love with Hollywood then," said Ringo—it also brought them some bad press. Despite tight controls on the band, when voluptuous blond starlet Jayne Mansfield shows up at the Beatles' rented mansion, she persuades the group (sans Paul) to accompany her to the Whisky a Go Go on their last night in Los Angeles.

They caravan to the club, with John, the actress, and journalist Larry Kane sitting together. "Before anyone knew what was happening," Kane recalls, "John grabbed Mansfield and they started making out like mad."

Mansfield had assured the Beatles they would have privacy at the club. She couldn't have been more wrong. Cameras are everywhere, and the place is in a frenzy.

She poses between John and George, one of her hands on each of their thighs. Irritated by the crush of people, George throws a drink at photographer Bob Flora—who perfectly captures the shot.

The next day, George's image is everywhere. "I remember sitting on the plane, reading the paper and there was the photo of me throwing the water," he says.

"When in future days someone would say—and someone often did say it—'You guys never go *out* anywhere. Don't you ever feel shut in?' We would recall the time we went nightclubbing with Jayne Mansfield and sigh," manager Derek Taylor recalled.

The following week, the Beatles return to New York, where John is hoping to meet Bob Dylan. He has asked Al Aronowitz, who covers music for the *Saturday Evening Post,* to make the introduction.

Meeting him has been on John's wish list since the spring of 1964, when a French DJ gave the Beatles *The Freewheelin' Bob Dylan.*

John is a published poet—his first book of drawings and verse, *In His Own Write,* was released in March of 1964, during the filming of *A Hard Day's Night*—and, according to Paul, "the fact that Bob Dylan wrote poetry added to *his* appeal."

The 1963 album—Dylan, now twenty-three, began recording it at age twenty—marked a notable shift, with Dylan joining John and Paul's ranks as a prolific songwriter. On his eponymous first album, Dylan had written two out of thirteen songs; on *Freewheelin',* he wrote *twelve* of thirteen.

Coincidentally, on Dylan's first album, released in

1962, one of the songs he'd recorded was "The House of the Rising Sun," an old folk ballad of unknown provenance. Earlier in 1964, another British band called the Animals relays its own innovative cover, which ends the Beatles' number-one run in America. "Congratulations from the Beatles (a group)," reads the telegram the Fab Four send the Animals, humbly masking a growing anxiety about losing their top place in the British Invasion. Dylan is so taken with the Animals version, in fact, that it's credited with inspiring him to pick up an electric guitar.

Dylan is one of the most distinctive folksingers around. *In case he's not sure of himself,* John thinks of Dylan's lyrics, *he makes it double entendre. So therefore he is secure in his Hipness.*

Brian Epstein has arranged a reception in their suite at the Hotel Delmonico, on Park Avenue, where various American folk groups such as the Kingston Trio and Peter, Paul and Mary—whose 1963 cover of Dylan's "Blowin' in the Wind" was a number-two *Billboard* single—mingle with the Beatles. At one point, the phone rings.

"That was Mr. Aronowitz," Brian tells John. "He's here with Mr. Dylan."

"*Zimmerman,*" John says. "Zimmerman is his name. My name isn't John Beatle. It's John Lennon. Just like that."

Though Al Aronowitz will later call the

introduction "the crowning achievement" of his career, it begins awkwardly, when Dylan's customary request for "cheap wine" is botched because Brian Epstein has only vintage champagne on hand.

That's when talk turns to another mind-altering substance.

"I really like that line in 'I Want to Hold Your Hand,'" Dylan tells them. "'I get high, I get high.'"

"Actually," John says, "it's 'I can't hide, I can't hide.'"

They share a laugh, then Dylan adds, "Here I was, thinking you were singing about smoking pot."

John and Paul exchange embarrassed glances. "We, ah, haven't really tried marijuana before," John says.

Dylan's road manager, Victor Maymudes, rolls a joint for each Beatle.

"Give it to my royal taster," John says, pointing to Ringo.

Ringo takes several hits . . . and can't stop laughing.

John joins in, then Brian.

As Paul spouts existential philosophy and wanders around hugging people, Ringo and George double over in hysterical laughter, especially when the room phone rings and Dylan answers it with, "This is Beatlemania here."

"It was such an amazing night," George later says. "I felt really good. That was a hell of a night."

"Paul came up to me and hugged me for ten

minutes," Maymudes recalls, "and said, 'It was so great, and it's all your fault because I love this pot!'"

"I don't remember much of what we talked about. We were smoking dope, drinking wine, and generally being rock 'n' rollers and having a laugh, you know, and surrealism," John said. "It was party time."

CHAPTER 23

I hope I die before I get old.
——"My Generation"

Paul's the only one left in London.

It's March of 1965. Last month, as the Beatles started work on their second feature film (the working title, *Eight Arms to Hold You,* eventually becomes *Help!*), Ringo married his eighteen-year-old girlfriend, Maureen Cox, a hairdresser from Liverpool, and moved into the same St. George's Hill estate where John lives with Cyn, their two-year-old son, Julian, and a cat named Mimi, after John's aunt. George is living at the Claremont estate, in nearby Esher, with his girlfriend, model Pattie Boyd (whom he'd met when she was an extra on *A Hard Day's Night*).

Although a former assistant claims that "John was basically a lazy bastard" who "was quite happy to stay down in Weybridge, doing fuck-all," John counters, "I wanted to live in London…but I wouldn't risk it until it's quietened down."

There's no sense of anything quieting down anytime soon, however. The Beatles have been on a tremendous roll—"I Feel Fine," their next single after "A Hard Day's Night," hits number 1 in both America and Britain, where it knocks the Rolling Stones' cover of the Howlin' Wolf classic "Little Red Rooster" from the top slot. Lennon and McCartney have coauthored seven number-one hits that year (in addition to "I Want to Hold Your Hand," "She Loves You," "Can't Buy Me Love," "Love Me Do," "A Hard Day's Night," and "I Feel Fine," there's "A World Without Love," a song they wrote but deemed not good enough for the Beatles, so they passed it along to the British duo Peter and Gordon—Peter being Peter Asher, brother of Paul's girlfriend, Jane), giving them the all-time songwriting record for most songs to top the US charts in a calendar year.

Bachelor Paul usually drives his own sporty Aston Martin to songwriting sessions at John's home in St. George's Hill, in Weybridge, but one morning he decides to have a car take him.

The chauffeur looks exhausted, offering a metaphorical description of his work schedule.

Eight days a week.

Like Ringo's "a hard day's night," the phrase

resonates with the band, though John says, "We struggled to record it and struggled to make it into a song." They end up releasing it in December of 1964, on their album *Beatles for Sale,* and in February of 1965 as a single in the United States, where it becomes their seventh US number-one hit. All this success has a punishing pace, however.

"The band," the BBC says in a review, referring to the album's cover photo, "looks, frankly, knackered" from two years of nearly nonstop recording, touring, and filming.

There has hardly been a moment to pause and reflect, yet ironically it was during this busy song-writing time that "I started thinking about my own emotions," John later says, pinpointing the subsequent change in his songwriting to a darker, more personal style.

Though in the past the band had relied "on pills"—like the "Prellies" (phenmetrazine) that got them through twelve-hour performances in Hamburg—to endure grueling performance schedules, it's later revealed that during *Help!* the Beatles were instead "on pot," on what director Dick Lester called "a happy high."

According to Ringo, they have all been "smoking pot for breakfast." To avoid arousing suspicion when they go through customs, the Beatles roadies devise an ingenious concealment: they buy a carton of cigarettes, fill each pack with joints, then use an iron to reseal the cellophane.

"I've always needed a drug to survive," John admits, adding, "The others, too, but I always had more, more pills, more of everything because I'm more crazy probably."

And in the spring of 1965, he and George are introduced to yet another mind-bending substance: LSD.

———— ∞ ————

"Let's go," George Harrison says to his wife, Pattie. The two of them, along with John and Cynthia Lennon, have just finished a nice meal as the dinner guests of London dentist John Riley. They have plans to meet Ringo at a club and catch some new musical acts Brian Epstein is promoting, including their Hamburg friend Klaus Voormann's new band.

"You haven't had any coffee yet. It's ready, I've made it—and it's delicious," their host's girlfriend protests as the group rises to leave.

They agree, but after drinking the coffee, John says they really do have to leave. "These friends of ours are going to be on soon. It's their first night."

"I advise you not to leave," Riley tells them, revealing that he's secretly dosed them with LSD. "It was in the coffee."

John is furious. *"How dare you fucking do this to us!"*

Despite the dentist's attempts to get the foursome to stay—"I think he thought that there was going to be a big gang bang, and that he was going to shag everybody. I really think that was his motive," says George—the four of them take off in Pattie's orange Mini Cooper.

"All the way the car felt smaller and smaller, and by the time we arrived we were completely out of it," Pattie remembers. Cyn is frightened by her altered perceptions, later saying, "It was as if we suddenly found ourselves in the middle of a horror film."

John, on the other hand, is rather enjoying himself. "We were cackling in the streets, and people were shouting 'Let's break a window,' you know, it was just insane. We were just out of our heads." George finds himself undergoing something transcendental: "It was as if I had never tasted, talked, seen, thought or heard properly before."

Eventually they make it to the Ad Lib Club, on Leicester Place, where they pile into an elevator. It has a small red light.

Cyn screams, succumbing to panic. "We all thought there was a fire, but there was just a little red light," John says. "We were all screaming like that, and we were all hot and hysterical."

When the door opens, they rush to tell Ringo about the fire they've hallucinated.

The whole experience feels like something out of John's favorite book, *Alice's Adventures in Wonderland*.

Later, "going about ten miles an hour, but it seemed like a thousand," John remembers, George somehow manages to steer the Mini back to the house. John and Cyn decide to stay the night.

John decides that George's house resembles "a big submarine" that seems "to float above his wall, which was eighteen foot, and I was driving it." He stays up late, making drawings "of four faces saying, 'We all agree with you!'"

"God, it was just terrifying, but it was fantastic."

CHAPTER 24

Hello, darkness, my old friend.
— "The Sound of Silence"

A s work on the *Help!* sound track continues, no one close to John realizes how much the title track mirrors his fraught emotional state. "I am singing about when I was so much younger and all the rest," when really, John says, "it was my fat Elvis period."

John's not himself lately—and he *has* put on weight. *It's stress.* John's second book, *A Spaniard in the Works,* is to be published in June of 1965, and he hasn't yet finished it, complaining that the writing feels like schoolwork.

During composition of the sound track, the ever-present Lennon-McCartney musical rivalry bubbles over, in part because of the rigors of their contractual obligations to EMI. As John later tells *Rolling Stone,*

"They would say well, you're going to make an album and get together and knock off a few songs, just like a job."

Paul remembers "Ticket to Ride"—the first Beatles song to run over three minutes—as a collaboration that took shape during a February 1965 afternoon session at John's house. "We wrote the melody together," he says. "Because John sang it, you might have to give him 60 percent of it."

Although in interviews, John stakes a greater claim, telling *Playboy,* "That's me, one of the earliest heavy-metal records," and that "Paul's contribution was the way Ringo played the drums," the two collaborate as well as ever. Even if their disagreements got to the level of name-calling, Paul recalls, "he'd let it settle for a second and then he lowered his glasses and he said, 'It's only me...'" and put his glasses back on again. "Those were the moments when I actually saw him without the facade," Paul says, "the John Lennon he was frightened to reveal to the world."

But John is itching to move on. He sees the strictures of touring as the artistic death of the Beatles. "That's why we never improved as musicians; we killed ourselves then to make it. And that was the end of it."

John has a point, but still, the band does put out good songs—crowd-pleasing pop songs, yes, but isn't it their job to give the fans what they want? Songs like "I Want to Hold Your Hand" and "Please Please Me" made them international superstars. "Eight Days a Week" is full of energy. Makes you feel good.

Is it mainstream? Sure. But Paul *likes* mainstream, enjoys being a commercial songwriter. He's so open to inspiration that when a song comes to him in a dream, he wakes himself up. "I got out of bed, sat at the piano, found G, found F sharp minor 7th—and that leads you through then to B and E minor, and finally back to E. It all leads forward logically." Paul finds his musical epiphany "the most magic thing."

In the morning, the tune still fresh in his mind, Paul gives it the offbeat title of "Scrambled Eggs."

On set, Paul works at the song constantly, much to director Richard Lester's annoyance. The budget is much bigger this time around, thanks to the massive success of *A Hard Day's Night,* and the film will be released in color, but they've only got four weeks to shoot it. Lester tells Paul to finish the bloody song or he'll have the piano on the set removed.

"Blimey, he's always talking about [that song]," George remarks. "You'd think he was Beethoven or somebody!"

On vacation in Portugal in June of 1965, Paul and his girlfriend, Jane Asher, take a long drive. As Jane naps, Paul sings to himself, "Da-da-da...yes-ter-day...

sud-den-ly...fun-ni-ly...mer-ri-ly..." until he has the lyrics.

"The song was around for months and months," John remembers, but Paul couldn't settle on a title. "Every time we got together to write songs or for a recording session, this would come up," he says. "Then, one morning, Paul woke up, and the song and the title were both there. Completed! I know it sounds like a fairy tale, but it is the plain truth. I was sorry, in a way, because we had so many laughs about it."

The recording session is on for later that month, right before Paul's twenty-third birthday. When George Martin hears the completed song, he doesn't think it has the Beatles sound. He preps Paul to sing it solo, replacing the band with a classical string quartet.

When they break for lunch, Paul approaches cellist Francisco Gabarro. "We have a winner with that 'Yesterday,'" he predicts.

Not immediately. Though "Yesterday" makes the *Help!* sound track, it's not played in the film, nor is it released as a single in the UK, though it hits number 1 in the United States.

When asked about his involvement in the song, John is explicit. "'Yesterday,'" he says, "I had nothing to do with."

CHAPTER 25

I know what it's like to be dead.
　　　　　—"She Said She Said"

"S top worrying!" United Artists' movie posters commanded. "*Help!* is on the way."

Not so for law enforcement assigned to cover the American tour in support of the sound track. "The Beatles may sing rock 'n' roll, but they've got the cops moaning the blues," the *Long Island Star-Journal* had reported on the Beatles' August 1964 tour stop in New York.

One year later, there are heightened procedures in place.

The Beatles are in a helicopter transporting them from Manhattan to the grounds of the World's Fair, in Queens, where they'll be whisked into an armored truck flanked by sixty officers and onto a stage built specially for tonight's show at Shea Stadium.

As the copter flies over Shea, John listens to the roar of the fans, which can be heard all the way up here, over the noise of the helicopter's engine. PAUL, THROW US A KISS, RINGO, THROW US A RING, one banner pleads. Flashbulbs pop like machine-gun fire.

The American promoter of the concert, Sid Bernstein, marvels at the sight.

"It's the top of the mountain, Sid," John says.

At the Olympic-size swimming pool on the grounds of the Beatles' rented mansion in Los Angeles, John and Paul are on a secret mission.

"There were good nights and bad nights on the tours," Ringo says. "But they were all the same. The only fun part was the hotels in the evening, smoking pot and that."

That is what John and George want to share with Paul and Ringo. On LSD, George recalls, "I had such an overwhelming feeling of well-being, that there was a God, and I could see him in every blade of grass. It was like gaining hundreds of years of experience in twelve hours."

Deeper experience, too. John has always treated George, the youngest Beatle, as "a kid who played guitar."

"After taking acid [we] had a very interesting relationship," George says. "I felt closer to him than all the others . . . just by the look in his eyes, I felt we were connected."

John agrees. "We are probably the most cracked," he says of himself and George, while "Paul is a bit more stable than George and I."

And though John and George make it clear that "we couldn't relate" to the uninitiated, Paul isn't swayed, though he "felt very left out," George later says. Still, while Ringo is willing to experiment, Paul holds back. "It was the way I'd been brought up," he explains. " 'Beware the demon drug.' " But George admits, "We were all slightly cruel to him," taunting Paul, "We're taking it and you're not." The other three all drop acid, along with musicians David Crosby and Roger McGuinn of the Byrds and actor Peter Fonda.

Fonda points up at a helicopter flying far too close to the mansion. It's a familiar sight. "They come over to the house with telephoto lenses and take pictures to see if I'm smoking pot or taking LSD," Fonda later tells *Esquire* magazine. *"Hello, fellas, you dirty bastards!"*

"You have to be a bastard to make it. That's a fact," John later says. "And the Beatles were the biggest bastards of all."

Now, only George is distressed.

To ease his thoughts, Fonda tells George a story about when he was ten years old and did something dangerous—he accidentally shot himself in the stomach. It must be true. Fonda has a four-inch scar across his midsection.

Fonda keeps whispering, "I know what it's like to be dead, man."

Alone, John writes a letter to Cyn, filled with longing and regret.

"We gave the whole of our youth to the Beatles," he laments, reflecting on his family—Cyn and Julian, who is now two and a half.

"I've missed years of Julian's life."

Back in 1963, he'd insisted that "touring was a relief, just to get out of Liverpool and break new ground." Now the pressures of that life are weighing on him.

"I spend hours in dressing rooms and things thinking about the times I've wasted not being with him...of those stupid bastard times when I keep reading bloody newspapers and other shit whilst he's in the room with me and I've decided it's ALL WRONG! He doesn't see enough of me as it is and I really want him to know me and love me, and miss me like I seem to be missing both of you so much...."

CHAPTER 26

A working class hero is something to be.
— "Working Class Hero"

It's October 26, 1965, and the police at Buckingham Palace are unprepared for the heaving crowd of thousands, including an intrepid few who even climb the palace gates. But it's not Queen Elizabeth they're hoping for a glimpse of—it's the Fab Four, who are among 189 individuals due to be receiving honors from Her Majesty that morning.

A few months earlier, each of the Beatles had received a nondescript brown envelope at his home address, alerting him to this news. The rest of the world found out on June 12, when the Beatles' names were included on the thirty-nine-year-old queen's annual "Birthday Honours List." The Beatles are to be distinguished as Members of the Order of the British Empire (MBE), which—though lowest among the five classes of appointment to the order—is an honor never before given to a pop band. In fact, an MBE has never before been given to anyone under the age of twenty-five.

Many esteemed MBE recipients don't want to share their honors with the boys from Liverpool. Some go so far as to return their awards to Buckingham Palace in protest. One of them, Colonel Frederick Wagg, declares, "Decorating the Beatles has made a mockery of everything this country stands for. I've heard them sing and play, and I think they're terrible."

Most attitudes are a little more tempered, however. While one Liverpool man interviewed says that "in some respects" he agrees with the argument that giving the award to the Beatles is debasing it, he also says, "I think they've done a lot of good. Nobody's had a bad word to say for them at all. They've not been a bad example to anybody." And unsurprisingly, the response from a female fan is that the award is simply "smashing! They should have got it and I think they're great!"

Among themselves, the band pronounces the MBE "daft," then decides "it all just seemed part of the game we'd agreed to play."

Although none of their families is present at Buckingham Palace—or Buck House, as John calls it—to watch the Beatles' investiture ceremony in the Great Throne Room that day, the four of them are accompanied by a proud and glowing Brian Epstein. And no matter how much they might want to downplay it, the truth is that they're all more than a bit overwhelmed to be in this situation.

"To start with," John says, "we wanted to laugh. But when it happens to you, when you are being decorated, you don't laugh anymore"—though they did have a smoke in a palace washroom. "Although we didn't believe in the Royal Family, you can't help being impressed when you're in the palace, when you know you're standing in front of the Queen," John adds. "It was like in a dream. It was beautiful."

John takes his medal, tucked inside its small presentation box, to Mendips, Aunt Mimi's home. Playing the role of the queen, he pins the medal on Mimi's chest and tells her she deserves it more than he does.

But if meeting the queen was something the Beatles hadn't initially cared much about one way or the other, meeting the *King* is a different story.

While they'd been on tour in Los Angeles, they'd had the evening of August 27 off from performing, and the opportunity arose to meet their hero: Elvis Presley. They'd all leaped at the chance to go to visit him at his home in Bel Air.

"We just idolized the guy so much," John says.

"We were all major fans, so it was hero worship of a high degree," Paul says in agreement.

George voices the band's sole condition. "If this is going to be another dirty big publicity circus, let's forget it."

Though Brian Epstein and Elvis's manager both agree to a photo- and recording-free secret event, fans and media catch wind of it anyway and tail the Beatles' limousines all the way from their rented mansion, in Benedict Canyon, to Elvis's, in Bel Air. But a few joints smoked en route calm the Beatles down over the unwanted intrusion.

Even so, John recalls that they were all "terrified" at the sight of Elvis Presley in the circular room where he receives guests. John's heart is pounding. *It's Elvis! It's Elvis!*

In addition to Elvis, his then girlfriend, Priscilla, is there, as are half a dozen or so members of his entourage, a.k.a. the Memphis Mafia. But after introductions are made, there's an awkward silence. No one knows exactly what to say.

Now what?

Elvis finally breaks the ice. "If you guys are just gonna sit there and stare at me, I'm goin' to bed. . . . I didn't mean for this to be like subjects calling on the King. I thought we'd sit and talk about music and maybe jam a little."

Everyone laughs, and the King starts picking out notes on a Fender bass and calls for someone to bring in some guitars.

John picks up a guitar, and Paul gives Elvis a few bass tips while Ringo "[taps] out the backbeat with his fingers on the nearest bits of wooden furniture" to the tune of "I Feel Fine." George plays for a while, then wanders around a bit. "I spent most of the party trying to suss out from the gang if anybody had any reefers," he later said, but he didn't have much luck. "They were 'uppers and whiskey' people."

Several hours later, around two in the morning, as the music carries them out of the house and onto the street, John has an observation to share. "Elvis was stoned."

To George, the answer is obvious. "Aren't we all?"

CHAPTER 27

Ah, you don't believe we're on the eve of
destruction.

—"Eve of Destruction"

The Beatles have run out of songs.

Yet the band is contractually obligated to put out its sixth studio album in time for Christmas.

And all the songs have to be great. Lennon-McCartney originals, not covers.

There is reason to worry. Rivals on two continents are spoiling for a takedown.

The Rolling Stones jokingly criticized the Beatles for the rigid, Liverpudlian way the band positions their guitars, high up on their chests. "No wonder you can only rock," Keith Richards tells John. "No wonder you can't roll."

In the summer of 1965, the Rolling Stones' single "Satisfaction" surpasses the Beatles' "Help!" on the

charts en route to becoming the Stones' first number-
one hit in America.

Keith Richards and Mick Jagger had even upped
the ante on songwriting. If the melody for "Scrambled Eggs" came to Paul in a dream, "I wrote
'Satisfaction' in my sleep," Richards says. "I pushed
rewind"—on the cassette player he kept next to his
bed—"and there was 'Satisfaction.'"

⁕

John lies on the king-size bed inside his mansion.
Five hours later, he's still empty of ideas, until
suddenly:

...a Nowhere Man...

He writes the song in minutes.

Paul remembers polishing up the chorus. "He'd
say, 'Nowhere land,' and I'd say, 'For nobody.' It was
a two-way thing."

In one week, the Beatles come up with seven songs.

George Martin is always with them in the studio,
listening and watching, giving advice, perplexed as
ever that "John couldn't be bothered even to tune his
guitar. He was a completely impractical man."

One night, when they're recording late, the control
room intercom switches on, and John hears Brian's
voice. He snaps into focus.

"Something doesn't sound quite right," Brian says.

An uncomfortable silence follows. Brian is clearly drunk. Just as clear is the fact that he's trying to impress his male companion.

Not for the first time, John reminds Brian who does what. "You just take care of your percentage and leave us to worry about the music."

Four weeks later, on November 12, the album is finished.

Now it needs a title. John says, "We should call it the *Pot Album.*"

They share a laugh about all the times they've "shared a laugh" during this recording.

Paul mentions something an old blues guy said of the Rolling Stones: "Mick Jagger, man. Well, you know they're good—but it's plastic soul."

John likes the wordplay of *Rubber Soul*. Rubber soles are very popular in Britain. The cobbler glues them to the bottom of people's shoes to fight the damp.

But when a dark piece of John's past resurfaces, it's not as easy to repair.

CHAPTER 28

Turn off your mind relax and float downstream.
　　　　　　　　—"Tomorrow Never Knows"

There's been an unexpected development on the home front.

Alfred (called "Alf" or "Freddie") Lennon, John's long-absent father, has emerged and told his life story to *Tit-Bits,* a weekly magazine that features scantily clad girls on the cover and eye-grabbing headlines such as HOW WOMEN TURN MEN INTO POOR LOVERS.

Alf, it seems, has ambitions to become a recording artist, just like his son. His single, "That's My Life (My Love and My Home)," is released at the same time as *Rubber Soul.*

"*Rubber Soul* broke everything open," Steve Winwood, then frontman of the Spencer Davis Group, says. "It crossed music into a whole new dimension and was responsible for kicking off the sixties rock era as we know it."

Alf's recording career, on the other hand, spans a single day. His record tanks—and he's not too pleased about it. Nor is John pleased to learn that kind Cyn has invited his father into their home when "the ignoble Alf" turned up unannounced one day.

He'd first resurfaced in John's life on April 1, 1964, when Brian had phoned to tell John that the elder Lennon was in his office. With a journalist.

John headed over to NEMS Enterprises in London to see his father—for the first time in seventeen years. "I don't feel as if I owe him anything," John's always said. "He never helped me. I got here by my-self, and this is the longest I've ever done anything, except being at school."

"It wasn't what you would call a happy reunion," a witness said. "It was very tense."

"What do you want, then?" John asked coldly.

Alf gave John his side of the story, describing how Julia Lennon left him for another man while he was out working at sea, how Mimi and the other Stanley girls were dead set against him from the very beginning, how they forced him to give up any sort of right to custody. John felt himself thaw a bit. He knew all about how tough Mimi and his aunts could be.

"The world deserves to know the truth," Alf said.

Alf has no idea he's being used.

Behind his father's approach is British tabloid the *Daily Sketch,* which offered to forgo printing Alf's story in exchange for exclusive interviews with John and the other Beatles.

And there it is.

Brian refused, and the story eventually went to *Tit-Bits.*

The next time Alf stops by the house, John *is* home—and his father's not alone. He's brought along his manager.

Alf, John notices, has also had extensive dental work done.

The record company "made me get my teeth seen to," Alf explains. "It cost £109. I'm still paying it up, £10 a month."

"It was only the second time in my life I'd seen him," John said later, describing the scene. "I showed him the door. I wasn't having him in the house."

"I know you're behind pulling my record," Alf accuses his celebrity son—an accusation Alf's manager later repeats to the *Daily Mail*—but John isn't having it.

"I had too many father figures," John later says, but that doesn't make his own struggle to be a father to Julian any easier.

Admittedly, "I'm not the greatest dad on earth; I'm

doing me best. But I'm a very irritable guy, and I get depressed. I'm up and down, up and down."

He slams the door on Alf in disgust.

⁂

During repeated acid trips—a thousand over time, John later estimates—"a lot of early childhood was coming out."

A 1964 book called *The Psychedelic Experience* pulls him even deeper. Lines jump out at John and seize his mind and soul:

Do not struggle.

Trust your divinity, trust your brain, trust your companions.

Whenever in doubt, turn off your mind, relax, float downstream.

Coauthored by Timothy Leary, Ralph Metzner, and Richard Alpert—former Harvard clinical psychologists ousted from the university not only for taking the psychotropics LSD and psilocybin alongside their research subjects but also for forcing their students to take them—*The Psychedelic Experience* is about the therapeutic uses of mild-altering drugs. John interprets the book's message as "I should destroy my ego and I did."

So he wants no part of the extensive tour UK Brian is proposing for December of 1965. The band agrees to only nine UK dates. Then they'll make three international stops before they reprise their American summer tour in 1966.

On April 6, 1966, the Beatles return to the studio to record what John dubs "the acid album."

John wishes Stu Sutcliffe were still alive to design the cover for the album they'll call *Revolver.* Between 1963 and 1965, photographer Robert Freeman had created covers for four British Beatles albums, including a "stretched" look for *Rubber Soul,* but John wants to push it further. So he calls up Klaus Voormann, their German artist friend from Hamburg, and tasks him to work with Robert Whitaker, who'd been the Beatles' official photographer since they'd met during the 1964 Australian tour, to create a distinctive new look that combines drawings and photographs.

John is "eating acid all the time," and he writes "a sad song, an acidy song," which opens "She said / I know what it's like to be dead"—about the story Peter Fonda told the year before in Los Angeles. And he plays George Martin the song he wants to close out the album. It's called "Tomorrow Never Knows." Accompanying himself on the acoustic guitar, he sings lines straight from *The Psychedelic Experience*: "Turn off your mind relax and float downstream..."

December 6, 1980

You gals are waiting for someone, I bet."
     He gives the two women standing in front of
the Dakota his best smile to put them at ease.
Now small talk.

Successful manipulation, Mark knows, requires that
the prey feel safe at all times. Charm, kindness, and
flattery must be used constantly in order to disarm
the victim.

When he met Gloria, at the travel agency in
Hawaii, he told her he wanted to take a trip around
the world. She worked with him for hours, days,
planning the fantasy voyage down to the last detail.
With every moment in his presence, Gloria was
falling deeper in love.

These two young women are eyeing him

suspiciously. Which is to be expected. He is a stranger, and this is New York. Bad, awful things happen here every day, every hour—especially to young, attractive women.

"As a matter of fact," the curly-haired brunette says, "we're waiting for you." She gives him the once-over. "It wasn't worth it."

Mark is genuinely stung by the insult. He shows it, too—it's important to display the psychic wound. Then, when the aggressor reveals vulnerability, brought on by innate niceness and strong desire to avoid appearing rude—overpower her.

He reaches for the gun.

"I was only teasing you," the brunette says and smiles. She offers her hand.

Mark releases his grip on the revolver, shakes her hand, and introduces himself.

"I'm Jude Stein," she says. "This is my friend Jeri Moll."

"Hey Jude, don't make it bad," Mark sings. He chuckles. "I bet nobody ever said that to you before."

Jeri Moll makes a groaning sound.

Mark knows she's thinking he's just like any other guy. *I'm not. She'll see.*

He'll play their game—for now. These two clearly have a sense of entitlement. They think their proximity to the Dakota makes them the most knowledgeable of all Lennon fans. The most special.

"I heard John Lennon lives here," he says, all innocence. "I was hoping to get his autograph. Is he in town?"

"You can be sure of one thing," Jude replies. "John Lennon is somewhere in New York City."

His heart surges with joy. His smile is genuine.

Mark tells them he's flown from Hawaii for a chance to meet his idol.

He gauges their reaction. They're falling for his normal act.

He gets the women to open up to him some more. They're both in their late twenties, and they tell him that for the past five years they've come here almost every single night to try to talk to John and Yoko.

"We're permanent fixtures here," Jude says. "And John and Yoko know us well."

"*Really* well," Jeri Moll adds. "We're like family."

Bullshit, Mark wants to scream. *Lennon doesn't care about his fans—he lies to them.*

"Back in October," Jude says, "we were waiting out here with birthday gifts for John and Sean. Yoko saw us, and when we told her about the presents? *She invited us up.*"

Jeri Moll squeals with excitement. "To their apartment!"

"I mean, we were *shocked*. I've never been more shocked in my entire life."

You will be, Mark thinks, smiling.

"Yoko called Sean over," Jude says, "and after we gave him the present, she invited us for tea, in their dining room. Can you believe it?"

You're so blind. So blind and stupid and mindless. Lennon is not Jesus, and I'm going to prove it to you.

"That's . . . wow," Mark says, putting on a face of bewilderment and wonder, like a child who has been invited inside Santa's secret workshop. "That is so amazing."

Mark keeps encouraging them to talk. If what they're saying is true—and it may very well be, because the two women seem to know not only the doorman but also everyone entering and leaving the building—they could prove useful. When Lennon arrives, he'll feel comfortable approaching them—will *want* to approach them. *Which will bring Lennon closer. To me.*

Mark's hand squeezes the gun, his skin tingling with excitement as Jude says, "Have you listened to *Double Fantasy?*"

"Not yet."

"You should buy a copy. I think it's John's greatest work. If you have a copy, I bet he'll sign it."

What a perfect ruse, Mark realizes. If he's holding it, Lennon will be more apt to stop and sign it. *I'll give Lennon the album and then, instead of removing a pen from my jacket pocket, I'll remove my gun and shoot him.*

Mark waves good-bye and walks up Columbus

Avenue, where he finds a record store with posters of Lennon in the windows. He purchases a copy of *Double Fantasy* and stares at the photo on the cover, a black-and-white shot of John and Yoko kissing.

He imagines his face on the cover.

Imagines himself leaning forward to kiss Yoko.

Imagines Lennon lying on the ground, dead, covered in blood.

It's late afternoon when he returns to the Dakota. The two young women are still there, standing vigil. As he waits with them, they study the album from front to back.

Jude and Jeri agree that "I'm Losing You" is the best song on the album. "It's John at his most emotional," they say with a sigh.

Mark's never listened to any of the songs, but he's read enough reviews. He counters with Yoko's harsh response song, which accuses John of "getting phony": "I'm Moving On."

Now it's time for him to do the same.

"I didn't come all this way to argue with the two of you," he says. "I imagine I'll be doing more than just meeting John Lennon."

A car pulls up to the front of the building.

Mark keeps his hand on the gun as the passenger steps out.

It's not Lennon.

Every time a car stops, he experiences an adrenaline

rush. Is this John Lennon? Will he step out and greet them? Each time Mark keeps his hand on the revolver.

By early evening, with no sign of Lennon, Mark decides to pack it in. There's a new day coming. He returns to the Y to strategize.

CHAPTER 29

Guess I got what I deserve.
— "Baby Blue"

At the end of February in 1966, twenty-five-year-old reporter Maureen Cleave asks twenty-six-year-old John Lennon for an interview. They've been friendly ever since she started covering the band for the *Evening Standard* in February of 1963, back when it was still a big deal to have a London paper mention them at all.

Even so, it's a major coup when John invites her to his house for a sit-down—not one but *four* exclusives (each of the Beatles agrees to speak with Cleave individually).

John is being generous to his friend, but he also has a point to make. Dubbed the "cheeky Beatle" or "the smart Beatle" because of his snappy one-liners and naughty double entendres, he wants to show that the members of the band, the so-called mop-tops, are free thinkers on the important issues of the day, such as the escalating war in Vietnam and social injustices happening around the world.

"How Does a Beatle Live? John Lennon Lives Like This" runs in the March 4 edition of the *Evening Standard*. Cleave reports on Lennon's intense bouts of self-education, most recently the Indian music George has introduced him to and his own reading on world religion.

"Christianity will go," John predicts in the midst of their wide-ranging conversation. "It will vanish and shrink. I needn't argue about that; I'm right and I will be proved right. We're more popular than Jesus now; I don't know which will go first—rock 'n' roll or Christianity. Jesus was all right, but his disciples were thick and ordinary. It's them twisting it that ruins it for me."

Says John later, "A few people wrote into the papers, and a few wrote back, saying, 'So what, he said that. Who is he anyway,' or they said, 'So he can have his own opinion.' And then it just vanished."

The band's prim image is starting to chafe. Beatles photographer Robert Whitaker observes, "All over the world I'd watched people worshipping like gods, four Beatles. To me they were just stock standard normal people. But this emotion that fans poured on them made me wonder where Christianity was heading."

When the opportunity arises to shoot something different with Whitaker, the Beatles are eager.

"There we were, supposed to be sort of angels. I wanted to show that we were really aware of life," John says.

Whitaker agrees. "I got fed up with taking squeaky-clean pictures of the Beatles, and I thought I'd revolutionize what pop idols are," he later says in an interview. Near the end of March, the band books a photo shoot with the twenty-six-year-old, and they take some surrealism-inflected photos of a smiling Fab Four dressed in white butcher coats, holding slabs of meat and dismembered baby dolls. Whitaker "knew we liked black humor and sick jokes," Paul recalls. "It didn't seem too offensive to us. It was just dolls and a lot of meat."

With the band's latest American tour scheduled for August, Capitol decides to release *Yesterday and Today,* a compilation of songs pulled from the American versions of *Help!, Rubber Soul,* and *Revolver* plus the previously released "We Can Work It Out" / "Day Tripper" single. Capitol needs a design for the cover.

John wants to send the record label Whitaker's "butcher" photograph as a cover image.

The Beatles, against Brian's wishes, have already included this photo in promotional materials for their tenth consecutive British number-one single,

"Paperback Writer." No one in Britain complained, but Capitol balks at using it for an album cover. Although they eventually give in and ship 750,000 albums ahead of the June 15, 1966, release, nearly every record store refuses to display them.

"It's as relevant as Vietnam," John explains to the press about the controversial image. "If the public can accept something as cruel as the war, they can accept this cover."

Nevertheless, Capitol can't. On June 14, the company recalls the record, incurring shipping and manufacturing costs to replace the controversial cover photograph with another one Whitaker shot, showing the band gathered around an open steamer trunk.

Though the "butcher cover" remains a highly sought-after Beatles collectible, the chart-topping album is a money loser for Capitol, the only Beatles record with that dubious distinction.

Ahead of the August tour dates, the Beatles' press officer, Tony Barrow—originator of the band's nick-name, the Fab Four—sends Maureen Cleave's *Evening Standard* profiles to *DATEbook,* an American teen magazine favored by the band for its progressive social vision. "I think the style and content is very much in line with the sort of thing *DATEbook* likes to use," Barrow writes to the editors, who agree. They reprint the profiles in their September issue (on stands in mid-July) with a quotation from John (the second of eight) on the cover: "I don't know which will go first—rock 'n' roll or Christianity."

The Associated Press picks up on the story, and two radio disc jockeys mobilize their teenage listeners to denounce John Lennon and defend Jesus Christ.

"This is Doug Layton and Tommy Charles reminding you that our fantastic Beatles boycott is still in effect," Layton broadcasts from WAQY-AM's Birmingham, Alabama, studio. "Don't you forget what the Beatles have said."

The disc jockeys organize a burning of Beatles records as a publicity stunt to boost ratings. Charles adds, "Don't forget to take your Beatles records and Beatles paraphernalia to any one of our fourteen pickup points in Birmingham, Alabama, and turn them in this week if possible."

The band has no idea the trouble these two men are about to cause.

CHAPTER 30

Every way you look at it you lose.
            —"Mrs. Robinson"

Ratings at WAQY-AM are up—in part because of the sensational efforts of station disc jockeys Doug Layton and Tommy Charles. They borrow a giant tree-grinding machine from the Birmingham town council and rename it "the Beatle grinder." On August 8, three days before the first American tour date, kids show up with records and photos and feed them into the machine, which chomps them into dust.

Pennsylvania senator Robert Fleming introduces a resolution to ban the Beatles—they're supposed to play Philadelphia's JFK Stadium on August 16—and pull their records from jukeboxes statewide.

"We can get along very well without the Beatles," Fleming tells reporters, "but there are multitudes of us that cannot get along without Jesus Christ."

When the city of Boston denies Democratic state representative Charles Iannello's request to revoke the Beatles' permit for a concert planned at Suffolk Downs (where the legendary thoroughbred Seabiscuit once ran), he asks, "Who are these four creeps to put themselves above the High and Mighty? Do you think they'll do anything for the morals of our teenagers? We've got enough problems."

<hr />

So does John.

Freda Kelly, Brian Epstein's personal secretary as well as the secretary for the Beatles fan club, delivers letters by the sackful to John's mock Tudor mansion in Weybridge. Cyn divides them into two piles—fan mail and hate mail.

Each day, John asks Cyn which pile is bigger. The answer is always the same: "Letters arrived at the house full of threats, hate, and venom," Cyn says.

Psychics are sending him their predictions. One foresees the Beatles will die in a plane crash, another that John will be shot while on tour in the United States.

On August 5, 1966 (August 8 in the United States), the album *Revolver* and the double A–side single "Eleanor Rigby" / "Yellow Submarine" are released in the UK. The Beatles' fourteen-city concert tour is set to begin in less than a week. They've already decided not to play any of the new music live, since it won't be heard over the screaming fans, but they haven't planned for the screaming press.

On August 6, Brian Epstein holds an ineffectual press conference at New York's Americana Hotel.

"What will it cost to cancel the tour?" Brian asks business associate Nat Weiss afterward.

"A million dollars," Weiss answers.

But there's another compelling financial reason to perform the American shows: British taxes.

During the spring recording sessions for *Revolver,* George Harrison contributed the song "Taxman," a biting commentary on the 95 percent "supertax" that Labour Party prime minister Harold Wilson proposed on high earners. "Should 5 percent appear too small," Harrison wrote, "be thankful I don't take it all."

"They were never happy with that," Beatles' accountant Harry Pinsker explains. "That's why George wrote 'Taxman.' They'd been poor boys who'd worked hard and made money, and now someone was trying to take it away."

The American tour will make them around $4 million (more than $32 million in today's dollars). And they won't have to contend with the supertax.

John and Cyn hug each other tightly as they say their good-byes at London's Heathrow Airport. The band arrives in Chicago and checks in to the Astor

Tower hotel, in Chicago's Gold Coast. It's August 11, 1966, the night before the Beatles are to play the first of two shows at the International Amphitheatre, and John is sitting in a wooden chair inside his suite on the twenty-seventh floor, fighting to gain control of his shaking hands.

"If anything were to happen to any of you," Brian tells them, "I'd never forgive myself."

CHAPTER 31

Nobody told me there'd be days like these.
　　　　　　　—"Nobody Told Me"

On August 12, John and his bandmates enter Tony Barrow's suite, where under the press man's watchful eye they'll face nearly three dozen reporters. John sits down solemnly and leans across a table into a solitary microphone.

"I wasn't saying the Beatles are better than Jesus or God or Christianity," John explains. "I could have said TV, or cinema, or anything else that's popular, or motorcars are bigger than Jesus. But I just said Beatles because, you know, that's the easiest one for me. I just never thought of the repercussions. I never really thought of it."

He tells the assembled reporters that when his words were "put into a kid's magazine [*DATEbook*]," his original intention "just loses its meaning or its context immediately . . . and everybody starts making their own versions of it."

Paul feels for his bandmate and friend. "Because John's quote was taken out of context, it was widely misunderstood," he'll say in a 2019 interview. "He was actually making a point about church congregations shrinking, therefore I felt very bad for John during the whole episode."

"I didn't want to talk because I thought they'd kill me," John later says of that face-off with the press, "because they take things so seriously [in the States]. I mean, they shoot you and then they realize it wasn't that important."

That night, thirteen thousand forgiving fans "hail Beatles in Chicago," as Salt Lake City's *Deseret News* reports. At the August 13 stop, Detroit's Olympia Stadium, picketers messaging JESUS SAVES—JOHN SINS and LIMEY GO HOME! are vastly outnumbered, the Associated Press reports, by nearly thirty thousand fans "not deterred by the story of protest kicked up recently by Beatle John Lennon."

Cleveland Municipal Stadium is to host the band on August 14. But even as a Baptist minister warns parishioners that any concert attendees among them face expulsion from the congregation, the Vatican sides with John: "It cannot be denied that there is some foundation to the latest observations of John Lennon about atheism or the distraction of many people."

But papal validation doesn't stop the large-scale burning of Beatles records known as Beatles bonfires. On August 11, the AP publishes a photo from Chester, South Carolina, of a KKK grand dragon feeding albums into the flames of a burning cross. And though WAQY-AM disc jockey Tommy Charles releases a statement accepting John's apology and canceling the Birmingham bonfire, the one organized by radio station KLUE in Longview, Texas, happens on August 13. Two days later, a picture of a teenage Longview girl armed with a torch, igniting a pile of albums, goes out over the UPI wire. By then, the Beatles are already at DC Stadium (later RFK Stadium) for their August 15 show.

In the clubhouse of baseball's Washington Senators, who were in the midst of a losing season in the American League, the Beatles face down a press corps primed to throw curveballs. Yet the *Washington Post*'s Leroy Aarons had scooped them all with an advance sympathetic interview headlined "CAN'T EXPRESS MYSELF VERY WELL"; BEATLE APOLOGIZES FOR REMARKS, which explained that the religious views of the twenty-five-year-old John were "more of a groping than a finding." Regarding the ten days of bonfires: "That was the real shock, the physical burning. I couldn't go away knowing that I created another little piece of hate in the world."

Hate personified appears at the stadium in the

form of five red-, white,- and green-robed members of the Prince George's County, Maryland, Ku Klux Klan. They picket but don't interrupt the concert. The music goes on in Philadelphia, Toronto, and Boston—where numerous Kennedys, including Robert and Ethel Kennedy's teenage children, Joseph and Kathleen, have traveled from Hyannis Port to join the audience of twenty-five thousand.

They are scheduled to perform two shows at the Mid-South Coliseum, in Memphis, on Friday, August 19, even though on August 10, local leaders issued a unanimous resolution to "advise the Beatles that they are not welcome in the City of Memphis."

Despite warnings made to Tony Barrow that "religious zealots . . . were actually threatening to assassinate John Lennon if the Beatles came to Memphis," the band boards its charter flight.

"Send John out first. He's the one they want," George suggests jokingly, while John plays the sacrificial martyr: "You might as well paint a target on me."

But John is truly fearful.

George is, too. "All the time, constantly," he feels "frightened by things" because it's been less than three years since President John F. Kennedy was assassinated.

"There was always an edge in America," Ringo says later. "We knew they did have guns."

Yet more than twenty thousand adoring fans have paid the ticket price of $5.50. One young woman tells a reporter, "I love Jesus, but I love those Beatles, too."

———— ∞∞∞ ————

Surrounded by a police detail, the Beatles file into the back of the armored van that will transport them to the Mid-South Coliseum. A member of their entourage remembers that "we had to lie down, because they thought snipers might shoot us."

The Beatles take the stage at 4:00 p.m. and play an uneventful show.

During their second performance, George is singing the first verse of "If I Needed Someone" (on the *Rubber Soul* album in the UK, *Yesterday and Today* in America), when a loud popping noise—the sound a gun would make—rips through the concert hall.

"Every one of us," John later recalls, "look[ed] at each other, because each thought it was the other that had been shot. It was that bad."

When they get offstage, the band learns that two teenagers had lobbed a cherry bomb from the upper balcony.

A pair of teenage girls had smuggled their own contraband into the coliseum: a cassette recorder. In 2007, the "cherry bomb tape" surfaces. Australia's

Sydney Morning Herald reviews the recording, and the moment the Beatles react to the explosion, "the men of the moment blast off into double-time, Lennon positively flogging his rhythm guitar," though a 1966 article from UPI notes that "the four performers didn't bat an eye or miss a note" when a "cherry bomb went off with a loud report at the booted feet of drummer Ringo Starr."

There are six more cities to play before the tour is complete. On August 21, contending with rainy conditions that caused the cancellation of the show at Cincinnati's Crosley Field—"The only gig we ever missed!" says George—and impeded travel to St. Louis's Busch Stadium, the band reaches its limit.

"After the gig," says Paul, "I remember us getting in a big, empty steel-lined wagon, like a removal van. There was no furniture in there—nothing. We were sliding around trying to hold on to something, and at that moment everyone said, 'Oh, this bloody touring lark—I've had it up to here, man.'"

When the band arrives in Los Angeles ahead of the August 28 show at the Hollywood Bowl, Capitol Records executive Ken Mansfield sees the stress on John's face. "When I hung out with him years before, he had this carefree, lighthearted attitude, but in '66, his mood was entirely different. He was struggling mightily to get out from the comments he made."

John says of the cumulative effect of the backlash,

"It was as if they were all in a big movie and we were the ones trapped in the middle of it."

There is one last show—a thirty-minute set—to be played at San Francisco's Candlestick Park on Monday, August 29. An AP photographer captures conflicting signage—GOD SAVE THE BEATLES and JESUS LOVES YOU—DO THE BEATLES?—while one fan declares: LENNON SAVES.

The Beatles need saving from the ordeal of this American tour. But first, a memento. Moments before the band takes the stage, Paul makes a first-ever request of press man Tony Barrow: "Tape it, will you? Tape the show."

Following the closing notes of "Paperback Writer," Paul steps to the microphone. "We'd like to ask you to join in and, er, clap, sing, talk, do anything. Anyway, the song is . . . good night."

They play "Long Tall Sally." Back in December of 1960, the song was their opening number at Litherland Town Hall. Barrow's tape ends before the band finishes the song.

John is the last to leave the stage. He stares at the crowd, taking it all in for one final time. Then he joins the others in their rush for the armored car that will take them to the airport.

On board their London-bound flight, George raises a glass. "Right—that's it, I'm not a Beatle anymore!"

Three years earlier, when the Beatles' popularity was first exploding, John had been sanguine when asked by a journalist about his future plans. "I'll just develop what I'm doing at the moment, although whatever I say now I'll change my mind next week," he'd stated. "This isn't show business. It's something else. This is different from anything that anybody imagines. You don't go on from this. You do this and then you finish."

By the time *Revolver* tops the American charts, on September 10, the Beatles are back in England.

For good.

CHAPTER 32

Love and hope and sex and dreams...
— "Shattered"

I f you wanted to, John, you could be a very interesting actor," director Richard Lester says, offering
him the role of the musketeer Gripweed in *How I
Won the War,* Lester's black farce about World War II.

John signs on. But when shooting gets under way
in Almeria, Spain, in September of 1966, he has
trouble on set, struggling to remember his lines and
fighting boredom in between scenes.

He drives around in his Rolls-Royce and trips on
acid nearly every day.

Gets nostalgic and daydreams about his childhood
in Liverpool.

What about Brian? John hasn't seen much of him
since Los Angeles, where an opportunistic ex of Brian's
stole his briefcase, filled with cash and incriminating

details about his sexuality. The thorny situation kept Brian from witnessing the Beatles' final concert.

John keeps music in his head—the brass band from the orphanage at Strawberry Field. He nostalgically recalls his forbidden (by Mimi) youthful forays to the old Gothic mansion, with its overgrown garden and trees made for climbing.

"I have visions of Strawberry Fields," he says, telling *Rolling Stone* in 1968 that "Strawberry Fields is just anywhere you want to go." But unlike the 1965 ballad "In My Life," which was also inspired by memories of Liverpool, this new song is penned by a hippie sage.

The lines roll off his pen. He makes a demo on a portable tape recorder.

On holiday in Spain with Ringo and Maureen, Cyn and John quarrel over his drug use. "John was still searching," Cynthia Lennon will later write, "whereas I thought I had found what I wanted out of life."

In his final on-screen moments in *How I Won the War,* John plays a death scene, speaking the line, "I knew it would end this way." He then addresses the audience directly: "You knew it would end this way, too, didn't you?" (When the film is released, in October of 1967, reviews are lackluster, but critics can't deny that the images of a dying Lennon hold profound emotional impact. And perhaps most influential: the round "granny glasses" his character wears, which John makes part of his personal style forever after.)

With the lyrics for what would become "Strawberry Fields Forever" spinning around in his head, John returns home from Spain. In a departure from his usual inclination to write quickly, he continues to work on the song.

———— ∞∞ ————

In the local newspaper, John reads an article describing a 1966 black-and-white movie directed by a Japanese avant-garde artist named Yoko Ono, a member of the interdisciplinary, experimental global artists collective called Fluxus. The five-and-a-half-minute *Four* (Fluxfilm no. 16), now archived in New York's Museum of Modern Art, is described by Fluxus founder George Maciunas as "sequences of buttock moment as various performers walked. Filmed at constant distance."

John laughs but is secretly intrigued by the artist's brashness and honesty.

So when John Dunbar (married to musician Marianne Faithfull, who in 1966 began a highly publicized romance with Mick Jagger), co-owner of a year-old Mayfair gallery called Indica, invites John to the November 8 opening of Ono's *Unfinished*

Paintings and Objects, the Beatle shows up a day early, while she's still installing the exhibition.

Yoko Ono is wearing a black sweater and black pants to match her long black hair, which is combed straight down around a center part.

"Never bring anybody until it's all ready," she chides Dunbar. She seems furious—until she takes a look at John, who says, "Maybe I should follow you and see what you're doing."

"He was shaved—and he was wearing a suit," she later recalls. "Up to then, English men had all looked kind of weedy to me. This was the first sexy one I met."

Yoko is seven years older than John and married to her second husband, an American artist. They have a daughter, Kyoko, the same age as Julian.

"Well," John says, "what's the event?"

She hands him a little card. He opens it and sees a single word:

Breathe.

"You mean, like, exhale?" he asks with an exaggerated pant.

"That's it. You've got it," she replies with a smile.

Yoko is also exhibiting an apple. When John sees the price—£200—he has a flash of fear that the artist is after his Beatles riches.

Yoko continues to follow until John stops at her *Ceiling Painting*. He climbs a white stepladder and uses a magnifying glass to inspect another small card suspended from the ceiling.

In the center, she's written YES—a very small YES.

John smiles at the artist's positive message—and he's completely enthralled. "I thought it was fantastic," John later says. "I got the humor immediately."

John goes home to his wife. That night, in bed, sleeping next to Cyn, he's still thinking about Yoko Ono.

Riding a wave of emotion, John returns to Studio Two at Abbey Road. On November 24, 1966, he performs a solo acoustic version of his new song for the band, the producers, and the sound engineers.

"When I first heard 'Strawberry Fields Forever,' I was sidesmacked," George Martin recalls. "Even with John singing it alone on his acoustic guitar, I thought it was a wonderful piece of work."

John isn't content with the sound. He leads the Beatles through multiple versions, from dreamy to metallic, ultimately calling on George Martin to combine two of the arrangements.

"Well, there are two things against it," the producer explains. "One is that they're in different keys. The other is that they're in different tempos."

With a "You can fix it, George," John doesn't have to choose.

This time.

But the pressures on the Beatles, his marriage, and his fragile psyche are mounting, and only John can decide his next move.

December 6, 1980

Jude Stein and her friend Jeri return to the Dakota shortly after 5:00 p.m. Their new friend from Hawaii, Mark Chapman, said he would meet them there and promised to take them to dinner at a Japanese restaurant.

"I don't see Mark anywhere," Jeri says.

"Let's wait a few minutes. Maybe he's running late."

"I hope he gets here soon. It's getting cold."

And dark, Jude thinks. The streets are barely safe during the day. At night, the city turns into a horror show. The "rotten apple" is setting record levels for murder, rape, burglary, and car theft. It's no wonder people are fleeing in droves.

There's no one normal here anymore. The city needs normal people—people like Mark Chapman. Nice and friendly. Kind. Polite. I would have definitely gone out with him.

Jeri wants to stick around to see if John Lennon makes an appearance. Jude, though, is eyeing a homeless guy who's approaching them. He's doing that creepy zombie walk, which makes her think he's on crack. The "poor man's cocaine" is everywhere. Crackheads are mugging and killing people.

"Where are the cops when you need them?" Jude says. "Let's get going."

They're about to leave when a yellow cab slides to the curb in front of the building. John Lennon emerges, wearing a tan jacket. He takes a drag from his cigarette—a Gitane for sure!—and waves to them.

But he doesn't rush inside the Dakota. He comes over to them.

John greets his two loyal fans by name. He chats with them for a few minutes about his new album.

"I believe it's my best work since the Beatles," John says. "I feel truly alive for the first time in twenty years."

You should have come back, Mark, Jude thinks. *You missed having your dream come true—standing right next to, and speaking with, John Lennon.*

CHAPTER 33

I'm not feelin' too good myself.
——"Feelin' Alright?"

For Christmas in 1966, paid members of the Beatles fan club receive their annual flexi disc from the band featuring a Christmas message. This year's, called "Pantomime: Everywhere It's Christmas," is a wacky six and a half minutes of skits and novelty tunes that the band recorded between takes of "Strawberry Fields Forever."

At Studio Two, the holiday spirit feels more like a burn. The Beatles have been putting in long hours there since the end of November.

The Beach Boys album *Pet Sounds* (released by Capitol on May 16, 1966) and John's song "Strawberry Fields Forever" have lit a pair of creative fires under Paul. Just a week later, on December 29, he comes in and lays down the piano tracks for his own tribute to bygone Liverpool, "Penny Lane."

This is how it had always been with John and Paul. "He'd write 'Strawberry Fields,'" says Paul, "I'd go away and write 'Penny Lane.'" No question that it was "to compete with each other. But it was very friendly competition."

Even so, the Beatles are many songs short of an album, but Brian is pressing for a new hit.

"I must have a really great single," the manager tells George Martin. "What have you got?"

"Well, I've got three tracks," the producer tells him, "and two of them are the best they've ever made. We could put the two together and make a smashing single."

The result is the double A–side single "Strawberry Fields Forever" / "Penny Lane." The record is slated for a February release.

On January 31, the band is in Kent, working on promotional materials. "We'd been filming a TV piece to go with 'Strawberry Fields Forever,'" John explains in a 1967 interview. "There was a break and I went into this shop and bought an old poster advertising a variety show that starred Mr. Kite."

He hangs it on the wall of his living room.

Driven by American radio play of "Penny Lane," the dual-side single hits number 1 in America—but in Britain it ranks behind "Release Me" by balladeer Engelbert Humperdinck. It's the first time that a Beatles single has taken second place since January 1963's "Please Please Me."

John says he isn't bothered. "There's room for everything. I don't mind Engelbert Humperdinck. They're the cats. It's their scene."

Throughout 1966, the band has been challenged by the achievements of new and established rivals on both sides of the Atlantic. The April 15 release of the Rolling Stones' chart-topping fourth UK (and sixth US) album, *Aftermath,* marks two firsts for Mick Jagger and Keith Richards: they cowrote every song and recorded the entire album at California's RCA Studios. On August 15, Jefferson Airplane introduced the "San Francisco sound" with RCA's release of its debut studio album, *Jefferson Airplane Takes Off.* On December 9, the Who's second album, *A Quick One,* climbs to number 4 on the UK charts.

The Jefferson Airplane lead singer, Grace Slick, who joined the band on October 16, 1966, recalls that if "you were in a rock 'n' roll band in the '60s, the only thing you couldn't do was kill people. Everything else was acceptable. You're being paid to travel around the world, and people admire you because you're a rock 'n' roll star."

The Beatles rose to fame on the strength of their

live performances. Now they must discover a way to enthrall fans from inside the studio.

"I was going through murder," John says of the uncertain transition.

Then Paul has a brainchild. "How about if we become an alter-ego band, something like, say, 'Sgt. Pepper's Lonely Hearts'"? he suggests to John, George, and Ringo. "I've got a little bit of a song cooking with that title."

Studio Two fills with smoke and teacups swimming in cigarette butts as they listen to Paul's idea for a symphonic concept record. While John strums his guitar, Paul sits close by, playing piano.

Suddenly it's clear to John how to work Paul's grand plan. Take "a bunch of songs, and you stick two bits of *Pepper* in it, and it's a concept."

Yet what's even more certain to all four of them is that the music is far too complicated to ever be performed live.

"Let Sgt. Pepper do the touring," Paul says, then calls George Martin over to the piano. He's working on the melody for a song based on that poster Paul saw in John's house in Weybridge.

"It was all there, the trampoline, the somersets, the hoops, the garters, the horse," Paul says. "It was Pablo Fanque's fair, and it said 'being for the benefit of Mr. Kite'; almost the whole song was written right off this poster."

John calls out, "It's a fairground sequence. I want to be in that circus atmosphere. I want to smell the sawdust when I hear that song."

"John would deal in moods, he would deal in colors," the producer notes, and he's learned to translate those signals into instruments.

Those will work, John thinks when he hears the organ, harmonium, and bass harmonica sounds that George Martin provides.

Paul goes to John's house for another of their traditional songwriting sessions. John is holding a drawing made by his son, Julian. It's a picture of his schoolmate with the handwritten title "Lucy in the Sky with Diamonds."

They go up to the music room.

"Cellophane flowers," Paul says. "Newspaper taxis."

John counters with "kaleidoscope eyes" and "looking glass ties," and suddenly they're riffing together like the old days.

Paul is happy to see a glimmer of the John he knows. "You're stuck out in suburbia, living a middle-class life," he tells his old friend.

Cyn, too, barely recognizes John, complaining that "it was becoming impossible to communicate" with her husband. "I think the drugs destroyed a lot of his creativity," she says, despite his connecting ever more deeply with fans on songs like "Strawberry Fields,"

"Being for the Benefit of Mr. Kite!," and "Lucy in the Sky with Diamonds."

On the evening of March 21, at Studio Two, John accidentally drops acid, mistaking it for the amphetamine he sought to combat the boredom of watching Paul and George finesse the vocals on "Getting Better." Suddenly, his roiling existential struggles burst into an immediate danger.

"George, I'm not feeling too good," John tells their producer. "I'm not focusing on me."

The ever-present fans are clustered outside. The only safe refuge is the rooftop, so that's where George Martin takes him.

John looks up at the clear night sky. "Aren't they fantastic?" he asks of the stars, pressing up against the eighteen-inch guardrail for a better view.

"They just look like stars to me," the producer says, gently guiding John away from the precipice.

⁂

"John always had a way of having an edge to his songs," George says.

The making of *Sgt. Pepper's Lonely Hearts Club Band* has further sharpened those edges. At John's insistence, the album is "one of the most important steps in our career. It had to be just right."

In contrast to the ten-hour recording session for the

Beatles' first studio album, *Please Please Me,* on February 11, 1963, the band logs seven hundred hours of studio time to create this thirteenth LP—at the astounding cost of $100,000 (more than $750,000 today).

Brian Epstein hosts two release parties for the album. The first is held for the press at his house in London on May 19, 1967. Based on the strength of her portfolio, Brian's assistant has invited a twenty-five-year-old American photographer, Linda Eastman, to attend. By chance, Paul had just met Linda a few days earlier at the Bag O'Nails club, where she was being shown around London by the Animals, another leading British music export and one of her first celebrity photo subjects. Paul and Linda hit it off, but Paul is still in a serious relationship with his long-time girlfriend, Jane Asher, to whom he'll announce an engagement on Christmas Day in 1967.

The second party is on May 28, at Brian's recently purchased country home. While Paul doesn't attend, John does—in spectacular fashion. He uses the occasion to unveil that he's had his enormous (nearly twenty-feet-long and six-and-a-half-feet-wide) 1964 Rolls-Royce Phantom V painted in vibrant colors reminiscent of a gypsy caravan. "It was sprayed all yellow first," John's chauffeur, Les Anthony, says, "then hand-painted" with ordinary latex house paint in elaborate Romany designs and astrological symbols. "The first time I drove it, I was followed by hordes of photographers and Pathé News."

"John and friends floated in on his gaudy yellow Rolls, through bucolic country lanes adrift with clouds of May blossoms, as if in a magic pumpkin on the way to the ball," says fellow party guest Tony Bramwell. Cynthia Lennon remembers that inaugural drive as having "all the feeling of a school outing. Every time the car passed through town or villages it stopped the traffic. Crowds of jeering, waving people pressed up against the tinted windows trying to get a better look at the occupants of this crazy car."

Not everyone approves of the paint job—"You swine! How dare you do that to a Rolls-Royce!" John often gleefully recounts an old woman once shouting at him—but there's no question that his "psychedelic Rolls" is as subversive and of-the-moment as *Sgt. Pepper's Lonely Hearts Club Band* itself.

The crescendo toward the June 1967 worldwide release is building as powerfully as the resounding orchestral chords that George Martin engineered to close the album's anchor track, "A Day in the Life."

EMI won't be releasing any singles from *Sgt. Pepper,* so disc jockeys and reviewers who receive advance copies are forced to listen to the album from start to finish—just as the Beatles intend.

Joe O'Brien, DJ at New York's WMCA, is the first to spin the record live. He tells *The New Yorker* that "listeners are unprepared because this album is not a teen-age album, but a terribly intellectual one."

The album soars to the top of the British and American charts. While the fans' warm embrace generates 2.5 million US sales in its first three months of release, and although it stays at number 1 on *Billboard*'s Hot 100 for fifteen weeks, critics engage in a protracted war of words.

Even as *Time* magazine reports that the album is touted by legendary composer and conductor Leonard Bernstein as being on par with the work of Robert Schumann, and even as *The Guardian* declares, "There is no longer any need, thank goodness, to apologize for talking seriously about Beatles music," *The Observer* argues, "The record is not perfect, even on pop terms" (calling out George Harrison for being increasingly under the influence of his Indian mentor, Ravi Shankar: "On the musical side there is tendency to overdo the curry power").

Twenty-two-year-old freelance music writer Richard Goldstein has the harshest words of all. His review, headlined WE STILL NEED THE BEATLES, BUT..., suggests the album is derivative of the artistry of Beatles' rivals. "There is a touch of the Jefferson Airplane, a dab of Beach Boys vibrations, and a generous pat of gymnastics from The Who."

"The music critic of the *New York Times* hated *Sgt. Pepper*," Paul says. "And we had to sit through that."

That being a mockery of John and Paul's greatest songwriting achievements. "There is nothing beautiful on *Sergeant Pepper.* Nothing is real and there is nothing to get hung about. The Lennon raunchiness has become mere caprice...Paul McCartney's soaring pop magnificats have become merely politely profound."

The BBC piles on, banning airplay of "A Day in the Life" over the suggestive lyric "I'd love to turn you on." British politicians disassemble the song line by line in search of hidden meaning. They seize on the line "four thousand holes in Blackburn, Lancashire," as Lennon's ode to needle marks.

"I'd like to meet the man who banned this song of ours," John says. "If they want to read drugs into our stuff, they will. But it's *them* that's reading it, *them*!"

The band's next project will premiere not on an album (though the band recorded the title track of their upcoming *Magical Mystery Tour* in April) but on the *Our World* television program.

"It will be the first worldwide satellite broadcast ever," Ringo tells the others.

The air date is June 25, 1967.

"Oh, God, is it that close?" John says, "I supposed we'd better write something."

John and Paul each scramble to write a song for the global broadcast. Paul comes up with "Your

Mother Should Know." John presents "All You Need Is Love." John wins.

Engineer Geoff Emerick is struck by the sharp contrast between the way Paul and John work yet how easily the two musicians seem able to write together. "Paul was meticulous and organized: he always carried a notebook around with him, in which he methodically wrote down lyrics and chord changes in his neat handwriting. In contrast, John seemed to live in chaos: he was constantly searching for scraps of paper that he'd hurriedly scribbled ideas on. Paul was a natural communicator; John couldn't articulate his ideas well. Paul was the diplomat; John was the agitator. Paul was soft-spoken and almost unfailingly polite; John could be a right loudmouth and quite rude. Paul was willing to put in long hours to get a part right; John was impatient, always ready to move on to the next thing."

On June 14, in Studio Two, the band does thirty-three takes of John's new song. "Keep it simple so viewers across the globe will understand," the television producers have instructed.

John delivers. He's written the anthem of the season, soon to be known as the Summer of Love, declaring—against the backdrop of the conflict raging in Vietnam and the aftermath of the Six-Day War smoldering in the Middle East—"All You Need Is Love."

"Well, it's certainly repetitive," George complains to Paul in rehearsal of the multiple choruses replicating the title of the song.

On June 25, 1967, John perches on a high stool, and with a little help from his friends in an all-star chorus, including the Rolling Stones, Marianne Faithfull, and Eric Clapton, begins to sing to four hundred million watchers and is anointed a pop-cultural prophet for peace.

One person who isn't witnessing it in person: Brian Epstein. That same evening, he is descending further into the depths of alcohol and amphetamine addiction. Though Epstein was recently treated and released from a clinic—where John sent an extravagant bouquet with a card reading *You know I love you...I really mean that*—the Beatles' management contract with him is set for renewal in a few months' time, on September 30, 1967. The band's drastic change in focus from touring to studio is certain to change the financial terms, and not in Brian's favor.

And it's not a good omen that the man who ushered the Beatles to stardom is currently too addled to attend the live broadcast of "All You Need Is Love."

CHAPTER 34

What's so funny 'bout peace love and understanding?
— "(What's So Funny 'Bout) Peace,
Love, and Understanding"

On August 24, 1967, John joins Paul, George, and Ringo near the front of the ballroom of the London Hilton. A diminutive guru named Maharishi Mahesh Yogi, surrounded by flowers and security guards, is getting ready to speak about Transcendental Meditation.

George has pushed the band to attend, and Paul reminds the others that their original pledge still holds. "George wants it. What one of us wants, the others go along with."

Their minds are blown.

"It's fantastic stuff, Cyn," John tells his wife. "The meditation's so simple, and it's life-changing."

The maharishi invites the Beatles and their wives and girlfriends (Paul is still dating Jane Asher) to

join him for a ten-day conference in Bangor, Wales.
Mick Jagger and Marianne Faithfull decide to go
along, and Brian Epstein plans to follow in a couple
of days.

London's Euston train station is packed with
screaming fans, reporters, and camera crews.

Every bloody move we make causes pandemonium, John
thinks as he jumps out of the car. He runs for the platform, leaving Cyn behind to manage their luggage.

She gets swallowed by the crowd, and a police
officer, convinced that she's just another groupie,
pushes her away from the platform.

"Tell him to let you on!" he yells to his wife. "Tell
him you're with us."

The train begins to pull away.

When she catches up with them at the retreat not
long afterward, John scolds her. "Why are you always
last, Cyn?"

On August 27, 1967, the phone rings at the
Beatles' dormitory on the grounds of the retreat.
There's terrible news from London: thirty-two-year-
old Brian Epstein has been found dead at home from
an overdose of sleeping pills.

John's first reaction is practical. "Now we're our
own managers; now we have to make all the decisions," he tells the others.

Then a horrible shock sets in, the same as he
experienced when his mother died.

When his uncle George died.

When Stu died.

And now Brian.

Complicating matters was that "I introduced Brian to pills—which gives me a guilt association with his death." John is desperately in need of guidance. "But then," he says, "the maharishi talked to us and, I don't know, cooled us out a bit."

"He just told us not to be overwhelmed with grief," John tells an interviewer. "Whatever thoughts we have of Brian...keep them happy, because whatever thoughts we have of him will travel with him, wherever he is."

The Beatles choose not to attend Brian's funeral, fearing a mob scene.

<hr />

Brian's absence is felt when the Beatles pursue their first project without him. Feeling like the group should push forward, Paul takes the reins and spearheads a project that has its beginnings in a song they recorded in April: "Magical Mystery Tour." The band agrees to make Paul's song the basis of a British TV movie in which the Beatles and an eccentric cast of characters take a Ken Kesey–inspired bus tour across the English countryside. When two weeks of shooting begins, on September 11, there's no script, so almost all the movie's promised "strange things" are improvised. Among the many bizarre scenes is a reenactment of one of John's dreams in which he keeps shoveling heaps of spaghetti onto a table in front of a heavyset "Aunt Jessie."

The new Beatles music—released as a six-song EP in England and padded with contemporaneous singles to create an American album—proves as popular as always. Paul supplies three of the sound track's songs plus the separately released number-one single "Hello, Goodbye," but the highlight belongs to John, who finally sets his Lewis Carroll obsession to music with the psychedelic milestone "I Am the Walrus."

When the fifty-two-minute movie airs in black-and-white (though it was shot in color) on BBC1, on December 26, viewers are baffled, and reviews—for the first time ever for a Beatles project—are uniformly terrible. The reception is so bad that US networks decline to show it, and Paul must go on Britain's *The Frost Programme* the following day to defend it. "We don't say it was a good film," he says later. "It was our first attempt. If we goofed, then we goofed."

Being disliked is a new phenomenon for John, Paul, George, and Ringo, and there's grumbling that this wouldn't have happened under Brian's watch.

On February 16, 1968, the Beatles opt to follow the guru all the way to India. They touch down in Delhi with their wives (in Paul's case, with his girlfriend, Jane), and a celebrity entourage including Mike Love of the Beach Boys, the folksinger Donovan, and actress Mia Farrow. Farrow is recovering from her own public loss—her marriage to Frank Sinatra. The fifty-year-old crooner and twenty-one-year-old actress had been married in 1966, but although the divorce won't be finalized until August of 1968, he'd already served her with divorce papers on the set of *Rosemary's Baby,* the supernatural thriller she was then filming inside New York's historic Dakota apartment building.

The ashram is halfway to Tibet and halfway around the world from Los Angeles. At the Beverly Hilton, on February 29, 1968, *Sgt. Pepper's Lonely Hearts Club Band* wins Album of the Year and Best Album Cover, Graphic Arts, at the tenth annual Grammy Awards.

The Beatles are in absentia. They are in the audience of the maharishi, who's insistent that they end all drug use.

George is a quick convert. "The meditation buzz is incredible," he says. "I get higher than I ever did with drugs."

Paul has trouble banishing the music from his mind. "The minute you clear it," he says, "a thought comes in and says, 'What are we gonna do about our next record?'"

Or two. During a month at the ashram in Rishikesh, he and John write most of the songs for what will become *The Beatles,* a double album known as the White Album after its minimalist white sleeve.

Their productivity causes George much consternation. He argues, "We're not fucking here to do the next album, we're here to meditate!"

"The way George is going he'll be flying on a magic carpet by the time he's forty," John jokes, though he does take the meditation seriously and practices it for eight hours at a stretch. His brain is then flooded with lyrics for what he calls "the most miserable songs on earth." He explains that "in 'Yer Blues,' when I wrote 'I'm so lonely I want to die,' I wasn't kidding. That's how I felt...up there, trying to reach God and feeling suicidal."

John is aching for Yoko. And then her letters start arriving.

"I'm a cloud," she writes on a postcard. "Look in the sky." He tells Cynthia he needs more space, soon moving out of the bungalow they'd been sharing.

But he doesn't stop making music. "John was keen to learn the finger-style guitar I played and he was a good student," Donovan recalls. "John wrote

'Julia' and 'Dear Prudence' [for fellow maharishi disciple Prudence Farrow, Mia's nineteen-year-old sister] based on the picking I taught him."

John tells Paul that he's waiting for the maharishi to "slip me the real secret mantra which would give me happiness."

The fantastical transaction never materializes, not even when John flies high over the Ganges on a helicopter ride with the guru.

"Why were you so keen? You really wanted to get in that helicopter," Paul says to John after he returns to the ashram.

John replies, "I thought he might slip me the answer!"

Cynthia has hers.

"Something had gone very wrong between John and me," she says. "It was as if a brick wall had gone up between us."

In April, on their return flight to London, John demolishes it. He makes a long, drunken confession detailing the numerous transgressions he's committed against their marriage—with groupies, with reporters, with other musicians, with the wives of friends, and countless others. In fact, he's never been faithful; he's "always had *some* kind of affairs going." In the close confines of the airplane, Cyn is forced to listen.

But it's a one-way street. "We had no problems

at home" is Cynthia's viewpoint. "We really didn't have a cross word." Though even she sees that John is slipping further and further away. "At home he would be lost in a daydream: present, but absent. I'd talk to him, but he wouldn't hear me."

"We are going in with clear heads and hoping for the best," Paul says as the band prepares to record the dozens of songs he and John wrote while in India.

But first, they fly to New York. On May 14, they'll announce the launch of Apple Records.

Though cynics hear the refrain of "Taxman," John emphasizes his creative, altruistic vision for the multifaceted company (incorporated in London in April of 1967 and headquartered at 94 Baker Street) that is to produce not only music but also film and even clothing. "We hope to make a thing that's free," he says in a television interview, "where people can come and do and record."

John has even more to do. He sends Cyn to relax with friends in Greece (Julian stays with the house-keeper), then goes on holiday—from his marriage. The gravitational pull of Yoko Ono is too strong for him to resist.

John calls Yoko. "Are you coming?" he asks. "Take a taxi."

It's midnight when she arrives at Weybridge.

John is normally cool. But in Yoko's presence, he's sweating, unsure of himself.

"We can do two things," he says to her while they're sitting in his living room, in the uncomfortable company of Pete Shotton, John's friend and former bandmate in the original Quarry Men. "One is sit here and chat, or go up and make music."

Yoko, the daughter of a successful concert pianist, studied musical composition at Sarah Lawrence College, in Bronxville, New York. Together they begin to improvise the sounds and vocals that in November of 1968 appear on their album *Unfinished Music No. 1: Two Virgins.*

They make love at sunrise. In the morning, Shotton finds John in the kitchen.

"We've been up all night," John tells him.

That much is obvious. What John says next is the real stunner. "I want to go and live with Yoko."

⬡

Cynthia opens the door to the sunroom. It's May 22, and she's returned one day early from Greece. She finds her husband and a Japanese woman dressed in robes and sitting cross-legged on the floor, facing each other.

Cynthia freezes. She recognizes the woman—the

artist Yoko Ono. They'd met once before at a meditation meeting.

Cyn stares, blinking rapidly, as if trying to wash the sight from her eyes.

No. No, this can't be happening.

"Oh, hi," John says.

Yoko looks in the opposite direction as Cyn stumbles out of the sunroom and leaves the house.

After a tenuous reconciliation that lasts only a few weeks, John sends Cyn on holiday again, this time to Italy.

Yoko moves into John's house. She's left her second husband, Tony Cox, and their young daughter, Kyoko.

John has never felt more alive—or happier. Yoko has *transformed* him.

They become inseparable.

CHAPTER 35

And while Lennon read a book on Marx...
                          —"American Pie"

"I want to put out what I feel about revolution," John tells Yoko.

That word, *revolution,* has been swirling in his head ever since his sojourn in India. John and Yoko follow the news. Every headline shouts of fresh violence. John F. Kennedy. *Assassinated.* Martin Luther King Jr. *Assassinated.* Twenty thousand of the nearly half million US troops in Vietnam. *Killed in action.*

John risks hostile fire on multiple fronts when on May 31, 1968, the Beatles begin recording a new album.

Yoko, seven years John's senior, has made it clear that her happiness is linked to his.

"I demand equal time, equal space, equal rights," she tells John.

"What do you want, a contract?" he asks.

"Well," she says, "the answer to that is that I can't be here."

Her absence is a situation John can't accept, so he breaks the band's long-held pact forbidding wives and girlfriends from recording sessions.

"She just moved in," George says, voicing what the rest of the group, along with George Martin and the studio engineers, is feeling.

Paul is more understanding. "It's not that bad," he says. "Let the young lovers be together." But knowing how tense things are in the band, he's prescient in joking, "It's gonna be such an incredible sort of comical thing, like in fifty years' time, you know. 'They broke up because Yoko sat on an amp!'"

The first song up is a bluesy, acoustic version of John's "Revolution," to be titled "Revolution 1" on the album. He envisions it as a single, but Paul and George think it's too slow, so they regroup to cut a raging electric version of the song. John plays his electric guitar at maximum volume, but he's not getting the sound he wants.

"No, no, I want that guitar to sound dirtier!" he shouts at engineer Geoff Emerick, who patches together two preamps and overloads the signals to create the distorted guitar sound John is after.

Miraculously, the console doesn't overheat and explode, but tempers routinely do. John and Yoko break off to work on "Revolution 9," a "sound collage" that springs from the swirl of tape loops, chants, and sound effects that closes out the original ten-minute version of "Revolution 1." (The number 9 holds meaning for John; he was born on October 9 and lived at 9 Newcastle Road in Liverpool.)

"It was as much Yoko's as it was John's," Emerick says. "Certainly it wasn't Beatles music." (A critic for *New Musical Express* calls this track "a pimple on the face of the [White] album" with "some character coming back every few minutes to tell us 'Number Nine, Number Nine.'")

John places supreme value on Yoko's contributions. "She inspired all this creation in me. It wasn't that she inspired the songs. She inspired me. The statement in 'Revolution' was mine." It's filled with the kind of ideas that John voices on a television interview with BBC2 to promote the opening of *In His Own Write*, the stage adaptation of his first two books, *In His Own Write* (1964) and *A Spaniard in the Works* (1965).

"I think we're being run by maniacs for maniacal ends, you know," John says on the June 6 broadcast. "If anybody can put on paper what our government, and the American government, and the Russian, Chinese...what they are all trying to do, and what they *think* they're doing...I think they're all insane."

"It's an overtly political song about revolution and a great one," Paul says, defending him.

—◦∞∞◦—

On June 18, John takes Yoko to the premiere of *In His Own Write* at London's Old Vic theater. They wear matching outfits and sit in the front row.

Only those in his inner circle know he has left Cyn for Yoko and that Yoko is already two months pregnant.

As the production begins, the actors onstage are drowned out by hecklers who point to John and shout, "Where's your wife?" and "Where's Cynthia?"

"I don't know!" he shouts back.

Outside the theater, the crowd of angry fans yells "Chink" and "River Kwai" and "Yellow" at Yoko. Someone extends a bouquet of yellow roses toward her stems first, puncturing her hands with thorns.

The next morning, their relationship is international news.

John finds himself locked in the biggest scandal since his comments about Jesus two years before. John takes Yoko to visit Mimi in Poole, England, where he had bought his aunt a waterfront bungalow for £25,000 in 1965 (in 2018, the property was listed for just under $9.5 million).

"Who's the poisoned dwarf, John?" Mimi asks.

"It's Yoko," John answers.

"I'm an artist," Yoko says.

"That's very funny," Mimi replies. "I've never heard of you."

Cynthia certainly has. When she returns from Italy, she takes to calling the Beatles' office and leaving messages. John doesn't return her calls. If she wants to hear her husband's voice, she'll have to buy his new record.

The A side is "Hey Jude." "[Paul] said it was written about Julian, my child. He knew I was splitting with Cyn and leaving Julian," John later remembers.

"But I always heard it as a song to me," he continues. "Yoko's just come into the picture...The words 'go out and get her'—subconsciously he was saying, Go ahead, leave me"—and their Beatles partnership.

Mick Jagger and a few lucky bystanders listen in when Paul spins an advance copy at the hashish-filled Club Vesuvio, in a London basement. "That's something else, innit?" Jagger says to Paul. "It's like two songs."

The seven-inch single pushes the boundaries of recording technology to contain the song's seven-minutes-plus running time. "It wasn't intended to go on that long at the end," Paul explains to the Rolling Stones frontman. "So then we built it with the orchestra but it was mainly because I just wouldn't stop doing all that 'Judy judy judy—wooow!' Cary Grant on heat!"

The summer of 1968 is burning with social unrest.

Two days after the August 26 US release (August 30 in the UK) of Paul's "Hey Jude" with John's "Revolution" on the flip side, violence erupts in Chicago when antiwar protesters clash with National Guard troops outside the Conrad Hilton hotel, site of the Democratic National Convention, where Hubert Humphrey wins the presidential nomination over Eugene McCarthy while continuing to support President Johnson's war efforts in Vietnam.

The demonstrators shout, "The whole world is watching. The whole world is watching."

They are listening, too. "Hey Jude," Apple Records' first release, is also the Beatles' most successful single, selling more than five million copies worldwide by the end of 1968.

<hr />

As the recording of the White Album continues, John and Yoko need a place to stay. Ringo is able to provide them with one.

In 1965, Ringo leased flat 1 at 34 Montagu Square, around a mile from Abbey Road, and kept it as a city pied-à-terre even after he moved to Weybridge, Surrey. He'd rented the apartment first to Paul, then to twenty-five-year-old Jimi Hendrix, who wrote "The Wind Cries Mary," a May 1967 British single that also appeared on his debut US album *Are You Experienced,* while living there. Ringo evicted Hendrix after the celebrity tenant damaged the apartment's walls during an acid trip.

Late in the morning of October 18, 1968, John, age twenty-eight, and Yoko, thirty-five, are in bed and half naked when a loud knock sounds on the door.

"I've got a message for you," John hears someone say.

John wonders if it's a reporter looking for an exclusive comment on the couple's recent public announcement about Yoko's pregnancy. She's now six months along and due in February.

John's not wearing his glasses, but he can make out a figure standing by their bedroom window. His first thought is that it must be one of the Kray twins, a pair of infamous London gangsters and stone-cold killers known for their violent shakedowns of business owners and entertainers.

Once John puts on his glasses and sees a police officer standing there, he knows why they've come knocking. He'd been forewarned by a reporter from the *Daily Mirror.*

The drug squad's coming to get you.

Yoko runs to fetch some clothes.

"Ring the lawyer, quick!" John tells her, refusing to open the front door.

The couple has been living on what John describes as "a strange cocktail of love, sex, and forgetfulness," or what Yoko calls "a diet of champagne, caviar, and heroin."

Officers led by Detective Sergeant Norman Pilcher of the Scotland Yard Drug Squad start to force their way in through a back window. Pilcher is famous for staging celebrity drug busts. He's already arrested Mick Jagger, Keith Richards, and Donovan.

Pilcher pushes his way past John and Yoko, trailed by a plainclothes detective, two detective constables, two canine handlers, and a policewoman. It's an incredible show of force—especially since Pilcher and his team are unable to find any drugs in the apartment.

Mindful that police may have been watching the apartment since back when Jimi Hendrix was in residence, John and Yoko have been careful to keep the place scrubbed. Even so, Yogi and Boo-Boo, the drug-sniffing dogs, zero in on forgotten traces of cannabis inside a cigarette roller, a film can, and a binoculars case.

Norman Pilcher can't hide his gap-toothed smile from the reporters crowded outside the apartment as John and Yoko are driven in a squad car to the Paddington Green police station.

LENNON AND FRIEND CHARGED IN POSSESSION OF MARIJUANA, the *New York Times* reports via the AP wire, detailing a further charge of obstructing the execution of a search warrant.

At Marylebone Magistrates Court, John agrees to plead guilty and pay a £150 fine.

"It was the most terrifying experience I have ever had," he says.

"John's drug bust," Ringo says, "was a reminder that a cop was lying in wait if anyone had a party."

Though charges against Yoko are dropped, on November 4, in the aftermath of the stressful arrest, she's admitted to Queen Charlotte's Hospital, where she suffers a miscarriage on November 21. John sleeps on the floor of Yoko's room rather than leave her side.

They name the unborn boy John Ono Lennon II and bury him in an undisclosed location.

Five years later, Detective Sergeant Norman Pilcher is the one who's on trial—for perjury in another drug case. At London's central criminal court, Old Bailey, the judge who will sentence Pilcher to four years in prison tells him, "You poisoned the wells of criminal justice and set about it deliberately."

December 6, 1980

Mark wants to be as close to Lennon as possible. To achieve that aim, he needs to find much nicer accommodations—with a vantage point that puts him eyeball-to-eyeball with the man who believes he's bigger and better than Jesus.

He leaves the Y with his suitcase and travels south around ten blocks to the Sheraton Centre, at 811 Seventh Avenue, on the corner of West 53rd Street.

At the reception desk, he asks for a room with a view of the westernmost edge of Central Park. The expense, $82 per night, is well worth it. Upstairs, he goes to the window of room 2730 and looks north past the bare branches that divide the park from Central Park West.

The hotel is visible from Lennon's living room, on

the seventh floor of the Dakota. And now Mark can look right back at his target.

Satisfied, he reaches for his Walkman and a bunch of cassettes. He grabs his camera and his copy of *Double Fantasy* and heads outside to take a short subway ride back to the Dakota.

Before leaving Hawaii, he'd taped fourteen hours of Beatles songs. For inspiration, he listened to them nonstop on the long flight to New York.

Outside, "Strawberry Fields Forever" begins to play. The song is one of his favorites. He especially enjoys the parts where he recorded himself screaming and chanting "John Lennon must die!" and "John Lennon is a phony."

Mark sees a familiar face at the 72nd Street subway station. He draws closer.

It's James Taylor.

Mark follows the famous singer up a flight of steps. Then he corners Taylor against the wall of the station.

"I'm a musician just like you," Mark says. He begins to sweat, and his pupils are dilated. "I'm working on a project with John Lennon. I have something that I need to get to him. You know him, right?"

Taylor seems unnerved. He tries to peel himself off the subway wall.

"I've gotta go, man," the singer says softly.

Taylor turns north on Central Park West. After

around twenty yards, Mark sees the man look over his shoulder. Mark stands alone across the street from the Dakota, muttering to himself, when their eyes lock.

Taylor looks away and picks up his pace.

"A creepy, sweaty guy recognized me and got in my face," Taylor will later recall. "He was talking fast, telling me about himself—that he was working on a project with John Lennon. I had spent nine months in a psychiatric hospital, and it seemed to me that he was mentally ill."

CHAPTER 36

I don't need to fight to prove I'm right.
— "Baba O'Riley"

I n US folklore, nothing has been more romanticized than guns and the larger-than-life men who wielded them," states *Time* magazine in its June 21, 1968, cover story titled "The Gun in America."

During the last week of September, the Beatles continue to record songs for their double album. Like the majority of the thirty songs on the White Album, "Happiness Is a Warm Gun" originated when John began writing it at the ashram in Rishikesh. He envisions its multiple distinct phases as "sort of a history of rock and roll."

When George Martin hands John a visual, the fragments become an ingenious whole. "A gun magazine was sitting around," John remembers, "and the cover was the picture of a smoking gun. The title of the article, which I never read, was 'Happiness Is a Warm Gun.'

"I thought, what a fantastic, insane thing to say. A warm gun means you've just shot something."

American gun laws have been static since 1939, but in the wake of the political assassinations of JFK, MLK Jr., and RFK, President Lyndon B. Johnson pushes for reform, sponsoring the Gun Control Act of 1968, which Congress passes into law on October 22.

On November 20, two days before EMI releases the White Album—pressed with Apple labels—Paul is interviewed on Radio Luxembourg, calling the song "a favorite of mine" while dismissing the content that inspired it.

"And it was so sick, you know, the idea of 'Come and buy your killing weapons,' and 'Come and get it.' But it's just such a great line, 'Happiness Is a Warm Gun,' that John sort of took that and used that as a chorus. And the rest of the words...I think they're great words, you know. It's a poem. And he finishes off, 'Happiness Is a Warm Gun, yes it is.'"

Critics agree. "'Happiness Is a Warm Gun' is one of the greatest numbers on the album," the *International Times* says, praising the Beatles' ninth studio album and latest chart topper, the reviewer catching John's musical intention that "the music has three distinct phases ending with a touch of the '50s...a snatch from 'Angel Baby' by Rosie and the Originals at the end."

"Obviously a Lennon composition," the *Record Mirror* states. "The firearm becomes feminine and the lyrics ambiguous," referencing the intrigue that has circled for decades as to whether the lyric "When I hold you in my arms / And I feel my finger on your trigger" is sexual—"Oh, well, by then I'm into double meanings," John later says.

According to the BBC, that's precisely what makes the White Album "the greatest and truest most popular work of art in the history of the world, with the greatest cover—both avant-garde and incredibly popular at the same time."

American rock critic Lester Bangs observes the passage of another creative milestone: "The first album by the Beatles or in the history of rock by four solo artists in one band."

Each Beatle is to receive one of the first four albums in the run, with a sequential number printed on each cover.

John wants the first of the first, calling out, "Bagsy No. 1!"

"John got 000001 because he shouted the loudest," Paul remembers.

Ringo keeps his double album in a bank vault. And there it stays until 2015, when the drummer discovers that his copy, not John's, is the original—number 000001.

That Saturday, December 5, 2015, Julien's Auctions, in Beverly Hills, sets a guide price of $40,000 to $60,000, which will go to Ringo's charity, the Lotus Foundation.

The bidding shatters records, bringing $790,000. Ringo has a message for the buyer: "Whoever gets it it will have my fingerprints on it."

⚬⚬⚬

Forty-seven years earlier, in December of 1968, Mick Jagger is asking musical stars to appear in a concert he's calling the Rock and Roll Circus. The BBC books twenty-eight-year-old Michael Lindsay-Hogg to direct the film at the Intertel Studios, Wembley. "All the performers in the show had basically come out of a little address book in Mick Jagger's back pocket," Lindsay-Hogg recalls. "He looks up L, he calls John, and then John says he'll do it."

On the afternoon of December 11, 1968, celebrity guests in costumes, including Yoko Ono and Marianne Faithful, gather in a studio space decorated as a circus tent. They watch as ringmaster Mick Jagger moves among the members of Sir Robert Fossett's Circus, including trapeze artists, a live tiger, and a fire eater.

Jethro Tull and the Who are slated to perform, but the main draw is the supergroup dubbed the Dirty Mac, featuring twenty-eight-year-old John Lennon on vocals and guitar, twenty-three-year-old Eric Clapton on guitar, almost-twenty-five-year-old Stones guitarist Keith Richards on bass, and twenty-one-year-old Mitch Mitchell of the Jimi Hendrix Experience on drums.

When one of the crew asks John for his choice of amp, he answers, "Oh, one that plays!"

The all-star quartet launches into John's "Yer Blues." It's John's first performance outside the Beatles. Their second song, "Whole Lotta Yoko," features Yoko Ono wailing over a blues-rock jam.

On New Year's Day in 1969, the British writer Barry Miles, whose byline was simply "Miles," reports on his recent visit to Apple's Trident Studios in Soho, where over the past few months the Beatles have been finishing the White Album while twenty-one-year-old musician James Taylor—who sang "Something in the Way She Moves" and passed a spring 1968 audition with Paul and George to become Apple's first American artist—was recording his eponymous debut album.

"I was pleased," Miles writes in his favorable review

in the *International Times,* "because it's nice to see and hear people working happily together, in close coordination, producing sounds which are good to hear, trying out ideas, getting it all down on tape for everyone to hear later."

The harmonious picture Miles paints of Taylor's recording sessions is perfectly in line with Paul's vision for Apple, though according to Ken Mansfield, the US manager of Apple Records, in reality "the atmosphere at Apple is utter chaos... 'We can't be more number one, we can't be more famous. We're going to start a business, and we're gonna do it right,'" Mansfield remembers Paul telling him. "Everything is about creativity."

John tests the boundary between art and commerce, insisting that a nude photo of him and Yoko taken at 34 Montagu Square appear on the cover of *Unfinished Music No. 1: Two Virgins.*

The idea came to him during a meditation session in India. "I wrote Yoko telling her that I planned to have her in the nude on the cover," John later says. "She was quite surprised, but nowhere near as much as George and Paul."

Sir Joseph Lockwood, head of EMI, grouses, "Well, I should find some better bodies to put on the cover than your two. They're not very attractive." In November of 1968, the album, which features the avant-garde recordings that John and Yoko made on their first night together, goes out in a plain brown wrapper—selling only five thousand copies in the UK.

On January 2, 1969, officials at Newark airport seize a shipment of thirty thousand copies, denouncing the album cover as "pornographic." The incident prompts the FBI to open a file on John.

"But it was worth it for the howl that went up," John says. "It really blew their minds. It cleared the air a bit. People always try to kill anything that's honest. The album wasn't ugly, it was just a point of view."

George and John's definitions of art are rapidly diverging. Since returning from the maharishi's ashram, George "was angry because he couldn't achieve the level of spirituality he wanted," his wife, Pattie Boyd, recalls.

"Fuck off—can't you see I'm meditating?" he lashes out at one stewardess who disturbs him during a transatlantic flight.

In the studio on January 8, George plays his song "I Me Mine" (also the title of his 1980 memoir) for John. It's a barbed commentary on the epic clash of egos that's crippling the band.

"I just got so fed up with the bad vibes," he explains.

And then George turns his anger on Yoko. "Dylan and a few people," he lights into her when they're all sitting in the Apple offices at 3 Savile Row, "said that [you've] got a lousy name in New York and you gave off bad vibes."

George and John sit and stare at each other.

"I didn't hit him," John remembers. "I don't know why."

"I Me Mine" would be the last new song the Beatles ever recorded.

"John had a tremendous weight on his shoulders," Ken Mansfield observes. "He wanted to use his fame to change the world. Unlike the others, he was becoming a real political force."

CHAPTER 37

Let's stay together.
　　　　　　— "Let's Stay Together"

The Beatles return to Twickenham Studios, where they'd filmed *A Hard Day's Night* and *Help!* Michael Lindsay-Hogg, who directed *The Rolling Stones Rock and Roll Circus* (which winds up shelved and not unveiled to the public until 1996), will film the making of the band's tenth British studio album, *Let It Be* (originally titled *Get Back*). "It's another of Paul's projects," says Barry Miles: the title song is inspired by a dream Paul had about his mother, Mary, ten years after her 1957 death.

"I think we should go back on the road," Paul says as the 1968 holidays approach. "Small band, go and do the clubs. Let's go back to square one and remember what we're all about."

There's a new kind of pressure behind his words: financial.

Back in October, the Beatles' accountants had issued an urgent warning: because of their extreme tax exposure, the band needs to earn £120,000 for every £10,000 it spends. The costs of running the sprawling Apple Corps have spiraled.

Director Lindsay-Hogg has grand ideas about the way to execute the film's concert finale. He's thinking of staging a multicultural tribute to world peace to be shot on an ocean liner or in the Sahara. "The Beatles were to start playing as the sun came up," he says, "and you'd see the crowds flocking toward them through the day."

"We can build a replica of the Roman Colosseum so the band can arrive with a group of lions," Paul suggests.

"Let's go back to Liverpool," Ringo puts in. "To the Cavern Club."

John says, "I'm warming to the idea of doing it in an asylum."

A movie about the world's greatest band needs a daring ending.

George has one.

"That's it," he says over lunch on the seventh day of tense rehearsals being captured on film. "See you 'round the clubs." Then he walks out of the meeting and out of the band he joined at age fourteen.

John isn't rattled. "I think if George doesn't come back by Monday or Tuesday, we ask Eric Clapton to play in it," he suggests. It's not an entirely out-of-the-blue idea; in early September, George had invited Clapton to play on "While My Guitar Gently Weeps" as part of the White Album sessions. "The point is, if George leaves, do we want to carry on the Beatles? I do. We should just get other members and carry on."

George quits on January 10, 1969. He returns on January 15. But he's still dead set against touring.

On January 29, a location for the concert scene still hasn't been chosen. Then it hits them, all of them. "What a great idea it would be to play on the roof—play to the whole of the West End," John says, with a knowing look to Ringo and a mischievous smile to Lindsay-Hogg.

The city of London is in for a surprise.

At one o'clock on the afternoon of Thursday, January 30, 1969, Apple executives are given short notice to report to the rooftop of 3 Savile Row. Engineers haul up a river of electric cables while carpenters build a makeshift stage.

John and the others go over the set list. *We haven't played live together in almost four years*. John's nervous as hell.

The others are, too. He can see it in their eyes.

"I don't want to go," George says.

"What's the point?" Ringo adds.

John makes the final decision. He borrows a fur coat from Yoko, adjusts his glasses, and climbs the stairs from the dressing room to the rooftop.

Wind whips off the Thames, and it's too dangerous for a helicopter to provide aerial shots. Filmmakers will have to divide the shoot into a series of close-ups of the band and reaction shots from the crowd gathering on the street.

Though his hands feel "too cold to play the chords," John grabs his guitar and sees the familiar face of Billy Preston. The American R&B keyboardist the Beatles met while touring with Little Richard in 1962 has been sitting in with the band on electric piano.

Ken Mansfield holds four lit cigarettes toward George to allow the lead guitarist to warm his fingertips.

They tear into the opening number, "Get Back."

Curious passersby stop dead in their tracks in front of the building. They crane their necks and point to the sky.

That's right, John wants to tell them. *The Beatles are giving you a free concert, their first concert since Candlestick in 1966, right above your heads.*

That's the precise location of American photographer Ethan Russell, who at John's invitation has trekked up to the rooftop and made a death-defying climb of an adjacent wall to get an overhead shot of the world's most famous rockers against the vastness of London, "mere mortals after all."

For forty-two minutes, the Beatles play five songs, including three versions of "Get Back" and two apiece of "Don't Let Me Down" and "I've Got a Feeling," for a total of nine performances.

The Metropolitan Police are circling the building, having told Apple employees, "You've got ten minutes." But the constables are Beatles fans, too. They let the band play on for a little while longer. Finally, officers make it inside and up the stairs to shut the performance down. Assistants scramble to flush drug stashes down the toilets, just in case.

Once police reach the rooftop, the Beatles finish playing.

John quips into the microphone, "I'd like to say thank you on behalf of the group and ourselves, and I hope we've passed the audition."

The four Beatles smile in agreement.

We're still the best damn rock 'n' roll band on earth.

When Paul is asked in 2019 if he sensed at the time that the rooftop concert would be the group's last, he says, "No, I don't think I did; I don't think any of us did. It was really just the culmination of a lot of writing and rehearsing that we had done up to this point."

But the end never needs an invitation.

CHAPTER 38

Keep me searching for a heart of gold...
                                    —"Heart of Gold"

pple's losing money every week," John tells Ray
Coleman, editor of *Disc and Music Echo,* in January of 1969. "If it carries on like this, all of us
will be broke within the next six months."

"That was my opening," Allen Klein later says.
The thirty-seven-year-old New Jersey–born music
executive has already guided the finances of the
Rolling Stones as well as those of Sam Cooke and
Bobby Darin, plus Donovan and the Animals. He's
become legendary in the music world as "the Robin
Hood of pop" for negotiating huge advances for his
recording artists—and for regarding a contract as
"just a piece of paper." A sign on Klein's desk in
New York reads: YEA, THOUGH I WALK THROUGH
THE VALLEY OF THE SHADOW OF DEATH, I SHALL

FEAR NO EVIL: FOR *I AM THE BIGGEST MOTHER-FUCKER IN THE VALLEY*.

Via his connections to Mick Jagger, Klein sets up a clandestine meeting with John and Yoko in the Harlequin Penthouse at the Dorchester hotel in London.

"He was very nervous, you could see it in his face," John remembers, but Klein, trained as an accountant, quickly succeeds in charming John because "he not only knew my work, and the lyrics that I had written, but he also understood them, and from *way* back. That was it."

John likes Klein's brashness and his bulldog mentality. So does Yoko, to whom Klein promises a solo art show.

"He's a fucking sharp man, and anyone who knew me that well, without having met me before, had to be the guy to look after me," John explains. He can't wait to document his commitment to Klein, writing a letter to all parties with a financial interest in the Beatles, including the record company EMI, saying that "I've asked Allen Klein to look after my things. Please give him any information he wants and full cooperation. Love. John Lennon."

George and Ringo are convinced that Klein is well suited. Like John, they sympathize with Klein's hardscrabble upbringing. "Because we were all from Liverpool," George reasons, "we favored people who were street people."

They especially like his promises that they'll be too rich to ever worry. "You should be able to say FYM—Fuck You, Money," Klein tells them.

"Rock 'n' roll specializes in that kind of, 'This guy's a twerp. We've got to have him on our team!'" Paul says, but he wants no part of any association with Klein.

When Paul tells John whom he'd rather have, John is struck by the obvious.

Of course Paul wants Lee Eastman. The Manhattan music lawyer is the father of Paul's fiancée, Linda Eastman, the New York photographer he'd first met in 1967, then reconnected with after he and Jane split up.

Paul reaches out to Mick Jagger, who it turns out is trying to get rid of Klein. "Don't go near him, he's a dog. He's a crook," the Rolling Stone tells Paul. Jagger also calls John to advise him against "making the biggest mistake of your life," but John's made up his mind.

And neither one of us is going to budge.

They come to a bizarre arrangement.

Both Lee Eastman and Allen Klein move their offices into Apple headquarters in London and carve out different slices—legal and financial, respectively—of the Beatles' pie.

On March 12, 1969, twenty-six-year-old Paul marries twenty-seven-year-old Linda.

None of the other Beatles is invited to the wedding. "Maybe it was because the group was breaking up," Paul says. "We were all pissed off with each other. We certainly weren't a gang anymore."

The press is chasing Paul and Linda. "It rained, and this was appropriate," *The Guardian* reports. "The pavements outside the Marylebone register office would have been wet in any case with the tears of fans thrown by the sudden reality of having failed to become Mrs. McCartney."

Instead, Paul tosses candy to the lovelorn, who compete for the sweet mementos.

News of Paul's wedding ignites John's competitive spirit.

John's divorce was only finalized on November 8, 1968, and Yoko's second divorce was finalized on February 2. John hasn't told his ex-wife, Cynthia, or their son, Julian, about his wedding plans. He envisions that he and Yoko will "get married on a cross-channel ferry. That was the romantic part."

John's driver rushes them to Southampton, where a ferry crosses the English Channel to France, but Yoko, who is not a British citizen, is denied a visa. Another plan, to get married in Amsterdam, is dashed when the couple can't meet the two-week residency requirement.

John's money and fame secure a private jet to Paris on March 16.

In London, George and his wife, Pattie Boyd, are dominating the headlines. On Paul's wedding day, Detective Sergeant Norman Pilcher led a drug raid on their home in Esher, where Yogi the police dog located a small amount of pot. On March 18, George and Pattie appear at a hearing on charges of cannabis possession.

On the morning of March 20, 1969, eight days after Paul's wedding, John and Yoko fly from Paris to Gibraltar, on Spain's southern peninsula—a British territory since 1713. There's no residency requirement, and as a British citizen, John can legally marry there. In "The Ballad of John and Yoko," John names his personal assistant as the one who saved the wedding by saying, "You can make it O.K. / You can get married in Gibraltar near Spain."

A warm wind blows off the Mediterranean Sea as they arrive at the British consulate. Yoko has dressed for the ten-minute ceremony in a white minidress, tall white boots, a wide-brimmed hat, and dark glasses; John is in a white suit jacket, corduroys, and tennis shoes.

With the Rock of Gibraltar as a backdrop, the couple poses for photos. John holds their marriage certificate overhead, victorious.

"Intellectually, we didn't believe in getting

married," John tells the reporters who've tracked them to this remote destination. "But one doesn't love someone just intellectually. For two people marriage still has the edge over just living together."

Best man Peter Brown hires a white Rolls-Royce to transport the newlyweds to Amsterdam, where they check in to the Hilton for a weeklong stay.

At a local pub, magazine reporter Rick Wilson and his editor are having lunch. "There's been some communication to the office about some happening at the Hilton," the editor says. "John Lennon's holding court about something or other."

He and Yoko have sent out cards to the press, inviting them to a daily discussion about peace from March 25 to March 31.

"We knew whatever we did was going to be in the papers," John reasons. "We decided to utilize the space we would occupy anyway, by getting married, with a commercial for peace.

"We would sell our production, which we call 'peace.' And to sell a product you need a gimmick, and the gimmick we thought was 'bed.' And we thought 'bed' because bed was the easiest way of doing it, because we're lazy."

Wilson dashes to the hotel, where he joins two dozen or so reporters and photographers on the way up to room 902, John and Yoko's honeymoon suite. They're in bed, wearing pajamas.

"Why not Saigon or Dallas if peace is the cause?" Wilson asks.

"Because I'm dead scared of Saigon or Dallas," John replies. "There's less chance of getting shot or crucified here."

On March 21, while John and Yoko are on their honeymoon, Allen Klein is appointed Apple's business manager. He begins firing Apple staff in anticipation of his new three-year arrangement, which allows him to collect 20 percent of Apple revenues (though none on existing Beatles contracts).

On the final day of John and Yoko's bed-in, March 31, George and Pattie stand trial. Rumors are swirling that Pilcher and his Drug Squad planted a stash in their home—"I'm a tidy sort of bloke. I don't like chaos. I kept records in the record rack, tea in the tea caddy, and pot in the pot box," George insists of the hash the police say they found on his floor—but the Harrisons plead guilty, are fined £250, and are sentenced to a one-year probation.

John and Paul meet at Paul's house on Cavendish Avenue. As songwriting partners, they take a walk in the garden.

On April 14, the two newly married men start recording "The Ballad of John and Yoko" at Abbey

Road studios. Though neither Ringo nor George is available that day, to the two original Beatles, it seems like the best of old times.

Over seven hours, John takes the lead on guitar and vocals while Paul handles the bass, the drums, and even the maracas.

"Go a bit slower, Ringo," John jokes.

"Okay, George," Paul replies with a cheeky smile.

Engineer Geoff Emerick is watching from the control room. "It was a great session, one of those magic times when everything went right and nothing went wrong."

The May 1969 single becomes the Beatles seventeenth number-one UK hit—and their last to top the charts in that country.

CHAPTER 39

> A time to be born, a time to die...
> — "Turn! Turn! Turn!"

T his is my story both humble and true," John writes in a poem he's calling "Alphabet." One line reads, "T is for Tommy who won the war."

There is a poetry stand in People's Park, a community garden created by students protesting for peace on the campus of the University of California at Berkeley. To clear the crowd, on May 15, 1969, police had turned guns loaded with bird shot and buckshot on the students, killing one and seriously wounding many more.

When John reads about Bloody Thursday, as it's called, his devotion to the peace cause only intensifies. "When I first got the news it stooned me, absolutely stooned me," he says.

He's eager to return to America, to advise the

demonstrators. But his repeated requests for a visa are all denied on the basis of his 1968 conviction for marijuana possession.

John's British passport grants him access to the Bahamas, but when he and Yoko arrive there, on May 24, they feel that the American press is too distant, so they fly to Toronto, where immigration authorities at first detain them before granting a ten-day visa.

On May 26, they check in to suite 1742 of Montreal's stately Queen Elizabeth Hotel to stage an eight-day bed-in—in close proximity to the New York press corps.

"What about talking to the people who make the decisions, the power brokers?" a reporter asks.

"Talk about what?" John answers. "It doesn't happen like that. In the US, the government is too busy talking about how to keep me out. If I'm a joke, as they say, and not important, why don't they just let me in?"

American and Canadian radio hosts welcome the Beatle to the airwaves. When he phones KSAN in San Francisco, members of the psychedelic band Quicksilver Messenger Service are listening. "The advice you gave was right on! Violence really does beget violence," the band writes John. "But the way the People's Park issue is being handled is not cool. I know your advice will save a lot of broken bones."

When he talks to a reporter from *Rolling Stone,* John

seems less than certain. "Yes, we're really scared to go to the US because people have become so violent, even our sort of people."

In the face of fear and uncertainty, his passion for songwriting never deserts him. "Why isn't somebody writing one for the people *now*?" he asks Yoko. "That's what my job is. Our job is to write for the people now."

On May 31, a full moon rises, illuminating John and Yoko's hotel room, where John scatters flower petals daily.

The next day, an impromptu recording session happens at the site of the bed-in. The equipment—four microphones and four-track Ampex recorder—is spartan in comparison to the setup at Abbey Road studios, but John is looking for a simple sound in the new song he's written with Yoko to promote peace.

"Sing along," he instructs his celebrity guests as he strums his acoustic guitar.

Some of them—including Yoko, comedian Tommy Smothers, LSD guru Timothy Leary, poet Allen Ginsberg, Beatles publicist Derek Taylor, and a dozen members of a local Hare Krishna temple—are namechecked in the lyrics of John's first solo single, which he records in a single take.

John is in his element leading this hopeful plea to the citizens of the world, but he makes it clear that the peace movement is bigger than any one person.

"Like Pete Seeger said, we don't have a leader but we have a song—'Give Peace a Chance.'"

Although the *Let It Be* sessions and rooftop concert have yet to be prepared for release, on July 1, 1969, the Beatles begin recording a new album.

Without John.

On July 4, Apple releases "Give Peace a Chance" (it carries the Beatles' standard Lennon and McCartney credit as well as a new one—the Plastic Ono Band) in the UK.

John misses its rise up the charts. He's in a Scottish hospital after swerving his Austin Maxi (carrying Yoko and their children, Kyoko and Julian) away from an oncoming car and into a roadside ditch. John jokes with the press—"If you're going to have a car crash, try to arrange for it to happen in the Highlands"—even through the pain of seventeen facial stitches.

On July 9, engineer Geoff Emerick sees movement at the studio doorway, where John and Yoko have appeared "like two apparitions dressed in black."

"Yes, I'm okay," John tells Emerick, George Martin, and the worried Beatles.

Then he places an order with Harrods and has a double bed installed at Abbey Road so that John can be close to Yoko while she recuperates from having fourteen stitches and a back injury. "Can you put a microphone up over here so we can hear her on the headphones?" he asks the astonished recording staff.

When a policeman patrolling the studio grounds makes his way into the control room during a late-night session, John is plunged into a terror reminiscent of his 1968 drug bust. "It's your job to keep people out of here!" he orders roadie Mal Evans.

Some people, such as Yoko's friend the American actor Dan Richter, are allowed in. "I couldn't help thinking that those guys were making rock 'n' roll history," Richter recalls, "while I was sitting on this bed in the middle of the Abbey Road studio, handing Yoko a small white packet."

Not long after their car accident, John starts writing a song he's calling "Come Together." Or, rather, rewriting it: the song had originally been intended for Timothy Leary's derailed campaign that year for the California governorship.

When recording begins, on July 21, John says to the band, "I've got no arrangement for you, but you know how I want it. Give me something funky."

He's taking all the vocals. When Paul asks him, "What do you want me to do on this track, John?" he replies, "Don't worry; I'll do the overdubs on this."

"It's an upbeat, rock-a-beat-a-boogie, with very Lennon lyrics," George says, and even Timothy Leary can't argue with the metaphor John gives him for repurposing the song—"he was a tailor and I was a customer who had ordered a suit and never returned. So he sold it to someone else." (Despite the song's pronounced Lennon flavor, he is sued for its similarity to Chuck Berry's "You Can't Catch Me," which includes the lyrics, "Here come a flat-top, he was movin' up with me." As part of a settlement, John agrees to cover three songs from Berry's publisher for a mid-'70s oldies album.)

Between sessions, John rests at home, listening to Yoko play Beethoven's "Moonlight" Sonata on the piano.

Inspiration strikes. "Can you play those chords backward?" he says.

She does, and John writes "Because" around them.

"'Because' is one of the most beautiful things we've ever done," George says. "It has three-part harmony—John, Paul, and George."

All four Beatles need to agree on a name for the album. *Everest,* after the world's highest mountain and also a popular brand of British cigarette, is the leading contender, but Paul is the only one enthusiastic about an international photo shoot.

"Well, if we're not going to name it *Everest* and

pose for the cover in Tibet, where are we going to go?" he asks.

Ringo offers an easy solution. "Let's just step outside and name it *Abbey Road*."

He's only joking, but Paul is inspired. He makes some rough sketches of an album cover showing the four of them walking a zebra crossing on Abbey Road.

John contributes the photographer, Iain MacMillan. Yoko had commissioned him to document her 1966 show at the Indica gallery, the same one where she and John met.

On the morning of August 8, MacMillan hauls a stepladder into the middle of the London street and waits while a police officer stops traffic. John, dressed all in white, leads a dark-suited Ringo, a barefoot Paul with cigarette in hand, and a denim-clad George on six passes back and forth while the photographer snaps away.

Only one photograph shows them stepping perfectly in time.

The next night, more than five thousand miles away in Los Angeles, three disciples of a thirty-five-year-old self-proclaimed messiah named Charles Manson follow a winding private road in the exclusive Benedict Canyon enclave in the Hollywood Hills.

Armed with a gun and knives, they enter the home at 10050 Cielo Drive. Manson, an aspiring singer and guitarist, knows the address as that of twenty-eight-year-old Terry Melcher, the record producer and son of film and recording star Doris Day. The two men had met the previous summer at the home of the Beach Boys drummer, Dennis Wilson. Following an audition, Melcher told Manson he "wasn't impressed enough to want to make a record."

Though Melcher had lived at 10050 Cielo Drive from May of 1966 until January of 1969, the current residents are film director Roman Polanski—whose most recent hit is *Rosemary's Baby,* starring Mia Farrow—and his wife, actress Sharon Tate. The twenty-six-year-old star of *Valley of the Dolls* is eight and a half months pregnant and in the company of three friends while Polanski is working on a new script in London.

Sharon Tate pleads for the life of her unborn child, but the murderers show no mercy, smearing the word *pig* in Tate's blood on the white front door of the house. The next night, in central Los Angeles, the killing spree continues, claiming the lives of Leno and Rosemary LaBianca. On a refrigerator at the LaBianca home, the killers leave another startling message in blood—a misspelling of "Helter Skelter," the title of a Beatles song off the 1968 smash White Album.

Paul wrote the intense hard-rock number in response to an interview that ran in *Melody Maker* with the Who's Pete Townshend proclaiming he'd just recorded "the raunchiest, loudest, most ridiculous rock 'n' roll record you've ever heard." (It was "I Can See for Miles.")

"So I said to the guys, 'I think we should do a song like that; something really wild.'"

Look out, warns the chorus. *Coming down fast.*

Though "Helter Skelter" is a song about a fairground slide, it also hints at the dark progression from innocence to violence.

CHAPTER 40

Johnny's in the basement
mixing up the medicine.
— "Subterranean Homesick Blues"

Leave John alone!"
   At Tittenhurst Park, a seventy-two-acre Ascot estate that John and Yoko purchased in May of 1969 for £150,000, Yoko is showing photographer Ethan Russell a disturbing package she's received from one of John's fans. It's a doll in her likeness, pins piercing the torso, with the message attached.

These are not happy times for them. Or for the band.

The *Abbey Road* sessions close on August 20 with a final recording of John's "I Want You (She's So Heavy)."

"Louder! Louder!" he yells at engineer Geoff Emerick. "I want the track to build and build, and then I want the white noise to take over and blot out the music altogether."

He succeeds. The response from the other Beatles is silence.

The mood hasn't lifted two days later, when the band gathers at Tittenhurst Park, graced with flowering gardens and a man-made lake stocked with ducks and fish, for a promotional photo shoot.

Ethan Russell lines the four long-haired bandmates against a carved wooden door on the estate. No one is smiling, and Russell doesn't force it.

Through his lens, it's clear that "this marriage had come to an end—and boy does it show."

It would be the last photo ever taken of the band together.

⬦

John and Yoko make a pact. They want to try again for a child, so they're quitting their heroin habit.

"We were very square people in a way," Yoko recalls. "We wouldn't kick it in a hospital because we wouldn't let anybody know. We just went straight cold turkey."

In an interview published on August 23, Apple recording artist James Taylor tells *Rolling Stone,* "John's gone away for two weeks, just to get away from it all."

The experience is a nightmare.

The gruesome withdrawal symptoms—fever, nausea, palpitations, sweats, chills, and intestinal distress—crash against them like a powerful wave. *We have to do it this way,* John keeps telling himself.

During his self-imposed exile, John writes "Cold Turkey," a song about his intense personal detox battle. "It took courage enough for John to go cold turkey on his own," Yoko's friend Dan Richter later comments. But writing a song about it? "To admit it, and tell you everything about it...that took real guts."

John proposes "Cold Turkey" to Paul and the others as a Beatles single on *Abbey Road*.

They decline.

"I'm gonna leave the band," John confides to Eric Clapton high over the Atlantic Ocean.

John had called Clapton that morning. "How would you fancy playing at a rock 'n' roll festival with the Plastic Ono Band in Toronto?"

Tonight.

Their first-class airline tickets are dated Saturday, September 13, a month after Woodstock, which the Beatles hadn't played. This Canadian festival will be the first public outing for the Plastic Ono Band. "Nothing's expected of John and Yoko or the Plastic Ono," John says. "They would be anybody or perform anything. So with that sort of freedom there's no hang-ups."

John in the leather gear he favors as a young rocker in Liverpool.

The original "Silver Beatles" in Liverpool (L to R: Stuart Sutcliffe, John Lennon, Paul McCartney, and George Harrison, with a sit-in drummer).

German poster advertising the Beatles alongside Rory Storm and the Hurricanes (the band Ringo Starr played in).

Everything clicks into place for the band once Ringo Starr joins as drummer.

John is initially delighted by the Beatles' rise to fame.

John with his wife, Cynthia, and their son, Julian. John finds the transition between rock star and family man difficult.

The Beatles (with manager, Brian Epstein, in Paris) tour almost constantly.

A 2-for-1 photo op in Florida for the Beatles and rising boxing star Cassius Clay (the future Mohammad Ali).

John's handwritten set list from the Beatles' first concert in America on February 11, 1964, on stationery from their hotel in Washington, DC.

Dr. Joyce Brothers interviews the Beatles at the Plaza Hotel in New York.

The Beatles chafe under their squeaky-clean image and cause controversy with the "Butcher Cover."

John grows weary with the constant demands of press.

A "Beatles Bonfire," where teens are urged to burn records and memorabilia in protest of John's observation that the band is more popular than Jesus.

The Beatles celebrate the release of their latest album, *Sgt. Pepper's Lonely Hearts Club Band,* which goes on to become the bestselling studio album in British history.

John and his son Julian in front of John's psychedelic Rolls-Royce.

In early 1968, the Beatles are among many celebrities who travel to India to study transcendental meditation with the Maharishi Mahesh Yogi (L to R: John, Mike Love of the Beach Boys, the Maharishi, George, actress Mia Farrow and her brother John Farrow, singer Donovan, and Paul).

During a month at the ashram, John and Paul write most of the songs for what will become *The Beatles*, aka the White Album.

John and Julian with Eric Clapton, during the December 1968 filming of the documentary *The Rolling Stones Rock and Roll Circus*.

Eric Clapton, Keith Richards, and John Lennon at the Rock and Roll Circus.

John with Mick Jagger in London.

On January 30, 1969, the Beatles give their last-ever live performance together, on the rooftop of Apple Records.

John Lennon and Yoko Ono, one of rock music's most famous pairings.

On March 20, 1969, John and Yoko get married in Gibraltar, then stage a lengthy "Bed-In" Peace Protest as part of their honeymoon.

John at the piano where he wrote *Imagine*, the most celebrated album and single of his solo career.

Eric Clapton, Klaus Voorman, John Lennon, and Yoko Ono goofing poolside in Toronto, the day after the Plastic Ono Band's first public performance.

John plays "Instant Karma! (We All Shine On)," which he wrote in less than an hour.

PEOPLE FOR PEACE

John wearing a "People for Peace" armband on the TV program *Top of the Pops* with the Plastic Ono Band.

At the New York Office of Immigration and Naturalization, fighting deportation in 1972.

This is to certify that

LENNON, JOHN WINSTON ONO

(REGISTRATION NUMBER)

A17 597 321

NO-DAY-YR OF BIRTH   SEX

10 09 40   M

has been duly registered according to law and was admitted to the United States as an immigrant at

PORT   NO-DAY-YR OF ENTRY

15 NYC   07 27 76

Four years later, John is issued a Green Card. Visible here is the "Ono" added to his legal name.

John with Alice Cooper, fellow member of the Hollywood Vampires, a celebrity drinking club.

Drinking Brandy Alexanders at the Troubadour in LA in 1974 (L to R: Peter Lawford, John, May Pang, and Harry Nilsson).

John's last live performance, with Elton John in Madison Square Garden on November 28, 1974.

David Bowie, Art Garfunkel, Paul Simon, Yoko Ono, John, and Roberta Flack at the 1975 Grammy Awards in New York.

John in New York City with Yoko and their toddler son Sean, born on John's 35th birthday in 1975.

John makes musical memories with Sean.

John and Yoko pose in front of the Dakota on November 21, 1980, days after their album *Double Fantasy*—John's first in five years—comes out.

John Lennon signs autographs for fans waiting outside his home in the Dakota—including Mark David Chapman, who murders him later that night.

Producer David Geffen escorts Yoko from Roosevelt Hospital after John is declared dead on arrival.

Huge crowds of mourners gather outside the Dakota before moving their vigil to nearby Central Park.

The logbook Chapman signs as "John Lennon" before setting off for New York.

Chapman is escorted from the police station in handcuffs.

Mark David Chapman's mugshot.

Chapman carries a new copy of *The Catcher in the Rye* (his previous copy is held in police evidence) to his 1981 court proceedings.

Except when it comes to preparing for the sold-out show.

In addition to Clapton, John's recruited drummer Alan White, and his old German pal Klaus Voormann to play bass.

"We tried to rehearse on the plane," John says, "but it was impossible."

At Varsity Stadium at the University of Toronto (capacity: 21,000), the Plastic Ono Band is a last-minute addition to a bill that includes the Doors as well as many of the musicians John once idolized, such as Jerry Lee Lewis and Gene Vincent.

John hasn't played to a crowd this size since the Beatles' 1966 American tour. He's pacing backstage, chain-smoking, feeling the pressure of slotting between two of his musical heroes, Chuck Berry and Little Richard.

"The show should be closed, by me, the King," Little Richard declares. "You know that, Mr. Lennon. You know that, Mr. Promoters. You know that, Mr. Doors. I am the King and I should close the show."

It's after midnight when American record producer Kim Fowley makes the new band's introduction. "Everyone get out your matches and lighters, please. In a minute I'm going to bring out John Lennon and Eric Clapton and when I do I want you to light them and give them a huge Toronto welcome."

The Plastic Ono Band walks onstage to the glow

of handheld lights. They play five songs, including the classics "Blue Suede Shoes" and "Dizzy Miss Lizzy"—"only with all of us blasting it. Fantastic. It's just pure sound."

"What's next?" John turns to Eric Clapton, who doesn't have an answer.

"C'mon!" John calls while he keeps jamming. They play his "Yer Blues" and "Cold Turkey," the song's live debut.

"Then we went into 'Give Peace a Chance,' which was just unbelievable," John says. "The buzz was incredible."

"I never felt so good in my life," he remembers, vowing, "I don't care who I have to play with, I'm going back to playing rock onstage!"

⸎

Allen Klein calls a Saturday meeting on September 20. The Apple offices are empty as the Beatles file into the boardroom.

Klein has hammered out a new deal with EMI's Capitol Records that will sharply raise the Beatles' cut of wholesale record prices from 17.5 to 25 percent.

John, with Yoko by his side, stares across the table at Paul. *Tell them now that you're done,* he wills himself.

Instead, John launches an attack on Paul and his contributions to *Abbey Road*.

"I liked the 'A' side but I never liked that sort of pop opera on the other side. I think it's junk because it was just bits of songs thrown together. 'Come Together' is all right, that's all I remember. That was my song."

Paul takes the slings and arrows.

The pain gets worse. As Paul tries to convince John that they can find compromises to his complaints, John's suddenly had enough. "You don't seem to understand, do you? The group is over. I'm leaving," he tells them.

"I must say I felt guilty at springing it on them at such short notice," he later reflects, though Paul says, "I remember him saying, 'It's weird, this, telling you I'm leaving the group, but in a way it's very exciting.' It was like when he told Cynthia he was getting a divorce."

On September 26, John returns to the studio. With Eric Clapton on guitar, Klaus Voormann on bass, and Ringo on drums, he records twenty-six takes of "Cold Turkey" and rejects them all.

That same day, *Abbey Road* gets its UK release.

"It's strange that we have now reached the point

where nobody worries TOO much about what the Beatles are doing on record," *Melody Maker* writes in its review of what will go on to become the group's bestselling album.

Many critics single out the album's second song, the one inspired by George's wife, Pattie. "'Something' is a song of mine," twenty-six-year-old George says in an interview with the *Detroit Free Press,* "probably the nicest melody I've ever written."

John and Paul don't agree on much these days, except that the song is indeed George's best work yet. Frank Sinatra elevates the praise for "Something," calling it "the greatest love song in the past fifty years" and covering the song in his own live performances.

Musically, it is a fine farewell. The big valedictory comes, fittingly, on "The End," with John, George, and Paul trading guitar solos (after an unprecedented Ringo drum solo) before landing on the line "And in the end / The love you take / Is equal to the love you make."

From his vantage point in the control room, engineer Geoff Emerick observed, "John, Paul, and George looked like they had gone back in time, like they were kids again, playing together for the sheer enjoyment of it. More than anything, they reminded me of gunslingers, with their guitars strapped on, looks of steely-eyed resolve, determined to outdo one another. Yet there was no animosity, no tension at all—you could tell they were simply having fun."

But that's all in the past when, on October 20, Apple releases the single "Cold Turkey." John's testament is uncomfortably received. "'Cold Turkey' talks about thirty-six hours rolling in pain," says the music coordinator of Detroit's WKNR-FM. The BBC bans its airplay.

"They thought it was a pro-drugs song," John later tells BBC1 radio DJ Andy Peebles. "To some it was a rock 'n' roll version of *The Man with the Golden Arm*," a 1955 Frank Sinatra film showing his character suffering from drug withdrawal.

That same day, Apple releases John and Yoko's *Wedding Album* in the United States (it comes out a few weeks later in the UK, on November 7). They'd recorded it in April and, during a break on the afternoon of the twenty-second, had gone up to the Apple rooftop to take part in a quick ceremony in front of a commissioner for oaths, ratifying John's formal name change from John Winston Lennon to John Ono Lennon. "Yoko changed her name for me. I've changed mine for her. One for both, both for each other," John declares.

Wedding Album, side 1 of which offers John and Yoko pronouncing each other's names for almost twenty-three minutes over a backing track of their heartbeats, marks the third of a trio of experimental albums that started with *Unfinished Music No. 1: Two Virgins* and continued with *Unfinished Music No. 2: Life with the Lions* (which also included a recorded heartbeat, that of their miscarried son).

The album is a critical and commercial dud, but John shrugs it off. "We didn't expect a hit record out of it," he later tells the BBC. It was more personal than that.

"When people get married they usually make their own wedding albums," John says, something to "show to the relatives when they come round. Well, our relatives are the . . . what you call fans."

He continues, "We're public personalities," and — referring to another celebrity couple that happens to be celebrating a first anniversary that same October 20 — "I'd enjoy reading Jackie and Onassis's album."

The chorus of "Give Peace a Chance" echoes through Washington, DC. On November 15, activist Pete Seeger leads 250,000 demonstrators through Lennon's lyrics in protest of the mounting death toll in the Vietnam War, in which American casualties surpass forty thousand.

John and Yoko are heartened that their message is making a difference, pledging, "We'll keep promoting peace in the way we do which, whichever way you look at it, is our way, because we're artists and not politicians."

John's unbothered when he and Yoko are mocked for their activism. "Laurel and Hardy, that's John and Yoko," he comments. Better not to be taken too seriously anyway, "because all the serious people like Martin Luther King and Kennedy and Gandhi get shot."

Ten days later, John has his chauffeur drive the psychedelic Rolls to Buckingham Palace to return the MBE medal awarded him by the queen in 1965, along with a note stating it was being done in protest of the British government's support of America in the Vietnam War "and against Cold Turkey slipping down the charts." He explains his decision in a live interview on BBC TV. "Really shouldn't have taken it," he says of the MBE medal. "Felt I had sold out. I must get rid of it, I kept saying, I must get rid of it. So I did. Wanted to get rid of it by 1970 anyway."

John and Yoko create an international ad campaign around the slogan "War is over! If you want it." The message, appearing in newspapers and on billboards, is signed "Happy Christmas, John and Yoko." Though some people find the message too facile—American antiwar activist John Sinclair sneers, "You are going to sound awfully fucking stupid trying to tell the heroic Vietnamese people that 'the war is over if you want it' while they are being burned and bombed and blown out of their pitiful little huts and fields"—John explains that it's not about ignoring reality but about taking action. "You've got the power," he says. "All we have to do is remember that: we've all got the power. That's why we said 'war is over if you want it.'... Don't believe that jazz that there's nothing you can do, 'just turn on and drop out, man.' You've got to turn on and drop *in*. Or they're going to drop all over you."

The *Daily Mail* names John Clown of the Year for his actions. But on December 30, ATV in England airs an hourlong special featuring three men, each chosen as a Man of the Decade: American president John F. Kennedy, Vietnamese leader Ho Chi Minh—and British rock star John Lennon.

Rather than focusing on the violence and turmoil of the past decade, John has a sunnier view. "Not many people are noticing all the *good* that came out of the last ten years," John tells the interviewer, famed zoologist Desmond Morris.

"And this is only the beginning," he continues, sounding optimistic about the future of the peace movement. "The sixties was just waking up in the morning, and we haven't even got to dinnertime yet. And I can't wait, you know, I just can't wait. I'm so glad to be around. And it's just gonna be great.

"It's gonna be wonderful and I believe it."

CHAPTER 41

Has anybody seen my old friend John?
—"Abraham, Martin and John"

John just wrote a great song and he wants to cut it as a single."

Beatles assistant Mal Evans puts out this call to Plastic Ono Band members Klaus Voormann (bass), Alan White (drums), and Billy Preston (organ).

The concept for the song came to John just that morning, and he'd completed the lyrics in less than an hour. He's calling it "Instant Karma!"

George Harrison wants in on the project once John tells him about it. "I've written this tune and I'm going to record it tonight and have it pressed up and out tomorrow—that's the whole point of 'Instant Karma,' you know," John says.

The musicians arrive at the Abbey Road studios on January 27, 1970, to begin recording John's cosmic take on the human condition, which is that "there really is a reaction to what you do now."

They're all rehearsing when White hears John say, "Alan, whatever you're doing, keep doing it. It's wonderful."

Then a new voice says to White, "Uh, could you put the cymbals down?"

The person speaking is not George Martin but producer Phil Spector, John's friend since 1964, when the two chatted during the Beatles' first flight to America.

Spector, who's stationed two bodyguards outside the door to the control room, wants no input from Apple engineers such as Geoff Emerick, who doesn't like the way Spector is maxing out the sound on the consoles.

"You're making Phil a bit uncomfortable," John tells Emerick, who promptly walks out of the session.

"How do you want it?" Spector asks John, who answers, "You know, 1950s."

Spector works his "wall of sound" technique, mixing and layering the reverberations of multiple instruments, until John pronounces the result "fantastic." When he hears the finished mix, in the early hours of January 28, he says, "It sounded like there was fifty people playing."

The whole thing is done with such speed, John says, "I wrote it for breakfast, recorded it for lunch, and we're putting it out for dinner."

On February 6, ten days after John first conceived of the song, Apple releases "Instant Karma! (We All Shine On)," credited to "Lennon/Ono with the Plastic Ono Band."

Before Christmas in 1969, Paul begins noodling around in the four-track studio recently installed at his home on Cavendish Avenue. He records forty-three seconds of an acoustic-guitar ditty called "The Lovely Linda," then a slightly more fleshed out song called "That Would Be Something," its lyrics consisting solely of the title phrase and the line "To meet you in the fallin' rain momma." Aside from the Apple and EMI engineers he consults, his sessions are secret, but the solo work lifts his spirits, which had been crushed by John's breakup announcement.

On February 11, John and Yoko perform their new song on the *Top of the Pops* program, propelling it toward a top-five ranking in both the UK and America. It's the first time one of the Beatles has performed on the program without the others.

Meanwhile, Paul continues creating thirteen songs to fill a homemade eponymous album, scheduled for release on April 17.

The rivalry between the two songwriting partners is ferociously rekindled.

———— ✺ ————

The supposedly back-to-basics songs that the Beatles recorded in the studio and performed on the rooftop, as well as the film documenting the making of this album, have yet to come out. All four Beatles have approval over who will polish the songs to create an album they'll call *Let It Be.* John and George propose Phil Spector, and Paul and Ringo agree.

But Paul is horrified at what Spector does to his songs.

When Spector begins work, on March 23, the George Martin–produced version of "Let It Be" (the Beatles' last single with their longtime producer) is already number 2 on the UK charts.

"Let It Be" is Paul's song, as is "The Long and Winding Road." Spector remixes both. When Paul hears "harps, horns, an orchestra, and women's choir" on "The Long and Winding Road," he's first astonished, then enraged that he wasn't consulted. "I would *never* have female voices on a Beatles record," he tells journalist Ray Connolly.

Things are further complicated when *McCartney,* Paul's solo album, is pushed from April to June so that *Let It Be* can come out first.

John and George write Paul a letter (addressed "From Us to You"), which Ringo delivers on their behalf. It reads, "We're sorry it turned out like this—it's nothing personal. Love John & George. Hare Krishna."

But Paul is still livid and takes it all *very* personally. In an effort to appease him, Ringo persuades the others to reinstate *McCartney*'s April 17 on-sale date.

On April 10, Apple issues a press release touting the health of the band: "The Beatles are alive and well and the Beat goes on, the Beat goes on."

The release of *McCartney* is a week away, but Paul can't face promoting the album with a press conference. He instead has Apple publicist Peter Brown (who'd orchestrated John and Yoko's wedding plans) craft a questionnaire.

When asked if this was the start of a solo career or a break with the Beatles, Paul replies "Time will tell" and "Both"; his response to whether his break with the Beatles will be temporary or permanent is "I don't really know." But his one-word answer to the follow-up question is a bombshell:

Q. Do you foresee a time when Lennon-McCartney will become an active songwriting partnership again?

A. No.

The *Daily Mirror* breaks the news—PAUL QUITS BEATLES—and he confirms it, telling the *Record Mirror* on April 18 how much working solo suits him. "I only had me to ask for a decision, and I agreed with me."

John is woken from a deep sleep when reporter Ray Connolly calls for his comment.

John is floored by the double cross. "Oh, Christ," he shouts into the phone. "He gets all the credit for it!"

Let It Be goes on sale May 8.

The next day, *New Musical Express* publishes a searing review titled "Have the Beatles Sold Out?," which decries the album, with its doubled sticker price and funereal black cover, as a "cardboard tombstone."

"Musically, boys, you passed the audition," assesses the critic for *Rolling Stone,* harking back to John's closing line atop the Apple roof before concluding that the flaw of overproduction "somehow doesn't seem to matter much anymore anyway."

Paul defends himself to the press: "I didn't leave the Beatles. The Beatles have left the Beatles, but no one wanted to be the one to say the party's over."

The next time John sees his former bandmate, he's larger than life.

With *McCartney* atop the US *Billboard* charts on the strength of the anticipation of Paul's solo effort, which includes the ballad "Maybe I'm Amazed," John and Yoko travel to San Francisco to meet with twenty-four-year-old *Rolling Stone* writer Jann Wenner about booking an interview.

The three of them (and Jann's wife, Jane) slip unrecognized into a nearly empty theater to see *Let It Be.* Though the film (which goes on to win an Oscar and a Grammy for Best Original Score) had premiered in New York on May 13, none of the Beatles attended. John is seeing it now for the first time. At the sight of Paul singing on the rooftop of Apple records, first John, then Yoko, dissolves into tears.

"He's crying, she's crying, and we're just trying to hold on to ourselves," Wenner says. "You're there helping come to the emotional rescue of the Beatles."

<hr />

Murder defendant Charles Manson gives a jailhouse interview that appears in the June 1970 issue of *Rolling Stone.* "This music is bringing on the revolution, the unorganized overthrow of the establishment," Manson says. "The Beatles know [what's happening] in the sense that the subconscious knows." At his trial, Manson says "Helter Skelter" is about confusion. "It's not my conspiracy. It is not my music.... Why blame it on me? I didn't write the music."

John also protests that he didn't write the song. Although he's on the witness list, he refuses to appear at the trial, asking, "What's 'Helter Skelter' got to do with knifing somebody?" then offering, "I've never listened to the words properly, it was just a noise."

CHAPTER 42

That'll be the day when I die.
                    —"That'll Be the Day"

At Tittenhurst Park, John and his son, Julian, row across the lake and explore the grounds on weekends. They drink Dr Pepper while they play on a Mellotron. Julian would later fondly remember this time: "When Dad moved to Tittenhurst, it was the first time he'd called me in quite a long time," he reflected. "It was an exciting thing for me to go and see him again after not seeing him for such a while. Tittenhurst was this enormous, palacelike place with 99 acres, golf-cart buggies, a lake, a little island. It was like a house of fun."

At seven years old, Julian possesses a curious mind.

"If you die, will I ever see you again?" Julian asks.

"If I can communicate from the dead, I will float a white feather straight across the room to you."

Julian smiles at his father's answer.

At Capitol Records in Los Angeles, executives couldn't be grimmer. In 1970, the year of the Beatles' breakup, they record a loss of $8 million (nearly $54 million today).

Still, John reveals in the second part of his first published interview with *Rolling Stone*'s Jann Wenner, "America is where it's at. I should have been born in New York, I should have been born in the Village, that's where I belong."

In early 1971, John is in bed at Tittenhurst, reading *Grapefruit,* Yoko's book of poetry from tiny Wunternaum Press, in Bellport, New York. She'd underscored her chosen American identity by selecting July 4, 1964, as her publication date.

John lands on a poem titled "Tunafish Sandwich Piece."

"Imagine one thousand suns in the / sky at the same time," Yoko writes.

The concept is simple, artful.

He reads another of Yoko's poems. This one is called "Cloud Piece."

"Imagine the clouds dripping," she writes.

John walks downstairs and over to the in-house Ascot Sound Studios. The word *imagine* is swirling in his head.

He sits at the Steinway piano, spray-painted white and inscribed "For Yoko, Happy Birthday, love John." He'd bought his wife the exquisite instrument when she turned thirty-eight, on February 19.

The sun is gently lifting over the trees, beaming through Tittenhurst's east-facing windows and reflecting off John's yellow-tinted glasses. Yoko sits close by while he presses the keys and begins to hum.

Late one foggy night in June, John summons session musicians to his mansion to work on his new album.

"I quickly jumped into a white Rolls-Royce with Nicky Hopkins [who'd played electric piano on the Beatles' 'Revolution']," acoustic guitarist Ted Turner recalls.

Another guitarist, Rod Lynton, marvels at John's fine collection of instruments, though he's shocked to find that the strings on John's Epiphone Casino are "crusty."

"It's a piece of wood with strings on it. You just play it, OK?" Lennon tells him.

———— ✺✺✺ ————

A troubled American named Curt Claudio has been writing to John. In the midst of these sessions, Claudio shows up in person, wearing a shabby coat. A film crew on hand to record the making of *Imagine* documents his arrival.

In the entryway of Tittenhurst, John agrees to have a chat with the intruder. Claudio, who has matted, scraggly brown hair and has come all the way from California, claims to be a traumatized Vietnam vet in search of some kind of universal truth.

"I'm just a guy who writes songs," John tells him. "I'm just a guy."

"At Tittenhurst, there was no particular security," Yoko recalls. "John always felt responsible for these people because they were the result of his songs."

If he assaults me right now, there's no stopping him.

———— ✺✺✺ ————

On July 3, John and Yoko fly to New York. They've booked the Record Plant, on West 44th Street, for more sessions on July 4 and 5.

A reporter from *The New Yorker* tours the facility and pronounces its contemporary furnishings and state-of-the-art equipment as having "the air of a luxurious space capsule" that is "designed specifically for rock musicians."

While Phil Spector mixes *Imagine* in quadraphonic sound, Yoko listens closely to the contrasting guitar work.

"George Harrison's guitar playing was more classically beautiful," she later observes. "But John's was restless—beautiful restless stuff."

Phil Spector is also helping George with another project.

George is taking up his guitar for a cause: the Concert for Bangladesh, with all proceeds going to a cause dear to Ravi Shankar. Shankar, George's musical mentor, was born in India to a Bengali family and is dedicated to aiding victims suffering from the multiple assaults of cholera, child hunger, and the war against Bangladeshi independence.

George invites all three of his former bandmates to join the all-star roster for two concerts at Madison Square Garden—at 2:30 and 7:00 p.m. on August 1, 1971.

Only Ringo accepts.

John worries the concert is a ruse to trick him into a Beatles reunion and refuses to appear, though Yoko is inclined to perform in support of the charity event—despite not having been included in the invitation. The couple fights over it bitterly. "She wants to go onstage at George's Bangladesh thing. I'm not gonna do it," John complains to Yoko's friend Dan Richter (now serving as the couple's butler at the Tittenhurst estate). "If she wants to go on without me, let her. I'll be in Paris."

In the end, neither goes, and the story circulates that John snubbed the invite because George hasn't included Yoko.

"We are not trying to make any politics," Shankar says when he greets the twenty thousand concertgoers who attend each sold-out show. "We are artists. But through our music we would like you to feel the agony . . . in Bangladesh."

When Bob Dylan steps forward, the mood at the Garden rises from elated to euphoric. He's making a surprise appearance after a self-imposed four-year absence from live performances to play an acoustic set of his beloved older songs, including "A Hard Rain's A-Gonna Fall." Originals and covers by renowned session keyboardists Leon Russell and Billy Preston, along with Eric Clapton, Shankar, Ringo, and George, make enough music to fill a triple album.

"What Woodstock was *said* to be," states a glowing review, "the Madison Square Bangladesh concert *was*."

To the media, manager Allen Klein—whom

George asks to help produce the concert—declares that the entirety of the $250,000 ($1.5 million today) they've raised in ticket sales will go to charity. "It was so much easier for me to say I'm not taking *anything,* so I don't have to answer any questions to anybody. Isn't that easy? If you do it, you do it; if you don't, you don't. I made it clean. It was easy," Klein boasts. (All very well in theory, though in reality Klein takes so much that he's eventually embroiled in several lawsuits—including one filed by George—and eventually serves prison time for making false statements on a tax return.) Furthermore, Apple plans to have Spector rush out a concert album, whose proceeds will all go to support the cause, as well as a concert film. Apple's *The Concert for Bangladesh* hits number 1 in the United States, number 2 in the UK.

Though John sits out both Woodstock and George's Concert for Bangladesh, he's still searching for ways his music can make a difference. Just such an opportunity may present itself with the September release of *Imagine.*

CHAPTER 43

I think I'm falling
In love too fast.
— "Help Me"

Y ou could say I fell in love with New York on a
street corner," John declares.

He and Yoko have been living in New York
since August 13, 1971, a few weeks after George's
Madison Square Garden event, on six-month B-2
tourist visas issued by the US Immigration and Naturalization Service to "Mr. and Mrs. John W.
Lennon," who are classified as "visitors for pleasure."

Despite the short-term visas, their intent has always
been to stay.

"Yoko and I were forever coming and going to New
York, so finally we decided it would be cheaper and
more functional to actually live here...so that's what
we did!" John tells reporters.

Yet there's also a more painful, personal reason.

Although Yoko has been given custody of her daughter, Kyoko, after a series of legal battles, her ex-husband Tony Cox has repeatedly absconded with the eight-year-old girl.

As best as John can determine, "Tony's attitude was, 'You can have my wife, but you can't have my child.'"

And now Yoko and John cannot find Kyoko or Tony anywhere.

The most reliable information they have is that Cox may have taken Kyoko to America, and therefore it makes sense for Yoko and John to base themselves somewhere in the United States.

Besides, John has been wanting to move to New York anyway. After all, "We love it, and it's the center of our world," John says of the city. "America is the Roman Empire and New York is Rome itself. New York is at my speed." He also feels a kinship to New Yorkers' brusqueness. "They're like me...they don't believe in wasting time."

Yoko agrees. "John has a New York temperament in his work. Liverpool is very much like New York, for an English city."

John credits Yoko, who lived in New York during her teens and twenties, with selling him on it. "She made me walk around the streets and parks and squares and examine every nook and cranny."

They both appreciate the "unbelievably creative

atmosphere" and diversity of the city, where their interracial marriage doesn't stand out as much as it does in England.

"Everywhere's somewhere, and everywhere's the same, really, and wherever you are is where it's at," John muses. "But it's more so in New York. It does have sugar on it, and I've got a sweet tooth."

———— ⌾ ————

John and Yoko encounter the kind of creativity they particularly enjoy while taking a Sunday walk in Washington Square Park.

"I'm proud to be a New York hippie!" they hear a raspy-voiced street singer declare. It's artist and activist David Peel, staging his weekly "happening."

Immediately charmed, John says, "We started singing with him in the street. And we got moved on by the police, and it was all very wonderful. He was such a great guy, you know."

Although Peel "can't sing, or he can't really play," John admits, it doesn't dampen the former Beatle's enthusiasm. "Picasso spent 40 years trying to get as simple as that."

He and Yoko offer Peel a contract with Apple Records. "We loved his music, his spirit, and his philosophy of the street," John says. "That's why we decided to make a record with him." The record, *The*

Pope Smokes Dope, by David Peel and the Lower East Side, peaks at number 191 on the *Billboard* 200, but Peel pronounces John an "excellent" producer. "He was deadly serious, but he knew how to have fun," Peel says, and he expresses his gratitude in music.

"John Lennon, Yoko Ono," he declares in a song titled "The Ballad of New York City," "New York City is your friend"—and John returns the favor by namechecking David Peel (and his record) in his own song "New York City," on his 1972 album with Yoko, *Some Time in New York City.*

<hr />

John and Yoko gravitate to Greenwich Village, where, John says, "everybody seems to know everybody." Though they initially take three hotel rooms (numbers 1701, 1702, and 1703) at the St. Regis in Midtown for themselves and their personal assistant, May Pang, after a couple of months they choose to instead rent a two-room apartment at 105 Bank Street in the West Village, as well as a studio in SoHo for work. Before they leave the St. Regis, however, they are able to film cameos of several celebrities—including Dick Cavett, Jack Palance, and dapper Hollywood dance legend Fred Astaire, who insists on more than one try at his cameo (walking Yoko to a hotel-room window), pleading, "I can do the scene better"—for the film they've been making to accompany *Imagine*.

The Bank Street apartment is where the counterculture activists Jerry Rubin and Abbie Hoffman (cofounders of the Youth International Party, known as Yippies) come calling. "The close friendship between Jerry Rubin and John Lennon (and Yoko)," Rubin's biographer says, "can't be underestimated." During 1971–72, the activist's personal calendars show "more often than not" that the three of them are "hanging out."

Rubin likes to tell the story of this symbiotic friendship: "Yoko Ono told me and Abbie that they considered us to be great artists." Abbie replied, "That's funny. We always thought of you as great politicians." Further connecting them is the fact that when Rubin brings John and Yoko to his own apartment, they discover that it's in the same building where a decade earlier, as a struggling young artist in the city, Yoko had once been the superintendent. The three of them and Hoffman talk about combining forces, organizing a singing and speaking tour to raise political awareness.

President Richard Nixon worries about just such a plan. Nixon, who is universally reviled by the Yippies, is up for reelection in 1972 and fears that John Lennon (whom he opened an FBI inquiry on back in 1969) and his friends will wield their considerable influence with the youth culture against him. The president feels especially vulnerable on that front, since he's recently signed into law the Twenty-Sixth Amendment, which lowered the voting age from twenty-one to eighteen, granting teenagers the right to vote for the first time.

⌒⌒⌒⌒

On John's thirty-first birthday, October 9, 1971, Yoko achieves a personal victory—the art show that Allen Klein had promised. Her first major exhibit, *This Is Not Here,* is mounted at Syracuse's Everson Museum of Art.

Ostensibly it's a solo show, though the catalog features numerous collaborative pieces, including *Baby Grand Guitar*—an oversize instrument of her own creation plus the neck of a second guitar displayed with Yoko's invitation to "imagine the body."

"She thinks up beautiful pure concept things, and I come up with a gimmicky reaction," John tells the *New York Times* in answer to the interviewer's question "Is Syracuse ready for Yoko Ono and John Lennon?"

Not entirely. "There was going to be a secret Beatles reunion concert, with everyone except Paul in the theater at the Everson," David Ross, then assistant to the museum's director, remembers. "One of my jobs was to get equipment ready, and have it ready, secretly."

On opening day, six thousand guests tour the exhibit, spreading rumors of the chance to see all four Beatles together again (and Yoko in "a black velvet hotpants suit").

The only other Beatle to attend, however—as was often the case—is Ringo.

He's not the only celebrity friend, though: in addition to Ringo and his wife, Maureen, there's Phil Spector, Klaus Voormann, Eric Clapton, and poet Allen Ginsberg on hand.

When the increasing size and frenzy of the crowd makes officials in the upstate city of 197,000 begin to fear a riot, John and Yoko move his birthday party over to the Hotel Syracuse, where the famous friends give a raucous semiprivate performance of more than twenty songs—including "Give Peace a Chance" and for George, in absentia, his "My Sweet Lord"—"commonly recognized," according to *The Guardian,* as "*the* single of the year."

John and Yoko have already been in New York for a few weeks when John's second solo album, *Imagine,* goes on sale in the United States, on September 9 (October 8 in the UK). It's both a critical and commercial success, and it becomes the most celebrated album and single of John's solo career, reaching number 1 on the UK album charts and number 3 as a US single.

Those paying attention to the ongoing feud among the ex-Beatles can't help but notice that this album, with its peace-loving title track, fires some vicious shots in the direction of John's former musical partner. John would claim that Paul started it with his album *Ram,* which was released in May of 1971 and opens with a track that complains of "Too many people preaching practices"—widely interpreted (correctly, as Paul would later confirm) as criticism of John and Yoko's activism. The cover art, aside from showing Paul grabbing a ram by the horns, includes a not-so-subtle photo of one beetle screwing another.

Lo and behold, the *Imagine* album comes with a postcard depicting John parodying Paul's cover pose by clutching a pig's ears. That's child's play compared to the brutal assault of "How Do You Sleep?," which namechecks several of Paul's songs ("The only thing you done was yesterday . . . ") while declaring, "Those freaks was right when they said you was dead" and "The sound you make is Muzak to my ears." Adding further injuries to the insults is that John's musical accomplice is George Harrison, who serves up some wicked slide-guitar solos.

Melody Maker isn't shy about proclaiming a victor:

"Lennon's won, hands down." In a piece titled "John Sings Long Track About Paul," a *New Musical Express* writer states, "Listening to this LP [*Imagine*] is like hearing McCartney ballads, and McCartney rockers, the way McCartney should be doing them."

Paul presents a musical olive branch a couple of months later with the December 7 release of *Wild Life,* the hastily recorded debut of his new band, Wings (which features his wife, Linda, on keyboards). Although its concluding song, "Dear Friend," apparently was recorded before the release of *Imagine,* Paul intends it as a peace offering to his longtime musical soul mate, singing, "I'm in love with a friend of mine."

Rolling Stone makes the distinction that while John seems eager "to represent himself as the spokesman for the politically conscious avant-garde," Paul appears "content to make straightforward pop music, to entertain," and that in answer to John's musical query, Paul "apparently sleeps soundly."

December 7, 1980

Mark puts on a bright, happy face as he approaches the doorman at Lennon's building.

"Is John Lennon around?" Mark asks casually.

"Don't really know; I think he may be outta town."

The doorman says the words by rote.

They probably told him to say that.

Mark feels certain that Lennon is home right now. His hand on the gun, he contemplates shooting the doorman and rushing inside. He knows exactly where Lennon lives, can reach the apartment easily.

But what if Lennon isn't home? What if Lennon's door is locked? There are a dozen things that could go wrong. Best to be patient, wait for the man to show up outside—and Lennon *will* come outside at some point.

I have all the time in the world. Lennon doesn't.

"Do you mind if I wait and see?"

"It's a public sidewalk," the doorman replies. "As long as you don't block the driveway, you can stand anywhere you want."

Mark waits with his copy of *Double Fantasy*.

Three hours pass.

Enough, he thinks. *John Lennon is hardly the only celebrity in New York City.*

He takes a self-guided walk of fame and adds a sound track—his edited and altered versions of Beatles songs.

He sees a crowded art gallery. He steps in, eyes peeled for celebrities or even rich people—though none of them is anywhere near as rich as Lennon.

A group of people is huddled around two men. *Probably famous artists,* he thinks and, wondering who they are, moves closer. The crowd is so large he has to crane his neck.

Mark spots two actors—Leslie Nielsen, whose *Airplane!* was last summer's comedy blockbuster, and Robert Goulet, who starred in *Camelot* on Broadway.

I can take anyone here.

Mark puts his hand on the singer's shoulder.

Goulet pulls away and turns.

"Excuse me?" Goulet says. "What is this?"

"You're no Lancelot," Mark says to the dashing baritone.

Goulet ignores the taunt. "I'm trying to have a conversation here."

Mark's hand is on the revolver. He imagines pulling it out and firing a shot into the actor's face, blowing his brains across the canvas behind him.

Goulet glares at him, then starts to turn his back.

It's like he's daring me to do it.

"Um, do you think we could take a quick picture?"

Goulet is annoyed. Finally, he relents and faces Mark.

"Well," the actor says, "come on, then."

Mark's hand grips the gun.

He pulls out his camera, hands it to an onlooker, and poses next to Goulet while the photo is taken.

Before Mark can shake the man's hand, Goulet has moved away.

Even though the man is famous, killing him won't achieve the result he desires. The actor isn't the purpose for his visit.

Outside, Mark hails a cab.

"I need to find a bookstore," he tells the driver.

"There's one near the Sheraton. Hop in."

At the shop, Mark heads straight for the fiction section to buy a copy of *The Catcher in the Rye,* his favorite book. When he sees a photograph showing Dorothy and the Cowardly Lion from *The Wizard of Oz,* his favorite movie, he's seized by inspiration.

While standing in the checkout line, he's jolted

a second time. John Lennon's name is on the cover of *Playboy* magazine. It's the January issue, featuring Lennon's interview with David Sheff.

They're coming together, he tells himself. *History and time.*

CHAPTER 44

Who on earth d'you think you are?
A superstar?
                    —"Instant Karma!"

I wanna come home," says twenty-nine-year-old John Sinclair.

Thousands and thousands of people witness his plea, his face and voice broadcast on a thirty-foot screen inside the University of Michigan's Crisler Arena, in Ann Arbor, in the early morning of December 11, 1971.

Getting him home is why they're all here. Fifteen thousand protesters pass joints around the smoke-filled stadium at a rally for Sinclair, who's more than two years into a ten-year prison sentence for a minor drug conviction that involved two marijuana cigarettes and an undercover police officer.

The political and musical roster kicked off at 8:00 p.m. on December 10 with speeches from activists such as Jerry Rubin, Allen Ginsberg, and Black Panther Bobby Seale and performances by artists ranging from Motown's own Stevie Wonder to New York street musician David Peel.

Now it's after 3:00 a.m., and John and Yoko are still waiting for their cue to go on.

But no one has been waiting for this moment as long as Sinclair, who's already spent years behind bars (although not in maximum security). The prisoner—speaking via a telephone hookup from his prison work farm, around fifty miles from the stadium—is a cofounder of the White Panther Party, an antiracist offshoot of the Black Panthers, and is dubbed by *Creem* magazine the "High Priest of Heavy."

The crowd gathered at the John Sinclair Freedom Rally is mesmerized.

So are the FBI informants embedded among them.

John and Yoko—dressed, a reporter observes, "in matching black leather jackets, unzipped to reveal 'Free John Now' T-shirts"—follow David Peel onstage.

In addition to being an activist, Sinclair is also known as a poet and a music reviewer and was the manager of the Detroit rock 'n' roll band MC5. He'd once commented that "rock musicians are often old, retired, and forgotten by the time they're thirty, and don't even have the benefit of a pension." With John

Lennon now thirty-one and Yoko thirty-eight, the rockers Sinclair is counting on to save him have, by his own standards, already aged out.

"Apathy won't get us anywhere," John tells the crowd. "So flower power failed, so what, let's start again." He picks up his acoustic guitar and launches into a set of four political songs, culminating with one he's written called "John Sinclair," with its imperative chorus, "Gotta, gotta, gotta set him free."

John later acknowledges that his radical period "almost *ruined* it [his music], in a way. It became journalism and not poetry." But on this night, fans pass immediate and harsh judgment.

They walk out.

"It was a rational act," *Creem* magazine writes in its review of the protest concert. "In a word, they were awful. The music was boring. And it was four a.m."

Clack, clack, clack go the typewriters as FBI agents compile reports based on informants' findings. The dossier is stamped CONFIDENTIAL and distributed to field offices in seven cities.

Clipped into the file is the lackluster review of the performance in the *Detroit News*. "Yoko can't even remain on key," notes one complaint lodged against

John's tribute to Sinclair, which the article dubbed "an interesting piece, but lacking Lennon's usual standards."

"Source advised this song ['John Sinclair'] was composed by Lennon especially for this event," the FBI report notes, a detail corroborated by the *Detroit News*—"They were so new that Lennon had to read the lyrics from a music stand as he sang."

"I wrote a ditty about John Sinclair and his plight," John told event organizers. "I'd like to come there and perform it."

"I heard the song while I was in prison," says Sinclair. "I made them bring me in a tape because I didn't believe Lennon had written it and that he was coming to Ann Arbor to sing it. It was a beautiful thing to do," he marvels.

Despite its less than enthusiastic reception, and although the unpolished songs won't be released by Apple until the following June (September in the UK), on John and Yoko's 1972 political double album, *Some Time in New York City,* the raw performance spurs the desired effect.

Within a week, the Michigan Supreme Court rules the state's marijuana laws unconstitutional, and the poet-activist becomes a free man.

"It was the culmination of two and a half years of agitating and organizing to get me out," Sinclair says of his release. "I just lucked into Lennon hearing about it and wanting to help. That meant a lot to me."

The idea that John has the kind of star power to influence cases like Sinclair's, however, is exactly what the Nixon administration fears most. They wanted him stifled.

Gone.

Out.

December 7, 1980

Mark is lying on his hotel bed, staring up at the ceiling, when someone knocks on his door.

The young blonde standing in the hallway is wearing a green dress that hugs her generous curves. She swallows nervously, and when she says hello, he catches a European accent. German, he thinks.

Good. He specifically told the madam who ran the escort service listed in the Manhattan Yellow Pages that he wanted a woman who came from another country—and she had to be quiet. He didn't want someone who talked.

Mark invites her inside. Her eyes flit across the room, looking for signs of trouble.

"I'm not kinky. I'm clean," he tells her. "I'm not a weirdo."

He explains that he hasn't asked her here for sex.

"I just want to be in the company of a woman tonight," he says. "I'm expecting that tomorrow will be a very difficult day for me. Now take off your clothes and get in bed."

She obeys. Mark disrobes and joins her.

The woman is clearly nervous. He gives her a massage. It takes a considerable amount of time to get her to relax. To trust him.

He moves his head closer to hers and whispers, "A real man doesn't have to use a woman. A real man doesn't have to take from a woman. He can give."

She begins to touch him. Her hand softly brushes up against his erection.

It's both pleasing and terrifying.

He enjoys women, but he has never enjoyed intercourse, even with his wife. That warm, wet cleft between a woman's legs is the entryway to a world he doesn't understand—a place that reminds him of a black hole that can swallow him if he isn't careful.

Mark lies on his back. As the woman begins moving her hand, his wife, Gloria, enters his mind, and he starts to lose his erection.

He closes his eyes and tries to push the image of Gloria away, but for some reason she won't leave.

He stares at the prostitute's neck, and he thinks of Gloria—all those times he'd grab her and throw her up against the wall when she disobeyed him or questioned something he did. Sometimes he'd spit on her.

Hit her.

His erection returns.

The young woman's neck is so delicate. He imagines himself snapping it. "It's easy if you try . . ."

That makes him giggle.

Makes him think of Lennon across the park in his castle.

But not for long.

He imagines he's John Lennon and that the woman touching him is Yoko. He sees himself as important because he is important.

And come tomorrow, the whole world will know.

The prostitute slips out of bed and pulls her dress over her head. It's 3:00 a.m.

"Your dress is the same color that the woman wore for Holden Caulfield," Mark says. "It's synchronicity."

"Who is Holden Caulfield?"

"The main character from *The Catcher in the Rye*." He studies her for a moment. "You haven't read it?"

She shakes her head.

He sighs. So many people don't read anymore. "It's a wonderful story about a teenager who goes insane because he can't cope that there's no love in the world."

She stares at him, dumbfounded, maybe even a bit frightened; he's not sure.

He smiles. "You should read it," he says as he pays her. "The book holds many answers."

After she leaves, he grabs his Bible and opens it to the New Testament.

The title "The Gospel According to John" jumps out at him from the page, as if it's glowing.

He studies the words for what seems like hours. Then he adds Lennon's name to the page in blood-red ink.

CHAPTER 45

I might not give the answer that you want me to.
—"Oh Well"

In August of 1971, John Dean, counsel to the president, had written a memo headed "Dealing with Our Political Enemies," proposing to Nixon, "We can use the available political machinery to screw our political enemies."

Six months after Dean wrote that memo, US senator Strom Thurmond answers with one of his own. On February 4, 1972, in his capacity as a member of the Senate Judiciary Committee, Thurmond—a Nixon loyalist who represents South Carolina, one of the Bible Belt states caught up in the August 1966 "Beatles bonfires" controversy—forwards to Attorney General John Mitchell a report he's overseen for the Senate Internal Security Subcommittee.

"This appears to me to be an important matter, and

I think it would be well for it to be considered at the highest level," the senator writes. "As I can see, many headaches might be avoided if appropriate action can be taken in time."

The report's chief finding: that John Lennon qualifies as one of said political enemies and that his association with "New Left leaders" links him to these "strong advocates of the program to 'dump Nixon.'"

And the "political machinery" available to "screw" him? "If Lennon's visa is terminated, it would be a strategy counter-measure," Thurmond recommends.

John and Yoko's original six-month visas are set to expire on February 29, 1972. They are granted a two-week extension, but Yoko hasn't been able to reunite with her daughter. Even though on March 3 yet another court determines that Yoko has custody, Kyoko's father, Tony Cox, has once again taken the girl and vanished. "It was terrible. I didn't know where she was. It was a kidnapping and a very difficult situation," Yoko recalls.

On March 6, Thurmond is notified that his "previous inquiry concerning the former member of the Beatles, John Lennon" has been looked into, and "the Immigration and Naturalization Service has served notice on him that he is to leave this country no later than March 15."

At the urging of John's business manager,

Allen Klein, Leon Wildes, the thirty-nine-year-old president of the American Immigration Lawyers Association, takes on the case. Though he has "never heard of John Lennon, much less Yoko Ono," Wildes is confident that he can reverse the canceled extension of his clients' visas, and on March 16 the US immigration authorities grant them four additional weeks.

But Wildes has the sense that "they were out to get John and Yoko from the first moment I got into the case."

Ever since Nixon first opened it, in 1969, John's FBI file has been growing. When John spoke on the 6:00 p.m. edition of WABC-TV's *Eyewitness News* on January 11 about a press conference where he, Yoko, and Jerry Rubin appeared, a special agent amended his event report to the special agent in charge of the New York FBI office with the urgent notation "All extremists should be considered dangerous."

Yet on February 23, a confidential informant filed a contradictory report. An "unnamed person" who had engaged in "numerous conversations with John Lennon and his wife about becoming active in the New Left movement in the United States" noted that "Lennon and his wife seem uninterested...Lennon and his wife are passé about United States politics."

Wilde places a call to the district director of immigration, who confirms the lawyer's suspicions. "The situation in Washington vis-à-vis your clients is not a healthy one," the official says. "They will not be given any further extensions and I suggest you tell them to get the hell out."

Get the hell out is what John and Yoko would like to say to the people they keep seeing outside their apartment. Though one February FBI report mangled their home address as "St. Regis Hotel, 150 Bank Street" (they'd left the hotel for their 105 Bank Street apartment four months earlier), they're nevertheless subject to ongoing observation by "large men in glasses across the street" and "an agent behind every mail box." It seems so over the top that when John first complained to his journalist friend Ray Connolly that his phones were being tapped, Connolly brushed it off. "I thought he was being paranoid. He sometimes was, but not this time," Connolly later wrote.

When the couple complains to Wildes about "two guys interminably fixing a bike, a broken bike across the street" as well as "two guys in a car" following their driver, the lawyer can only surmise that the FBI was being so blatant on purpose because they "wanted them to feel that they were under surveillance."

John agrees, saying as much when he appears on *The Dick Cavett Show.*

"I felt followed everywhere by government agents," John tells the host. "Every time I picked up the phone, there was a lot of noise...I'd open the door and there'd be guys standing on the other side of the street. I'd get in the car and they'd be following me and not hiding...They wanted me to see that I was being followed..."

Wildes, who regards John as "a guy of major principle," relates that his client "understood that what was being done to him was wrong. It was an abuse of the law, and he was willing to stand up and try to shine the big light on it." It was a case of the government abusing power, of "the Nixon administration [making] life intolerable for John Lennon and Yoko Ono." Never, Wildes later says, had he seen "the government so determined to remove anyone from the United States."

John and Yoko gain another fighter in their corner in their simultaneous ongoing search for Kyoko. Outside their Immigration and Naturalization Service hearing on April 18, John elaborates on what he told reporters in March. "We want to stay permanently because New York is the center of the earth and also because we want to find Yoko's daughter, Kyoko." John gives an interview to Geraldo Rivera, a twenty-nine-year-old reporter for ABC-TV *Eyewitness News,* explaining that it's because Yoko "is married to an English citizen"—referring to himself, of course—"and that's caused all the trouble" before reiterating, "But we love to be here."

Rivera has earned praise and notoriety (and a Peabody Award) for his March 1972 investigative exposé, *Willowbrook: The Last Disgrace,* detailing the inhumane treatment of residents at a Staten Island school for the mentally disabled. That same month, Willowbrook parents filed a class-action lawsuit against the facility (though it would be another fifteen years before the state ultimately shut it down, in 1987).

John and Yoko, Rivera says in 2019, "appreciated the work I was doing on behalf of the developmentally disabled and vowed to help."

But first it would be Rivera who, they hoped, could help them.

JOHN & YOKO WAIT & WAIT is the New York *Daily News* headline on July 14. The paper reports that after months of immigration hearings, a decision on the couple's status will be postponed until September.

The delay allows them more time to search for the missing Kyoko. From August 3 to 6, accompanied by Rivera and his *Eyewitness News* camera crew, John and Yoko fruitlessly scour San Francisco, unknowingly following the trail of the FBI (who in late May had responded to an informant's claim that Kyoko was in the vicinity of Monterey — "I know the whereabouts of Kyoko Cox" — only to dismiss the assertion as the "vision" of a "flower child").

Unfortunately, they are no more successful than the

FBI had been. "I could tell they were very distressed by what was happening to them," Rivera says, "but also [by] what was happening around the country because of Nixon's endless war."

John and Yoko seek treatment from a Chinese acupuncturist introduced to them by the editor and publisher of *SunDance* magazine. Visits to the healer's family home in San Mateo, are kept secret by referring to John "as J. L. so people wouldn't know who we were talking about."

When they return to New York, John and Yoko begin preparing right away for what they call the One to One concert (their answer to George's Concert for Bangladesh) to benefit the mentally disabled, especially those Willowbrook State School residents for whom Geraldo Rivera continues to crusade. Like George's concert, this one will feature a lineup of other guests—including Stevie Wonder, Roberta Flack, and Sha Na Na—and consist of two Madison Square Garden performances, a movie, and a record. Rivera tells the *New York Post,* "We raised about a quarter of a million dollars." John rewards volunteer fund-raisers and students from the school with $60,000 worth of tickets to the shows and has tambourines distributed so that concertgoers can shake the percussion instruments in time to the music.

"Now more than ever, baby, Nixon now!" Sammy Davis Jr. is onstage at Miami Marine Stadium. It's August 22, the second day of the 1972 Republican National Convention, and Davis, a former Kennedy Democrat, is debuting for delegates the incumbent president's campaign song. ("Hate to get personal about it," a *Rolling Stone* reporter observes, "but the only other time I ever saw the fellow [Davis] was back in San Francisco" at a fund-raising event for a losing effort by an Old Left judicial candidate.)

"I don't think the youth vote is in anybody's pocket," Nixon tells the assembled party delegates. In Flamingo Park, five thousand "nondelegates" are amassing, though John and Yoko are not among them, being back up in New York furiously getting ready for their charity concert. These "zippies, Yippies, hippies, crazies," according to a local resident, are protesters reclaiming the ground they'd recently occupied when Miami Beach had also hosted the Democratic National Convention, from July 10 to July 13.

"People who want to have bloody hands go over to the tent on my right," an antiwar organizer announces from a Flamingo Park soundstage. "People who want death masks go over just behind that. We still need people for the bombing and the dike building."

When John appeared on *The Dick Cavett Show,* months earlier, he'd made it clear that he was bowing out of any protest activities planned around the Republican National Convention and would not be attending. Nevertheless, the FBI has agents scouring Miami Beach for the man identified in Senator Strom Thurmond's report as "a member of the former musical group known as 'The Beatles.'"

Despite John's being one of the world's most recognizable celebrities, a flyer is distributed so that he can be easily identified by the police and FBI. Except it's not even John's face pictured on the cheat sheet but rather a publicity still of David Peel (who has his own FBI file) saying, in a speech balloon, "The pope smokes dope"—the title of his 1972 album, released by Apple. In later years, Peel remarks that it was "rock's greatest flattery" to have been confused with John, though the closest resemblance between them is that both sport long hair and round eyeglasses.

On election night, November 7, John and Yoko can barely watch as the incumbent, Richard Nixon, defeats fifty-year-old South Dakota senator George McGovern in a landslide, carrying forty-nine out of fifty states for a second term in the White House.

"I just really trust him, you know?" a youthful Nixonette says of the chief executive.

John never has and never will.

The one benefit to him from Nixon's reelection, however, is that the administration no longer seems to consider him a "political enemy." On December 8, the special agent in charge of New York's FBI office notifies the Bureau's acting director that "in view of subject's inactivity in Revolutionary Activities and his seemingly [sic] rejection by NY Radicals, captioned case is being closed in the NY Division."

Within a month of Nixon's reelection, John's FBI file is closed. But his visa troubles continue.

CHAPTER 46

We gotta get out of this place
If it's the last thing we ever do.
— "We Gotta Get Out of This
Place"

It's time to move.

In February of 1973, John and Yoko's Bank Street apartment is robbed, which leaves them shaken. They have next to no security at their bohemian loft, plus the lingering effect of the FBI surveillance on top of a decade of international fame and its invasion of privacy—it's all left John feeling too exposed in Greenwich Village. "You just couldn't go out the front door, because there would be something weird at the door," he complains.

His social circle in the Village is also not what it once was. He's disillusioned with his ability to have an effect on American politics, and his friendship with the Yippies, especially Jerry Rubin, has soured. "As he didn't lead the revolution, I decided to quit answering the phone," John states. He's been feeling used, manipulated, taken advantage of—and his own recent behavior has been worst of all.

Rubin hosted a party on the night of what turned out to be Nixon's landslide win over McGovern. He recalls John "came into the house screaming" about the defeat, "crazy with rage."

"I can't believe this is fuckin' IT," John explodes, and when other guests encourage him not to lose heart and to throw himself back into organizing, saying that people will listen to him, John shoots back, "Listen to me? Man, where've you been? They haven't been listening to me!"

John's devastated by the loss, and though Yoko usually monitors his alcohol intake, on that night he gets uncharacteristically drunk and high on cocaine. By the time they arrived at Rubin's apartment, "John was totally out of his head with drugs and pills and drink because he couldn't stand the fact that George McGovern lost," Yoko explains. To the shock of all the party guests—especially his wife—John walks into the room, immediately targets a woman (purportedly Rubin's girlfriend), and takes her into the bedroom. "She didn't come on to him at all," says Yoko. "He just pulled her [up] and went into the next room. And then they were groping and all that, and we were all quiet."

Someone tries to cover the noise by putting on a

Bob Dylan record, to no avail. "We heard it anyway. And everybody had their coats in the next room, where John and this girl are making out, so nobody can go home."

"It was very embarrassing," Yoko tells journalist friend Ray Connolly.

An understatement.

The next day John is remorseful, but Yoko needs to take some time to mull over how best to handle his behavior. Meanwhile, they get word that an apartment on the Upper West Side is available at 1 West 72nd Street: the Dakota, the 1884 structure regarded as the city's first luxury apartment building. They'd noticed and admired the building before, but nothing had been available then. Now the seventh-floor apartment across the hall from Roberta Flack is being vacated by actor Robert Ryan after the death of his wife. Its twelve rooms and sweeping views of Central Park immediately captivate the couple.

Most important, the Dakota has guards and robust security in place. While the building is "chockablock full of famous people"—in addition to Flack, other residents include Leonard Bernstein, Rex Reed, and Lauren Bacall—it offers a sense of privacy, too.

That April, John and Yoko pass a stringent co-op board review and move uptown. John happily tells a German reporter, "It is a big apartment, and it's beautiful, but it doesn't have grounds...you know, it's secure."

⌘

Although moving uptown may have eased some of the couple's concerns, it certainly hasn't addressed their biggest problems. The episode at Jerry Rubin's place has been festering.

"That situation really woke me up," Yoko says. "I thought, 'Okay, we were so much in love with each other and that's why we sacrificed everything, my daughter, everything. It was worth it if we were totally in love with each other. But if he wants to make it with another girl or something, what am I doing?'"

Yoko confides in their twenty-two-year-old assistant, May Pang. "Listen, May," she says. "John and I are not getting along. We've been arguing. We're growing apart."

The rift has also been apparent to lawyer Leon Wildes. "They had a loving relationship and it broke down because of all that pressure," he says, "Nixon being reelected and so on."

Regardless of their marital troubles, the couple's shared revulsion for Nixon—who has maintained since June 22, 1972, that the White House had no involvement in the failed attempt to bug the

Democratic National Committee headquarters at the Watergate—is stronger than ever. The Watergate hearings begin on May 17, 1973, and a month later, on June 18, John and Yoko are given an opportunity to attend in person.

They accept, surely pleased at the chance to observe the people who've been persecuting them being held to the fire.

John and Yoko travel together to Washington, DC, to witness testimony from John Dean, who has been ousted as White House counsel over his role in the Watergate scandal. In the first row of spectators sits Dean's wife—Mrs. Maureen "Mo" Dean, who's wearing a towering hairdo—and just behind her is Elvin Bell, an adviser to Nixon during his nego-tiations with Soviet Union general secretary Leonid Brezhnev (resulting in the Strategic Arms Limitation Talks, a.k.a. SALT). Bell has a security clearance high enough to win him a second-row seat, but while he is craning his neck to see around Mrs. Dean, a woman taps him on the shoulder and says, "Pardon me, please," as she moves past.

He glances at her and is startled to notice that she and her male companion look familiar.

Suddenly, Bell makes the connection. It's John Lennon and Yoko Ono, the famous antiwar artists, who've taken the two seats beside his.

John and Yoko strike up a conversation with Bell

during a break in the testimony, and their back-and-forth continues throughout the day, mostly a barrage of questions, from the benign—"Are you a baritone or bass when you sing?"—to the more pressing: "Why is your country fighting in Vietnam?," a concern that Bell can't fully answer.

Several photos are snapped of John and Yoko in the Washington, DC, audience that day. They will be the last taken of the two of them together for quite some time.

CHAPTER 47

I can't live
If living is without you.
　　　—"Without You"

The thing to do, Yoko decides, is give them both some time apart.

"I needed a rest. I needed space," she tells *The Telegraph* many years later. "I was very aware that we were ruining each other's careers and I was hated and John was hated because of me. We did everything together and we did everything publicly together. The Bed-In was our work for peace but we weren't liked for it," she reflects. "It was a very difficult time."

As for John's recent behavior, "I started to notice that he became a little restless on top of that, so I thought it's better to give him a rest and me a rest."

Though stories vary, Yoko maintains that she's the one who orchestrates the next steps. It's obvious they'll never really succeed in staying apart as long as John remains in New York, "So then I suggested L.A., and he just lit up," Yoko says.

She also knows that being left to his own devices would not be good for John. He doesn't know how to be single; he's never been fully on his own. Yoko decides he needs someone to look after him, a woman to keep him interested (and in line). So she casts about and decides to approach one of their assistants—the always friendly and helpful May Pang, who is single and pretty—to take on the role of John's new girlfriend. "May Pang was a very intelligent, attractive woman and extremely efficient. I thought they'd be OK," Yoko reasons.

She pitches the idea to May. "John will probably start going out with other people. Who knows who he will go out with? I know he likes you a lot. So...?"

Twenty-two-year-old May—a Chinese American woman from Spanish Harlem, who is first and foremost a "gung-ho rock fan"—is startled and confused by the proposition.

"I just looked at her and said, 'Not me. I'm not interested,'" May tells interviewers in 2008. But Yoko is undeterred. "I know you're not after him, but you need a boyfriend," May recalls Yoko telling her. "I let that pass because I thought this is one of those crazy moments, and I had hoped her idea would pass."

The thought of having an affair with her boss,

a married man, has never even crossed the young Catholic girl's mind.

Though monumentally out of her depth, once John approaches her himself to make it clear that he is in fact interested in her, May decides she's willing to be part of this strange situation. In the late summer of 1973, John and May decamp for Los Angeles—but *not* on Yoko's orders, May insists—because there are obvious benefits for the new couple in another city. Plus, John has recording projects lined up in LA, so Capitol Records fronts the expense of the trip with a loan to John of $10,000 in traveler's checks.

Friend and local radio DJ Elliot Mintz picks them up at the airport. With John and Yoko, Mintz was accustomed to talking "not about me or them but the state of the world." Now John surprises him by cutting straight to the state of his marriage and telling Mintz that Yoko has "kicked him out and he didn't know when or even if they'd be getting back together."

Meanwhile, John's with May and finishing up a new album he recorded at the Record Plant before leaving New York. He's self-producing it under the title *Mind Games*.

Over a steady stream of his signature French cigarettes—unfiltered brands such as Gauloises and Gitanes, which he feels make his voice deeper—John tells a reporter for *Melody Maker* that his intention is "to sit on Capitol, to do the artwork and to see to things like radio promotion."

The sitting part was certainly accomplished. "It was a big blow when they [the Beatles] split up, of course," says Don Zimmerman, executive director of Capitol Records. "But after that, we got to know them more on an individual level. When John was splitting up with Yoko, he spent time at the Tower [the Capitol Records Building]. He'd come in and put his feet up on the coffee table, the only problem being that you couldn't get any work done."

As for the music, "It's rock at different speeds. It's not a political album, or an introspective album," John says of *Mind Games*. "Someone told me it was like *Imagine* with balls, which I like a lot."

In Los Angeles, John is relaxed, reconnecting with dozens of old friends and making scores of influential new acquaintances. Although he would eventually come to characterize the following year and a half as a "lost weekend" of depression and debauchery—and there *are* bouts of both—there's also a great deal of creativity, productivity, and fun.

For the first time in his adult life, John is defined neither as a Beatle nor as the husband of Yoko Ono. "He reached artistic heights and healed a lot of his personal relationships," recalls May. "Most important," she adds, in contrast to the way media reports present it, "he wasn't miserable for 18 months."

Journalist Larry Kane concurs, revealing that in 1975, John tells him his months with May were among the "happiest times of my life."

John finishes three solo albums and produces two others for friends. "It wasn't by any means a lost weekend," says Elliot Mintz. "Just a very long one."

"I know that period in his life is supposed to have been really troubled and unpleasant and dark, but I've got to be honest, I never saw that in him at all," agrees Elton John, who meets Lennon for the first time in Los Angeles early that fall of 1973 through their mutual friend Tony King—Apple's US manager at the time, though he soon leaves to manage Elton's fledgling Rocket Records.

Elton is spending a month in Los Angeles in advance of MCA's October 5, 1973, US release of his double (and seventh studio) album, *Goodbye Yellow Brick Road*. "Elton John and his wordsmith Bernie Taupin," *Creem* magazine says in its review, "now have perched a short tier below the BeatleStones on the mass pop scale (not enough heterosexual good looks; too many ballads)."

The two men have more in common than simply being chart-topping British rock stars. "Elton's notorious for being a very fast writer," says his guitarist Davey Johnstone, "and also a little impatient in the studio." *Yellow Brick Road* was recorded in two weeks; Lennon has clocked some even faster speeds in the studio (his single "Instant Karma!" and the Beatles' *Please Please Me* were both done in a single day).

At their first meeting, Elton recalls walking into the Capitol offices to find Lennon waltzing with Tony King, who's dressed in full drag as Queen Elizabeth, complete with tiara, shooting a TV ad for John's new album, *Mind Games*.

"I took to him straightaway," Elton recalls. Not only because the Beatles were among his idols, but also specifically because Lennon "was a Beatle who thought it was a good idea to promote his new album by dancing around with a man dragged up as the Queen, for fuck's sake. I thought: we're going to get along like a house on fire. And I was right."

Elton teasingly calls the pair of them "Fred Astaire and Ginger Beer" (i.e., queer) and snaps a few Polaroids.

"I'm gonna impound all those pictures till I get me green card," John jokes.

"Behave yourself, Sharon Cavendish!" Tony King calls out to Elton. "It's her drag name," he explains to Lennon, who looks puzzled, then intrigued.

"I want to be Morag," John declares.

"It doesn't work like that," Elton chides. "You can't choose your drag name—someone has to give it to you. She's the one who named me Sharon Cavendish," Elton says, pointing at King, who nods and adjusts his tiara.

"'Cavendish' comes from a keyboard player in the fifties called Kay Cavendish, who was always billed as 'Kitten on the Keys,'" King explains with a laugh.

"I love giving people drag names," says Elton, declaring to Lennon, "You're . . . Carol Dakota!"

May encourages John to reestablish a relationship with his son, Julian, whom John hasn't seen since he and Yoko moved to the United States. Julian and Kyoko are the same age, and seeing Julian is a painful reminder for Yoko of her missing daughter, so John has limited himself to occasional phone calls.

Very occasional.

"It was thanks to my mum that we started having conversations again," Julian later says, but it's never easy closing the gaps that open when too much time passes between communications.

So Cynthia doesn't know what to expect when she reaches out in early 1974 to inform John that she and Julian are planning to come over on the SS *France*, a luxury liner launched by Madame Charles de Gaulle in 1960, now making its final crossing from Southampton to New York.

To Cyn's relief, John not only encourages it but also upgrades their passage and makes sure that he and May are at the dock to meet the ship in New

York when it arrives. Upon discovering that Elton John and Tony King will be aboard for the same voyage, John requests that they watch over his son and ex-wife along the way, and they oblige.

When the ship docks, ten-year-old Julian immediately embraces his father, easing the tension for all of them. Though it's been years since they were last together, Julian's relieved to find his father as "charming, funny, and warm" as he remembered. John, May recalls, is "shocked to see 'a little man' and not the small child he remembered."

The four of them head back to Los Angeles, where John and Julian spend "a lot of time getting reacquainted as father and son, playing the guitar and making music," going swimming, and taking repeated trips to Disneyland. When asked by an interviewer around this time if he has any regrets in life, John hesitates, then admits that "if he had his time over, he'd be different to Julian."

Says friend Elliot Mintz, "He realized he should have been there more for him, but as he once said to me, 'some of us just can't handle that.' And I think when he realized it, a part of himself was able to forgive his own father, who hadn't been there for him."

John is a warm host to Julian and, with May's encouragement, accommodating to Cynthia, for which she remains forever grateful. "May was wonderful, even though she was young and inexperienced in having to deal with such sensitive and emotional issues," Cyn says. "May was open, caring, and compassionate to me and my son Julian....She was a good friend when my son and I needed one."

But while May is a positive influence on John, many things remain beyond her control. She is sorely lacking, for example, the ability to *prevent* John from doing just about anything.

She can show him the right path, but she can't stop him from going down the wrong one.

CHAPTER 48

It's better to burn out
Than to fade away.
    —"My My, Hey Hey (Out of the
                                Blue)"

The trouble begins even before Phil Spector pulls out the gun.

John's so pleased to be working with the legendary producer of *Imagine* again—on an oldies album this time—that he cedes total control to Spector, something he's never done before. He also starts drinking in the recording studio, something he's never done before, either, but Spector encourages it. Besides, who's going to stop him? May? Hardly.

The mood in Spector's LA studio couldn't be more different from the one at the studio in London. Far from the serious, private affairs John's used to—where even the presence of wives and girlfriends had been frowned upon—Spector holds open-door sessions at A&M Studios that double as parties, with alcohol and celebrity visitors flowing nonstop. The producer himself shows up in costumes—as a priest or surgeon or karate champion—and wears a gun in a shoulder holster.

"The guys were all drinking—and John was being one of the guys," May says. "Everyone was as blitzed as he."

"John was exercising all his bad habits, as were we all, including Phil," admits drummer Jim Keltner. "The only problem with that was that Phil was the producer, and somebody had to be, you know, sane."

Spector doesn't inspire confidence on that front. Privately, John calls him "the Vampire." May worries about the gun, but John assures her it's just for show—until the night Spector pulls it out and shoots it into the ceiling.

Fellow producer Mark Hudson recalls, "Spector pulled out a large gun and started chasing John through the hallways. John was trying to laugh it off but it was horrible."

"Listen, Phil, if you're gonna kill me, kill me. But don't fuck with me ears. I need 'em," John deadpans.

When Spector later disappears with the recordings and can't be found, it's almost a relief.

Another notorious group John falls in with also includes vampires: the Hollywood Vampires.

"The original Hollywood Vampires was a drinking club, a last-man-standing kinda thing," says the club president, Alice Cooper. "People started calling us the Hollywood Vampires because we'd never see daylight. We figured instead of drinking the blood of the vein, we were drinking the blood of the vine."

The club is made up of Hollywood rockers such as Cooper, Bernie Taupin (Elton John's songwriting partner), Mickey Dolenz of the Monkees, and Keith Moon of the Who (often clad in outrageous costumes, including a Queen Elizabeth getup). Whenever he's in town, Ringo is a welcome member. They all congregate for endless rounds of late-night drinks in the upstairs loft at Hollywood's Rainbow Bar & Grill, which is adorned with a plaque reading THE LAIR OF THE HOLLYWOOD VAMPIRES.

John finds his way into the club through his good friend Harry Nilsson, the Grammy-winning singer-songwriter famed for his version of the folk-rock song "Everybody's Talkin'" (from the Oscar-winning 1969 film *Midnight Cowboy*) and his more recent orchestral smash-hit cover of "Without You," a ballad by the Beatles' Apple label signees Badfinger.

Alice Cooper—who's just covered the Beatles' "A Hard Day's Night" during the tour promoting his *Billion Dollar Babies* album—often falls into the uneasy role of mediator between Harry and John. "They were the best of friends, but when they drank, they liked to get political and talk about religion and everything else that causes fights."

Cooper notes, "Everybody's personality changes a little bit when they drink." In John and Harry's case, "It was funny because neither one was a fighter; they just had a belligerent streak in them every once in a while. Most of the time they were laughing."

"The difference between the two was that Harry loved to drink and was good at it," explains Elliot Mintz. "John also loved to drink, but was no good at it. At the beginning of an evening with the two of them, the conversation would be brilliant...Then suddenly it would flip, and the insanity would start."

⸺⸻⸺

One such night is March 12, 1974, when John and Harry show up at the Troubadour, a favorite night-club in West Hollywood, for a midnight comedy show.

Sitting next to them is Rat Pack actor (and fellow Brit) Peter Lawford, whose former beach house John is currently renting in Santa Monica.

"Brandy Alexanders for the table!" Harry orders. He and John are already pretty blitzed.

"What's that?" John asks. He's never heard of the drink, let alone tried one.

"Brandy and cream with chocolate liqueur. Don't worry, you'll love it," Harry assures him.

"They taste like milk shakes," John exclaims when they arrive. Several more rounds of the unexpectedly potent cocktails go down with dangerous ease.

May Pang sits by, helpless. "Harry would keep feeding John drinks until it was too late."

The Smothers Brothers come onstage to perform a comedy routine.

Tommy Smothers is an old friend of John, having sung in the chorus on "Give Peace a Chance."

Instead of giving them a friendly greeting, John and Harry start heckling Tommy and Dick Smothers. "I think we almost screwed up the act," John later admits.

"It was horrendous," recounts Tom Smothers. "They came in pretty ripped to see our show, and, as Harry later explained to me, he told John, 'He needs some heckling to make this thing work.' He didn't think I had an act. Well, they start heckling, and it was some of the worst language I've ever heard—and they had a real buzz on...It was a mess."

Lawford tries and fails to intervene, then John gets into a scuffle with a local photographer, who claims he hit her.

"Don't you know who I am?" he shouts to the

parking attendant when he's hauled out of the club. "I'm Ed Sullivan!"

Waking up full of regret, with the story splashed across the tabloids, John sends a bouquet of flowers to Tommy and Dick Smothers, along with an apology: "With Love & Tears!"

In New York, Yoko has even less to say to the reporters who come calling: "No comment!"

In Los Angeles, the district attorney investigates the events surrounding John's highly publicized night at the Troubadour. Though there is insufficient evidence to justify criminal charges, with his visa still in limbo, he settles out of court with the photographer who's accused him. "I had to pay her off," John says, "because I thought it would harm my immigration."

At Burbank Studios, John is dealing with a different kind of damage. With Phil Spector still on the lam, John is instead producing his friend Harry Nilsson's album *Pussy Cats*. But in the midst of the first recording session, it's clear that Harry's famously gorgeous voice is shot. Drummer Jim Keltner recalls him saying that he and John had been out "doing a lot of screaming the night before, which John is really good at."

"Where is all that yooooooo-deeeee-dooooo-dahh stuff?" John asks.

"Croak" is all Harry Nilsson can manage.

John suggests they wrap it up and get back home for the night.

"Home" is a clubhouse of sorts—for months after arriving in LA, John and May hotel- and house-hopped around town, but now they've landed a Santa Monica beach house large enough to accommodate a good portion of John's fellow Hollywood Vampires. At his suggestion, in an effort to avoid the kinds of troubles that beset the earlier recording sessions with Phil Spector, half the people playing on the new album are also shacked up together.

John's old friend Klaus Voormann has joined them. So has the always outrageous Keith Moon. And Ringo Starr, along with his business manager, Hilary Gerrard, is there to both help his friends and escape his own marital troubles (George Harrison has confessed that he and Ringo's wife, Maureen, are having an affair. A distraught Ringo leaves Tittenhurst, which he's recently bought from John, and heads to see his friends in LA).

The two-story white stucco beach house has an impressive pedigree. Originally built in the 1930s by MGM studio head Louis B. Mayer, the five-bedroom villa then belonged to actor Peter Lawford back when he was married to Patricia Kennedy, one of John F.

Kennedy's younger sisters. Lawford is known to have let the president (and possibly his other brother-in-law Bobby) use the house, allegedly for trysts with Marilyn Monroe.

"John and I took the master bedroom," May says. "When we first saw it, he said, 'So, this is where they did it,' referring to the former presidential guest and Monroe." It's a piece of trivia that John delights in sharing with visitors. Chris O'Dell, a tour manager and former Apple employee who was a frequent visitor to the beach house, recalls, "We were all sort of spooked by the legend of Marilyn, especially John, who was convinced that her ghost haunted the house. He said something woke him up every morning, and we all just assumed it was Marilyn."

Harry, Keith, Klaus, and Hilary take the other four bedrooms, and the library, "complete with an official portrait of President Kennedy on the wall," is converted into Ringo's room.

With May as den mother, the group settles into a surreal sort of domesticity: days full of visitors, nights in the studio, and not infrequent wild after-hours.

John's starting to feel worn down.

"This is my brilliant idea, to have us all live together and work together. And we'd all be in tune," John recalls. "But it was a madhouse."

The situation he's in finally lands on him. "I've got this great singer with no voice, and a house full of drunken lunatics. So, I suddenly got sober in the middle of it. *I'm responsible, I'm the producer, man! I'd better straighten out.* So I straightened out."

⸺ ⸙ ⸺

On March 28, a new session musician drops in to the studio.

Paul McCartney.

It's been years since they've seen each other—ironically, just as John's old drug conviction stands in the way of his visa application, effectively trapping him in the United States (he fears he won't be allowed back in if he were to leave), Paul's own arrests for cannabis possession have been keeping him out. But now Paul's in town for the forty-sixth Academy Awards: his Wings song "Live and Let Die" (cowritten with Linda and produced by George Martin) is nominated in the Best Music (Original Song) category.

The tuxedos can wait. He picks up a set of sticks and sits behind the drum kit. Both Ringo and Keith Moon are absent, but prodigy Stevie Wonder, who's been recording in a different studio nearby, comes over to sit in.

They play "Midnight Special," a song that takes them back to Liverpool days.

"Don't get too serious, we're not getting paid," John

tells his friends. It turns into a spirited jam session with Paul and Linda, Stevie Wonder, and May Pang on tambourine, among other session musicians.

It's been more than four years since the former bandmates have played together, and while a bootleg recording of the session—eventually released under the title *A Toot and a Snore in '74*—reveals a set heavy on the blues and sloppily executed, "they made joyous music together that night," May remembers.

They certainly make history. And everyone there is acutely aware of it. Even though others were also playing, John notes, "they were just watching me and Paul."

CHAPTER 49

Light of the love that I found...
— "Fool in the Rain"

T he affair was something that was not hurtful to me," Yoko insists. From the start, she says, "I was prepared to lose him, but it was better he came back. I didn't think I would lose him."

But now she feels it's gone on long enough. Although it's been more than six months since John left for LA, Yoko's been in constant communication with him. And with May Pang. And with several other friends, such as radio DJ Elliot Mintz and photographer Bob Gruen.

May finds the calls from Yoko increasingly controlling.

"First they were directives to keep our relationship quiet, which was fine with me," recalls May. But John was too openly affectionate with her for that to last long. Once that news got out, Yoko's "crisis mode kicked in. She would call with instructions of what to say, that she had thrown John out. She'd call every day to remind us what to say. One drama after another," May says in exasperation.

Yoko's explanation for calling John so often was much simpler: "We missed each other. We were calling each other every day. Some days he would call me three or four times," Yoko tells reporters.

And while by all accounts John isn't nearly as unhappy or out of control as some people make him out to be, he has never expressed anything other than a desire to reconcile with Yoko. "The sense with him all the time was 'What do I have to do to get out of here and back to her?'" says Mintz.

Now that she's convinced John's "lost weekend" must come to an end, Yoko needs advice. In addition to the psychics and numerologists she's always consulted, she begins making recurring appointments with her tarot card reader, John Green. Green, who joins Yoko's staff in 1974, is able to provide multiple readings a day on any subject of her choice.

She also reaches out to John's friends to ask for help.

"Yoko came to our house in England and asked if I would do her a favor," Paul says in 2019. "When I went to LA, would I mention to John that she was prepared to take him back as long as he would make the effort to court her?"

When Paul conveys that message to John privately, he can see the relief on his old friend's face.

On April 2, 1974, when the Oscar statuette for Best Song is handed out at Los Angeles's Dorothy Chandler Pavilion to "The Way We Were" rather than to "Live and Let Die," John is waiting backstage to console Paul.

Though music insiders spin visions of a renewed partnership, Paul's role as an envoy for Yoko remains under wraps.

By late April, the Hollywood glitter is fading. John can no longer resist the powerful pull of New York.

***

John returns to New York, but not to Yoko. Instead, he and May stay at the Pierre hotel on Fifth Avenue, in a suite right above Elton John's. He remixes Harry Nilsson's *Pussy Cats* and starts work on a new album, *Walls and Bridges*.

John stays up late watching TV, wondering if he'll ever have another hit record. Paul, George, and Ringo have all achieved multiple number-one hits as solo artists (including Paul's "Uncle Albert/ Admiral Halsey" and "My Love," George's "My

Sweet Lord" and "Give Me Love (Give Me Peace on Earth)," and Ringo's "Photograph" and "You're Sixteen")—but John hasn't had any, and the exclusion stings. "I'm out of favor at the moment," he laments to Elton.

John flips the channels, stopping on Reverend Ike, a thirty-nine-year-old black minister who preaches out of a converted Loews movie theater uptown, on 175th Street.

"Let me tell you, guys, it doesn't matter," Reverend Ike is saying. "It's whatever gets you through the night." John takes down the minister's words and starts writing.

On June 17, 1974—shortly after Paul slips in a third US number-one single with Wings' "Band on the Run"—John's at the Record Plant working on the rough mixes for his new album, *Walls and Bridges*. As he's "fiddling about," Elton John and Tony King walk in. John plays them several of the new songs, including "Whatever Gets You Thru the Night," inspired by that line from the TV evangelist. It's not his favorite of the songs, but Elton seems to like it.

John's producing the record himself, and since Elton likes how he works—"fast, and he got bored easily, which was right up my street"—he pipes up.

"Say, can I put a bit of piano on that?"

"Sure, love it!" John replies. Though the two of them are good friends by now, this is the first time he's ever actually seen Elton play the piano, and he's blown away.

"He zapped in. I was amazed at his ability," John recalls. "We had a great time."

Elton also adds piano and harmony to "Surprise, Surprise (Sweet Bird of Paradox)," John's love note to May, but it's "Whatever Gets You Thru the Night" that he thinks has real hit potential.

"That'll be your Number One," Elton predicts.

John scoffs, but Elton is serious. He's so sure of it, in fact, that the two friends make a steep wager as to just how high it will chart.

If the single hits number 1, John has to perform live onstage at one of Elton's upcoming tour dates.

"He sang harmony on it and he really did a damn good job," John explains. "So, I sort of half-heartedly promised that if 'Whatever Gets You Thru the Night' became No. 1, which I had no reason to expect, I'd do Madison Square Garden with him."

When Apple releases the album, on September 26 (October 4 in the UK), critics marvel at the pairing. "Elton John—*Elton John????*—on keyboards and back-up vocals," *New Musical Express* announces, picking up on "a real, desperate rocking edge to" the song, which *Rolling Stone* calls "the ice cream that follows a tonsillectomy."

On October 9, 1974, John celebrates his thirty-fourth birthday. A series of music milestones follows in fast succession: *Walls and Bridges* is certified gold on October 22, and then on November 16, "Whatever Gets You Thru the Night" tops the *Billboard* charts at number 1, just as Elton predicted.

Elton calls John up. "Remember when you promised…"

To make good on his bet, John will be working on Thanksgiving. At Madison Square Garden.

Before the Elton John show on November 28, John's stage fright comes roaring back, and he's gripped with nausea. Elton gives John an onyx medallion inscribed with the name Dr. Winston O'Boogie, an alias John sometimes used, and Yoko sends both musicians gardenias, her favorite flower. When John makes his unannounced appearance, he's wearing the medallion and has Yoko's gardenia affixed to his lapel.

The crowd cheers, stunned at the sight of the superstar, who's about to amaze them one more time.

"I just went up and did a few numbers"—the first being "Whatever Gets You Thru the Night"—"but the emotional thing was me and Elton together," John says.

The two then sang "Lucy in the Sky with Diamonds," a Lennon song from *Sgt. Pepper* that Elton had just covered (with Dr. Winston O'Boogie on guitar and backing vocals) and released as a single. For the concert finale, "we thought we'd do a number of an old estranged fiancé of mine called Paul," John

Lennon tells the crowd. "This one I never sang, it's an old Beatle number, and we just about know it."

Elton's band launches into "I Saw Her Standing There."

After the show, Yoko joins the concert after-party at the Pierre, and she and John are photographed sitting together, talking and holding hands. The barriers between them are crumbling.

Although John and Yoko do not reconcile immediately after the Elton John show, the stage is set for a reunion.

But even as the two of them are coming back together, the Beatles are moving further—forever—apart.

A few weeks after John's show with Elton, George Harrison is in New York, also booked to play Madison Square Garden to promote his album *Dark Horse*. Paul is in town as well. (For once, Ringo is the only Beatle not in attendance.) They plan to meet at the Plaza Hotel on December 19, 1974, along with their lawyers, to sign the papers that will formally dissolve the Beatles.

It's the last step in a legal process that Paul began on December 31, 1970, when he filed a lawsuit in London's High Court, an action that turned "these true buddies of mine from way way back, these truest friends of mine" into "my firmest enemies overnight." Despite the trauma, though, Paul maintains "I had to do it. It was either that or [let] Klein have the whole thing, all the fortune we'd worked for all our lives since we were children."

And for the most part, the hurt feelings have begun to dissipate over the past four years. After that jam session in LA, Paul and John are on good terms again. John has accepted George's invitation to perform with him onstage at the Garden tonight. Ringo is friendly with all of them and is now on the phone, having already signed the papers in England. George and Paul are at the Plaza, waiting for John so they can all sign and be done.

But John doesn't show up. There's a tax issue that he's worried will disproportionately affect him. Yet when his lawyers finally reach him, at home with May, John gives them the message that he can't sign because the stars aren't properly aligned. "I didn't sign it because my astrologer told me it wasn't the right day," he later explains. (As friend and journalist Ray Connolly points out, "This was the first anyone had ever heard of him having an astrologer. But Yoko had one.")

The group at the Plaza is shocked and annoyed—especially George, who immediately lets John know he's no longer wanted onstage tonight.

(George has been having an especially rough time; the tour has not been a success, and his wife, Pattie Boyd, has left him for his best friend, Eric Clapton.) Paul, the peacemaker, comes over to John and May's apartment to work out what—other than astrology—is at issue.

Luckily, the hurt feelings blow over quickly, even for George, who reconciles with John the next day.

"Everybody changes," May reflects. "With John things changed on a daily basis. It's a question of time. Five years earlier," in 1969, when John was the one pushing for a breakup, "was not the same situation. In 1974 he had just seen everyone. The friendship was still there. They were brothers. There was no animosity."

While the lawyers revise the documents, John and May take Julian, now eleven and visiting the United States for the holidays, down to Florida.

"We wanted to give Julian a good time for his Christmas holiday, somewhere warm," May tells the *Palm Beach Post* in 2018. They stay in a borrowed unit at the Sun and Surf condominiums on Sunrise Avenue. "We were there for a week. A few days in Palm Beach, a day or two at Disney World, then we came back to Palm Beach and then home to New York."

In Palm Beach, they swim and relax, go to a few restaurants, attend a few parties on the island. On

Worth Avenue, John buys May some jewelry. It's a nice break. Just as he enjoyed Disneyland, in California, John enjoys Disney World (especially the Pirates of the Caribbean ride), but he especially appreciates the benign anonymity the crowds afford him. "I don't like being famous," he tells a Palm Beach photographer. "I just want to be like you guys."

On December 29, 1974, while they're at the Polynesian Village Resort at Disney World, the lawyers catch up to John.

With the revised documents in front of him, he hesitates, aware of what he's about to do.

"Take out your camera," John suggests to May.

And then he hesitates again, looking out the window. "I could almost see him replaying the entire Beatles experience in his mind," she says.

"Even though they all felt they had to break up to get to the next level of their musical careers, John had started this band that changed the world. It changed pop culture. It changed how we live and how we dress. And he knew that. So when he sat down to sign, he knew that this was it. His was the last signature. As he had started the group, he was the one to end it."

And so it comes to an end in the Magic Kingdom: with a final autograph placed just under the other three, John Lennon signs away the Beatles.

CHAPTER 50

Gotta be rock and roll music
If you wanna dance with me.
— "Rock and Roll Music"

In January of 1975, John's guitar and backing vocals appear on another number-one song in America—Elton John's reggae-esque cover of "Lucy in the Sky with Diamonds."

That same month, John welcomes Londoner David Bowie back to New York. They'd met a few months earlier, on September 20, 1974, at the twenty-first birthday party Dean Martin threw for his son Ricci in Los Angeles. Other guests had included Ringo, Elton John, Elizabeth Taylor, Arthur Ashe, and Brian and Carl Wilson of the Beach Boys.

The big draw at the event for John are the stars Dean Martin and Elizabeth Taylor. "He really wanted to go," May says. "He loved the old-time Hollywood stars."

Forty-two-year-old Elizabeth Taylor, in between marriages to Richard Burton, has recently met Bowie and taken a strong liking to him. "Miss Taylor had been trying to get me to make a movie with her," Bowie says, though he isn't interested. (He later tells Cameron Crowe, in an interview for *Rolling Stone,* "I mean she was a nice woman and all, even if I didn't get much of a chance to know her. She did tell me I reminded her of James Dean.") She makes the introduction between the two musicians at the party.

"So John was sort of 'Oh, here comes another new one,'" Bowie later says, imitating John's Liverpool accent. "And I was sort of, 'It's John Lennon! I don't know what to say. Don't mention the Beatles, you'll look really stupid.' And he said, 'Hello, Dave.' And I said, 'I've got everything you've made—except the Beatles.'

"In the early 1970s," Bowie admits sheepishly, "that would have been most uncool to actually say you liked the Beatles in any way, shape, or form."

Despite that awkward first meeting, the two quickly find common ground and become close friends. "I guess he defined for me, at any rate, how one could twist and turn the fabric of pop and imbue it with elements from other art forms, often producing something extremely beautiful, very powerful and imbued with strangeness," Bowie recalls. "Also, uninvited,

John would wax on endlessly about any topic under the sun and was over-endowed with opinions. I immediately felt empathy with that."

Bowie says John "was probably one of the brightest, quickest witted, earnestly socialist men I've ever met in my life. Socialist in its true definition, not in a fabricated political sense, a real humanist.

"And he had a really spiteful sense of humour which of course, being English, I adored."

Bowie, who on January 8 had celebrated his twenty-eighth birthday (Elvis Presley turned forty that same day), has returned to the Pierre, on Fifth Avenue, where—in two $700-per-week suites—he had built the elaborate sets for his Diamond Dogs Tour, which wrapped on December 1, 1974.

Though critical and popular perceptions hold that "a new album release by David Bowie is today looked on with as much awe as a release by the Beatles in the sixties," John enjoys ribbing Bowie about his recent concept albums, including 1972's multiplatinum *The Rise and Fall of Ziggy Stardust and the Spiders from Mars,* the story of a fictional rock star named Ziggy, one of Bowie's many alter egos.

"What the bloody hell are you doing, Bowie? It's all so negative, your shit. All this Diamond Dogs mutant crap. Ha, ha, ha."

"What do you think of glam rock?" Bowie asks John.

"It's just fooking rock and roll with lipstick," he answers in his Liverpool accent.

"Very succinct, but not all that accurate," Bowie says with a laugh.

Bowie's latest evolution is a shift toward a style he's calling "plastic soul," the same phrase that Paul used in a different context in advance of *Rubber Soul*. Fascinated by the popular "sound of Philadelphia," Bowie began recording his new album, *Young Americans,* at Sigma Sound Studios in that city. Now he's returned to New York to finish it at the hallowed Electric Lady Studios, which Jimi Hendrix had opened for business in 1970, just three weeks before his death by accidental overdose.

Bowie hasn't consulted his producer, Tony Visconti (who later marries May Pang), who's departed for London under the impression that the album is complete, but he wants to add a cover of "Across the Universe"—the song John brought to the studio in early 1968 (eventually appearing on the final Beatles album, *Let It Be*), spurred by his irritation one night at his first wife, Cynthia.

"It's so interesting," John says about the songwriting. "'Words are flying [*sic*] out like [*sings*] endless rain into a paper cup, they slither wildly as they slip away across the universe.' Such an extraordinary meter and I can never repeat it! It's not a matter of craftsmanship; it wrote itself."

Bowie skips one part of the tune, eliminating the Sanskrit mantra "Jai guru deva om," which John had learned from his studies with the maharishi and included in the original chorus.

John likes the cover ("I thought, great," he says when he heard that Bowie wanted to cover it. "It's one of my favorite songs, but I didn't like my version of it") and accepts Bowie's invitation to collaborate. They talk for hours about the concept of fame, Bowie breaking down the paralyzing paradox of celebrity as "How much you want to be known before you are, and then when you are, how much you want the reverse: 'I don't want to do these interviews! I don't want to have these photographs taken!'"

Bowie builds the rhythm around a guitar riff he'd originally earmarked for "Footstompin'" (his cover of the 1961 Flares song, which he eventually released on his 1995 album *RarestOneBowie*).

"What was that riff you had?" Bowie asks his long-time guitarist Carlos Alomar, whose motto is "I play any guitar that pays." John listens to Alomar's guitar work, then finds his way in, repeating the word *aim,* which Bowie then morphs into *fame,* the song's driving theme, lyric, and title.

"He goes in with about four words and a few guys," John says, "and starts laying down this stuff, and he has virtually nothing—he's just making it up in the studio. So I just contributed whatever I contributed—you know, like, backwards piano and oooohhh [hits a high note] and a couple of things like the repeat of 'fame.'"

The structure of the session may have been Bowie's, but the pacing is all John's. "God, that session was fast," Bowie marvels. "That was an evening's work!"

He calls his producer in London, saying, "Er, Tony. I don't know how to tell you this, but John and I wrote a song together and we recorded and mixed it. It's called 'Fame.'"

On July 25, RCA Records issues "Fame," with Bowie and John credited as coauthors. When on September 20, 1975, the song becomes Bowie's first number-one hit in America, he insists, "I wouldn't know how to pick a single if it hit me in the face."

"And we made a record out of it, right?" John says. "So he got his first number one so I felt that was like a karmic thing, you know. With me and Elton, I got my first number one so I passed it on to Bowie and he got his."

And even better: "I like that track."

<hr>

These collaborations are revitalizing for John. So although the ink is barely dry on the severed Beatles relationship, when Paul suggests that John come down to record with him in New Orleans on his new Wings album, John very seriously considers it—talking it over with May, Art Garfunkel, and even the Beatles' old press officer Derek Taylor.

Had he gone to New Orleans, an entirely unknown future could have been explored. But instead, he's enticed into a very different collaboration, one he cannot turn away from.

CHAPTER 51

Shake it up, baby, now...
— "Twist and Shout"

John's newest collaboration is of a more personal nature. Yoko is pregnant.

Given her advanced maternal age of forty-two and her history of miscarriages, John takes tender care of her fragile health and that of her unborn child. "When I got pregnant I had to concentrate on being pregnant for a whole nine months," Yoko says. She's on bed rest most of the time, which prevents her from working, so "John got a wheelchair and he would push me around into the kitchen where there would be lunch," she recalls. "Isn't that sweet?"

"We got back together, decided this was our life, that having a baby was important to us and that anything else was subsidiary to that. We worked hard for that child," John says. "We went through all hell trying to have a baby, through many miscarriages and other problems. He is what they call a love child in truth. Doctors told us we could never have a child. We almost gave up."

John books a country house where Yoko can rest, and he cancels all their plans.

"Stay alive in '75. That's my motto," he tells an interviewer. "I just feel good now, I'm writing well, so I'm happy."

John presents his wife with his Los Angeles diary, chronicling all the highs and lows of his separation from her.

He pulls out a book of matches. Strikes one. Touches the lit match to the edges of the paper, sparking a flame. He carries the burning diary to the kitchen sink and watches the pages burn, the past turning to ash.

John and Yoko go public with their reunion on March 1, 1975, live and on television. The occasion is the seventeenth Grammy Awards, held at the Uris Theatre, in Manhattan.

Wearing a black suit and black beret, Elton's medallion, a pin that spells "Elvis" in sparkling letters, and a gold ring on his left ring finger, John takes the stage with Paul Simon (formerly of the duo

Simon and Garfunkel, who split in 1970 while Art Garfunkel was pursuing an acting career) to present the night's top honor, Record of the Year.

"Hello, I'm John. I used to play with my partner, Paul," John says.

"I'm, uh...I'm Paul. I used to play with my partner, Art," responds Simon.

When Olivia Newton John's "I Honestly Love You" wins, things appear to get a little tense as Garfunkel himself comes onstage to accept the award on her behalf.

"Are you ever getting back together again?" John asks the famous duo, in an obvious joke, and Simon immediately returns the question, "Are *you guys* getting back together again?" "No," John says with a laugh. "It's terrible, isn't it?"

Paul McCartney, who earlier in the evening won in absentia for "Band on the Run" (Best Pop Performance by a Duo, Group, or Chorus), isn't around to comment on John's response.

But John's other reunion is newsworthy. The press picks up on the "Thank you, Mother" (John's term of endearment for Yoko), which he called out as he made his entrance, and snaps photos of the couple, Yoko in a floor-length white gown with ostrich-feather trim.

Of that Grammy appearance with Yoko, John says, "I was glad it was big, and it was quick, so we got maximum effect and it sort of said it without having to go through a big routine—it just sort of went in all the right papers and magazines, and there we were, and that's it."

John's legal entanglements with the US government can at best be termed a stalemate. The three-year limbo rankles all the more given that one of John's most treacherous adversaries was convicted on January 1, 1975, of conspiracy, obstruction of justice, and perjury relating to the Watergate scandal and is currently serving a thirty-month-to-eight-year prison sentence. That man is John Mitchell, who stepped down from the office of attorney general (in order to head Nixon's reelection campaign) on February 15, 1972—eleven days after receiving and acting upon Senator Strom Thurmond's recommendations regarding deportation proceedings against John Lennon.

On June 19, John files suit against Mitchell and officials of the US Immigration and Naturalization Service, stating in his affidavit that "I have been the subject of illegal surveillance activities on the part of the government; that as a result, my case" has "been prejudged for reasons unrelated to my immigration status."

Five days later, on June 23, immigration officials

grant a stay on the humanitarian grounds of Yoko's pregnancy.

"It would have been unconscionable to deport him now," says an INS spokesman. "Yoko Ono has had a difficult pregnancy."

⌘

In the United States Court of Appeals for the Second Circuit, a panel of three judges hears John's case in open court. It's October 7, 1975, two days before John's thirty-fifth birthday. The baby is due any day now. Their attorney, Leon Wildes, argues that "there is substantial reason to believe that official governmental action was based principally on a desire to silence political opposition squarely protected by the First Amendment."

The judges rule two to one in John's favor; the twenty-four-page decision is written by Chief Judge Irving Kaufman. Kaufman, a career-long proponent of First Amendment rights, was appointed to the court in 1961 by President John F. Kennedy, though he earned his most notorious judicial credential ten years earlier, at the height of the Cold War, when he sentenced Julius and Ethel Rosenberg to death following their conviction on espionage charges for providing atomic secrets to the Soviet Union.

"The courts will not condone selective deportation

based on secret political grounds," Kaufman finds, adding, "Lennon's four-year battle to remain in our country is testimony to his faith in the American dream."

⌘

John puts out a statement that "It's a great birthday gift from America for me, Yoko, and the baby," but his attention is elsewhere when the verdict is issued. After a touch-and-go pregnancy and a difficult delivery, Yoko gives birth to a healthy eight-pound, ten-ounce boy by cesarean section at New York Hospital on October 9. They name him Sean Taro Ono Lennon.

John and his son not only share a birthday, they also share a name ("Sean" being an Irish variation of "John"; Julian's rarely used first name is also John).

"I feel higher than the Empire State Building!" John declares, beaming at his new son.

While Yoko recovers, John starts sharing the news. He types a postcard and sends it to *Rolling Stone,* thanking fans for "all...your help in the immigration 'battle'" and commemorating "the great triple event. (judges decision/baby Sean/on J.L.s' birthday!!!) What a week!"

He signs it "John and Yoko and Sean (three virgins)."

December 8, 1980

Mark arrives at the Dakota and finds a new man working the morning security shift. There's something off about him—something that makes Mark wonder if the guy is an undercover cop.

Have I been flagged as a threat? Let's find out.

He slips into his disarmingly pleasant and polite persona, leaning into his southern drawl.

Mark smiles. "You wouldn't happen to know whether John Lennon might be planning on coming out today, would you?" He pulls out his shiny new record. "I've got this album here. I'm hoping to get it autographed while I'm here in New York City."

Mark adds that he's traveled all the way from Hawaii to meet his idol.

The guard doesn't give him any information about

Lennon, but the man appears relaxed. He's not an undercover cop. Mark is sure of it.

Which is a good thing. If a cop or anyone here tries to pull anything, Mark will kill him. He will shoot his way in, do whatever it takes to get to Lennon.

Wearing a T-shirt promoting Todd Rundgren's 1978 solo album, *Hermit of Mink Hollow,* he retreats across the street. It's another unseasonably warm day in Manhattan, where the temperature, according to the weathermen, will reach sixty degrees.

Such a great day to be alive. He sits on a park bench in view of the Dakota. He starts to play a game he calls "How is John Lennon spending his final hours?"

Is John at home playing his grand piano?

Is he eating some indulgent culinary creation prepared for him by a private chef?

Is he doing interviews for Double Fantasy*?*

Or is he having sex with Yoko?

The questions are nonstop. They keep invading his mind.

Mark pulls out the copy of *The Catcher in the Rye* he picked up this morning. With the clerk as his witness, he used a brand-new Bic pen to inscribe the inside cover:

To Holden Caulfield from Holden Caulfield. This is my statement—The Catcher in the Rye.

He reads the line again. It makes him smile.

History and time, he reminds himself. *Synchronicity.*

He has no plans to return to the hotel. In a semicircle on the dresser, he laid out a few personal items for the cops he knows will go looking for him there: two photographs of him posing with the Vietnamese refugee children he counseled; a YMCA letter of commendation; his old passport; and the *Wizard of Oz* photo he purchased at the bookstore—none of it is important, except his final clue.

He's left his Bible open to the Gospel of John—*Lennon*.

This is who I am, Mark thought as he looked at his room for the final time. *This is who I was.*

After a walk through Central Park, Mark returns to the Dakota. He opens his copy of *The Catcher in the Rye* and is looking down into the pages when the doorman calls to him.

"Did you see him?" the man asks. "John Lennon just stepped out of a cab and went inside the building."

The news doesn't bother him. The timing, he feels, isn't right.

A short time later, a little boy appears in the archway of the Dakota.

The boy is Sean Lennon. He's heading out for a morning walk with his nanny.

Mark approaches the boy and gets down on one knee, feels the gun tucked in his jacket pocket bump against his leg. He slides his hand inside his pocket to make sure the revolver doesn't fall out.

"I came all the way across the ocean from Hawaii, and I'm honored to meet you," Mark says, shaking Sean's tiny hand.

Sean's brow furrows, confused. He runs his sleeve across his nose.

"You'd better take care of that runny nose," Mark says. "You wouldn't want to get sick and miss Christmas."

Mark looks up at Sean's governess.

"He's a beautiful boy," he tells her. "He's such a beautiful boy."

CHAPTER 52

A splendid time is guaranteed for all.
— "Being for the Benefit of Mr. Kite!"

Christmas carols have never sounded as sweet as they do this season, when Sean is a newborn. They should, coming from voices beloved worldwide. The singers are Paul and Linda McCartney, who are making a surprise visit to the Dakota to meet the baby.

It has taken a long while for the chilliness between the two old friends to thaw. While Paul has made occasional friendly overtures over the years, John has always held his former bandmate at arm's length. "You're all pizza and fairy tales," John sneered at Paul once when he phoned the Bank Street apartment.

"He'd become sort of Americanized by then, so the best insult I could think of was to say, "Oh, fuck off, Kojak," and slam the phone down," Paul recalls. At the same time, though, he mused over the turn of phrase. "'Pizza and fairy tales'—I almost made that an album title."

Now John's friend Elliot Mintz is among the holiday guests mingling and eating take-out pizza in the Dakota, watching the winter sun descend over the Hudson River and "paying close attention to John and Paul and the way they looked at each other." Mintz says that "during this Christmas sunset, it was obvious to me that the two of them had run out of things to say."

When they're dancing to the jukebox, there's no need to talk. On New Year's Eve, John plays an old 78 recording of "As Time Goes By." Mintz recalls the indelible image: "John was wearing a long black tuxedo with tails, it was snowing, and up in the sky there were flashing fireworks going off."

After the holidays, John studies up on his old bandmate, telling Yoko that he "had read somewhere that Paul McCartney had made $25 million."

"OK," she says, "I'll try to make the same, but it's going to take me at least two years."

John's made his own timeline. "I wanted to be with Sean the first five years, which are the years that everyone says are the most important in a child's life." He teaches himself to cook so that he can prepare Sean's meals, including fresh bread, saying, "I took a Polaroid of my first loaf. It was like an album coming out of the oven." Yoko has about as much experience with business as John does with full-time fatherhood, but she's determined—and armed with a unique asset. "She's the world's most famous unknown artist," John says. "Everyone knows her name, but no one knows what she actually does."

And what she actually does is: Make money.

They accumulate property—at the Dakota, they amass five apartments: two seventh-floor residences, plus one for guests, another for storage, and a ground-floor studio they use as an office (given its association with Charles Manson, neighbors are startled to see the words *helter skelter* written in large letters across a wall of the studio; later, it's painted over to look like a serene blue sky with clouds).

"John and Yoko were as bad as me when it came to shopping," Elton John says. He rewrites the lyrics to "Imagine" and sends them a card that says, "Imagine six apartments, it isn't hard to do, one is full of fur coats, another's full of shoes."

As John explains, "My insecurity is having too many clothes. That's a physical manifestation of my insecurity—a closet full of clothes I cannot possibly wear."

But they're largely homebodies. Dakota neighbor Roberta Flack, who can often hear the couple rehearsing music, observes, "Most artists like myself tend to keep to themselves." Film critic Rex Reed, who also lives in the building, says of the couple, "They were home all the time watching TV."

John and Yoko have few visitors, but on April 24, 1976, the McCartneys drop in and once again find John and Yoko at home. It's almost midnight when Paul and John tune in to *Saturday Night Live*. Raquel Welch is hosting the eighteenth episode of the comedy show's first season, and John Sebastian of the Lovin' Spoonful is booked to sing his hit theme song "Welcome Back" (from the TV classroom comedy *Welcome Back, Kotter*).

Suddenly, producer Lorne Michaels starts speaking—directly to the two ex-Beatles and their former bandmates. Unbeknownst to Michaels, his comedy routine has turned into a reality show, because Paul and John are sitting together in front of a television less than two miles from NBC's studios at 30 Rockefeller Plaza.

It's been in the news that (in addition to numerous other offers) the band turned down $230 million from Sid Bernstein—the promoter who'd organized the Beatles' 1964 American tour—to perform a series of bicentennial concerts in the summer of 1976.

"Well, if it's money you want," Michaels deadpans, holding up a certified check for $3,000, "all you have to do is sing three Beatles songs. 'She Loves You,' yeah, yeah, yeah—that's $1,000 right there. You know the words. It'll be easy."

Michaels has stationed a staffer to watch for any Beatles entering the lobby.

The producer's wish nearly comes true.

"Wouldn't it be funny if we went down," John says to Paul, "just as a gag."

"I was visiting John at their apartment, and it came on TV," McCartney recalls in 2019. "He [John] asked if I knew about this. I didn't, as I had been in the UK, and for a moment we thought we might run down to the TV studio. But we decided it was too much like work and that it would be more fun to have the night off."

They wonder if John Sebastian wishes he had also passed on the gig. It's an awkward moment in the live performance when the studio audience refuses to sing along to Sebastian's hit TV theme song.

John and Paul can agree that the Beatles never faced a lack of audience participation, but when Paul shows up again at the Dakota the next day, carrying his guitar, John finds reason to quarrel.

"Please call before you come over," John tells him. "It's not 1956 and turning up at the door isn't the same anymore."

Paul turns back, hiding his hurt at the fresh wounds John has cut.

Some relationships, though, John tries to heal.

When word comes via the Apple offices that John's sixty-three-year-old father, Alf Lennon, has a diagnosis of terminal stomach cancer, there is little time to make amends. He places a transatlantic call to the hospital.

"I'm sorry I treated you the way I did, Dad," John says.

Alf pushes off the apology, saying, "It's just bloody marvelous to talk to you again."

A large bouquet of flowers arrives in Alf's room, with a card signed by John, Yoko, and Sean, but Alf will never meet his new grandson. On April 1, 1976, he dies, twelve years to the day since he walked into Brian Epstein's office at NEMS looking for John.

Because of his unresolved immigration status, John can't travel to attend the funeral.

———— ⦵⦵⦵ ————

It's summer in the city, and John's only thoughts are of Sean and Yoko.

"They'd go to Central Park for picnics: ham sandwiches and Dom Pérignon," a neighbor observes, adding a critique of their outdoor table manners: "They would drink out of the bottle, passing it back and forth like hippies."

John and Yoko clean up when, after months of silence from the US government, a hearing is called for July 27 at 20 West Broadway, the Immigration and Naturalization Service building.

With Judge Ira Fieldsteel presiding, attorney Leon Wildes helps his star witness make the case that the United States should finally issue him a green card.

WILDES: Have you ever been convicted of any crime, anywhere in the US?

LENNON: No.

WILDES: Have you ever been a member of the Communist Party or any other organization that may seek to overthrow the US government by force?

LENNON: No.

WILDES: Do you intend to make the US your home?

LENNON: I do.

WILDES: Will you continue your work here?

LENNON: Yes. I wish to continue to live here with my family and continue making music.

A parade of celebrity supporters details the extent of the good John has already done for his adopted country.

"Justice for John & Yoko!" says Bob Dylan in a handwritten plea to the INS, applauding their "great voice and drive for this country's so called ART IN-STITUTION" and insisting, "Let them stay and live here and breathe."

"We had to prove that John was an important figure to the well-being of American society," Geraldo Rivera, a witness on Lennon's behalf, says in a 2019 interview. "I told the judge how important Lennon was to the cause of deinstitutionalizing the mentally disabled in New York through his work in the Willowbrook case."

Gloria Swanson, a screen siren in the golden age of Hollywood, who'd met and befriended John over their shared passion for health food, also comes to his defense. "We must educate the country," she tells the judge, "and the Lennons will help do something about it."

"He is one of the great artists of the Western world," the writer Norman Mailer states.

After ninety minutes of testimony, the judge grants John's petition.

"It's great to be legal again!" John exclaims with a kiss for Yoko.

<hr />

A few months later, George delivers the *Saturday Night Live* punch line.

"See, I thought you would understand," Lorne Michaels tells his musical guest in the show's cold open on November 20, in a follow-up to his comedic enticement to the Beatles in April, "that it was $3,000 for four people, and that it would just be $750 for each of you. As far as I'm concerned, you could have the full $3,000."

"That's pretty chintzy," George jokes with the producer.

Later in the show, George performs an acoustic duet with fellow musical guest Paul Simon. They open with "Here Comes the Sun," from the Beatles' *Abbey Road,* a song that came to him in April of 1969, when he skipped a meeting at Apple to visit Eric Clapton in his Surrey garden.

The performance resonates for more than a quarter century.

When the White Stripes are invited to perform on the October 19, 2002, episode of *SNL,* a friend of the band remembers guitarist and songwriter Jack White rhapsodizing "about seeing George Harrison on *SNL* just sitting down and doing 'Here Comes the Sun.' God, it'd be cool to do something like that," White tells producers, "playing the acoustic guitar."

CHAPTER 53

People say I'm crazy
Doing what I'm doing.
— "Watching the Wheels"

I'm crazy for trying and crazy for crying," Linda
Ronstadt sings onstage at the Kennedy Center, in
Washington, DC. John and Yoko are listening to
her cover of Willie Nelson's "Crazy" at Jimmy
Carter's inaugural gala. The taped program will be
broadcast while politicos and celebrities clad in for-
mal wear, including Cher and Gregg Allman,
Loretta Lynn, Aretha Franklin, and Muhammad
Ali, mingle at the January 1977 festivities.

Carter, who led his inaugural parade wearing a
$175 suit he brought with him from his home
state of Georgia, doesn't recognize John when John
steps forward to congratulate America's thirty-ninth
president, even with the prompt, "I used to be a
Beatle."

True to the spirit of the 1971 Plastic Ono Band song "Power to the People," Carter styles himself as the "people's president." Long gone is the armed guard, nearly ten thousand strong, that Nixon marshaled in 1969 for his first inauguration.

"We're living in a more tranquil period of society," Don Zimmerman, executive director of Capitol Records, observes to the *New York Times.* "The average age of the artists is older. Most rock stars are over thirty."

One of them is thirty-six-year-old John, who says, "I'm talking to guys and gals that have been through what we went through, together—the sixties group that has survived. Survived the war, the drugs, the politics, the violence on the street—the whole she-bang—that we've survived it and we're here. And I'm talkin' to them."

John is also talking to the younger generation. The much younger generation. John is not releasing records, but he's still making home recordings with and for his toddler son, Sean.

"Do you need anybody?" the little boy sings with feeling. "I need somebody to love."

"Very good," John says when Sean names the tune as "my favorite song," the one off *Sgt. Pepper* that his father has played for him over and over.

"Who's singing? You?" Sean asks.

"No. Ringo," John answers, "but Paul and I are singing it with him."

When Sean asks the name of the song, John has a flash of forgetfulness.

"Oh," he remembers. "'A Little Help from My Friends,' that's what it's called."

John tries to be Sean's best friend as well as his teacher. John plays him the guitar, and they watch *The Muppet Show* together—but never the commercials. "Anything you ever see on a commercial is a lie," John always tells him.

He makes a nighttime ritual for the two of them, flicking the lights off and on in a rhythm that means it's time to go to bed.

"Good night, Sean," he says in a soothing voice.

<hr />

A mysterious letter finds its way to the Dakota on November 29, 1977.

John unseals the envelope with a kitchen knife. He extracts the letter, reaches for his glasses, and reads the first two lines.

WE ARE THE TERRORISTS [FROM] THE FALN PUERTO RICAN INDEPENDENCE MOVEMENT. This letter is a positive (THREAT) to your life.

The group is targeting all three members of the Lennon family. There is also a demand—that John leave $100,000 in a "strong package" at the front entrance to "Dakota House."

A nine-day countdown is already ticking away.

If John tries "to play any trick to us" by contacting the FBI or the police, the note warns, "we are good preparedly for it."

John's pulse starts to race as he runs through his options, seeing none other than to contact the FBI, the US government agency that had previously placed him under surveillance because the Nixon administration didn't like his politics.

In consultation with the FBI, John decides not to comply with the demands.

On December 19, a second letter arrives, claiming that on the day the cash should have been delivered, "your building was surrounded by 23 armed man's of our troop," then acknowledging the holiday season: "This is Christmas time, do your normal life, don't be afraid is no body outside looking for you, on this you can have our trust."

The threat, though the FBI can't identify its source, turns John's heart to lead.

Now I'll be looking over my shoulder no matter where I go.
Now it's no longer safe to go outside.
Now I need to get Yoko and Sean away from the city.

John acts quickly, and in February of 1978 he

purchases a thousand acres of land in Delaware County, three hours north of Manhattan. Yoko can look after her latest investment there, a herd of registered Holstein cattle. The dairy cows are prize-winners at the New York State Fair.

"Only Yoko," John marvels, "could sell a cow for $250,000."

Even as they reside in the secluded Catskills, thoughts of looming danger cloud John's mind. He donates $1,000 to the New York Patrolmen's Benevolent Association so the police can buy bullet-proof vests.

They also purchase property in Florida, where John's experienced bursts of true happiness on his several trips down there over the years. "I really don't want to leave Palm Beach," he'd told a local reporter during a visit in 1974. "I'd like to own a piece of it."

On January 31, 1980, he does, buying a property that, a year earlier, Yoko had toured and rented under the pseudonym Mrs. Green. Here, at the historic twenty-two-room mansion built in 1919 by renowned architect Addison Mizner and known as El Solano, Julian meets his half brother, Sean, for the first time. It's a doubly special trip for Julian, and John marks (one week early) the occasion of his son's sixteenth birthday, April 8, 1979, with a family party on a chartered yacht.

Looking out over the ocean in the early morning hours, John says, "Sunrises rejuvenate you. It recharges the batteries!"

"Welcome, my dear!" John says to Yoko.

She's arrived in early 1980 to spend her first night at their newest property, a three-story Tudor-style home called Cannon Hill on the north shore of Long Island, overlooking Cold Spring Harbor.

As they pour tea and light their morning cigarettes, they agree that they've found "a gorgeous place."

"So different than waking up in New York," Yoko says.

Studio One, the first-floor office where Yoko keeps busy running Lenono Music and growing their fortune, is where Yoko spends most of her time.

"If I'm lucky, maybe she'll come up and we'll do something but she's a workaholic," John says. "Sometimes she'll start again at twelve midnight, 'cause she's always callin' the West Coast, or England or Tokyo or some Godforsaken place that's on a different time zone from us."

This morning John looks out toward the private beach. "It's better here than real life—you know, the sea is bluer."

CHAPTER 54

Go Johnny go!
— "Johnny B. Goode"

Twenty-five-year-old Tyler Coneys carries boxes filled with aspiring artists' demo tapes into the basement of Cannon Hill. He picks up extra cash sometimes by helping John and Yoko around their Cold Spring property. "John and Yoko would send stuff, fan mail, to the house on Long Island for storage," Coneys says in 2019. "A box came, and on top of the parcel that I was bringing down to the basement was a mocked-up album cover. On the cover was an overweight young guy with dark glasses. His name was Mark Chapman."

John has recently been a customer at the marina that Coneys's family owns in nearby Huntington. Coneys has been teaching John basic seamanship, bringing Sean along for the ride. John has a fourteen-foot single-sail boat named *Isis* after his and Yoko's passion for Egyptian art. "All my life I've been dreaming of having my own boat," he says. "I can't wait to learn how to sail!"

They sail past Billy Joel's home on Cooper's Bluff, overlooking Oyster Bay.

"Billy, I have all your records!" Lennon shouts toward the Piano Man's modern glass mansion.

"I'd like to go say hi to Billy Joel but I don't want to bother him," John tells his assistant, Fred Seaman. Ironically, Billy Joel feels exactly the same way. "We both respected each other's privacy," Joel says ruefully. "And due to that, we never got to meet."

John loves the freedom of sailing. Out on the open ocean, fans can't grab for a piece of him, drag him down.

At the Dakota, photographers are a particular nuisance, especially Paul Goresh, a twenty-one-year-old student of criminal justice at Middlesex County College who once faked his way into John's apartment by posing as a TV repairman.

Goresh is no longer allowed on Dakota property.

When John sees him snapping photos from across the street, he confronts Goresh.

A young woman is taking photos of the tense exchange. John grabs her camera, threatening to smash it on the ground—right after he smashes Goresh's.

"Okay, John, I'll give you my camera roll," Goresh says. He pulls out the film from his Minolta XG-1 and hands it to him. "We're good now, right?"

Yoko consults Takashi Yoshikawa, a Japanese expatriate whose New York clinic advises on macrobiotics—the Lennons' principal diet—and the ancient Chinese divination method ki-ology. The system holds that "energy numbers," derived from an individual's birthday, open the way to a harmonious existence. To clear the clouds that are "casting a shadow over his life and creativity," Yoshikawa prescribes that John sail southeast—a straight course to the island of Bermuda.

They set sail out of Newport Harbor, Rhode Island, on June 5, 1980, for a voyage expected to cover 650 nautical miles over five days.

Tyler Coneys is aboard the *Megan Jaye,* a forty-three-foot Hinckley sloop, along with two of his cousins, a small but experienced crew whose birthdays Yoko all finds auspicious. The captain of the vessel is a sailor close to John's age named Hank Halsted.

"John, since you're the least experienced sailor on board, I'm appointing you ship's cook," Captain Hank announces.

Captain Hank knows the ocean, but he also knows rock 'n' roll music. In his twenties, he was a concert promoter for the Allman Brothers and Big Brother and the Holding Company.

The captain isn't afraid to ask tough questions. "You just affected 50 million people there to the positive, big boy," he says to John. "What are you going to do to follow that up?"

"I'm going to raise my son," John says.

That plan is in for a drastic shift.

John is performing his duties in the galley when a powerful mid-Atlantic storm barrels down on the *Megan Jaye*. As thunder cracks, the crew joins John belowdecks to don their severe-weather gear.

While Captain Hank steers the small yacht through a force 8 gale, John straps himself to the cockpit rails.

The boat pitches violently, and one by one, the crew succumbs to seasickness.

Only Captain Hank and John remain to face the giant waves, some of them cresting past a height of twenty feet. John follows Halsted's orders as the relentless seas continuously pound the ship over the next forty-eight hours.

In his haze of fatigue, Captain Hank Halsted fears he'll make a mistake that could cost the lives of everyone on board.

He turns to the last person still standing, the sailor whose only previous experience is guiding a fourteen-footer through Cold Spring Harbor. "I'm gonna need some help here, big boy," Halsted barks at John, gesturing for him to take the wheel. "I'll tell you what to do."

Lennon fights his way toward the helm, gripping the rails, treading gingerly to prevent himself from being hurled over the side. There is no protection now that the stainless-steel dodger, or windshield, has been ripped apart by the frothing ocean.

"Don't jibe," Halsted explains. "Never let the wind cross the back of the boat."

With that, Halsted withdraws.

"He was thin, but very wiry and strong," Tyler Coneys recalls of John. "This was a terrifying situation for all of us, but Lennon took responsibility and truly stepped into his role as a leader."

John is alone. He faces down the waves, as if they are the stage fright that so often gripped him. *It won't go away,* he tells himself. *You can't change your mind. It's like being onstage; once you're on there's no gettin' off.*

A huge wall of water breaches the bow and crashes

over him as he stands at the helm. John grips the wheel, and the torrent of water buckles his knees. When the swell subsides, he pulls himself up and shakes his fist at the sky.

"I feel like a Viking!" he shouts. "Jason and the Golden Fleece."

Baptized by the storm, he grows more confident with the passing of each massive wave and each desperate hour.

"Freddie!" he calls in tribute of his dead sailor father.

When Captain Hank regains his strength, he returns to the helm to find signs of a calming ocean and "a man who was just enraptured."

I was having the time of my life, he realizes. *I was screaming sea chanteys and shoutin' at the gods!*

When the sloop glides safely into St. George's Harbour, Bermuda, on June 11, John races from the dock to place a call to the Dakota. He tells his assistant, Fred Seaman, to book himself and Sean on a flight to Bermuda. John also requests a guitar that for the past five years has been hanging in his bedroom, untouched.

It's time to launch a comeback.

CHAPTER 55

It's been a long time since I rock and rolled.
— "Rock and Roll"

John welcomes his four-year-old son to Bermuda with a long hug. Under the pseudonym John Green, he's rented Undercliff, a house two miles from Bermuda's capital, Hamilton.

By day, he plays with Sean on the sun-splashed beach, searching for sea glass and building castles in Bermuda's famous pink sands.

With the evening serenade of whistling tree frogs, he sits alone on the veranda with his Ovation acoustic guitar—the one he's avoided for so long. He sets up two Panasonic boom boxes to record his music.

He dedicates a song called "Nobody Told Me" to Ringo, speaking into the demo tape, "This one's for Mister Starkey."

John fights to get rid of his self-consciousness, the

scolding inner voice that for the last five years has relentlessly criticized: *You can't do that. That song's not good enough. Remember, you're the guy who wrote "A Day in the Life." Try again.*

It's a lonely battle. He calls Yoko in New York. She doesn't answer.

He's plunged into emotional distress, then remembers a song he started and abandoned more than ten years earlier. He reworks the music and lyrics to "Stranger's Room" into "I'm Losing You," a passionate reflection on love in its final throes, adding a powerful guitar riff.

"I'm getting all this stuff," he says when he finally reaches Yoko. She listens quietly as he plays back the tape of John singing directly to her, "Don't want to lose you, now."

"Incredible song," Yoko says. "It's so beautifully written and the emotion is so powerful."

Two hours later, John's phone rings. Yoko has written a companion song to "I'm Losing You"—"I'm Moving On," her personal take on the complexity of adult relationships.

Suddenly, John's feelings of despair lift into freeform creativity. "I like it to be inspirational—from the spirit," he says, and as the calls fly between Bermuda and New York, they keep making songs.

John is feeling so good that he goes out to a dance club—"for the first time since 1967," he says. The

DJ is spinning a song from an American group's debut album. "I suddenly heard 'Rock Lobster' by the B-52's for the first time," John says, and he feels an instant connection. "It sounds just like Yoko's music."

This person's studied her, he thinks. *They've finally caught up to where we were.*

Not knowing that the B-52's had indeed created the song as a "tribute to Yoko," John takes the similarities as another sign that it's time to get back in the studio.

More inspiration appears. When John takes Sean to the Bermuda Botanical Gardens, a sanctuary for local foliage that dates from the turn of the twentieth century, they walk through cedar and palmetto trees to enter a flowering garden.

He bends down to inspect a bed of sweet-smelling trumpet-shaped blossoms. FREESIA DOUBLE FANTASY, he reads from the identifying plaque.

Double Fantasy—that's a great title, he thinks to himself.

He and Yoko talk it over and share the excitement over the phrase, with its layered meanings. Not only is it a flower, John points out, but also, "without really saying anything, it says everything."

Yoko likes that it references "a dream that we have—which we share."

John is almost ready to go home.

CHAPTER 56

Our life together
Is so precious together.
—"(Just Like) Starting Over"

I'm interested in doing something extra special," John tells producer Jack Douglas.

He's calling from Bermuda with some highly unusual directions for the recording wizard, who engineered *Imagine* and who throughout the 1970s was making records with the Who, Miles Davis, and Patti Smith as well as Aerosmith and Cheap Trick.

John directs the curious producer to a noon seaplane landing at Manhattan's 30th Street pier. Douglas boards the plane, which is routed to Cold Spring Harbor and comes in for a landing on an unfamiliar beach. When Yoko meets the plane with a message, Douglas realizes he's at Cannon Hill.

"John wants to do a record; he wants you to

produce it." She hands him an envelope marked "For Jack's ears only."

Douglas listens to the cassettes, mesmerized by the primitive yet affecting sounds of John playing his guitar and singing into two Panasonic cassette recorders, keeping time on pots and pans. Douglas can't resist taking on the project. Once John is assured of Douglas's participation, he reels off his requirements for recruiting the session musicians. They all have to be around John's age, and they can't know who's behind the new record.

"I don't want to make a rock album," John says. "What I want to make here is a record about a middle-aged man. I want it to have that feel, a man who's putting together his life, who's survived, for me. The Beatles. And all of this other crap that's going on in my life. I survived it all, I'm now a family man. I'm facing middle age, I'm looking at forty."

Douglas rehearses bassist Tony Levin and Hugh McCracken on lead guitar, then leads them to an astonishing destination. At the Dakota, John Lennon greets the musicians: "I've been a househusband for the last five years and I want to get back to the music."

And he's relentless about the details. To Levin, John says, "They tell me you're good, just don't play too many notes"—and he hears every one of them. Levin comes away from the session marveling, "John

Lennon had more of a clear vision of what he wanted from the bass than anybody."

McCracken feels like he's back in October of 1971, when John asked him to "pretend it's Christmas" to set the mood for his session work on "Happy Xmas (War Is Over)." Tonight, John's getting a feel for the new track, "Beautiful Boy (Darling Boy)," stopping McCracken on a guitar figure he's improvised. "I like that a lot, don't forget it."

There's no chance.

The meeting at the Dakota is winding down when John calls the departing musicians over to his portable Fender Rhodes electric piano, saying, "Wait, I just wrote it."

He plays "(Just Like) Starting Over" and asks Douglas, "Do you think it'll make the record?"

"I think it's a smash," Douglas says. "Probably the first single."

<hr>

Photographers compete for position outside the Hit Factory on 48th Street and Ninth Avenue. It's August 7, 1980, more than four years since John has recorded new music. Paul Goresh is among the lucky ones who capture a shot, though John's face is obscured by a wide-brimmed hat.

Only one cameraman is allowed inside—someone

outside the New York music scene whose date of birth is approved by Yoko's astrologers. "Secrecy was the No. 1 issue," Boston's Roger Farrington confirms. "I was the first photographer authorized to photograph John Lennon in five years."

Farrington likes the Lennon he sees through his lens. "He was energized, witty, and looked fit and tan—he had been sailing in Bermuda. And with the long hair he looked every bit a rock star."

For the album cover, Yoko chooses Japanese high-art photographer Kishin Shinoyama. His depiction of *Double Fantasy* is a black-and-white portrait of the couple, eyes closed and lips touching in a sensual kiss.

On August 10, John calls videographer Jay Dubin. Dubin answers, but he doesn't trust the sound on his newfangled mobile phone. He assumes the street noise where he's standing, in front of the Waverly Theater in Greenwich Village, is making him mishear the name of the caller.

"Okay, let me sing a little bit of a song for you," John says.

The celebrity sound check sends Dubin on his way to the Hit Factory.

CHAPTER 57

Life is what happens to you when
you're busy making other plans.
— "Beautiful Boy (Darling Boy)"

Two days later, on August 12, John and Yoko announce their new project. They pitch the fourteen tracks (seven are his; seven are Yoko's) as "dialog songs, meaning that we were writing as if it were a play and we were two characters in it."

Executives vie for the rights to release *Double Fantasy*. The benchmark is Paul's 1979 contract. Columbia had paid him $10.8 million to make the switch from Capitol (the US distribution arm of Apple). Paul even negotiated a secret (until 2005) clause that would allow for a hypothetical Beatles reunion.

Ringo has also signed with the label, which is angling to represent all four ex-Beatles. "Whatever

John wants for this record, we'll give it to him!" one Columbia executive tells Jack Douglas.

Thirty-seven-year-old David Geffen is equally motivated. As a cofounder of Asylum Records in 1971 and a former vice chairman of Warner Bros. Pictures, he has an impressive pedigree and shrewd business instincts. He understands that if he is to win the deal, Yoko is the one he needs to convince.

He sends her a telegram, and she invites him to a meeting at the Dakota. He arrives dressed all in white—Yoko's favorite color, according to his research.

Yoko, wearing all black, makes a positive assessment of Geffen, determining that he has "good numbers." He also boasts a roster of top talent, including five-time Grammy winner Donna Summer, the first singer to sign with the label.

John's a fan. He plays *The Wanderer*—Summer's eighth studio album and Geffen Records' inaugural release—over and over again. Its title single is out on September 27. He brings a 45 into Yoko's office so she can hear Summer's vocal technique. "Listen! She's doing Elvis!"

Without hearing *Double Fantasy,* Geffen agrees to Yoko's terms. John and Yoko's album will be a Geffen Records release.

Yoko has one final condition. She wants control over where the record is made. "You can do it anywhere in the world except for the Record Plant," she tells Jack Douglas's business partner, Stan Vincent, "and not California" (referencing her disagreements with the Record Plant's owner as well as John's "lost weekend").

John and Yoko take over the Hit Factory's sixth floor, equipped with keyed private elevators for security.

Sean later remembers those special days. "Everything's there; it's carpeted and warm; the lighting is dim. It's very cozy. My parents are both there. The music's loud and clear and exciting. It's a very magical environment for a kid."

On the days Sean can't be in the studio, John tapes a color photo of his son inside the glass-paneled control booth. "He was looking at me all the time," John says, struggling with guilt over their first extended separation. He keeps a tight watch on the clock so he can be home in time to take part in their beloved good-night ritual.

When John rehearses the song "Beautiful Boy (Darling Boy)," he decides to perform the closing lyric in a whisper. "Good night, Sean, see you in the morning."

⟨⟨⟨⟩⟩⟩

"Here's David Sheff," John sings to the tune of "Eleanor Rigby," "come to ask questions with answers that no one will hear."

After a summer of legwork, the reporter has opened the door to the Dakota with his words. As David Geffen had done during the bidding for the rights to *Double Fantasy,* Sheff impressed Yoko with a compelling telegram. September 10 is the first day of a conversation that will run three weeks, the interviews to be published in *Playboy* magazine.

"This will be *the* reference book!" John predicts.

John's certainty is warranted, and it underscores security specialist Doug MacDougall's deepest fear—that John and Yoko will be dangerously revealing of their daily schedule.

"It's been a long time since we've done this kind of thing," Yoko tells Sheff of his access to the couple. But she's also, for the first time since the spring of 1975, granted sit-downs with the BBC, *Newsweek,* and other media outlets.

A parallel concern for MacDougall is the surge in the number of fans who have recently taken to congregating outside the Dakota, clamoring for John's attention as he travels between the Dakota and the Hit Factory. All MacDougall's years of FBI experience have failed to prepare the former agent for the complexity of a rock star's popularity.

CHAPTER 58

Fame, what you get is no tomorrow.
— "Fame"

John Lennon wakes up, reaches for his eyeglasses. At first the day seems like any other until he realizes it's a special one. October 9, 1980, is his fortieth birthday—and Sean's fifth.

Over morning tea, he indulges in a moment of happy reflection, counting "only two artists I've ever worked with for more than a one night's stand, as it were: Paul McCartney and Yoko Ono." He takes a little credit, too, joking, "So, I think as a talent scout I've done pretty damned well!"

Yoko laughs, and moments later, John's hearing another of those two familiar voices. He picks up the kitchen phone to greet his old songwriting partner, who's called to wish him all the best for the record launch.

"I believe the last time I spoke to John was when I was in England and we spoke on the phone," McCartney says in 2019. "It was a pleasant conversation about mostly domestic matters. We had been experiencing a bread strike in England, so I was into making my own bread. He told me he was also doing the same thing around that time in New York, so we talked bread."

Five-year-old Sean, whose diet is strictly macrobiotic—sugar-free and dairy-free—doesn't want baked bread today. He wants birthday cake and ice cream.

And he'll have his treats, as soon as his parents make a big announcement: in the spring of 1981, "John and Yoko will be touring Japan, USA, and Europe."

But the family has an earlier flight to catch.

Yoko entices John and Sean onto the rooftop of the Dakota. A small plane flies in from the north. Yoko waves at the pilot. He's Wayne Mansfield, whom she first hired to skywrite "War is over! If you want it" over the city during their 1969 antiwar campaign.

The skywriter spells out HAPPY BIRTHDAY JOHN AND SEAN—LOVE YOKO. He skillfully traces the letters until they are repeated in full nine times, for the shared birth date and for John's lucky number 9.

John tells his son, "We're almost like twins."

On a walk down Central Park West, the Lennons bump into Geraldo Rivera.

"There they were, John, Yoko, and their child," Rivera recalls in 2019. "I couldn't have been happier to see them and how happy and lighthearted they were. They reminded me of college kids or honeymooners. His love for her cannot be overstated. John was head over heels for Yoko. They were a beautiful family, and we had a great chat."

After the Upper West Siders share a few laughs in front of the entrance to Geraldo's apartment building, on 64th Street, they bid one another farewell.

"Here was one of the Beatles and one of the most famous people in the world walking around New York City without security, without bodyguards," Rivera remembers. "I did not have a good feeling about that."

John's still making records with old friends. He and Yoko have produced David Peel and the Super Apple Band's new single, "John Lennon for President," to be released by Peel's Orange label in November.

John's feeling nostalgic, too, for the music that inspired him. "This one's for Gene, and Eddie, and

Elvis. . . . and Buddy," he says of "(Just Like) Starting Over," the first single off *Double Fantasy*.

"It's a fifties song made with an eighties approach," John says, likening the sensibility to "Bruce Springsteen's 'Hungry Heart'—which I think is a great record—is, to me . . . it's the same kind of period-sound as 'Starting Over.'"

John's target listeners send the single to number 4 on the *Billboard* charts.

⸺⸺⸺ ⚬⚭⚬ ⸺⸺⸺

In San Francisco, Jann Wenner is in his office preparing a new cover story about John. The *Rolling Stone* editor and publisher is on the phone to New York. He's assigned the shoot to his chief photographer, Annie Leibovitz, and he has a particular look in mind.

"Please get me some pictures without Yoko," Wenner says.

Leibovitz objects. "You never tell me what to do."

Wenner won't back down.

He's dishing out the tough treatment to the entire staff. Panicked editors are talking to friends at other music magazines. "Two different writers had been sent to cover Lennon," the gossip goes, "but neither had gotten the hard story [*Rolling*] *Stone* wanted."

The reason is *Double Fantasy*: "They like the album too much."

CHAPTER 59

Still I look to find a reason to
believe.

— "Reason to Believe"

I'm happy to be forty years old," John says when he
calls producer Jack Douglas on November 10, one
week ahead of the worldwide release of *Double Fantasy*. "I'm in the best shape I've ever been in my life
and I feel the best I ever felt."

Critics pounce on John's advanced age in rock 'n'
roll years—"The old bugger still has a wonderful
voice by the way," says *New Musical Express*. John,
still celebrating, is unfazed. One recipient of his
generosity is Paul Goresh. On their way to the Hit
Factory, John and Yoko pose for the photographer in
front of the Dakota.

In Poole, England, John's aunt Mimi receives an
extravagant gift. She opens the fancy silver box labeled CARTIER to discover an exquisite pearl necklace

and matching brooch. An engraved card reads, "Double Fantasy—Christmas 1980—NYC—John and Yoko."

"You're daft!" Mimi scolds John when she reaches him on the phone at the Dakota.

"Go on, Mimi, spoil yourself," he says, "just for a change."

December 8, 1980

Mark is standing outside the Dakota when he is joined by a familiar face: the woman he met his first day there, Lennon superfan Jude Stein.

"Jeri and I came to meet you the other night," Jude says. "What happened?"

He feels a lie tingling on his lips. But no, he'll tell the truth this time. Keep them guessing.

"I went back to my room and fell asleep." He changes the subject. "We both missed seeing a glimpse of Lennon earlier this morning."

"And you missed seeing John the other night." With great delight, Jude describes her conversation with Lennon.

Mark feels the news wash over him.

It's almost noon, and a crowd is gathering near

the Dakota's entrance, waiting for a chance to see the famous ex-Beatle. A heavyset man with a camera seems annoyed.

"That's Paul Goresh," Jude tells him. "He's some freelance photographer."

Mark doesn't like the looks of him.

The cameraman looks right back. He not so casually wanders into their orbit and introduces himself.

Mark keeps to his practiced story—that he's from Hawaii and here to get Lennon to autograph his album.

"Where are you staying in New York?" Goresh asks.

Why is he interrogating me?

Mark gets in his face. "Why the hell did you ask me that question? What do you want to know that for?"

"Easy, man. Take it easy. I was only making conversation, you know?"

Cool down, he tells himself. *Focus.*

Mark turns to Jude. "Would you like to join me for lunch? It'll be my treat."

They choose a restaurant just one block down from the building—the Dakota Grill. He can keep a close eye on the entrance.

He takes off his hat and his trench coat. The coat holds the gun, so he folds it on his lap.

He orders two beers and a hamburger. Jude has an omelet and coffee.

"I'd love to visit Hawaii," she says. "But it's such a long plane ride and I'm a little scared to fly."

"You can do anything you want if you set your mind to it." Mark flicks his attention back to the Dakota's entrance. "The human mind is an incredible thing. Once it's made up, nothing can stop it from doing what it wants to do."

CHAPTER 60

I've been waiting so long to be where I'm
going...
— "Sunshine of Your Love"

John has a scheduled photo shoot with Annie Leibovitz for the cover of *Rolling Stone* magazine. To
prepare, he visits his local barber and requests a
style reminiscent of the Teddy Boy look he favored
during his teenage years in Liverpool.

When he returns to the Dakota, Sean is there.
John takes a few minutes to watch cartoons with
him in bed.

"D'ya know what I wanna be when I grow up?"
Sean asks, sitting up straight, clutching a soft pillow
in his tiny hands.

"No, what's that?" John asks.

"Just a daddy."

"Ya' mean ya' don't like it that I'm working now,
right, and goin' out a lot?"

"Right," Sean answers.

"Well, I'll tell you something, Sean, it makes me happy to do the music and I might be more fun with ya' if I'm happier, right?"

"Uh-hum." The boy nods.

Annie Leibovitz sets up her camera equipment in John and Yoko's bedroom.

It's a reunion of sorts. Though Leibovitz is now chief photographer for the magazine, she and John had first worked together in 1970, when she was a freelance photographer and he was newly an ex-Beatle. She had persuaded Jann Wenner (who claimed the negatives from the shoot) to book her a student fare from San Francisco to New York. Leibovitz's portrait of John appeared on the cover of the January 21, 1971, issue, which also contained Wenner's first major interview with him.

"Listen, I know they want to run me by myself on the cover, but I really want Yoko to be on the cover with me," John tells her. "It's really important."

Leibovitz tries to promote her boss's mandate, but John is insistent. 'I want to be with *her*.'"

The photographer pivots to another idea—to reprise the nude *Two Virgins* shot that appeared on *Rolling Stone* in 1968.

John agrees to strip down, but not Yoko. She decides to keep her black top and blue jeans on. Leibovitz chronicles the pose as it evolves, moment by moment. John wraps his naked body around his fully clothed wife and kisses her affectionately on the cheek while lying on the carpeted floor next to their bed. Yoko's eyes remain open, contemplative.

"This is it," John exclaims. "This is our relationship."

⬥⬥⬥

"One more, one more," Annie Leibovitz says, turning her camera for a better angle.

John puts on his leather jacket. He's out of time. A radio crew is arriving for an interview.

"Ooh, can I have one with the jacket?" Leibovitz asks.

The shot captures him turning up his collar, launching a determined stare directly into the camera lens.

⬥⬥⬥

RKO radio announcer Dave Sholin and his crew are escorted into Lennon's apartment. They follow house rules and take off their shoes before they begin setting up their recording equipment.

"I hope to God that I die before Yoko," he tells Sholin and his crew. "I don't know what I would do if she left before I did."

Over the next three hours, conversation covers a wide swath of topics. "He was just bubbling over with enthusiasm with everything in his life," Sholin recalls. "He felt like that was it; he had turned the page and was starting another chapter."

"I'm ready to start all over again and get this thing going," John tells them. "Who knows what's going to happen next?"

The late afternoon sun gives way to twilight. John and Yoko depart with the radio crew. It's after 4:00 p.m., and the Dakota is shrouded in darkness.

December 8, 1980

J ude Stein has given up any hope of seeing Lennon today.

"Good luck getting your album signed," she tells Mark.

"You sure you won't have dinner with me?"

"I've gotta go, Mark. Good luck!"

"I plan to stay for as long as it takes."

Mark is now alone with Paul Goresh. The fat cameraman is doing his best to ignore him.

John Lennon emerges from the Dakota. Yoko is with him, along with a small group of people— reporters, Mark thinks. They're all holding cassette recorders.

Mark's heart is pounding, his hand dripping with sweat as he glares at Lennon. The man he's admired and scorned is finally here, just a few feet away, wearing dark sunglasses and a brown bomber jacket over his thin frame.

Mark can't talk.

Can't move.

Goresh is looking at him now. "Hey, man, I thought you wanted your album autographed. What the heck are you waiting for? There he is!"

Lennon and Yoko look past them, out to the street, at the traffic.

They're looking for their limo.

The night watchman moves up next to the famous couple and says, "I'm sorry, but your car hasn't shown up yet."

Lennon glances at his watch, displeased. Then he turns to the bearded man standing next to him and says, "Can we get a lift?"

"We're headed to the airport," the man replies. "You both are welcome to hitch a ride with us."

As the group begins loading their recording gear into the trunk of a car, John and Yoko walk into the street.

Mark follows.

Waves his copy of *Double Fantasy* in Lennon's direction.

Lennon takes the album. Mark offers the Bic pen that he'd used earlier this morning to inscribe *The Catcher in the Rye*.

This is it.

Lennon attempts to sign the album, but the pen won't write.

This is the moment.

Lennon makes a few circles, and finally the ink begins to flow.

History and time, coming together.

Lennon writes "John Lennon, 1980." Mark watches, smiling. Goresh snaps a photo and captures the moment.

Synchronicity.

Mark slips a hand inside his pocket. His gaze flicks to Yoko, and he's reminded of a dream he's had several times, the one where he knocks on the apartment door, and when it opens Yoko smiles at him. She is friendly, happy to see him.

In that moment, he feels loved.

"Is that all?" Lennon asks. "Do you want anything else?"

Mark shakes his head.

John and Yoko climb into the back seat of the car and drive off into the night.

CHAPTER 61

I've looked at life from both sides now...
—"Both Sides Now"

At 4:30 p.m., Jack Douglas is waiting for John and Yoko inside the Hit Factory.

David Geffen arrives with good news. "*Double Fantasy* has just gone gold!" he tells John and Yoko after they show up.

The announcement triggers a round of applause and hugs. For the two weeks since the release, John had been sleepless, worrying about sales for the new album. But achieving gold-album status—five hundred thousand copies sold—returns him to the top of the pop music mountain.

Over and over, they listen to Yoko's master vocal and John's guitar licks and keyboards for "Walking on Thin Ice."

"John, are you all right?" Yoko says, wondering why he's playing the song so many times.

He doesn't answer the question. Instead, he tells his wife, "I think you just cut your first number one!"

John, Yoko, and Douglas make plans to finish mixing the song the next day so that they can release Yoko's new single by Christmas.

At 10:30, John wraps the session.

"Should we stop at Wolf's for a hamburger?" he asks a sound engineer. "If I ate it, it would go right to my knee," he adds, deploying one of his Britishisms to let everyone know how hungry he is.

He'll get dinner with Yoko later.

First, John has a promise to keep. "I want to go home and kiss Sean good night."

December 8, 1980

The security guard's name is Jose Perdomo. Unlike the other Dakota watchmen, Jose, a Cuban refugee who speaks broken English, is friendly and talkative.

They're discussing Fidel Castro, the disastrous Bay of Pigs invasion, and the assassination of John F. Kennedy.

"What would compel Lee Harvey Oswald to shoot the president?" Mark asks.

"I don't know."

The temperature has dipped. Mark tightens the scarf around his neck and shuffles his feet in an attempt to stay warm.

"Do you think Castro had a role in it?"

"Probably," Jose replies. "He has a role in everything."

Mark thinks back to the moment when Lennon signed his album. He had the perfect opportunity to kill him, but something about it didn't feel right.

It makes him question whether he has the strength—the courage—to go through with this.

He feels like the Cowardly Lion in *The Wizard of Oz*.

"It must be incredible seeing a great star like John Lennon all the time," Mark says, eyes on the traffic. "Lennon is probably the most popular person in the world right now. He's like a god or something. I wish I had your job."

Jose nods respectfully.

A black limousine rolls up and stops at a traffic light on the corner.

Mark reaches into his pocket.

Waits.

The light changes from red to green.

The limo takes a wide turn left, heading his way.

Mark feels adrenaline flooding his veins. He's seen other fancy cars carrying Dakota residents like Lauren Bacall and Leonard Bernstein, but he has a strong feeling that Lennon is inside that limo, coming back home.

Coming back to me.

History and time, coming together.

Mark tightly grips the .38 Charter Arms as the limo pulls against the curb. He stands at an angle midway between the building and the street.

Yoko steps out of the car.

Mark is twenty feet away. He tries to get her attention by nodding.

She doesn't nod back.

Lennon gets out of the vehicle and follows after his wife. He turns to Mark and gives him a cold, hard stare.

For some reason it brings to mind the *Wizard of Oz* photograph he left behind on the hotel-room dresser—Dorothy wiping away the tear of the Cowardly Lion.

Lennon walks past him. There is dead calm.

Mark takes five steps toward the street.

Stops.

Turns.

Gets in a combat stance and pulls out his .38 revolver, loaded with hollow-point bullets.

<hr />

John Lennon has his back to him; doesn't see the move or the gun.

At close range, Mark fires.

The sound is loud—and thrilling. He didn't know if the bullets would actually work. He feared one or more of them had been damaged during the flight and would malfunction.

"Help him, help him," Yoko yells. "He's been

shot, he's been shot," she screams. "Somebody come quickly."

Mark pulls the trigger again—hears the loud gunshot and sees Lennon stumble.

They're working, he thinks as he fires shot after shot into Lennon's back and shoulder.

Lennon, incredibly, is still standing. The man stumbles away toward the front steps of the Dakota. He drops several cassettes and collapses inside the doorman's guardhouse.

You won't survive this. You're as good as dead.

Mark stares after him, the gunshot ringing in his ears. He is not the Cowardly Lion. He is no longer Mark David Chapman or ordinary by any human measures. Now he is something other—something transcendent. Eternal. Now, in this moment, he has become the world's most famous celebrity.

Finally, I am known.

Through history and time.

The doorman, Jose Perdomo, rushes him and grabs his arm—the one holding the gun. The .38 falls from Mark's hand. The night watchman kicks it away.

"Do you know what you've done?" Jose asks incredulously, tears streaming down his face. *"Do you know what you've done?"*

"I've just shot John Lennon."

"Just get outta here, man. *Just get outta here!*"

Mark cocks his head to the side, confused. "But where will I go?"

Jose doesn't stick around to answer.

Mark pulls out his paperback copy of *The Catcher in the Rye* from his back pocket and starts to read.

CHAPTER 62

It's just a shot away.
— "Gimme Shelter"

On the Upper West Side of Manhattan, NYPD officer Peter Cullen and his partner, Steve Spiro, are on night patrol. They're parked at the corner of Broadway and 72nd Street when their police radio squawks.

"Shots fired, 1 West 72nd Street."

Cullen and Spiro know the address — the Dakota.

With lights flashing and siren wailing, they race east, toward Central Park.

⁂

From a terrace twenty-two stories above street level, a young girl and her parents are watching and listening. "I heard the gunshots, the first I'd ever heard.

They sounded so much different than on TV. *Crack-crack-crack*...It was the first time I saw my parents both cry at the same time."

⚬⚬⚬

At the Langham, 135 Central Park West, James Taylor hears gunfire.

He leans his head out the window and looks toward the building across the street to the south. He's pretty sure the gunfire came from the Dakota.

⚬⚬⚬

Spiro and Cullen draw their weapons and slowly pass through the archway of the Dakota.

Cullen sees a familiar face. It's Jose Perdomo.

"Jose, what the hell is going on here?"

The security guard points to a doughy man in an overcoat with his nose stuck in a paperback book.

"He shot John Lennon!" Perdomo cries through trembling lips.

Cullen motions his partner to stay with the suspect. Steve Spiro points his gun at the man, who throws his hands up in surrender.

"Don't hurt me," he pleads. "I'm unarmed. Please don't let anyone hurt me."

Spiro grabs the suspect and faces him against the wall, kicking his feet apart.

Cullen enters the Dakota guardhouse, where John is lying facedown. Porter Jay Hastings is ready to apply a tourniquet to John's wounds, but there is little more he can do than remove John's glasses and cover him with his uniform coat.

"It's okay, John, you'll be all right," Hastings whispers. Trickles of blood are beginning to seep from the corners of John's mouth.

Cullen searches the suspect for weapons, and when he's clear, shouts, "Cuff him, Steve!"

Spiro slaps a pair of handcuffs on the suspect's wrists.

The man winces. "I acted alone," he says. "I'm the only one."

A third officer, from the Twentieth Precinct, on West 82nd Street, responds to the call. His name is Tony Palma.

The victim's situation is critical, and there's no time for Palma to make the connection that he's met the wounded man once before, at a coffee shop near the Dakota. There's no time to call an ambulance.

"Like weight lifters," Cullen observes as he and Spiro stay behind with the suspect, Palma and his partner, Herb Frauenberger, carry the bleeding gunshot victim "to a radio car, threw him in the backseat."

December 8, 1980

The police officers' names are Spiro and Cullen. They lead Mark into the street.

"Nobody's gonna hurt you," Spiro tells him. "Just do as you're told."

Mark freezes.

"My book, *my book*!" he says frantically. His life is contained inside those pages.

Cullen reaches down and grabs *The Catcher in the Rye* from the pavement. He hands it to Mark as they put him into the back of the squad car.

He feels safe. And he has his book—his message—to keep him company.

The enormity of what he's done settles on him. The dream is no longer a dream but an unshakable, unalterable reality.

He has gone from unseen to *seen*.

From unknown to *known*.

From nobody to *somebody*.

There will be fan clubs, of course, and psychiatrists. Lots of famous psychiatrists who will all fight for a chance to speak to him, to get in his mind and try to answer the unanswerable question of *why*. He will never provide them with a direct answer. He has to keep them guessing, because once they figure him out, they'll move on to someone else.

That's how the celebrity game is played.

Soon, everyone in this city will be battling one another to get a glimpse of him, the man who killed John Lennon. His name will be all over the papers, all over the news—all over the world—in just a few hours.

Mark takes in a deep breath.

Smiles.

From the corner of his eye he catches movement outside his window. He turns his head slightly to his right, hears some commotion, and then he sees someone crouching, looking at him.

It's Yoko.

She stares at him through the glass.

Mark stares back.

CHAPTER 63

You stole my heart, and that's what really hurts.
— "Maggie May"

Officer Frauenberger lays John Lennon across the back seat of the patrol car, manned by officers Jim Moran and Bill Gamble.

"Are you John Lennon?" Moran asks him.

Lennon nods, his chest soaked with blood.

They pull off the curb and speed the mile between the Dakota and Roosevelt Hospital.

Officer Tony Palma follows close behind. His back-seat passenger is a stunned and silent Yoko.

In the lead car, Moran radios ahead that police are bringing in a gunshot victim.

Third-year general surgery resident Dr. David Halleran is making his rounds when his emergency pager goes off. He runs to trauma room 115.

"I waited for the next few minutes, expecting to see an ambulance pulling in," he recalls in 2019. "Instead, I see a cop car."

Nurse Deartra Sato is part of the team that puts the victim "on a stretcher, pulled him into our minor OR, which was room 115. Then we cut the clothes off and opened his chest."

Halleran tells his team, "Four entry wounds over his left chest, three exit wounds. Either you do nothing or you crack his chest and find something that might be salvageable."

With no blood pressure and no pulse, every moment is critical.

"The patient didn't come in dead; he came in mortally wounded," he explains. "And I had nothing to lose. I was hoping that we could find something that we could repair, fix, or patch until we got him up to the operating room. For me, there was very little downside."

He makes an incision in the left side of the victim's chest and works to separate the ribs to expose the heart. With one hand flat underneath and the other hand over the vital organ, the surgeon squeezes the heart gently and rhythmically at one hundred beats per minute, trying desperately to increase blood flow to the coronary arteries.

It's not working.

A nurse leans over the operating table and is startled to recognize the victim, calling him by name.

"No, it's not," Halleran says while continuing to hold the victim's heart in his hands. "It can't be."

Nurse Sato checks his wallet and finds an ID that verifies his identity.

CHAPTER 64

Tomorrow I'll miss you.
  —"All My Loving"

TV producer Alan Weiss is lying on a gurney in the hallway of the Roosevelt Hospital ER. He's awaiting X-rays following a motorcycle accident he suffered an hour before in Central Park.

"My ears are still ringing from the impact of the road," Weiss later recalls, "and two police officers come out and they are literally standing over my head. I got my eyes closed, and I hear one officer say to the other one, 'Can you believe it? John Lennon.'"

Weiss's mind begins to race. *Did he say John Lennon, my favorite Beatle?*

"At first, I didn't believe it," Weiss explains in a 2019 interview. "I banged my head. My ears were ringing. I wasn't sure I heard it correctly."

Weiss, a recent graduate of Northwestern University's Medill School of Journalism, works in the fast-paced television newsroom at WABC, located in the nearby Lincoln Square neighborhood. He begins peppering passersby with questions, trying to investigate this developing story from the confines of his gurney.

Finally, he slips a janitor some cash, saying, "Here's my press card; here's twenty bucks. Call this number, ask for [assignment editor] Neil [Goldstein], tell him Alan's in the hospital and I believe John Lennon's been shot."

The worker never makes the call, but within minutes Weiss gets powerful confirmation when he sees "Yoko Ono in a full-length fur coat on the arm of a police officer, and she's sobbing."

⁂

In trauma room 115, Dr. David Halleran is working steadily to keep John Lennon alive. Though Halleran's hands are steady, with every pump of the ex-Beatle's heart, his faint vital signs diminish.

Cardiovascular surgeon Dr. Richard Marks steps in to assist. A resident of the Upper West Side, he had returned to the hospital after seeing the commotion at the Dakota. Attending physician Dr. Stephan Lynn, who had left the hospital at 10:30 that night, remembers that he was called to return just before the eleven o'clock news.

With the assistance of a police officer, Weiss gets through to his editor on a hospital telephone. "Neil, I think John Lennon's been shot."

As the doctors work to save John Lennon's life, John's voice can be heard harmonizing around them as the Beatles' "All My Loving" plays over the hospital sound system.

Twenty minutes pass. With every medical intervention "totally ineffective," they have no choice but to declare him dead. "I stepped away from the table at that moment," Halleran remembers. "I felt exhausted and defeated. It was a Hail Mary pass, but I couldn't shake the feeling that we had failed this great man."

It falls to Dr. Lynn, as the director of the Roosevelt Hospital emergency room, to tell Yoko Ono what transpired in the last minutes of her husband's life.

In the emergency thoracotomy, he tells her, "all of the major blood vessels leaving the heart were simply destroyed. There was no way that we could repair them."

"He can't be dead, he was just alive," she says.

At that moment, Dr. Lynn begins to learn "more and more about how much John Lennon affected the rest of the world."

CHAPTER 65

I know a man ain't supposed to cry...
—"I Heard It Through the
Grapevine"

Live from South Florida, ABC is broadcasting the final minutes of a matchup between the New England Patriots and the Miami Dolphins. The game is tied 13–13 in the fourth quarter when the phone rings in the production truck parked outside Miami's Orange Bowl stadium.

"John Lennon has been shot in front of his apartment building and died on the way to the hospital," *Monday Night Football* producer Bob Goodrich is told over the phone by WABC-TV's Neil Goldstein.

Is this the truth? Is this some kind of hoax? Goodrich thinks.

With less than a minute to go on the game clock, the tragedy is communicated to the broadcast booth.

It's manned by NFL greats Fran Tarkenton and Frank Gifford—and legendary announcer Howard Cosell.

Before Cosell breaks into the game with the tragic announcement, the announcer's mind flashes to his 1974 *Monday Night Football* interview with John, when the singer said the rowdiness of an NFL crowd "makes rock concerts look like tea parties."

With three seconds remaining and the Patriots' kicker, an Englishman named John Smith, warming up to attempt a field goal, Cosell begins speaking.

"Remember this is just a football game, no matter who wins or loses," Cosell announces. "An unspeakable tragedy, confirmed to us by ABC News in New York City: John Lennon, outside of his apartment building on the West Side of New York City, the most famous, perhaps, of all of the Beatles, shot twice in the back, rushed to Roosevelt Hospital, dead...on...arrival."

John Smith's kick is blocked.

Geraldo Rivera sits in the living room of his apartment, overlooking Central Park West. From his location on 64th Street, he hears gunshots in the vicinity of the Dakota but is unfazed by the sound.

"There was a lot of crime in that area back in those days, and gunfire wasn't uncommon," he recalls.

His phone rings. Rivera's assignment editor is calling him in to the television studio on West 66th Street. He's to report live, via satellite, on the murder of John Lennon, joining British-born anchor Ted Koppel, who is broadcasting live from Washington.

Geraldo hangs up the phone, fighting off shock as he makes the connection between the shots he heard earlier and the breaking tragedy.

"The most tragic aspect of this terrible thing is the ironic thing about the fact that John Lennon was back; John Lennon, after a five-year absence, was finally back in the studios, had finally released a record album," he tells Koppel on the air. "[He was] one of the cornerstones of one of the most incredible musical units in the history of the planet. Changed the course of rock 'n' roll, changed the course of many of our lives...I'm trying to put my thoughts in order and give them to you in a logical way, but the painful aspect of what's happened has really skewed my reasoning on this."

Decades later, when Rivera recalls that moment with Koppel, he says, "Attempting to put John's life into context in real time was very challenging and extremely emotional. I tried to prevent myself from breaking down and crying, but it was very difficult."

As John Lennon lies wounded and bleeding inside the Dakota, Philip Michael, a maintenance man for the building, stands outside, watching in horror and trying to piece together everything that has happened.

Suddenly, he sees an object in motion. He approaches a decorative stone flower urn sculpted into the building entryway.

What's fallen out is a record—John Lennon's *Double Fantasy* album.

And it's signed.

This belongs to someone, Michael thinks, putting the album back inside the urn.

The damn thing keeps falling out, no matter how many times he replaces it. He decides to take it home with him for safekeeping.

On the way, he hears someone mention that the police are looking for a signed album. It's a piece of evidence from the crime scene. Michael contacts the police and gives them the album.

The following year, after Chapman's trial, Michael fills out paperwork in an effort to have the album returned to him. His request is granted. The district attorney thanks him in writing for turning in this crucial piece of evidence.

The album he gets back is a bit worse for wear. It's

been handled throughout the police investigation. The killer's forensically enhanced fingerprints are visible, as are notations from the crime lab.

He now has in his possession the last autograph John Lennon ever signed.

Michael puts the album away.

"It's the most valuable artifact in rock and roll history," a gallerist later tells the New York *Daily News*.

<hr />

Jay Dubin, the videographer who filmed the *Double Fantasy* sessions, is with his fiancée. They are waiting for a table at a restaurant when the news of John's murder breaks.

"I was just with him," Dubin says to her, stunned.

Later, Dubin realizes there was a cassette player recording the whole session. He puts the audiotape in his closet, eventually digitizing it for safekeeping, but otherwise leaving it be.

If ever he wants to hear John's voice, it will always be near.

<hr />

Jack Douglas is at the Hit Factory continuing work on Yoko's "Walking on Thin Ice." At 11:35 p.m., his wife gets through to him. Though the news she shares plunges Douglas into shock, the producer's sharp mind jumps back to the moment when Yoko, toward the end of the session, asked John what was wrong. Douglas recalls that John was acting strangely, and the producer feels compelled to act. He wipes clean the session tapes dated December 8.

It's after midnight when the chief of Manhattan detectives, Richard Nicastro, sits down with Yoko at the Dakota. With producer David Geffen nearby, the detective tries to question Yoko about the events of the day.

"The shock is too great!" is all she can say. "I can't, I can't do this right now."

CHAPTER 66

All I want is the truth.
      — "Gimme Some Truth"

Officer Tony Palma returns to the Twentieth Precinct.

John Lennon's killer sits in his tiny cell, sweating and clutching his book.

Palma still cannot comprehend what has happened. Can't get the image out of his head from back at the hospital — Yoko, after learning her husband was dead, collapsing and then banging her head repeatedly on the floor.

"Do you realize what you just did?" he asks, shaking his head in disbelief.

"Yeah," Chapman replies with a vacant stare. "I just killed myself. I am John Lennon."

I am John Lennon. The chilling words hit Palma right in the gut.

———— ⊗⊗⊗ ————

Lead homicide detective Ron Hoffman heads back to the Twentieth, where the alleged assassin will be charged with violation of New York penal law 125.10—criminally negligent homicide.

Hoffman looks into the interrogation room where Chapman is seated, wearing a white thermal undershirt. The suspect is refusing a formal interview.

The detective is working from the premise that "Chapman shot John Lennon because he wanted his moment of glory in the sun."

In a city filled with grief-stricken fans, Hoffman has to deal with the reality that his prisoner may himself become a target, "another Jack Ruby."

———— ⊗⊗⊗ ————

Assistant district attorney Kim Hogrefe is assigned the case, which is being treated as a "premeditated execution." Hogrefe must immediately contend with the press. "We felt he was criminally responsible," he says, explaining that Chapman "borrowed a substantial sum of money—of which $2,000 was found on him—for the purpose of coming to New York City to do what he has done."

———— ⊗⊗⊗ ————

At 6:00 a.m., a caller from California gets through to Yoko's office in the Dakota, saying, "I am flying to New York to finish the job Chapman started. I'm going to get Yoko Ono."

CHAPTER 67

The love you take
Is equal to the love you make.
—"The End"

At his country estate in the small village of Peas-marsh, East Sussex, Paul receives a phone call. The words he's hearing make no sense. How can his lifelong friend be gone?

A few minutes later, Linda finds him standing in their driveway. Paul breaks down in her arms.

"I can't take it in," he says.

The lifelong peacemaker takes on the pain the world is feeling. "That was like a really big shock in most people's lives, a bit like Kennedy...For me, it was just so sad that I wasn't going to see him again."

George gives a brief statement saying that he's "shattered and stunned" and that "to rob life is the ultimate robbery." He retreats into his grief.

"Something's happened to John." Ringo and his fiancée, Barbara Bach, are in the Bahamas when Barbara's daughter calls them. Ringo is on hiatus from recording a new album, *Stop and Smell the Roses*. John had offered Ringo two songs for the album, and was scheduled to join Ringo in the studio in January to record "Nobody Told Me." (Neither this nor the other John Lennon song, "Life Begins at 40," winds up on the album.)

"Cyn, I'm so sorry. John's dead." Cynthia Lennon happens to be in London, visiting Ringo's ex-wife, Maureen, when Ringo calls with the awful news.

Cyn immediately thinks of her and John's seventeen-year-old son, Julian, back home in North Wales. Everyone says he's the spitting image of his father. And Cyn knows firsthand what it's like to lose a parent at that age.

It's barely 6 a.m., so Cyn calls her third husband

and asks him to keep the news from Julian until she can make the four-hour drive home.

As soon as Julian wakes, though, and sees all the reporters outside the house, he knows that something terrible has happened to his father.

———

Ringo charters a private plane and flies with Barbara to New York.

"Don't run from them, it will just make it more difficult," advises friend Elliot Mintz as he helps Ringo and Barbara navigate the media swarming the Dakota. But the celebrity photographers don't miss a face as famous as Ringo's.

"I want to do what I can to help," Ringo tells Yoko when they're inside, away from the glare of the cameras.

"Well, you just play with Sean," she tells him. "Keep him busy."

Ringo and Barbara follow the child into his play area, equipped with a trampoline, and spend hours trying to make the little boy smile.

———

Elton John's plane touches down in Melbourne, Australia, but he and his entourage are ordered to stay on board. An eerie feeling comes over him immediately.

Someone's dead.

Elton's manager climbs out of his seat and heads straight to the cockpit to demand answers. Moments later, he returns crying and relays the tragedy.

"I couldn't believe it," Elton John says. "It wasn't just the fact of this death, it was the brutality of how it happened."

Hours after learning of his father's murder, Julian Lennon boards a passenger jet bound for New York.

The press are respectful of the teenager's grief as he departs, but he is unprepared for the mob scene that greets him at the Dakota, where hundreds of mourners have already started to gather to sing his father's songs.

December 9, 1980

Inside the Twentieth Precinct, Mark reads his copy of *The Catcher in the Rye*. He is dressed in the same clothes he wore last night, and he still smells pleasantly of gunpowder.

In the early afternoon, he is given a bullet-proof vest.

He understands its significance. The vest, however, won't protect him from a head shot. There could be one or more snipers waiting for him outside.

It's not out of the realm of possibility. People in this city are crazy.

After he slips on the vest, he is handcuffed and led through a phalanx of armed cops. The faces watching him are not friendly.

The police, he knows, are openly calling him a

wacko in the press. Others are quoted as saying he is a "loner" who "had a screw loose."

They put a jacket over his head and lead him outside, into a riot of howls, rage, and raised voices that drill into his ears. The cops escorting him dig their fingers deeper into his arms. Eyes on the ground, he sways back and forth as police around him push forward, through the crush of media. Flashbulbs go off like machine-gun fire. TV cameras, he's sure, are everywhere.

People scream "killer" and "monster" and "loser."

Someone yells, "I hope you rot in hell!"

Another: "I'm going to kill you, Chapman!"

Closer is another set of voices that belong to reporters shouting questions they hope he'll answer so that they, too, can get the inside scoop and become famous.

Everyone here is shouting his name.

Everyone on the planet now knows who he is. Like John Lennon and Jesus Christ, he has done what few people in this world are able to do.

He has left his mark. He will be remembered. Always and forever. Eternal.

He smiles underneath the jacket.

He is treated to the same grand reception at the courthouse. Inside, he is ushered into a soundproof pen to meet his court-appointed lawyer.

His name is Herbert Adlerberg. He has represented

highly unpopular defendants in high-profile cases before, including members of the Black Liberation Army, who were accused of terrorism and murdering police officers in the early 1970s, and the Harlem Six, a group of youths charged in a race-fueled double murder in 1964.

The courtroom is absolutely packed. Every single person is looking at him. Pens are scribbling furiously across notepads. Blinking back tears of joy, he takes a seat next to his lawyer.

Adlerberg asks to have him committed to a mental hospital. Assistant district attorney Kim Hogrefe asks that he be held without bail and sent to Rikers Island.

"He committed a deliberate, premeditated execution of John Lennon," Hogrefe tells the court, "and acted in a cool, calm, and calculated manner in killing Mr. Lennon by shooting him several times with a .38-caliber pistol."

Adlerberg tells Judge Martin Rettinger that he, Mark David Chapman, twice tried to kill himself.

The judge consents to Adlerberg's request. Mark is sent to Bellevue Hospital for psychological examination.

The psychiatrist at the hospital, Dr. Naomi Goldstein, seems pleasant enough.

They talk. A lot.

It's so interesting to have people not only listen to

him but also hang on his every word, analyzing its significance, weighing its importance.

He knows they're trying to decide whether he's sane.

Shortly thereafter, Mark is told that his attorney has decided to quit. Apparently, Adlerberg has received many death threats. Several promise to have him lynched.

His new lawyer, Jonathan Marks, can stomach fear. Most important, the man lusts for the limelight.

He'll do just fine.

Mark begins to confide in his attorney. The young Harvard Law School graduate and former assistant US attorney in Brooklyn listens intently.

There are reports that grieving Lennon fans are planning to storm Bellevue. The hospital can't protect him, so he's transferred to Rikers Island. He refuses to eat, fearing he'll be poisoned. The windows in his room are painted black. The prison is worried about snipers.

Alone in his cell, he thinks strategy.

"People are always eager to move on to the next bright, shiny object."

That won't be the case with me. I'm going to shine on, like the moon and the stars and the sun.

CHAPTER 68

Hey, kid, rock and roll
Rock on.
    — "Rock On"

On Yoko's orders, security expert Doug Mac-
Dougall has taken charge of John's remains. To
confuse the press, the bodyguard has deployed
multiple decoy hearses from a funeral chapel on Madison Avenue. He brings John's body to the crematory
at Ferncliff Cemetery, in Hartsdale, New York, without being followed.

Under cover of darkness, MacDougall returns to
Studio One, carrying a large box wrapped with a
big bow.

"What's that?" John's assistant, Fred Seaman, asks.

"That," the bodyguard replies, "was the greatest
rock musician in the world."

Sean's runny nose has spiked into a fever, and he's been recovering in his bedroom. Yoko hasn't been able to leave her room for days, so she sends the nanny to bring the boy to her.

"Why's Julian here? Where's Dad?" he's been asking. Sean approaches Yoko's bed, which is strewn with blankets and newspapers. At five years old, he's just learning to read, but he sees the letters *l-e-n-n-o-n* repeated over and over.

"Your dad's dead," Yoko tells him. "He's been killed." She doesn't soften the truth.

"Don't worry, Mom," Sean says with age-defying wisdom. "You're still young. You'll find somebody."

"Well, I'm glad you feel that way about it," she says.

The pressure Sean's feeling is too much. He runs to his room and cries.

<hr>

"There is no funeral for John," Yoko announces. "John loved and prayed for the human race. Please do the same for him."

She scatters his ashes in a spot in Central Park that can be viewed from their apartment.

"Maybe he is watching me from above," Julian reflects. "It would be nice if he was. I guess I'll find out someday."

Before dawn on Sunday, December 14, the first

mourners begin to gather in Central Park for the silent vigil scheduled for 2:00 p.m. At that hour, one hundred thousand people stand with their heads bowed. The only sounds are the buzzing of news helicopters and the flapping of American flags lowered to half-staff.

On a white poster board, one man has sandwiched a youthful photo of Lennon between two peace signs. The hand-lettered sign pleads, WHY?

Mourners begin to disperse, spreading a trail of flowers in their wake. "The dream is over," they sing, repeating the chorus from "God," the song that climaxes John's emotionally raw first solo album.

"Now Daddy is part of God," Sean tells his mother. "I guess when you die you become much bigger because you're part of everything."

August 24, 1981

Life has been good to him these past eight months. Wonderful, in fact. He has never slept better in his entire life.

The psychiatrists retained by both sides can't figure him out. They give conflicting reports, with defense experts declaring him to be mentally unfit and government experts rejecting his insanity claims. He is diagnosed by one defense doctor as a paranoid schizophrenic.

It's all quite entertaining.

Prosecuting attorneys Kim Hogrefe and Allen Sullivan believe he is a coldhearted, calculated killer. Key to their case is the fact that he bought the gun in Hawaii, made multiple trips to New York, had the presence of mind to fly to Atlanta to buy bullets, and knew to smuggle the gun in his luggage so it would not be found.

"If he was obsessed with anything, it was bringing attention to himself," Hogrefe has said. "He was narcissistic, he was grandiose. He wanted to bring attention to himself. The fact that John Lennon was the victim here was simply because John Lennon was available, publicly available, and others were not."

Mark has an epiphany one night while sitting in a lounge at Rikers Island, watching a movie called *The Bunker*. It's about the last days of Hitler. He talks about the movie with his defense attorney's cocounselor, David Suggs.

"It's quite amazing, when you think about it," Mark says.

"I'm not following."

"Hitler. Look at what he was facing, and yet he did not give up his principles and his ideas." Mark smiles. "And then it hit me, like a joyful thing, that I was called out for a special purpose, to promote the reading of the book."

Mark pens a letter to the *New York Times*. "It is my sincere belief that this written statement will not only stimulate the reading of J. D. Salinger's *The Catcher in the Rye,* but will also help many to understand what has happened."

A trial will bring lots of attention from around the world. He imagines people holding the book, waving and laughing and cheering. He shares his promotional plans with Bantam, the publisher of the paperback edition—and with psychiatrists.

"Everyone will read *The Catcher in the Rye*," he tells one psychiatrist. "*The Catcher in the Rye* will become the No. 1 best-seller and will probably become one of the biggest motion pictures in the history of literature."

He has the guards check the stock in bookstores. Some bring copies for him to sign. He signs them all the same way: "Mark Chapman, the Catcher in the Rye."

Two weeks before the date set for his trial, he tears up his copy of *The Catcher in the Rye* and tells his lawyer that he has changed his mind about an insanity plea.

On June 22, inside a closed courtroom and against his attorney's advice, he pleads guilty. He arrived at this decision, he explains, because he received a message from God.

The judge allows Assistant DA Sullivan to question him.

"This is your own decision?"

"It is my decision," Mark replies, "and God's decision."

Mr. Sullivan has more questions—about voices, prayer, and religion. Mark plays along accordingly.

"Why do you use hollow-point bullets?" Sullivan asks.

"To ensure Lennon's death."

Back at prison, he refuses to see anyone, including Gloria, who has traveled all the way from Hawaii for the trial. He shaves his head and tears up his Bible and stuffs the pages into his toilet. He destroys a radio and a TV. He jumps around his cell, manic, and screams at everyone that they're going to hell.

That he's possessed by a demon.

It's all reported vividly in the papers and on the news.

Now it's time to receive his sentence.

On the morning of August 24, he puts on his bullet-proof vest and dresses for court. The turnout, he keeps hearing, will be like nothing the world has ever seen.

It's going to be a beautiful day.

"Is there anything you'd like to say?" Judge Dennis Edwards Jr. asks him in court.

He pulls out a copy of *The Catcher in the Rye* and reads a section—a quotation from the main character, Holden Caulfield.

"Anyway, I keep picturing all these little kids playing some game in this big field of rye and all," Mark says, his heart swelling. "Thousands of little kids, and nobody's around—nobody big, I mean—except me. And I'm standing on the edge of some crazy cliff. What I have to do, I have to catch everybody if they start to go over the cliff—I mean if they're running and they don't look where they're going I have to come out from somewhere and *catch* them. That's all I'd do all day. I'd just be the catcher in the rye and all. I know it's crazy, but that's the only thing I'd really like to be."

Mark knows they don't understand the passage, don't understand him—how, like John Lennon, he has become this generation's voice, the one to speak out about phoniness and corruption. They lack the ability to understand, and he can't be angry at them. They lack his superior intelligence.

Judge Edwards says he must serve a minimum of twenty years. After that, he is eligible for parole.

What follows next is testimony regarding his mental state. He tunes it out, has nothing more to say.

He has promised never to speak again.

He is taken to a maximum-security cell.

He sits on his new bed. Closing his eyes, he takes in a deep breath.

Here, he will be protected from the ugliness of the outside world. People will bring him food. Books. He'll have all the time he could ever want to read, watch TV. To think.

It's wonderful.

The cell door slides shut and locks.

Mark David Chapman smiles.

I'm home.

NOTES

PROLOGUE

vii *Well, if you get a .22*: Jack Jones, *Let Me Take You Down: Inside the Mind of Mark David Chapman, the Man Who Killed John Lennon* (New thYork: Villard Books, 1992), 192.

vii The safest way to transport: Associated Press, "How John Lennon's Killer Mark David Chapman Brought Legal Gun to NY 35 Years Ago," Syracuse.com, December 8, 2015.

ix his thoughts turning to the five bullets: In this scene and others without available firsthand accounts, the reflections or words of Mark David Chapman and the people he interacts with have been reconstructed based on available third-party sources and interviews.

ix changes in air pressure: E. R. Shipp, "Chapman Given 20 Years in Lennon Slaying," *New York Times,* August 25, 1981.

ix "I'm a recording engineer": James R. Gaines, "Descent into Madness," *People,* June 22, 1981.

ix "I'm working with John Lennon and Paul McCartney": Gaines, "Descent into Madness."

x bag of coke: Gaines, "Descent into Madness."

x "But I'd plug him anyway": Gaines, "Descent into Madness."

xi "I'm Mark Chapman": Gaines, "Descent into Madness."

CHAPTER 1

1   "a great fellow": Philip Norman, *John Lennon: The Life* (New York: Ecco, 2008), 103.

3   "You lose a mother—and you find a guitar?": Hunter Davies, *The Beatles: The Authorized Biography* (New York: McGraw-Hill, 1968), 28.

3   *If you can sing or play an instrument*: Editors of *People, The Beatles: Celebrating Beatlemania, America 1964* (New York: Time Home Entertainment, 2019), 28.

4   *a fat schoolboy*: Norman, *John Lennon,* 108.

4   "Like I'm writing an essay or doing a crossword puzzle": Robin Hilton and Bob Boilen, "All Songs +1: A Conversation with Paul McCartney," *All Songs Considered,* NPR.org, June 10, 2016.

4   *He's drunk*: Barry Miles, *The Beatles Diary Volume 1: The Beatles Years* (London: Omnibus Press, 2001), 11.

4   *He'll get you into trouble, son*: Barry Miles, *Paul McCartney: Many Years from Now* (New York: Henry Holt, 1997), 32.

4   *You saw him rather than met him*: Editors of *People, The Beatles*, 28.

CHAPTER 2

5   "We never get auditions because of the jazz bands": Hunter Davies, *The Beatles: The Authorized Biography* (New York: McGraw-Hill, 1968), 60.

6   Bill Haley and His Comets: "The Startling Blast of 'Rock Around the Clock,' Sixty Years Later," David Cantwell, *The New Yorker,* July 27, 2015.

7   "A guitar's all right, John, but you'll never earn a living by it": Warren Hoge, "Liverpool Journal; The House That Can't Forget a Boy with a Guitar," *New York Times,* May 6, 2003.

7   "I wanted to write *Alice in Wonderland* and be Elvis Presley":
     Ray Connolly, *Being John Lennon: A Restless Life* (New York:
     Pegasus Books, 2018), 31.

7   *you'll regret it when I'm famous*: Philip Norman, *John Lennon:
     The Life* (New York: Ecco, 2008), 67.

7   gingery hair: Mark Lewisohn, *Tune In*, vol. 1, *The Beatles: All
     These Years* (New York: Crown Archetype, 2013), 181.

7   "It went through my head that I'd have to keep him in
     line": Connolly, *Being John Lennon*, 39.

8   "They'll eat you alive if you start playing rock 'n' roll in the
     Cavern!": Bob Spitz, *The Beatles: The Biography* (New York:
     Back Bay, 2006), 65.

8   *Cut out the bloody rock 'n' roll*: Spitz, *The Beatles*, 65.

8   New Clubmoor Hall: Lewisohn, *Tune In*, 144–45.

9   "It wiped me out as a lead guitar player": Paul McCartney,
     interview by Roger Scott, Capital Radio (London), November 17, 1983.

9   "John, your little friend's here": Barry Miles, *Paul McCartney:
     Many Years from Now* (New York: Henry Holt, 1997), 44.

9   "John and Mimi had a very special relationship": Lewisohn,
     Tune In, 14.

10   "I think she quite liked me": Lewisohn, *Tune In*, 14.

10   "taking the mickey": Philip Norman, *Paul McCartney: The
     Life* (New York: Little, Brown, 2016), 74.

10   *drawing gorgeous girls for toothpaste posters*: Lewisohn, *Tune
     In*, 137.

10   "Front porch, John Lennon, front porch": Norman, *Paul
     McCartney*, 82.

10   "the echo of the guitars": Barry Miles, *The Beatles Diary Volume
     1: The Beatles Years* (London: Omnibus Press, 2001), 12.

11   Paul Anka used in his hit "Diana": Austin O'Connor, "10
     Things You May Not Know About Paul Anka," *AARP*,
     April 17, 2013.

CHAPTER 3

12   *Face up to your dad!*: Mark Lewisohn, *Tune In,* vol. 1, *The Beatles: All These Years* (New York: Crown Archetype, 2013), 149.

14   "Can you give me guitar lessons?": Lewisohn, *Tune In,* 14.

CHAPTER 4

15   "holding a mirror up": Philip Norman, *Paul McCartney: The Life* (New York: Little, Brown, 2016), 83.

15   "I was aggressive because I wanted to be popular": Hunter Davies, *The Beatles: The Authorized Biography* (New York: McGraw-Hill, 1968), 13.

16   "eyeball to eyeball": Mark Lewisohn, *Tune In,* vol. 1, *The Beatles: All These Years* (New York: Crown Archetype, 2013), 11.

17   "I'd either sit down with a guitar or at the piano": Robin Hilton and Bob Boilen, "All Songs +1: A Conversation with Paul McCartney," *All Songs Considered,* NPR.org, June 10, 2016.

17   "I've got a mate who can play 'Raunchy'": Lewisohn, *Tune In,* 150.

18   Little George is *cool*: Lewisohn, *Tune In,* 158.

18   "Cocky": Lewisohn, *Tune In,* 158.

18   "George was just too young": The Beatles, *The Beatles Anthology* (San Francisco: Chronicle Books, 2000), 13.

18   "I didn't dig him on first sight": Hunter Davies, *The Beatles: The Authorized Biography* (New York: McGraw-Hill, 1968), 158.

18   "George looked even younger than Paul": Ray Connolly, *Being John Lennon: A Restless Life* (New York: Pegasus Books, 2018), 52.

18   the Eddie Clayton Skiffle Group: Lewisohn, *Tune In,* 157.

18   "John said if I could play like that, I could join them": Davies, *The Beatles,* 44.

18   "Go on, George, show him!": Lewisohn, *Tune In,* 158.

18   "I played 'Ranchee' [sic] for them": Davies, *The Beatles,* 44.

18   "knew more chords, a lot more": Connolly, *Being John Lennon,* 52.

19   "Now there were three of us": Davies, *The Beatles,* 45.

CHAPTER 5

21   "Are you Julia Dykins's son?": Mark Lewisohn, *Tune In,* vol. 1, *The Beatles: All These Years* (New York: Crown Archetype, 2013), 182.

21   *We'd caught up so much, me and Julia*: Hunter Davies, *The Beatles: The Authorized Biography* (New York: McGraw-Hill, 1968), 52.

22   Mimi looks at Clague and shouts, "Killer!": Ray Connolly, *Being John Lennon: A Restless Life* (New York: Pegasus Books, 2018), 61.

23   only $16.50 a night: Pete Hamill, "The Death and Life of John Lennon," *New York,* March 18, 2008.

23   Mr. Lennon was "out of town": Keith Badman, *The Beatles Diary Volume 2: After the Break-Up, 1970–2001* (London: Omnibus Press, 2001), 267.

24   *I'm coming home*: CNN Special Report: Killing John Lennon, CNN.com, December 8, 2015.

24   *Come home*: James McMahon, "The Shooting of John Lennon: Will Mark David Chapman Ever Be Released?" *The Independent,* March 2, 2020.

24   a .38-caliber Charter Arms: Bill Prochnau, "A Strange Young Man Who Stopped the Music," *Washington Post,* December 10, 1980.

26   *He told us to imagine no possessions*: McMahon, "The Shooting of John Lennon."

26   Lennon admitted as much: Olivia B. Waxman, "Behind the Photo: How John Lennon and Yoko Ono Came Up with the Idea of Their Bed-In for Peace," *Time,* March 25, 2019.

27   signed out as "John Lennon": McMahon, "The Shooting of John Lennon."

27   Practices withdrawing the weapon: McMahon, "The Shooting of John Lennon."

27   "Mr. Lennon?": Badman, *The Beatles Diary,* 272.

28   his cop friend, Dana: Jack Jones, *Let Me Take You Down: Inside the Mind of Mark David Chapman, the Man Who Killed John Lennon* (New York: Villard Books, 1992), 197–98.

CHAPTER 6

29   Jacaranda Club: Mark Lewisohn, *Tune In,* vol. 1, *The Beatles: All These Years* (New York: Crown Archetype: 2013), 225–26.

29   "why don't you do something for us?": Lewisohn, *Tune In,* 299.

30   John's inspiration comes from the Crickets, Buddy Holly's band: Lewisohn, *Tune In,* 292.

30   "What's your group's lineup?": Lewisohn, *Tune In,* 299.

30   painted the murals in the basement: Michael Braun, *"Love Me Do!": The Beatles' Progress* (Los Angeles and New York: Graymalkin Media, 2019), 71–72.

30   a Hofner 333 four-string bass: Lewisohn, *Tune In,* 276.

30   "looks so cool": Ryan Steadman, "One of These Beatles Could've Been the Next Jackson Pollock (No, Not Pete Best)," *The Observer,* January 13, 2016.

30   "Who's the drummer?": Lewisohn, *Tune In,* 299.

30   Tommy Moore: Lewisohn, *Tune In,* 299–300, 307.

31   Paul purchased an Elpico amplifier: Lewisohn, *Tune In,* 308.

31   "If you want it": Lewisohn, *Tune In,* 218.

31   Long John and the Silver Beatles: Lewisohn, *Tune In,* 300–301.

31   "doing a moody": Lewisohn, *Tune In,* 301.

32   "Because I wear three rings": Lewisohn, *Tune In,* 233.

32   "He looked like a tough guy": Philip Norman, *Paul McCartney: The Life* (New York: Little, Brown, 2016), 118.

CHAPTER 7

33   quiet and relaxed: Mark Lewisohn, *Tune In,* vol. 1, *The Beatles: All These Years* (New York: Crown Archetype, 2013), 310.

33   "We were crummy, horrible": The Beatles, *The Beatles Anthology* (San Francisco: Chronicle Books, 2000), 44.

34   "They're a scruffy no-good group": Lewisohn, *Tune In,* 309.

34   "fine up to the middle-eight": Lewisohn, *Tune In,* 312.

34   sleep in the van: Lewisohn, *Tune In,* 311.

34   "a vital experience for us": *The Beatles in Scotland,* BBC Radio 2, September 24, 1996.

34   "Don't bother coming back next September": Lewisohn, *Tune In,* 334; originally from interview by Lisa Robinson, September 29, 1980.

34   John's future is blacker than ever: Lewisohn, *Tune In,* 334.

35   Allan Williams comes to them a week later: Lewisohn, *Tune In,* 334.

35   No drummer: Allan Kozinn, "Allan Williams, First Manager of the Beatles, Dies at 86," *New York Times,* December 31, 2016.

35   "He's got his own drum kit": Hunter Davies, *The Beatles:*

The Authorized Biography (New York: McGraw-Hill, 1968), 70.

35   "keep one beat going for long enough": Ray Connolly, *Being John Lennon: A Restless Life* (New York: Pegasus Books, 2018), 84.

CHAPTER 8

36   ferry from Harwich to the Hook of Holland: Hunter Davies, *The Beatles: The Authorized Biography* (New York: McGraw-Hill, 1968), 75–76.

36   the Bambi porno theater: Mark Lewisohn, *Tune In,* vol. 1, *The Beatles: All These Years* (New York: Crown Archetype, 2013), 352.

36   "a pigsty…a run down fleapit": Ray Connolly, *Being John Lennon: A Restless Life* (New York: Pegasus Books, 2018), 86.

36   Bruno Koschmider: "The Beatles' First Performance in Hamburg," BeatlesBible.com.

37   "We kept that big heavy four-in-a-bar going all night long": Connolly, *Being John Lennon,* 88.

37   204 stage hours: Lewisohn, *Tune In,* 366.

37   "Your voice began to hurt with the pain of singing": Davies, *The Beatles,* 78.

37   "Hamburg throat": Lewisohn, *Tune In,* 362.

37   "keep it up for twelve hours at a time": Davies, *The Beatles,* 93.

37   "We were the best bloody band there was": Connolly, *Being John Lennon,*143.

38   "Where are we going, fellers?": David Sheff, "*Playboy* Interview with John Lennon and Yoko Ono," *Playboy,* January 1981.

CHAPTER 9

39   "Our band would be great": Mark Lewisohn, *Tune In,* vol. 1, *The Beatles: All These Years* (New York: Crown Archetype, 2013), 375.

40   a bit peeved: Lewisohn, *Tune In,* 374.

40   "The guy really couldn't play bass to save his life," Lewisohn, *Tune In,* 375.

40   "looked the nasty one": Hunter Davies, *The Beatles: The Authorized Biography* (New York: McGraw-Hill, 1968), 86 (79).

40   "We liked his style": John Lennon, interview by Malcolm Searle, Melbourne, June 14, 1964, quoted in Lewisohn, *Tune In,* 381.

41   teaching his guitar part to John: "George Harrison Is Deported from Germany," BeatlesBible.com.

41   "I felt terrible": Davies, *The Beatles, 92.*

42   picked up by the police: Philip Norman, *Paul McCartney: The Life* (New York: Little, Brown, 2016), 123.

42   *Is this what I want to do? Is this it?*: John Lennon, interview by Elliot Mintz, January 1, 1976, quoted in Lewisohn, *Tune In,* 387.

CHAPTER 10

43   Tony Sheridan and the Beat Brothers: Philip Norman, *John Lennon: The Life* (New York: Ecco, 2008), 239–40.

43   proudly play the "My Bonnie" single: Lewisohn, *Tune In,* 544.

44   "lumbered": Ray Connolly, *Being John Lennon: A Restless Life* (New York: Pegasus Books, 2018), 107.

44   "I wasn't too keen on reaching twenty-one": Connolly, *Being John Lennon,* 109.

44   *I'm too old. I've missed the boat*: Lewisohn, *Tune In,* 562.

44   *I'm gonna make it*: Lewisohn, *Tune In,* 469.

44   'The Singing Rage'!: Lewisohn, *Tune In,* 496.

45   "keeping a watch on the crotch": Lewisohn, *Tune In,* 499.

45   hand over groceries and instructions: Philip Norman, *Paul McCartney: The Life* (New York: Little, Brown, 2016), 131.

45   "some very posh rich feller": The Beatles, *The Beatles Anthology* (San Francisco: Chronicle Books, 2000), 65.

46   "signed all sorts of contracts when we were about eighteen": Lewisohn, *Tune In,* 450.

46   "It seems to me with everything going on, someone ought to be looking after you": Bob Spitz, *The Beatles: The Biography* (New York: Back Bay, 2006), 272.

46   "75p each per night": Brian Epstein, *A Cellarful of Noise* (London: Souvenir Press, 1964; reprinted New York: Pocket Books, 1998), 103.

46   "I could at least secure a decent rate for their performance": Epstein, *A Cellarful of Noise,* 104.

46   Paul isn't that keen on Brian: Lewisohn, *Tune In,* 513.

46   "a good flair": Barry Miles, *Paul McCartney: Many Years from Now* (New York: Henry Holt, 1997), 96.

47   "imagine you're like on a cliff-top and you're thinking about diving off": Lewisohn, *Tune In,* 513.

47   "star quality": Laura Snapes, "The Beatles' First Contract with Manager Brian Epstein Sells for £275k," *The Guardian,* July 10, 2019.

47   "You're going to be bigger than Elvis, you know": Michael Braun, *"Love Me Do!": The Beatles' Progress* (Los Angeles and New York: Graymalkin Media, 2019), 55.

47   "This is where Brian was good. He knew how to get it happening": George Harrison, *I, Me, Mine* (San Francisco: Chronicle Books, 2002), 33; quoted in Lewisohn, *Tune In,* 514.

48   "We were in a daydream till he came along": Lewisohn, *Tune In,* 637.

48   "Manage us": Norman, *Paul McCartney*, 142.

CHAPTER 11

49   "My little bit to get you all on in time": Mark Lewisohn, *Tune In,* vol. 1, *The Beatles: All These Years* (New York: Crown Archetype: 2013), 530.

50   "it felt *complete*": Lewisohn, *Tune In,* 530.

50   "If I get a huge offer, they won't take you in leather": The Beatles, *The Beatles Anthology* (San Francisco: Chronicle Books, 2000), 73.

51   "I'll wear a fucking *balloon* if somebody's going to pay me!": John Lennon, interview by Lisa Robinson, *Hit Parader,* December 1975, quoted in Lewisohn, *Tune In,* 554.

51   "It was a bit old-hat anyway, all wearing leather gear": Paul McCartney, interview for *The Mersey Sound,* August 28, 1963, quoted in Lewisohn, *Tune In,* 553.

51   "I just saw it as playing a game": Lewisohn, *Tune In,* 554.

51   "stop eating onstage, stop swearing, stop smoking": Lewisohn, *Tune In,* 552.

51   "Brian was trying to clean our image up": Ray Connolly, *Being John Lennon: A Restless Life* (New York: Pegasus Books, 2018), 115.

51   "they wanted their trousers *extremely* narrow": Lewisohn, *Tune In,* 555.

52   "Ha-ha, John Lennon, no more scruffs for you": Connolly, *Being John Lennon,* 115.

52   "Groups of four guitarists are on the way out": Brian Epstein, *A Cellarful of Noise* (London: Souvenir Press, 1964; reprinted New York: Pocket Books, 1998), 108.

52   "These boys are going to explode": Lewisohn, *Tune In,* 558.

52   "The boys won't go, Mr. Epstein. We know these things": Epstein, *A Cellarful of Noise,* 110.

53   "Do you know Tony Meehan?": "Tony Meehan," *The Telegraph,* November 30, 2005.

53   "firsthand experience of what the teenagers want": *Melody Maker,* December 9, 1961, quoted in Lewisohn, *Tune In,* 559.

53   "the Group have received an offer of a recording Contract from another Company": Lewisohn, *Tune In,* 560.

53   "It was just a complete mess, as things generally are—a dreadful corporate blunder": Lewisohn, *Tune In,* 561.

CHAPTER 12

54   "I hope he kicks himself to death": Michael Braun, *"Love Me Do!": The Beatles' Progress* (Los Angeles and New York: Graymalkin Media, 2019), 35.

54   "I think Decca expected us to be all polished": Hunter Davies, *The Beatles: The Authorized Biography* (New York: McGraw-Hill, 1968), 132.

54   "We didn't sound natural": Braun, *"Love Me Do!,"* 60.

55   "John was always a little bit sarcastic": "Beatles' Photographer Astrid Kirchherr Opens Up," *Fresh Air,* NPR.org, January 15, 2008.

55   "Pete couldn't have the hairstyle anyway because he had curly hair": "Beatles' Photographer Astrid Kirchherr Opens Up."

56   "The Beatles were the stuff that screams were made of": Davies, *The Beatles,* 94.

56   the best FM: Mark Lewisohn, *Tune In,* vol. 1, *The Beatles: All These Years* (New York: Crown Archetype: 2013), 581.

56   "We weren't just recording stars": Lewisohn, *Tune In,* 582.

CHAPTER 13

57   "as the name Beatles doesn't mean anything they'll have to change it": Mark Lewisohn, *Tune In,* vol. 1, *The Beatles: All These Years* (New York: Crown Archetype: 2013), 590.

57   "the shorter the name the bigger the print": Lewisohn, *Tune In,* 590.

57   "It was *Us against Them*": Hunter Davies, *The Beatles: The Authorized Biography* (New York: McGraw-Hill, 1968), 137.

58   "What are we going to do?": Lewisohn, *Tune In,* 591.

58   "Hello, where's Stu?": Ray Connolly, *Being John Lennon: A Restless Life* (New York: Pegasus Books, 2018), 125.

58   "saying 'No, no, no!' and lashing out with his hands": Philip Norman, *John Lennon: The Life* (New York: Ecco, 2008), 263.

58   "Paul tried to be comforting": Lewisohn, *Tune In,* 603.

59   "sitting on a bench, huddled over": Lewisohn, *Tune In,* 603.

59   "Not many of our contemporaries had died": The Beatles, *The Beatles Anthology* (San Francisco: Chronicle Books, 2000), 69.

59   John and the boys remain in Hamburg: Davies, *The Beatles*, 111.

59   "Could you take a picture of me there?": Lewisohn, *Tune In,* 617.

59   "a little lonely feller": Lewisohn, *Tune In,* 617.

59   "so much strength in his face": Lewisohn, *Tune In,* 617.

60   "I depended on him to tell me the truth": The Beatles, *The Beatles Anthology*, 69.

60   "people he loved the most always left him": Norman, *John Lennon,* 269.

60   "You can't just cry all the time, you've got to *get on*": Lewisohn, *Tune In,* 618.

60   "so many pills that he literally wouldn't be able to shut his eyes": Philip Norman, *Paul McCartney: The Life* (New York: Little, Brown, 2016), 155.

61   "John came onstage dressed like a cleaning-woman": Lewisohn, *Tune In,* 608.

61   "It gave me shivers to watch it": Lewisohn, *Tune In,* 608.

61   **CONGRATULATIONS BOYS**: Connolly, *Being John Lennon,* 128.

CHAPTER 14

63   "It was like *heaven,* where the great gods live": Mark Lewisohn, *Tune In,* vol. 1, *The Beatles: All These Years* (New York: Crown Archetype, 2013), 641.

63   "None of us really knows how to read or write music": Al Aronowitz, "Beatlemania in 1964: 'This Has Gotten Entirely Out of Control,'" *Saturday Evening Post,* March 1964; reprinted in *The Guardian,* January 29, 2014.

64   "not all that impressed": Lewisohn, *Tune In,* 643.

64   "pick up George from the canteen": Lewisohn, *Tune In,* 643.

64   "That was how my mind was working at the beginning": Hunter Davies, *The Beatles: The Authorized Biography* (New York: McGraw-Hill, 1968), 161.

65   "a load of noise, hum, and goodness-knows-what": "Recording: Besame Mucho, Love Me Do, PS I Love You, Ask Me Why—The Beatles' first Abbey Road Recording Session," BeatlesBible.com.

65   "you're going to have a song called Love Me *Waahhh*": Lewisohn, *Tune In,* 644.

66   puts aside his electric guitar and picks up an acoustic: Geoff Emerick and Howard Massey, *Here, There and Everywhere: My Life Recording the Music of the Beatles* (New York: Gotham Books, 2006), 45.

66   *Everything stopped, no backing*: Lewisohn, *Tune In*, 644.

66   "Well that was twenty minutes of torture": Lewisohn, *Tune In*, 645.

66   "We've got to change this drummer": Lewisohn, *Tune In*, 643.

67   "He was giving them a good talking to": Lewisohn, *Tune In*, 645.

67   "They didn't say a word back, not a word": Lewisohn, *Tune In*, 645.

67   "Well, for a start, I don't like your tie": Mark Savage, "When George Martin Met the Beatles: The Story of Love Me Do," BBC, March 9, 2016.

67   "Phew! What do you think of that lot then?": Lewisohn, *Tune In*, 645.

67   "it wasn't their music, it was their charisma": Lewisohn, *Tune In*, 645–46.

CHAPTER 15

69   "unable to deal with the emotional side of that": Mark Lewisohn, *Tune In*, vol. 1, *The Beatles: All These Years* (New York: Crown Archetype, 2013), 651.

69   keep Pete: Lewisohn, *Tune In*, 651.

69   "Paul was showing Pete the drum pattern he wanted": Bob Spitz, *The Beatles: The Biography* (New York: Back Bay, 2006), 326.

70   "Pete was holding us back": Paul McCartney, interview by Tony Fletcher, *Jamming* 14 (1983), quoted in Lewisohn, *Tune In*, 651.

70   "We want Pete out and Ringo in": Brian Epstein, *A Cellarful of Noise* (London: Souvenir Press, 1964; reprinted New York: Pocket Books, 1998), 126.

70   "I knew the Beatles were gonna go places": Lewisohn, *Tune In*, 674.

71   "they weren't at the dismissal": Lewisohn, *Tune In,* 674.

71   "To be so *aware,* with so little education": Michael Braun, *"Love Me Do!": The Beatles' Progress* (Los Angeles and New York: Graymalkin Media, 2019), 43.

72   "From that moment on, it gelled": Lewisohn, *Tune In,* 678.

72   "Pete Best forever, Ringo never!": Philip Norman, "The Nowhere Men," *Daily Mail,* March 5, 2002.

72   "why get a bad-looking cat when you can get a good-looking one": Hunter Davies, *The Beatles: The Authorized Biography* (New York: McGraw-Hill, 1968), 151.

72   "the most hated man in Liverpool": Philip Norman, *John Lennon: The Life* (New York: Ecco, 2008), 275.

73   "I sneaked in and sneaked out again": Lewisohn, *Tune In,* 684.

73   *"You're too young!"*: Lewisohn, *Tune In,* 684.

73   "Cyn is having a baby": Davies, *The Beatles,* 153.

CHAPTER 16

74   "what are we going to do with *this*?": Mark Lewisohn, *Tune In,* vol. 1, *The Beatles: All These Years* (New York: Crown Archetype, 2013), 671.

75   "Double the speed": Debbie Geller, *In My Life: The Brian Epstein Story,* ed. Anthony Wall (New York: Thomas Dunne Books, 2000), 54.

75   "We want to record our own material": Geoff Emerick and Howard Massey, *Here, There and Everywhere: My Life Recording the Music of the Beatles* (New York: Gotham Books, 2006), 45.

76   "write something as good as that song": Ray Connolly, *Being John Lennon: A Restless Life* (New York: Pegasus Books, 2018), 139.

76   straight to number 1: Connolly, *Being John Lennon,* 139.

CHAPTER 17

77   "make your name with that": Mark Lewisohn, *Tune In,* vol. 1, *The Beatles: All These Years* (New York: Crown Archetype, 2013), 715.

77   "Remember I said I'd be famous": Rupert Christiansen, *The Complete Book of Aunts* (New York: Twelve, 2007), 37.

77   "The whole of Liverpool went out": Lewisohn, *Tune In,* 720.

78   "thought there was a fiddle on": Lewisohn, *Tune In,* 721.

78   "almost paralyzed with devotion": Ray Connolly, *Being John Lennon: A Restless Life* (New York: Pegasus Books, 2018), 141.

78   deems both Paul and George "sweet": Philip Norman, *Paul McCartney: The Life* (New York: Little, Brown, 2016), 164.

78   "They have a real authentic Negro sound": Barry Miles, *The Beatles Diary Volume 1: The Beatles Years* (London: Omnibus Press, 2001), 73.

79   "most startling of all the American city folk singers": Lewisohn, *Tune In,* 640.

79   the Ealing Club: Vincent Dowd, "The Club Where the Who First Rocked," BBC, November 12, 2017.

79   "The Stones were playing little clubs in London": Lewisohn, *Tune In,* 722.

80   "I want a long coat like that": Barry Miles, *Paul McCartney: Many Years from Now* (New York: Henry Holt, 1997), 101.

80   "Twenty-seven was the *height*": Lewisohn, *Tune In,* 749.

80   "We went in young boys": Lewisohn, *Tune In,* 803.

81   "would it be better to keep it simple?": The Beatles, *The Beatles Anthology* (San Francisco: Chronicle Books, 2000), 96.

82   "It's a good logo, like Rodgers and Hammerstein": Alex Bilmes, "Paul McCartney Is *Esquire*'s August Cover Star," *Esquire,* February 7, 2015.

82   "'We're the grooves and you two just watch it'":
      George Harrison, interview by Alan Freeman, BBC
      Radio 1, December 6, 1974, quoted in Lewisohn, *Tune
      In,* 831.

82   "The thing I like about the Beatles is their great sense
      of humor": George Martin, interview by Alan Smith in
      Mersey Beat, January 3, 1963, quoted in Lewisohn, *Tune
      In,* 774.

82   "Gentlemen, you've just made your first number one record":
      George Martin with Jeremy Hornsby, *All You Need Is Ears:
      The Story of the Recording Genius Who Created the Beatles* (New
      York: St. Martin's Press, 1979), 130.

CHAPTER 18

84   "I was always bitterly ashamed of it": Jody Rosen, "The
      Beatles' 'Please Please Me' 50th Anniversary," *Rolling Stone,*
      March 22, 2013.

84   won't tour America until they've achieved a number-one
      hit: Chris Ingham, *The Rough Guide to the Beatles* (London:
      Rough Guides, 2003), 25.

84   "We knew we would wipe you out if we could just get a
      grip on you": Richard Harrington, "The Lennon Legend,"
      Washington Post, December 14, 1980.

84   September 1963 visit to Benton, Illinois: "George Harrison
      Holidays with His Sister Louise in Benton, IL, USA,"
      BeatlesBible.com.

84   "They don't know us": "How the Beatles Took America: In-
      side the Biggest Explosion in Rock & Roll History," *Rolling
      Stone,* January 1, 2014.

84   the size of the crowds gathered to welcome them: "February
      7, 1964: Beatlemania Arrives in the US," On This Day,
      BBC.co.uk.

85   "I'd like to ask your help": The Beatles, *The Beatles Anthology* (San Francisco: Chronicle Books, 2000), 105.

85   "rattle their fucking jewelry": Michael Braun, *"Love Me Do!": The Beatles' Progress* (Los Angeles and New York: Graymalkin Media, 2019), 58.

85   "The Beatles are most intriguing": Andrew Grant Jackson, "The Beatles Play for the Queen," *Slate,* November 4, 2013.

85   "these rumbustious young Beatles": Braun, *"Love Me Do!,"* 11.

85   "the Year of the Beatles": Braun, *"Love Me Do!,"* 81.

86   "We all went potty about Dylan": Alan Light, "'The Freewheelin' Bob Dylan': Inside His First Classic," *Rolling Stone,* May 27, 2016.

86   "Everyone will think I copied it from him": Mark Lewisohn, *Tune In,* vol. 1, *The Beatles: All These Years* (New York: Crown Archetype, 2013), 106.

86   "Beat-les! Beat-les! Beat-les!": Barry Miles, *The Beatles Diary Volume 1: The Beatles Years* (London: Omnibus Press, 2001), 127.

86   ever skeptical that Beatlemania is likely to spread: Miles, *Beatles Diary,* 126.

86   "I Want to Hold Your Hand" is the number-one single in America: "How the Beatles Took America: Inside the Biggest Explosion in Rock & Roll History," *Rolling Stone,* January 1, 2014.

86   "They always act this way when anything big happens": Miles, *Beatles Diary,* 127.

87   "I wondered if the bastard had picked up on it": Harry Benson interview by the authors, 2019.

87   "How about a pillow fight?" Harry Benson interview by the authors, 2019.

89   the seventh floor, where Lennon lives with Yoko: Christine Haughney, "Sharing the Dakota with John Lennon," *New York Times,* December 6, 2010.

89   A bomb threat: Jack Jones, *Let Me Take You Down: Inside the Mind of Mark David Chapman, the Man Who Killed John Lennon* (New York: Villard Books, 1992), 206.

CHAPTER 19

91   "In a way I'm sorry they've been so successful": Michael Braun, *"Love Me Do!": The Beatles' Progress* (Los Angeles and New York: Graymalkin Media, 2019), 77.

91   "a shrewd young man who has caught the lightning": Braun, *"Love Me Do!,"* 54.

92   "I've this old-fashioned idea that marriage is a private thing": Jacqueline Edmondson, *John Lennon: A Biography* (Santa Barbara, CA: Greenwood, 2010), 59.

93   "talking about things like life and death": Philip Norman, *John Lennon: The Life* (New York: Ecco, 2008), 326.

93   "The Beatles Are Coming": Hunter Davies, *The Beatles: The Authorized Biography* (New York: McGraw-Hill, 1968), 194.

93   "the impression of an angry young man": Andrew Grant Jackson, "The Beatles Play for the Queen," *Slate,* November 4, 2013.

94   "the first spot of joy to come to a nation that is still very much in mourning": Braun, *"Love Me Do!,"* 170.

94   American television debut: Randy Lewis, "The Beatles, JFK and Nov. 22, 1963," *Los Angeles Times,* November 22, 2013.

94   "a big octopus with tentacles that were dragging us

down into New York": Jim Farber, "Beatles' Historic Arrival in New York City 50 Years Ago Gave Big Apple Unforgettable Lift," *Daily News* (New York), January 24, 2014.

94   a jet carrying the British pop stars had to be crash-proof: Mick Brown, *Tearing Down the Wall of Sound: The Rise and Fall of Phil Spector* (London: Bloomsbury, 2007), 53.

94   "may be the greatest rock and roll singers that we've ever had": Jann S. Wenner, "Phil Spector: The *Rolling Stone* Interview," *Rolling Stone,* November 1, 1969.

95   the Crawdaddy Club: "The Beatles See the Rolling Stones Perform for the First Time," BeatlesBible.com.

95   "went off in the corner of the room and finished the song off": David Sheff, "*Playboy* Interview with John Lennon and Yoko Ono," *Playboy,* January 1981.

96   "Mick and Keith decided they should write songs together themselves": Jann S. Wenner, "Lennon Remembers, Part Two," *Rolling Stone,* February 4, 1971.

96   "Tell the boys there's a big crowd waiting for them": Bob Spitz, "The Beatles Invasion, 50 Years Ago: Friday, Feb. 7, 1964," *Time,* February 7, 2014.

CHAPTER 20

97   "The only thing that's different is the hair": James Barron, "Historic Hysterics: Witnesses to a Really Big Show," *New York Times,* February 7, 2014.

97   "every group with long hair will be sought by American companies": Barry Miles, *The Beatles Diary Volume 1: The Beatles Years* (London: Omnibus Press, 2001), 127.

98   "almost seem a shade on the feminine side": Barbara Ehrenreich, Elizabeth Hess, and Gloria Jacobs, "Screams Heard 'Round the World," *Chicago Tribune,* December 14, 1986;

from *Re-Making Love: The Feminization of Sex* (New York: Anchor Books, 1986).

98   "Look at them comb their hair!": Jim Farber, "Beatles' Historic Arrival in New York City 50 Years Ago Gave Big Apple Unforgettable Lift," *Daily News* (New York), January 24, 2014.

98   "the only ones with real dandruff": Michael Braun, *"Love Me Do!": The Beatles' Progress* (Los Angeles and New York: Graymalkin Media, 2019), 14.

98   Ed Sullivan don a mop-top wig: Braun, *"Love Me Do!,"* 138.

98   airplane pilot also puts on a Beatles wig: Braun, *"Love Me Do!,"* 171.

98   promotional "Beatle Kits": Braun, *"Love Me Do!,"* 119.

98   "You have to be a real sour square not to love the nutty, noisy, happy, handsome Beatles": Braun, *"Love Me Do!,"* 10.

99   "The Americans will never understand it": Randy Lewis, "Ringo Starr, the Beatles and the Spirit of America," *Los Angeles Times,* October 24, 2014.

99   ALONZO TUSKE HATES THE BEATLES: Thomas Buckley, "Beatles Prepare for Their Debut: Police Patrol Their Hotel and Guard Theater," *New York Times,* February 9, 1964.

100 JOHN, DIVORCE CYNTHIA: Ehrenreich, Hess, and Jacobs, "Screams Heard 'Round the World."

100 "Us guys had to play it kind of cool": Brian Wawzenek, "The Beatles' First 'Ed Sullivan' Appearance: 10 Rock Stars Remember," UltimateClassicRock.com, February 9, 2016.

100 "I remember noticing John that first time on the Sullivan Show": Philip Norman, *John Lennon: The Life* (New York: Ecco, 2008), 350.

100 "Couldn't you sing, 'She loves you, yes, yes, yes?'": "Paul McCartney Blows 'Kisses' to His Father's Era," *Fresh Air,* NPR.org, March 29, 2012.

101 "the most piercing, uncomfortable sound I've ever heard":

Bob Spitz, "The Beatles Invasion 50 Years Ago: Wed., Feb. 12, 1964," *Time,* February 12, 2014.

101 "that terrible screech the BMT Astoria train makes": Braun, *"Love Me Do!,"* 135.

101 "two .38 caliber bullets from his belt and placed them in his ears": Braun, *"Love Me Do!,"* 154.

101 "They never did sound checks": Vincent Dowd, "Larry Kane: The Reluctant Beatles Fan," BBC, September 16, 2016.

101 "No theater ever got it how we liked it": Hunter Davies, *The Beatles: The Authorized Biography* (New York: McGraw-Hill, 1968), 174–75.

102 "John blew me a kiss and the window slid shut": *Miami Herald* archives, "What Happened When the Beatles Came to Miami? We Went Nuts and They Fell in Love," *Miami Herald,* February 3, 2019.

102 "four of the nicest youngsters we've ever had on our stage": John C. Winn, *Way Beyond Compare: The Beatles' Recorded Legacy,* vol. 1, *1957–1965* (New York: Three Rivers Press, 2008), 145.

102 "It was all part of being a Beatle, really": George Varga, "Muhammad Ali Knocked Out the Beatles in 1964," *Morning Call* (Lehigh Valley, Pennsylvania), June 4, 2016.

102 "lugged around and thrust into rooms full of press men": Varga, "Muhammad Ali."

102 "quite cute": The Beatles, *The Beatles Anthology* (San Francisco: Chronicle Books, 2000), 123.

103 "When Liston reads about the Beatles visiting me": Varga, "Muhammad Ali."

103 "My dog plays drums better than that kid with the big nose": George Kimball, "1964 World Heavyweight Title Fight 'I Shook Up the World!,'" *Irish Times*, February 21, 2004.

CHAPTER 21

104   The movie shoot is scheduled to take seven weeks: Philip Norman, *John Lennon: The Life* (New York: Ecco, 2008), 355.

104   written over the course of a few hours: Michael Braun, *"Love Me Do!": The Beatles' Progress* (Los Angeles and New York: Graymalkin Media, 2019), 171.

104   the first British single to hit number 1 simultaneously: Kenneth Womack, "50 Years of Beatles: 'I Had a Hard Day Last Night,'" *Penn State News,* February 24, 2014.

105   "the extension of that rebellion": Sam Kashner, "Making Beatlemania: *A Hard Day's Night* at 50," *Vanity Fair,* July 2, 2014.

105   "a famous street in Liverpool where the whores used to be": The Beatles, *The Beatles Anthology* (San Francisco: Chronicle Books, 2000), 128.

105   "The trouble is, it's only us who can write for us": Braun, *"Love Me Do!,"* 62.

105   "fucking stupid, isn't it?": Kashner, "Making Beatlemania."

105   "They had this great thing of gangs": Vanessa Thorpe, "Why on Earth Should We Moan? *A Hard Day's Night* Is Back...," *The Guardian,* July 6, 2014.

106   "Ringoism": The Beatles, *The Beatles Anthology,* 129.

106   "while I was saying one thing, have another thing come into my brain": The Beatles, *The Beatles Anthology,* 130.

106   It takes them twenty-four hours: Norman, *John Lennon,* 357.

106   "When I get home to you / I find my tiredness is through": Maureen Cleave, "Nowhere Boy: Maureen Cleave Remembers John Lennon," *The Telegraph,* December 14, 2009.

106   "I did practically every single with my voice": David Sheff, *All We Are Saying: The Last Major Interview with John Lennon and Yoko Ono* (New York: St. Martin's Griffin, 2000), 175.

107   "because I couldn't reach the notes": Sheff, *All We Are Saying,* 175.

107   "Sometimes we write together. Sometimes not": Braun, *"Love Me Do!,"* 28.

107   "John needed Paul's attention to detail and persistence": Joshua Wolf Shenk, "The Power of Two," *The Atlantic,* July/August 2014.

107   "I'm obsessed with them": Jon Savage, "The Fifth Beatle, Derek Taylor," *GQ,* May 20, 2018.

107   "it was as if de Gaulle had landed, or better yet, the Messiah": Savage, "The Fifth Beatle."

108   "I owe her a lot": Keith Altham, "John Lennon: Happy Birthday to the Head Beatle," *Fabulous,* October 10, 1964.

108   "lots of girls who were very keen to party with anybody from the tour": Philip O'Brien, "The Beatles Let It Be in Australia: 1964," *Sydney Morning Herald,* June 3, 2014.

108   makes $5.8 million in six weeks: Kashner, "Making Beatlemania."

109   "misleading air of off-the-cuff spontaneity": *Variety* staff, "A Hard Day's Night," *Variety,* December 31, 1963.

109   The Cavern, where they haven't performed since August of 1963: Hunter Davies, *The Beatles: The Authorized Biography* (New York: McGraw-Hill, 1968), 177.

109   "That's Liddypool for you": Braun, *"Love Me Do!,"* 69.

109   "only like people when they're on the way up": Jonathan Cott, "John Lennon: The Last Interview," *Rolling Stone,* December 23, 2010.

109   "'You're finished in Liverpool'": Bob Spitz, *The Beatles: The Biography* (New York: Back Bay, 2006), 512.

109   "not as good as James Bond": Spitz, *The Beatles,* 511.

CHAPTER 22

110 "He seemed so intelligent and witty": Hunter Davies, *The Beatles: The Authorized Biography* (New York: McGraw-Hill, 1968), 189.

111 "George is the handsomest and he's loving it all": Maureen Cleave, "How the Frenzied, Furry Beatles Took Over England," *San Francisco Examiner,* February 2, 1964.

111 "sexy eyelashes": *The Beatles: Eight Days a Week—The Touring Years,* directed by Ron Howard (2016).

111 "We reckoned we could make it because there were four of us": Richard Williams, "John & Yoko: Part One," *Melody Maker,* December 6, 1969.

111 "We don't like Jelly Babies": "Why George Harrison Begged One Young Fan to Stop Throwing Jelly Babies at the Beatles," *Daily Mail,* May 15, 2009.

112 "They just felt like hailstones": Al Aronowitz, "Beatlemania in 1964: 'This Has Gotten Entirely Out of Control,'" *Saturday Evening Post,* March 1964; reprinted in *The Guardian,* January 29, 2014.

112 "Mustn't spoil the image": Michael Braun, *"Love Me Do!": The Beatles' Progress* (Los Angeles and New York: Graymalkin Media, 2019), 52.

112 contact lenses painfully knocked out: Cynthia Lennon, *John* (New York: Crown, 2005), 191.

112 "You feel a clonk on the back of the head": The Beatles, *The Beatles Anthology* (San Francisco: Chronicle Books, 2000), 153.

112 "entirely out of control": Aronowitz, "Beatlemania in 1964."

112 "I had been in one of the back dressing rooms": Alyssa Bray, "Photographer David Magnus shares rare photos of the Beatles in 1967," *The JC,* February 17, 2017.

112 "What happened to us in the States was just like Britain": Davies, *The Beatles,* 196.

112 "madness from morning to night with not one moment's peace": Philip Norman, *Paul McCartney: The Life* (New York: Little, Brown, 2016), 243.

113 "really weird characters": Bob Spitz, *The Beatles: The Biography* (New York: Back Bay, 2006), 514.

113 "I feel safe as long as I'm plugged in": Philip Norman, *John Lennon: The Life* (New York: Ecco, 2008), 370.

113 "John always got really involved and excited": Norman, *John Lennon*, 371.

113 "standing outside every situation": Norman, *John Lennon*, 353.

113 "what a helluva lot John already knew about this country": Norman, *John Lennon*, 372.

114 "I could see the soul of an activist building up in him": Norman, *John Lennon*, 372.

114 "I always hated all the social things": Davies, *The Beatles*, 208.

114 "These people have no bloody manners": Aronowitz, "Beatlemania in 1964."

114 tickets had sold out in less than four hours: Randy Lewis, "Bob Eubanks on Bringing the Beatles to Hollywood Bowl in 1964," *Los Angeles Times*, August 21, 2014.

114 "We could be heard in a place like the Hollywood Bowl": The Beatles, *The Beatles Anthology* (San Francisco: Chronicle Books, 2000), 150.

115 "putting a microphone at the tail end of a 747 jet": The Beatles, *The Beatles Anthology*, 150.

115 "I used to have to follow their three bums wiggling": The Beatles, *The Beatles Anthology*, 150.

115 "I fell in love with Hollywood then": Jordan Runtagh, "*Eight Days a Week*: The Beatles' Touring History in 8 Concerts," *People*, November 21, 2017.

115 "John grabbed Mansfield and they started making out like mad": Spitz, *The Beatles*, 530.

116 "sitting on the plane, reading the paper and there was the photo of me": The Beatles, *The Beatles Anthology,* 150.

116 "'You guys never go *out* anywhere'": Spitz, *The Beatles,* 530–31.

116 "that Bob Dylan wrote poetry added to *his* appeal": The Beatles, *The Beatles Anthology,* 158.

116 on *Freewheelin',* he wrote *twelve* of thirteen: Alan Light, "'The Freewheelin' Bob Dylan': Inside His First Classic," *Rolling Stone,* May 26, 2013.

117 "Congratulations from the Beatles (a group)": Obituaries: "Mickie Most: Record Producer Who Scored Hit After Hit," *The Independent*, June 2, 2003.

117 *double entendre*: Jann Wenner, "The *Rolling Stone* Interview: John Lennon, Part One—The Working Class Hero," *Rolling Stone,* January 1971.

117 "Zimmerman is his name. My name isn't John Beatle": Wenner, "The *Rolling Stone* Interview."

118 "the crowning achievement": Valerie J. Nelson, "Al Aronowitz, 77; Rock Writer Introduced Dylan to Beatles," *Los Angeles Times,* August 5, 2005.

118 "cheap wine": Norman, *John Lennon,* 375.

118 "I get high, I get high": Norman, *John Lennon,* 375.

118 "royal taster": Norman, *John Lennon,* 376.

118 "This is Beatlemania here": The Beatles, *The Beatles Anthology,* 158.

118 "That was a hell of a night": Derek Taylor, *Fifty Years Adrift,* edited and annotated by George Harrison (London: Genesis Publications, 1984), quoted in "Bob Dylan turned the Beatles on to cannabis," BeatlesBible.com.

118 "Paul came up to me and hugged me for ten minutes": Andy Greene, "6 Things We Learned from the New Bob Dylan Tell-All," *Rolling Stone,* September 9, 2014.

119 "smoking dope, drinking wine, and generally being rock

'n' rollers": Jeff Giles, "55 Years Ago: Bob Dylan Introduces the Beatles to Marijuana," UltimateClassicRock.com, August 28, 2015.

CHAPTER 23

120 "John was basically a lazy bastard": Philip Norman, *Paul McCartney: The Life* (New York: Little, Brown, 2016), 224.

121 "I wanted to live in London": The Beatles, *The Beatles Anthology* (San Francisco: Chronicle Books, 2000), 159.

121 number 1 in both America and Britain: Philip Norman, *John Lennon: The Life* (New York: Ecco, 2008), 294.

122 "We struggled to record it and struggled to make it into a song": The Beatles, *The Beatles Anthology,* 160.

122 "looks, frankly, knackered": "The Beatles: *Beatles for Sale* Review," BBC.co.uk.

122 "I started thinking about my own emotions": Jann S. Wenner, "Lennon Remembers, Part Two," *Rolling Stone,* February 4, 1971.

122 "Prellies": Dan McQuade, "The Drug That Helped Turn the Beatles into the World's Greatest Band," *Village Voice,* August 14, 2014.

122 "on pot": Jann Wenner, "The *Rolling Stone* Interview: John Lennon, Part One—The Working Class Hero," *Rolling Stone,* January 1971.

122 "a happy high": Norman, *Paul McCartney,* 219.

122 "smoking pot for breakfast": Scott Beauchamp and Alex Shephard, "Bob Dylan and John Lennon's Weird, One-Sided Relationship," *The Atlantic,* September 24, 2012.

122 to avoid arousing suspicion: Norman, *John Lennon,* 396.

123 "I've always needed a drug to survive": Wenner, "The *Rolling Stone* Interview."

123 "Let's go": Pattie Boyd, *Wonderful Tonight: George Harrison,*

Eric Clapton, and Me (New York: Crown Archetype, 2007), 101.

123 London dentist John Riley: Mikal Gilmore, "Beatles' Acid Test: How LSD Opened the Door to 'Revolver,'" *Rolling Stone,* August 25, 2016.

123 Klaus Voormann's new band: Norman, *John Lennon,* 422.

123 "You haven't had any coffee yet": Boyd, *Wonderful Tonight,* 101.

123 "These friends of ours are going to be on soon": Boyd, *Wonderful Tonight,* 101.

123 "I advise you not to leave": Wenner, "The *Rolling Stone* Interview."

123 "It was in the coffee": Boyd, *Wonderful Tonight,* 101.

124 *"How dare you fucking do this to us!"*: Gilmore, "Beatles' Acid Test."

124 "I think he thought that there was going to be a big gang bang": Legs McNeil and Gillian McCain, "The Oral History of the First Two Times the Beatles Took Acid," Vice.com, December 4, 2016.

124 Pattie's orange Mini Cooper: Boyd, *Wonderful Tonight,* 101.

124 "All the way the car felt smaller and smaller": Boyd, *Wonderful Tonight,* 101.

124 "suddenly found ourselves in the middle of a horror film": McNeil and McCain, "The Oral History."

124 "We were cackling in the streets": Wenner, "The *Rolling Stone* Interview."

124 "as if I had never tasted, talked, seen, thought or heard properly before": Boyd, *Wonderful Tonight,* 102.

124 "just a little red light": Wenner, "The *Rolling Stone* Interview."

125 John's favorite book, *Alice's Adventures in Wonderland*: Norman, *John Lennon,* 423.

125 "ten miles an hour, but it seemed like a thousand": Wenner, "The *Rolling Stone* Interview."

125 "a big submarine": Wenner, "The *Rolling Stone* Interview."

125 "God, it was just terrifying, but it was fantastic": Wenner, "The *Rolling Stone* Interview."

CHAPTER 24

126 "my fat Elvis period": David Sheff, "*Playboy* Interview with John Lennon and Yoko Ono," *Playboy,* January 1981.

127 "get together and knock off a few songs, just like a job": Jann Wenner, "The *Rolling Stone* Interview: John Lennon, Part One—The Working Class Hero," *Rolling Stone,* January 1971.

127 "Because John sang it, you might have to give him 60 percent of it": David Rybaczewski, "Ticket to Ride," Beatlesebooks.com.

127 "That's me, one of the earliest heavy-metal records": Sheff, "*Playboy* Interview."

127 "lowered his glasses": Philip Norman, *Paul McCartney: The Life* (New York: Little, Brown, 2016), 221.

127 "the John Lennon he was frightened to reveal to the world": Norman, *Paul McCartney,* 221.

127 "why we never improved as musicians": Wenner, "The *Rolling Stone* Interview."

128 "I got out of bed, sat at the piano": Alice Vincent, "Yesterday: The Song That Started as Scrambled Eggs," *The Telegraph,* June 18, 2015.

128 "You'd think he was Beethoven or somebody!": The Beatles, *The Beatles Anthology* (San Francisco: Chronicle Books, 2000), 175.

129 "The song was around for months and months": The Beatles, *The Beatles Anthology,* 175.

129 "I was sorry, in a way, because we had so many laughs about it": The Beatles, *The Beatles Anthology,* 175.

129   "We have a winner with that 'Yesterday'": Vincent, "Yesterday."

129   "I had nothing to do with": Jann S. Wenner, "Lennon Remembers, Part Two," *Rolling Stone,* February 4, 1971.

CHAPTER 25

130   "they've got the cops moaning the blues": Michael Perlman, "When the Beatles Landed at Forest Hills Stadium," ForestHillsStadium.com, January 31, 2018.

131   PAUL, THROW US A KISS, RINGO, THROW US A RING: John McGee and Leeds Moberly, "The Beatles Play at Shea Stadium in 1965," *Daily News* (New York), August 16, 1965, reprinted August 14, 2015.

131   "It's the top of the mountain, Sid": Philip Norman, *John Lennon: The Life* (New York: Ecco, 2008), 403.

131   Olympic-size swimming pool: Bob Spitz, *The Beatles: The Biography* (New York: Back Bay, 2006), 578.

131   "The only fun part was the hotels in the evening, smoking pot and that": Hunter Davies, *The Beatles: The Authorized Biography* (New York: McGraw-Hill, 1968), 206.

131   an overwhelming feeling of well-being: Mikal Gilmore, "Beatles' Acid Test: How LSD Opened the Door to 'Revolver,'" *Rolling Stone,* August 25, 2016.

131   "a kid who played guitar": Carol Clerk, "George Harrison," *Uncut,* February 2002.

132   "a very interesting relationship": Norman, *John Lennon,* 426.

132   "We are probably the most cracked": Jann Wenner, "The *Rolling Stone* Interview: John Lennon, Part One—The Working Class Hero," *Rolling Stone,* January 1971.

132   "we couldn't relate": Spitz, *The Beatles,* 580.

132   "felt very left out": Philip Norman, *Paul McCartney: The Life* (New York: Little, Brown, 2016), 223.

132   "'Beware the demon drug'": Norman, *Paul McCartney*, 223.

132   "We're taking it and you're not": Norman, *Paul McCartney*, 223.

132   a helicopter flying far too close: Spitz, *The Beatles*, 580.

132   *"Hello, fellas, you dirty bastards!"*: Rex Reed, "'Holden Caulfield at 27': *Esquire*'s 1968 Profile of Peter Fonda," Esquire.com, August 17, 2019.

132   "You have to be a bastard to make it": Wenner, "The *Rolling Stone* Interview."

133   "I know what it's like to be dead, man": Spitz, *The Beatles*, 581.

133   "We gave the whole of our youth to the Beatles": John Lennon, *The John Lennon Letters*, edited by Hunter Davies (New York: Little, Brown, 2012), 89.

133   "touring was a relief, just to get out of Liverpool": Davies, *The Beatles*, 171.

133   "I spend hours in dressing rooms and things thinking about the times I've wasted": Lennon, *The John Lennon Letters*, 89.

CHAPTER 26

135   an MBE has never before been given to anyone under the age of twenty-five: Philip Norman, *John Lennon: The Life* (New York: Ecco, 2008), 400.

135   "a mockery of everything this country stands for": Dave Lifton, "The Day the Beatles Received Their MBEs," UltimateClassicRock.com, October 26, 2015.

135   "They've not been a bad example to anybody": "Should the Beatles Have Been Awarded MBEs?," BBC.co.uk, October 26, 2015.

135   "They should have got it and I think they're great!" "Should the Beatles Have Been Awarded MBEs?"

135   "part of the game we'd agreed to play": Hunter Davies, *The Beatles: The Authorized Biography* (New York: McGraw-Hill, 1968), 207.

136   "when you are being decorated, you don't laugh anymore": The Beatles, *The Beatles Anthology* (San Francisco: Chronicle Books, 2000), 181.

136   "can't help being impressed when you're in the palace": The Beatles, *The Beatles,* 181.

136   "You deserve this far more than I do": Rupert Christiansen, *The Complete Book of Aunts* (New York: Twelve, 2007), 38.

137   "We just idolized the guy so much": Michael K. Bohn, "50 Years Ago: When the Beatles Met Elvis," *Daily Gazette* (Schenectady, New York), August 7, 2015.

137   "We were all major fans, so it was hero worship of a high degree": Frank Mastropolo, "The Day the Beatles Met Elvis," UltimateClassicRock.com, August 27, 2015.

137   "another dirty big publicity circus": Ian Youngs, "When the Beatles Met Elvis Presley," *BBC News,* October 5, 2011.

137   *It's Elvis! It's Elvis!*: Francis Schoenberger, "He Said, She Said: An Interview with John Lennon," *Spin,* October 9, 2019 (reprint of 1975 interview).

137   "like subjects calling on the King": Bohn, "50 Years Ago."

138   "the backbeat with his fingers on the nearest bits of wooden furniture": Youngs, "When the Beatles Met Elvis Presley."

138   "trying to suss out from the gang if anybody had any reefers": Mastropolo, "The Day the Beatles Met Elvis."

138   "Elvis was stoned": Youngs, "When the Beatles Met Elvis Presley."

CHAPTER 27

139   "No wonder you can only rock": Keith Richards, *Life* (New York: Little, Brown, 2010), 207.

140   the Stones' first number-one hit in America: Rich Cohen, "How the Rolling Stones Found 'Satisfaction,'" *Slate,* May 10, 2016.

140   "I wrote 'Satisfaction' in my sleep": Cohen, "How the Rolling Stones Found 'Satisfaction.'"

140   writes the song in minutes: Philip Norman, *John Lennon: The Life* (New York: Ecco, 2008), 417.

140   "It was a two-way thing": Rob Sheffield, "50 Years of 'Rubber Soul': How the Beatles Invented the Future of Pop," *Rolling Stone,* December 3, 2015.

140   In one week, the Beatles come up with seven songs: Sheffield, "50 Years of 'Rubber Soul.'"

140   "a completely impractical man": Norman, *John Lennon,* 410.

140   "Something doesn't sound quite right": Norman, *John Lennon,* 412.

141   "just take care of your percentage and leave us to worry about the music": Ray Connolly, *Being John Lennon: A Restless Life* (New York: Pegasus Books, 2018), 155.

141   on November 12, the album is finished: Sheffield, "50 Years of 'Rubber Soul.'"

141   "We should call it the *Pot Album*": Norman, *John Lennon,* 415.

141   "Well, you know they're good—but it's plastic soul": David Rybaczewski, "'Rubber Soul' History," Beatlesebooks.com.

CHAPTER 28

142   told his life story to *Tit-Bits*: Philip Norman, *John Lennon: The Life* (New York: Ecco, 2008), 420.

142   "*Rubber Soul* broke everything open": Bob Spitz, *The Beatles: The Biography* (New York: Back Bay, 2006), 595.

143   "the ignoble Alf": Michael Braun, *"Love Me Do!": The Beatles' Progress* (Los Angeles and New York: Graymalkin Media, 2019), 43.

143   "I don't feel as if I owe him anything": Braun, *"Love Me Do!,"* 64.

143   "It wasn't what you would call a happy reunion": Ray Connolly, *Being John Lennon: A Restless Life* (New York: Pegasus Books, 2018), 179.

143   "What do you want, then?" Connolly, *Being John Lennon,* 179.

144   "made me get my teeth seen to": Hunter Davies, *The Beatles: The Authorized Biography* (New York: McGraw-Hill, 1968), 240.

144   "only the second time in my life I'd seen him": Maureen Cleave, "How Does a Beatle Live? John Lennon Lives Like This," *Evening Standard,* March 4, 1966.

144   an accusation Alf's manager later repeats: Tony Cartwright, "How Lennon Sabotaged His Dishwasher Dad's Bid to Be a Pop Star: Close Friend Tells Story of the Beatle's Hard-Drinking Father," *Daily Mail,* July 30, 2012.

144   "I had too many father figures": Jann S. Wenner, "Lennon Remembers: Part Two," *Rolling Stone,* February 4, 1971.

144   "I'm not the greatest dad on earth; I'm doing me best": Jonathan Cott, "John Lennon: The Last Interview," *Rolling Stone,* December 23, 2010.

145   "a lot of early childhood was coming out": Jann Wenner, "The *Rolling Stone* Interview: John Lennon, Part One—The Working Class Hero," *Rolling Stone,* January 1971.

145   *relax, float downstream*: Norman, *John Lennon,* 421.

145   "I should destroy my ego and I did": Wenner, "The *Rolling Stone* Interview."

146   "the acid album": Norman, *John Lennon,* 432.

146   covers for four British Beatles albums: Matt Schudel, "Robert Freeman, Photographer Who Helped Define the Image of the Beatles, Dies at 82," *Washington Post,* November 9, 2019.

146   "eating acid all the time": Wenner, "The *Rolling Stone* Interview."

147 "You gals are waiting for someone, I bet": Jack Jones, *Let Me Take You Down: Inside the Mind of Mark David Chapman, the Man Who Killed John Lennon* (New York: Villard Books, 1992), 8.

147 When he met Gloria: *CNN Special Report: Killing John Lennon,* CNN.com, December 8, 2015.

148 "As a matter of fact": Jones, *Let Me Take You Down,* 8.

148 "I bet nobody ever said that to you before": Jones, *Let Me Take You Down,* 8.

149 "I heard John Lennon lives here": Jones, *Let Me Take You Down,* 8.

149 the presents: Vicki Sheff, "The Betrayal of John Lennon," *Playboy,* March 1984.

151 Imagines himself leaning forward to kiss Yoko: Clyde Haberman, "Of Lennon, Time, Loss and Parole," *New York Times,* September 30, 2000.

CHAPTER 29

154 "How Does a Beatle Live?": Maureen Cleave, "How Does a Beatle Live? John Lennon Lives Like This," *Evening Standard,* March 4, 1966.

154 "Christianity will go": Cleave, "How Does a Beatle Live?"

154 "We're more popular than Jesus now": Cleave, "How Does a Beatle Live?"

154 "And then it just vanished": "The Beatles—A Day in the Life: March 4, 1966," BeatlesRadio.com.

154 "I'd watched people worshipping like gods, four Beatles": Jordan Runtagh, "Inside Beatles' Bloody, Banned 'Butcher' Cover," *Rolling Stone,* June 20, 2016.

155 "There we were, supposed to be sort of angels": Philip

Norman, *John Lennon: The Life* (New York: Ecco, 2008), 444.

155   "fed up with taking squeaky-clean pictures": Runtagh, "Inside Beatles' Bloody, Banned 'Butcher' Cover."

155   "It was just dolls and a lot of meat": Runtagh, "Inside Beatles' Bloody, Banned 'Butcher' Cover."

156   750,000 albums: Norman, *John Lennon,* 445.

156   "It's as relevant as Vietnam": Runtagh, "Inside Beatles' Bloody, Banned 'Butcher' Cover."

156   a money loser for Capitol: Douglas Martin, "Robert Whitaker, the Beatles' Photographer, Dies at 71," *New York Times,* October 1, 2011.

156   the band's nickname, the Fab Four: Allan Kozinn, "Tony Barrow, Beatles Publicist Who Coined the Term 'Fab Four,' Dies at 80," *New York Times,* May 16, 2016.

157   "the sort of thing *DATEbook* likes to use": Jordan Runtagh, "When John Lennon's 'More Popular Than Jesus' Controversy Turned Ugly," *Rolling Stone,* July 29, 2016.

157   "our fantastic Beatles boycott is still in effect": "John Lennon Sparks His First Major Controversy," History.com, November 16, 2009.

157   "your Beatles records and Beatles paraphernalia": "John Lennon Sparks His First Major Controversy."

CHAPTER 30

158   "the Beatle grinder": Jack Doyle, "Burn the Beatles, 1966: Bigger Than Jesus?," PopHistoryDig.com, October 11, 2017.

158   "We can get along very well without the Beatles": Doyle, "Burn the Beatles, 1966."

159   "Who are these four creeps to put themselves above the High and Mighty?": Doyle, "Burn the Beatles, 1966."

159 "Letters arrived at the house full of threats, hate, and venom": Cynthia Lennon, *A Twist of Lennon* (London: Star Books, 1978), quoted in "The Beatles—A Day in the Life, March 4, 1966," BeatlesRadio.com.

159 Psychics are sending him their predictions: Cynthia Lennon, *John* (New York: Crown, 2005), 190.

160 "What will it cost to cancel the tour?" Jordan Runtagh, "When John Lennon's 'More Popular Than Jesus' Controversy Turned Ugly," *Rolling Stone,* July 29, 2016.

160 "They'd been poor boys who'd worked hard and made money": Peter Taylor-Whiffen, "The Beatles' Accountant Fifty Years On: They Were Scruffy Boys Who Didn't Want to Pay Tax," *The Telegraph,* July 23, 2017.

160 around $4 million: Doyle, "Burn the Beatles, 1966."

161 "If anything were to happen to any of you": Runtagh, "When John Lennon's 'More Popular Than Jesus' Controversy Turned Ugly."

CHAPTER 31

162 "I wasn't saying the Beatles are better than Jesus or God or Christianity": John Dodge, "On This Day in Chicago, 1966: John Lennon Apologized for 'Jesus' Comment," CBS Chicago, August 12, 2014.

162 "just loses its meaning or its context immediately": "The Beatles—A Day in the Life, March 4, 1966," BeatlesRadio.com.

163 "I felt very bad for John during the whole episode": Paul McCartney, interview with the authors, 2019.

163 "I didn't want to talk because I thought they'd kill me": Jordan Runtagh, "When John Lennon's 'More Popular Than Jesus' Controversy Turned Ugly," *Rolling Stone,* July 29, 2016.

163 "hail Beatles in Chicago": Jack Doyle, "Burn the Beatles, 1966: Bigger Than Jesus?," PopHistoryDig.com, October 11, 2017.

163 "the story of protest kicked up recently by Beatle John Lennon": Doyle, "Burn the Beatles, 1966."

163 "some foundation to the latest observations of John Lennon": Doyle, "Burn the Beatles, 1966."

164 Beatles bonfires: Doyle, "Burn the Beatles, 1966."

164 "I created another little piece of hate in the world": Leroy Aarons, "'Can't Express Myself Very Well,' Beatle Apologizes for Remarks," *Washington Post,* August 15, 1966.

165 "not welcome in the City of Memphis": John Beifuss, "Memphis Leaders Gave Beatles Icy Reception," *Commercial Appeal* (Memphis), August 10, 2006.

165 "actually threatening to assassinate John Lennon": Bob Spitz, *The Beatles: The Biography* (New York, Back Bay, 2006), 632.

165 "You might as well paint a target on me": Runtagh, "When John Lennon's 'More Popular Than Jesus' Controversy Turned Ugly."

165 "frightened by things": Carol Clerk, "George Harrison," *Uncut,* February 2002.

165 "There was always an edge in America": Runtagh, "When John Lennon's 'More Popular Than Jesus' Controversy Turned Ugly."

166 ticket price of $5.50: Steve Pike, "The Beatles in Memphis," WKNOFM.org, August 23, 2013.

166 "I love Jesus, but I love those Beatles, too": UPI, "Beatles Win Contest," *Daily News Journal* (Murfreesboro, Tennessee), August 20, 1966.

166 "they thought snipers might shoot us": Spitz, *The Beatles,* 635.

166 "each thought it was the other that had been shot": The

Beatles, *The Beatles Anthology* (San Francisco: Chronicle Books, 2000), 227.

167   "blast off into double-time": "Bang That Turned the Beatles Off," *Sydney Morning Herald,* July 2, 2008.

167   "The four performers didn't bat an eye or miss a note": UPI, "Beatles Win Contest."

167   "The only gig we ever missed!": Jordan Runtagh, "Remembering Beatles' Final Concert," *Rolling Stone,* August 29, 2016.

167   "I remember us getting in a big, empty steel-lined wagon": Jeff Giles, "The Day the Beatles Decided to Stop Touring," UltimateClassicRock.com, August 21, 2017.

167   "He was struggling mightily to get out from the comments he made": Ken Mansfield, interview with authors, 2019.

168   "all in a big movie and we were the ones trapped": The Beatles, *The Beatles Anthology.*

168   conflicting signage: Doyle, "Burn the Beatles, 1966."

168   LENNON SAVES: Runtagh, "Remembering Beatles' Final Concert."

168   "Tape it, will you? Tape the show": Runtagh, "Remembering Beatles' Final Concert."

168   "We'd like to ask you to join in and, er, clap, sing, talk, do anything": Runtagh, "Remembering Beatles' Final Concert."

168   "Right—that's it, I'm not a Beatle anymore!": Runtagh, "Remembering Beatles' Final Concert."

169   "This isn't show business. It's something else": Michael Braun, *"Love Me Do!": The Beatles' Progress* (Los Angeles and New York: Graymalkin Media, 2019), 64.

CHAPTER 32

170   "If you wanted to, John, you could be a very interesting actor": Sam Kashner, "Making Beatlemania: *A Hard Day's Night* at 50," *Vanity Fair,* July 2, 2014.

170   an opportunistic ex of Brian's: Jordan Runtagh, "Remembering Beatles' Final Concert," *Rolling Stone,* August 29, 2016.

171   "I have visions of Strawberry Fields": David Rybaczewski, "Strawberry Fields Forever," BeatleseBooks.com.

171   "John was still searching": Philip Norman, *John Lennon: The Life* (New York: Ecco, 2008), 462.

171   "I knew it would end this way": Roger Ebert, "How I Won the War," RogerEbert.com, January 7, 1968.

172   "granny glasses": Ray Connolly, *Being John Lennon: A Restless Life* (New York: Pegasus Books, 2018), 228.

172   "sequences of buttock moment": "Fluxfilm No. 16: Four (1966/1967)," FluxusFoundation.com.

173   "Never bring anybody until it's all ready": Museum of Modern Art, "Yoko Ono. London. 1966–69," audio transcript from "Yoko Ono: One Woman Show, 1960–1971," MoMa.org.

173   "This was the first sexy one I met": Philip Norman, "Emotionally Tormented and Painfully Insecure—the Unknown Lennon," *Daily Mail,* October 7, 2008.

174   a very small YES: Museum of Modern Art, "Yoko Ono. London. 1966–69."

174   "I thought it was fantastic": Jann S. Wenner, "Lennon Remembers, Part Two," *Rolling Stone,* February 4, 1971.

174   "When I first heard 'Strawberry Fields Forever,' I was sidesmacked": Norman, *John Lennon,* 481.

174   "Well, there are two things against it": Colin Fleming, "Revisiting Beatles' Rare, Revelatory 'Strawberry Fields Forever' Early Take," *Rolling Stone,* November 22, 2016.

———

176   dinner at a Japanese restaurant: Jack Jones, *Let Me Take You Down: Inside the Mind of Mark David Chapman, the Man Who Killed John Lennon* (New York: Villard Books, 1992), 11.

176   Record levels for murder: Leonard Buder, "1980 Called Worst Year of Crime in City History," *New York Times,* February 25, 1981.

177   *I would have definitely gone out with him*: Jones, *Let Me Take You Down,* 11.

177   "poor man's cocaine": "Crack Cocaine: A Short History," DrugFreeWorld.org.

177   a Gitane for sure: Harry Cockburn, "France Considers Banning Gitanes and Gauloises Cigarettes for Being 'Too Cool,'" *The Independent,* July 21, 2016.

177   "truly alive for the first time in twenty years": Jones, *Let Me Take You Down,* 11.

CHAPTER 33

178   annual flexi disc from the band featuring a Christmas message: Jordan Runtagh, "Beatles' Rare Fan-Club Christmas Records: A Complete Guide," *Rolling Stone,* December 15, 2017.

179   "He'd write 'Strawberry Fields'": Joshua Wolf Shenk, "The Power of Two," *The Atlantic,* July/August 2014.

179   "We could put the two together and make a smashing single": The Beatles, *The Beatles Anthology* (San Francisco: Chronicle Books, 2000), 239.

179   "an old poster advertising a variety show that starred Mr. Kite": David Rybaczewski, "Being for the Benefit of Mr. Kite!," Beatlesebooks.com.

180   "I don't mind Engelbert Humperdinck. They're the cats": The Beatles, *The Beatles Anthology,* 239.

180   "the only thing you couldn't do was kill people. Everything else was acceptable": Dave Swanson, "50 Years Ago: Jefferson Airplane Release Their Debut Album, 'Takes Off,'" UltimateClassicRock.com, August 15, 2016.

181   "I was going through murder": Bob Spitz, *The Beatles: The Biography* (New York: Back Bay, 2006), 665.

181   "an alter-ego band": The Beatles, *The Beatles Anthology,* 241.

181   "you stick two bits of *Pepper* in it and it's a concept": The Beatles, *The Beatles Anthology,* 241.

181   "Let Sgt. Pepper do the touring": The Beatles, *The Beatles Anthology,* 241.

181   "It was all there, the trampoline, the somersets, the hoops, the garters, the horse": Barry Miles, *Paul McCartney: Many Years from Now* (New York: Henry Holt, 1997), 317.

182   "I want to be in that circus atmosphere. I want to smell the sawdust": The Beatles, *The Beatles Anthology,* 247.

182   "John would deal in moods, he would deal in colors": The Beatles, *The Beatles Anthology,* 247.

182   "Cellophane flowers": The Beatles, *The Beatles Anthology,* 242.

182   "You're stuck out in suburbia, living a middle-class life": Spitz, *The Beatles,* 666.

182   "it was becoming impossible to communicate": Spitz, *The Beatles,* 666.

182   "I think the drugs destroyed a lot of his creativity": Ray Connolly, *Being John Lennon: A Restless Life* (New York: Pegasus Books, 2018), 237.

183   "George, I'm not feeling too good": Spitz, *The Beatles,* 671.

183   "They just look like stars to me": The Beatles, *The Beatles Anthology,* 242.

183   "John always had a way of having an edge to his songs": The Beatles, *The Beatles Anthology,* 242.

183   "It had to be just right": "John Lennon Sgt. Pepper Album Cover Sketch," Juliensive.com, May 20, 2017.

184   seven hundred hours of studio time to create this thirteenth LP: David Rybaczewski, "Sgt. Pepper's Lonely Hearts Club Band," BeatleseBooks.com.

184   a twenty-five-year-old American photographer, Linda East-man: Philip Norman, *Paul McCartney: The Life* (New York: Little, Brown, 2016), 272–73.

184   the Animals, another leading British music export: Philip Norman, *Paul McCartney,* 266.

184   longtime girlfriend Jane Asher: "Paul McCartney and Jane Asher Announce Their Engagement," BeatlesBible.com.

184   Brian's recently purchased country home: "The Beatles Attend a Party at Brian Epstein's Country House," Beatles-Bible.com.

184   1964 Rolls-Royce Phantom V: Jordan Runtagh, "John Lennon's Phantom V: The Story of the Psychedelic Beatle-Mobile," *Rolling Stone,* July 27, 2017.

184   "It was sprayed all yellow first": John Lennon, *The John Lennon Letters,* edited by Hunter Davies (New York: Little, Brown, 2012), 234.

184   ordinary latex house paint: Brett Berk, "John Lennon's Psychedelic Rolls-Royce Returns to the U.K. to Celebrate Sgt. Pepper's 50th Anniversary," *Billboard,* July 12, 2017.

185   "The first time I drove it, I was followed by hordes of photographers": Lennon, *The John Lennon Letters,* 234.

185   "John and friends floated in on his gaudy yellow Rolls": Runtagh, "John Lennon's Phantom V."

185   "Crowds of jeering, waving people pressed up against the tinted windows": "The Beatles Attend a Party at Brian Epstein's Country House."

185   "How dare you do that to a Rolls-Royce!": Tom Hawthorn, "The Magical History Tour of Lennon's Rolls-Royce," *Globe and Mail* (Canada), January 18, 2011.

186   "not a teen-age album, but a terribly intellectual one." Lillian Ross, *"Sgt. Pepper,"* *The New Yorker,* June 24, 1967.

186   legendary composer and conductor Leonard Bernstein: Olivia B. Waxman, "How the Beatles Made *Sgt. Pepper's Lonely Hearts Club Band* Work," *Time,* June 1, 2017.

186   "There is no longer any need, thank goodness, to apologize": Richard Nelsson, "The New Beatles' Dazzler: Sgt. Pepper Reviewed—Archive 1967," *The Guardian,* June 1, 2017.

186   "tendency to overdo the curry power": Nelsson, "The New Beatles' Dazzler."

186   "a touch of the Jefferson Airplane, a dab of Beach Boys vibrations": Richard Goldstein, "We Still Need the Beatles, but..." *New York Times,* June 1, 1967.

186   "The music critic of the *New York Times* hated *Sgt. Pepper*": Geoff Edgers, "Meet the Critic Who Panned 'Sgt. Pepper' Then Discovered His Speaker Was Busted. He's Still Not Sorry," *Washington Post,* May 11, 2017.

187   "The Lennon raunchiness has become mere caprice": Goldstein, "We Still Need the Beatles, but..."

187   "If they want to read drugs into our stuff, they will": The Beatles, *The Beatles Anthology,* 247.

187   "It will be the first worldwide satellite broadcast ever": Gavin Edwards, "The Beatles Make History with 'All You Need Is Love': A Minute-by-Minute Breakdown," *Rolling Stone,* August 28, 2014.

187   "I suppose we'd better write something": Edwards, "The Beatles Make History with 'All You Need Is Love.'"

188   "In contrast, John seemed to live in chaos": Shenk, "The Power of Two."

188   "Keep it simple so viewers across the globe will understand": Spitz, *The Beatles,* 700.

189   "Well, it's certainly repetitive": Spitz, *The Beatles,* 702.

189   *You know I love you...I really mean that*: Philip Norman, *John Lennon: The Life* (New York: Ecco, 2008), 504.

CHAPTER 34

190   "What one of us wants, the others go along with": Barry Miles, *Paul McCartney: Many Years from Now* (Henry Holt, 1997), 403.

190   "It's fantastic stuff, Cyn": Cynthia Lennon, "The Beatles, the Maharishi, and me," *The Sunday Times* (UK, February 10, 2008).

191   "Tell him you're with us": Bob Spitz, *The Beatles: The Biography* (New York: Back Bay, 2006), 711.

191   "Why are you always last, Cyn?": Ray Connolly, *Being John Lennon: A Restless Life* (New York: Pegasus Books, 2018), 246.

191   "Now we're our own managers; now we have to make all the decisions": Miles, *Paul McCartney*, 406.

192   "I introduced Brian to pills—which gives me a guilt association with his death": Connolly, *Being John Lennon*, 248.

192   "cooled us out a bit": Miles, *Paul McCartney*, 406.

192   "He just told us not to be overwhelmed with grief": Connolly, *Being John Lennon*, 247.

193   "If we goofed, then we goofed": Adam Behr, "Magical Mystery Tour: A Rare Beatles Flop—but It Paved the Way for Monty Python," *The Conversation*, December 22, 2017.

194   "I get higher than I ever did with drugs": David Chiu, "The Beatles in India: 16 Things You Didn't Know," *Rolling Stone*, February 12, 2018.

195   "The minute you clear it": Miles, *Paul McCartney*, 414.

195   "We're not fucking here to do the next album, we're here to meditate": Miles, *Paul McCartney*, 414.

195   "The way George is going he'll be flying on a magic carpet by the time he's forty": Connolly, *Being John Lennon*, 261.

195   "the most miserable songs on earth": Philip Norman, *John Lennon: The Life* (New York: Ecco, 2008), 534.

195   "I'm a cloud": Spitz, *The Beatles,* 755.

195   "keen to learn the finger-style guitar I played": Miles, *Paul McCartney,* 421–22.

196   "slip me the real secret mantra which would give me happiness": Sandip Roy, "Fifty Years on, India Is Celebrating the Beatles' Infamous Trip to the Country," *Pittsburgh Post-Gazette,* March 6, 2018.

196   "I thought he might slip me the answer!" Miles, *Paul McCartney,* 426.

196   "Something had gone very wrong between John and me": Spitz, *The Beatles,* 755.

196   "always had *some* kind of affairs going": David Sheff, *All We Are Saying: The Last Major Interview with John Lennon and Yoko Ono* (New York: St. Martin's Griffin, 2000), 178.

197   "We had no problems at home": Connolly, *Being John Lennon,* 237.

197   "he would be lost in a daydream: present, but absent": Connolly, *Being John Lennon,* 237.

197   "We are going in with clear heads and hoping for the best": Jordan Runtagh, "The Beatles' Revelatory White Album Demos: A Complete Guide," *Rolling Stone,* May 29, 2018.

197   "We hope to make a thing that's free": Joel Rose, "The Beatles' Apple Records: Forty Years Later," NPR.org, May 14, 2008.

197   "Take a taxi": Carol Clerk, "The Ballad of John and Yoko," *Uncut,* September 2003.

198   "We can do two things": Clerk, "The Ballad of John and Yoko."

198   "I want to go and live with Yoko": Spitz, *The Beatles,* 765.

199   met once before at a meditation meeting: "In Her Life After John, Cynthia Lennon Didn't Stop Loving Him," *Fresh Air,* NPR.org, April 2, 2015.

199   "Oh, hi": Spitz, *The Beatles,* 772.

199   Yoko moves into John's house: Norman, *John Lennon,* 541.

CHAPTER 35

200   "I want to put out what I feel about revolution": The Beatles, *The Beatles Anthology* (San Francisco: Chronicle Books, 2000), 298.

200   "I demand equal time, equal space, equal rights": Philip Norman, *John Lennon: The Life* (New York: Ecco, 2008), 548.

201   "She just moved in": Bob Spitz, *The Beatles: The Biography* (New York: Back Bay, 2006), 777.

201   "It's not that bad": Rob Sheffield, "And in the End," *Rolling Stone*, August 17, 2020.

201   "because Yoko sat on an amp": Sheffield, "And in the End."

201   "No, no, I want that guitar to sound dirtier!": Geoff Emerick and Howard Massey, *Here, There and Everywhere: My Life Recording the Music of the Beatles* (New York: Gotham Books, 2006), 252.

202   "It was as much Yoko's as it was John's": Emerick and Massey, *Here, There and Everywhere*, 240.

202   "a pimple on the face of the [White] album": Alan Smith, "The Beatles: *The Beatles*," *New Musical Express*, November 9, 1968.

202   "It wasn't that she inspired the songs. She inspired me": David Sheff, "*Playboy* Interview with John Lennon and Yoko Ono," *Playboy*, January 1981.

202   "I think we're being run by maniacs for maniacal ends, you know": John Lennon, interview with Peter Lewis, *Release*, BBC-2, June 6, 1968.

203   "It's an overtly political song about revolution and a great one": Barry Miles, *Paul McCartney: Many Years from Now* (New York: Henry Holt, 1997), 466.

203   "Where's your wife?" Spitz, *The Beatles*, 774.

203   a waterfront bungalow: Beckie Strum, "Waterfront Property

John Lennon Bought His Aunt Selling for £7.25 Million," *Mansion Global,* October 4, 2018.

203   "Who's the poisoned dwarf, John?" "John's Aunt Met Yoko and Thought 'God, What Is That?'" *Irish Daily Mail,* March 21, 2020.

204   "He knew I was splitting with Cyn and leaving Julian": David Sheff, *All We Are Saying: The Last Major Interview with John Lennon and Yoko Ono* (New York: St. Martin's Griffin, 2000), 189.

204   "subconsciously he was saying, Go ahead, leave me": Sheff, *All We Are Saying,* 189.

204   "That's something else, innit?": Miles, *Paul McCartney,* 466.

205   "Cary Grant on heat!" Miles, *Paul McCartney,* 466.

205   "The whole world is watching": Maggie Astor, " 'The Whole World Is Watching': The 1968 Democratic Convention, 50 Years Later," *New York Times,* August 28, 2018.

206   Ringo evicted Hendrix: Amanda Uren, "1967: Hanging Out with Hendrix," *Mashable,* April 16, 2015.

206   a figure standing by their bedroom window: "John Lennon and Yoko Ono Are Arrested for Drugs Possession," Beatles-Bible.com.

206   forewarned by a reporter: Barry Miles, *The Beatles Diary Volume 1: The Beatles Years* (London: Omnibus Press, 2001), 312.

206   "Ring the lawyer, quick!": Miles, *The Beatles Diary,* 312.

207   "a strange cocktail of love, sex, and forgetfulness": "John Lennon: In a Hard Day's Light Part I," *People,* April 1, 2008.

207   Yogi and Boo-Boo, the drug-sniffing dogs: Ed Tracey, "Top Comments: The Norman Pilcher Edition," *Daily Kos,* February 8, 2018.

207   LENNON AND FRIEND CHARGED IN POSSESSION OF MARIJUANA: Associated Press, "Lennon and Friend Charged in

Possession of Marijuana," *New York Times,* October 19, 1968.

208   "It was the most terrifying experience I have ever had": Anthony Fawcett, *John Lennon: One Day at a Time* (New York: Grove Press, 1976), 39.

208   "a reminder that a cop was lying in wait if anyone had a party": The Beatles, *The Beatles Anthology,* 303.

208   suffers a miscarriage: Miles, *The Beatles Diary,* 314.

208   "poisoned the wells of criminal justice": Tracey, "Top Comments."

——

209   Sheraton Centre: Pete Hamill, "The Death and Life of John Lennon," *New York,* March 18, 2008.

209   $82 per night: Hamill, "The Death and Life of John Lennon."

209   room 2730: Hamill, "The Death and Life of John Lennon."

210   reaches for his Walkman: James R. Gaines, "In the Shadows a Killer Waited," *People,* March 2, 1987.

211   "A creepy, sweaty guy recognized me": Angie Martoccio, "5 Highlights from James Taylor's New Audio Memoir," *Rolling Stone,* February 7, 2020.

CHAPTER 36

212   "nothing has been more romanticized than guns": Olivia B. Waxman, "How the Gun Control Act of 1968 Changed America's Approach to Firearms—and What People Get Wrong About That History," *Time,* October 25, 2018.

212   "sort of a history of rock and roll": John Lennon, "Lennon-McCartney Songalog: Who Wrote What," *Hit Parader,* April, 1972.

213   "The title of the article, which I never read, was 'Happiness

Is a Warm Gun'": David Sheff, *All We Are Saying: The Last Major Interview with John Lennon and Yoko Ono* (New York: St. Martin's Griffin, 2000), 188–89.

213   "I thought, what a fantastic, insane thing to say": Barry Miles, *Paul McCartney: Many Years from Now* (New York: Henry Holt, 1997), 496.

213   "so sick, you know, the idea of 'Come and buy your killing weapons'": Paul McCartney, interview by Radio Luxembourg, November 20, 1968.

213   "one of the greatest numbers on the album": Barry Miles, "The Beatles: *The Beatles* (*White Album*)," *International Times,* November 29, 1968.

214   "the music has three distinct phases ending with a touch of the '50s": Miles, "The Beatles."

214   "The firearm becomes feminine and the lyrics ambiguous": "The Beatles: *The Beatles* (*White Album*)," *Record Mirror,* November 16, 1968.

214   "Oh, well, by then I'm into double meanings": Sheff, *All We Are Saying,* 189.

214   "both avant-garde and incredibly popular at the same time": Peter Silverton, "Ringo Starr Auctions Off the First Copy of the Beatles' White Album: The Story of a Revolutionary Record," *The Independent,* December 1, 2015.

214   "four solo artists in one band": Miles, *The Beatles Diary,* 315.

214   "John got 00001 because he shouted the loudest": Miles, *Paul McCartney,* 502.

215   his copy, not John's, is the original: Silverton, "Ringo Starr Auctions Off the First Copy of the Beatles' White Album."

215   "Whoever gets it, it will have my fingerprints on it": Daniel Kreps, "Ringo Starr's Personal 'White Album' Sells for World Record $790,000," *Rolling Stone,* December 5, 2015.

215   "a little address book in Mick Jagger's back pocket": Kat Aaron, "Resurrected Stones Film Finds Pivot Point in Rock History," NPR.org, July 25, 2019.

216   "Oh, one that plays!": Keith Altham, "Rolling Stones: The Greatest Show on Earth," *New Musical Express,* December 21, 1968.

217   "it's nice to see and hear people working happily together": Barry Miles, "James Taylor: *James Taylor,*" *International Times,* January 1, 1969.

217   "We can't be more number one, we can't be more famous": Ken Mansfield, interview by the authors, 2019.

217   "Everything is about creativity": Ken Mansfield, interview by the authors, 2019.

217   "I wrote Yoko telling her that I planned to have her in the nude on the cover": Ritchie Yorke, "John Lennon: Ringo's Right, We Can't Tour Again," *New Musical Express,* June 7, 1969.

217   "find some better bodies to put on the cover than your two": Miles, *Paul McCartney,* 527.

218   selling only five thousand copies in the UK: Christopher Hooton, "Two Virgins: The Story Behind John Lennon and Yoko Ono's Intentionally 'Unflattering,' Banned Nude Album Cover," *The Independent,* November 23, 2018.

218   "pornographic": Dave Lifton, "Why John Lennon and Yoko Ono's 'Two Virgins' was Seized by Police," UltimateClassicRock.com, January 2, 2016.

218   FBI to open a file on John: Miles, *The Beatles Diary,* 327.

218   "But it was worth it for the howl that went up": Yorke, "John Lennon."

218   "angry because he couldn't achieve the level of spirituality he wanted": Philip Norman, *Slowhand: The Life and Music of Eric Clapton* (New York: Back Bay, 2019), 204.

218   "Fuck off—can't you see I'm meditating?": Norman, *Slowhand,* 204.

218   "I just got so fed up with the bad vibes": Jordan Runtagh, "10 Things You Didn't Know George Harrison Did," *Rolling Stone,* November 29, 2016.

219   "a lousy name in New York and you gave off bad vibes": Andrew Grant Jackson, "Book Excerpt: George Harrison Realizes It's Time to Move On from the Beatles," *Rolling Stone,* August 17, 2012.

219   "I didn't hit him": Jackson, "Book Excerpt."

219   "John had a tremendous weight on his shoulders": Ken Mansfield, interview by the authors, 2019.

CHAPTER 37

220   "It's another of Paul's projects": Barry Miles, *Paul McCartney: Many Years from Now* (New York: Henry Holt, 1997), 21.

220   "I think we should go back on the road": Bob Spitz, *The Beatles: The Biography* (New York: Back Bay, 2006), 804.

221   The costs of running the sprawling Apple Corps: Miles, *Paul McCartney,* 528.

221   Director Lindsay-Hogg has grand ideas: Miles, *Paul McCartney,* 529.

221   "The Beatles were to start playing as the sun came up": Jordan Runtagh, "Beatles' Famous Rooftop Concert: 15 Things You Didn't Know," *Rolling Stone,* January 29, 2016.

221   "a replica of the Roman Colosseum": Runtagh, "Beatles' Famous Rooftop Concert."

221   "go back to Liverpool": Philip Norman, *John Lennon: The Life* (New York: Ecco, 2008), 578.

221   "I'm warming to the idea of doing it in an asylum": Norman, *John Lennon,* 578.

221   "See you 'round the clubs": Spitz, *The Beatles,* 806.

222   "I think if George doesn't come back": Rob Sheffield, "And in the End," *Rolling Stone,* August 17, 2020.

222   "The point is, if George leaves": Sheffield, "And in the End."

222   "What a great idea it would be to play on the roof": Spitz, *The Beatles,* 815.

223   "What's the point?": Runtagh, "Beatles' Famous Rooftop Concert."

223   "too cold to play the chords": Runtagh, "Beatles' Famous Rooftop Concert."

224   "mere mortals after all": Thomas Hobbs, "I Took the Last Ever Shot of the Beatles—and They Were Miserable," *The Guardian,* February 10, 2019.

224   "You've got ten minutes": Runtagh, "Beatles' Famous Rooftop Concert."

224   flush drug stashes down the toilets: Runtagh, "Beatles' Famous Rooftop Concert."

224   "I hope we've passed the audition": Marisa Iati, "The Beatles Played on a London Rooftop in 1969. It Wound Up Being Their Last Show," *Washington Post,* January 30, 2019.

224   "It was really just the culmination of a lot of writing and rehearsing": Paul McCartney, interview by the authors, 2019.

CHAPTER 38

225   "If it carries on like this, all of us will be broke within the next six months": Ray Connolly, *Being John Lennon: A Restless Life* (New York: Pegasus Books, 2018), 299.

225   "That was my opening": John McMillian, "You Never Give Me Your Money: How Allen Klein Played the Beatles and the Stones," *Newsweek,* December 17, 2013.

225   "the Robin Hood of pop": Philip Norman, *Paul McCartney: The Life* (New York: Little, Brown, 2016), 371.

225   "just a piece of paper": McMillian, "You Never Give Me Your Money."

226 *THE BIGGEST MOTHERFUCKER IN THE VALLEY*: McMillian, "You Never Give Me Your Money."

226 "He was very nervous, you could see it in his face": Jann S. Wenner, "Lennon Remembers: Part Two," *Rolling Stone*, February 4, 1971.

226 "knew my work, and the lyrics that I had written": Wenner, "Lennon Remembers."

226 "anyone who knew me that well, without having met me before": Connolly, *Being John Lennon*, 300.

226 "I've asked Allen Klein to look after my things": Barry Miles, *Paul McCartney: Many Years from Now* (New York: Henry Holt, 1997), 544.

226 "we favored people who were street people": Bob Spitz, *The Beatles: The Biography* (New York: Back Bay, 2006), 820.

227 "FYM—Fuck You, Money": Norman, *Paul McCartney*, 373.

227 "Rock 'n' roll specializes in that kind of, 'This guy's a twerp. We've got to have him on our team!'": Miles, *Paul McCartney*, 545.

227 "Don't go near him, he's a dog. He's a crook": Miles, *Paul McCartney*, 545.

227 "making the biggest mistake of your life": Norman, *Paul McCartney*, 373.

228 "We were all pissed off with each other. We certainly weren't a gang anymore": Frank Mastropolo, "The Day Paul McCartney Married Linda Beatles Diary Volume 1: The Beatles Years (London: Omnibus Press, 2001), 337.Eastman," UltimateClassicRock.com, March 12, 2019.

228 "the sudden reality of having failed to become Mrs. McCartney": Mastropolo, "The Day Paul McCartney Married Linda Eastman."

228 "get married on a cross-channel ferry. That was the romantic part": The Beatles, *The Beatles Anthology* (San Francisco: Chronicle Books, 2000), 332.

229 Yogi the police dog: Norman, *Paul McCartney,* 380.

229 "Intellectually, we didn't believe in getting married": Spitz, *The Beatles,* 829.

230 "John Lennon's holding court about something or other": Rick Wilson, "The Day I Saw John and Yoko's 'Bed-In' Peace Demonstration," *The Guardian,* February 26, 2017.

230 "We knew whatever we did was going to be in the papers": Olivia B. Waxman, "Behind the Photo: How John Lennon and Yoko Ono Came Up with Their Idea for a Bed-In for Peace," *Time,* March 25, 2019.

230 "the space we would occupy anyway, by getting married, with a commercial for peace": Waxman, "Behind the Photo."

231 "Why not Saigon or Dallas if peace is the cause?": Wilson, "The Day I Saw John and Yoko's 'Bed-In' Peace Demonstration."

231 Allen Klein is appointed Apple's business manager: Barry Miles, *The Beatles Diary Volume 1: The Beatles Years* (London: Omnibus Press, 2001), 337.

231 "I'm a tidy sort of bloke": Rob Sheffield, "And in the End," *Rolling Stone*, August 17, 2020.

232 "Go a bit slower, Ringo": Norman, *Paul McCartney,* 386.

232 "one of those magic times when everything went right and nothing went wrong": Geoff Emerick and Howard Massey, *Here, There and Everywhere: My Life Recording the Music of the Beatles* (New York: Gotham Books, 2006), 270.

232 the Beatles' seventeenth number-one UK hit: "The Ballad of John and Yoko by the Beatles," Songfacts.com.

CHAPTER 39

233 "This is my story both humble and true": "John Lennon—Signed, Numbered Poets Lithograph, 1969," Record-Mecca.com.

233 "T is for Tommy who won the war": Anthony Fawcett, *John Lennon: One Day at a Time* (New York: Grove Press, 1976), 163.

233 a poetry stand in People's Park: Clara Bingham, "The Battle for People's Park, Berkeley," *The Guardian,* July 6, 2019.

233 "When I first got the news it stooned me, absolutely stooned me": Ritchie Yorke, "Bedding In for Peace: John and Yoko in Canada," *Rolling Stone,* June 28, 1969.

234 suite 1742 of Montreal's stately Queen Elizabeth Hotel: Fiona Tapp, "What It's Like to Stay in the Montreal Hotel Suite Where John Lennon and Yoko Ono Held Their Bed-In," *The Independent,* May 9, 2019.

234 "If I'm a joke, as they say, and not important, why don't they just let me in?": Yorke, "Bedding In for Peace."

234 "Violence really does beget violence": Barry Miles, *The Beatles Diary Volume 1: The Beatles Years* (London: Omnibus Press, 2001), 345.

235 "Yes, we're really scared to go to the US because people have become so violent": Yorke, "Bedding In for Peace."

235 "Our job is to write for the people now": Frank Mastropolo, "When John and Yoko's Bed-In Led to 'Give Peace a Chance," UltimateClassicRock.com, May 26, 2019.

235 scatters flower petals daily: Tapp, "What It's Like to Stay in the Montreal Hotel Suite."

235 four microphones and a four-track Ampex recorder: Bob Boilen, "Old Music Tuesday: 40 Years of Giving Peace a Chance," *All Songs Considered,* NPR.org, June 30, 2009.

235 "Sing along": Paul Williams, "Eyewitness: John and Yoko Record 'Give Peace a Chance,'" *Q,* November 1995.

235 namechecked in the lyrics of John's first solo single: Bob Boilen, "Old Music Tuesday."

236 "we don't have a leader but we have a song—'Give Peace

a Chance'": Richard Williams, "John & Yoko (Part 2)," *Melody Maker,* December 13, 1969.

236   "If you're going to have a car crash, try to arrange for it to happen in the Highlands": "The Day John Lennon Crashed His Car in the Highlands," *Press and Journal* (Aberdeen), December 8, 2015.

236   "like two apparitions dressed in black": Geoff Emerick and Howard Massey, *Here, There and Everywhere: My Life Recording the Music of the Beatles* (New York: Gotham Books, 2006), 279.

236   "Yes, I'm okay": Emerick and Massey, *Here, There and Everywhere,* 270.

237   "put a microphone up over here so we can hear her on the headphones": Miles, *The Beatles Diary,* 347.

237   "It's your job to keep people out of here": Emerick and Massey, *Here, There and Everywhere,* 291.

237   "in the middle of the Abbey Road studio, handing Yoko a small white packet": Kenneth Womack, "In 1969 the Fifth Beatle Was Heroin: John Lennon's Addiction Took Its Toll on the Band," *Salon,* February 15, 2019.

237   "Give me something funky": Barry Miles, "My Blue Period: John Lennon," *MOJO,* 1995, from original interviews on September 23 and 24, 1969, at Apple.

237   "Don't worry; I'll do the overdubs on this": Emerick and Massey, *Here, There and Everywhere,* 285.

237   "It's an upbeat, rock-a-beat-a-boogie, with very Lennon lyrics": Ritchie Yorke, "George Harrison Talks About the Beatles' Album, *Abbey Road,*" *Detroit Free Press,* September 26, 1969.

238   "he was a tailor and I was a customer who had ordered a suit and never returned": Adam Clark Estes, "John Lennon Wrote 'Come Together' for Timothy Leary but Pot Ruined It," *Gizmodo,* August 8, 2014.

238 "Can you play those chords backward?": David Sheff, *All We Are Saying: The Last Major Interview with John Lennon and Yoko Ono* (New York: St. Martin's Griffin, 2000), 191.

238 "one of the most beautiful things we've ever done": Yorke, "George Harrison Talks About the Beatles' Album, *Abbey Road*."

239 "name it *Everest* and pose for the cover in Tibet": Emerick and Massey, *Here, There and Everywhere*, 297.

239 "Let's just step outside and name it *Abbey Road*": Emerick and Massey, *Here, There and Everywhere*, 297.

239 the photographer, Iain MacMillan: June Scott, "Iain Mac-Millan," *The Guardian*, June 20, 2006.

239 Only one photograph shows them stepping perfectly in time: "The Scot Who Took the Beatles' *Abbey Road* Photo," *BBC News*, August 8, 2019.

240 "wasn't impressed enough to want to make a record": Earl Caldwell, "Record Producer Rejected Manson," *New York Times*, October 24, 1970.

241 "raunchiest, loudest, most ridiculous rock 'n' roll record you've ever heard": "Helter Skelter," BeatlesBible.com.

241 " 'I think we should do a song like that; something really wild' ": Miles, *The Beatles Diary*, 319.

CHAPTER 40

242 "Leave John alone!": Thomas Hobbs, "I Took the Last Ever Shot of the Beatles—and They Were Miserable," *The Guardian*, February 10, 2019.

242 Tittenhurst Park: Linda Serck, "Beatle John Lennon's Time at Tittenhurst Park in Ascot," *BBC News*, May 11, 2011.

242 a disturbing package: Hobbs, "I Took the Last Ever Shot of the Beatles."

242 "I want the white noise to take over and blot out the music

altogether": Geoff Emerick and Howard Massey, *Here, There and Everywhere: My Life Recording the Music of the Beatles* (New York: Gotham Books, 2006), 300.

243   "this marriage had come to an end—and boy does it show": Hobbs, "I Took the Last Ever Shot of the Beatles."

243   "We were very square people in a way": Kenneth Womack, "In 1969 the Fifth Beatle Was Heroin: John Lennon's Addiction Took Its Toll on the Band," *Salon,* February 15, 2019.

243   "John's gone away for two weeks, just to get away from it all": Jerry Hopkins, "James Taylor on Apple: The Same Old Craperoo," *Rolling Stone,* August 23, 1969.

244   "It took courage enough for John to go cold turkey on his own": Philip Norman, *John Lennon: The Life* (New York: Ecco, 2008), 619.

244   leave the band: David L. Ulin, "All You Need Is Love, and a Good Lawyer," *Tampa Bay Times,* July 16, 2010.

244   "How would you fancy playing at a rock 'n' roll festival with the Plastic Ono Band in Toronto?": Philip Norman, *Slowhand: The Life and Music of Eric Clapton* (New York: Back Bay, 2019), 220.

244   "Nothing's expected of John and Yoko or the Plastic Ono": Barry Miles, "My Blue Period: John Lennon," *MOJO,* 1995, from original interviews on September 23 and 24, 1969, at Apple.

245   "We tried to rehearse on the plane": Bob Spitz, *The Beatles: The Biography* (New York: Back Bay, 2006), 845.

245   Varsity Stadium at the University of Toronto: Barry Miles, *The Beatles Diary Volume 1: The Beatles Years* (London: Omnibus Press, 2001), 352.

245   hasn't played to a crowd this size since the Beatles' 1966 American tour: Norman, *Slowhand,* 221.

245   "I am the King and I should close the show": Juliette

Jagger, "The Domino Effect: How One of Toronto's Most Iconic Rock Concerts Almost Never Happened," *Noisey,* April 13, 2015.

245   "Everyone get out your matches and lighters, please": Jagger, "The Domino Effect."

246   "only with all of us blasting it. Fantastic. It's just pure sound": Miles, "My Blue Period."

246   "What's next?" Miles, *The Beatles Diary,* 352.

246   "Then we went into 'Give Peace a Chance,' which was just unbelievable": Miles, *The Beatles Diary,* 352.

246   "The buzz was incredible": Norman, *John Lennon,* 622.

246   "I don't care who I have to play with, I'm going back to playing rock onstage!": Spitz, *The Beatles,* 846.

246   a new deal with EMI's Capitol Records: Miles, *The Beatles Diary,* 353.

247   "I never liked that sort of pop opera on the other side": Jann Wenner, "The *Rolling Stone* Interview: John Lennon, Part One—The Working Class Hero," *Rolling Stone,* January 1971.

247   "You don't seem to understand, do you?": Norman, *John Lennon,* 624.

247   "I felt guilty at springing it on them at such short notice": Norman, *John Lennon,* 624.

247   "'It's weird, this, telling you I'm leaving the group, but in a way it's very exciting'": Norman, *John Lennon,* 624.

247   Eric Clapton on guitar, Klaus Voormann on bass, and Ringo on drums: Norman, *Slowhand,* 222.

247   Twenty-six takes: "Cold Turkey by John Lennon," Songfacts.com.

248   "reached the point where nobody worries TOO much about what the Beatles are doing": Chris Welch, "Natural Born Beatles," *Melody Maker,* September 27, 1969.

248   "probably the nicest melody I've ever written": Ritchie

Yorke, "George Harrison Talks About the Beatles' Album, *Abbey Road*," *Detroit Free Press,* September 26, 1969.

248 "the greatest love song in the past fifty years": Barry Miles, *Paul McCartney: Many Years from Now* (New York: Henry Holt, 1997), 553.

248 "John, Paul, and George looked like they had gone back in time": Emerick and Massey, *Here, There and Everywhere,* 295.

249 "'Cold Turkey' talks about thirty-six hours rolling in pain": Mike Gormley, "Are We Burying McCartney Before He Is Dead?" *Detroit Free Press,* October 17, 1969.

249 "They thought it was a pro-drugs song": "Cold Turkey by John Lennon," Songfacts.com.

249 "One for both, both for each other": Miles, *The Beatles Diary,* 341.

249 a backing track of their heartbeats: Jason Farago, "Hearing Yoko Ono All Over Again," *New York Times,* June 25, 2015.

250 "We didn't expect a hit record out of it": "Wedding Album," BeatlesBible.com.

250 "When people get married they usually make their own wedding albums": Richard Williams, "John and Yoko (Part 2)," *Melody Maker,* December 13, 1969.

250 "I'd enjoy reading Jackie and Onassis's album": Williams, "John and Yoko."

250 Pete Seeger leads 250,000 demonstrators through Lennon's lyrics: Jon Wiener, "'War Is Over! If You Want It': John and Yoko, 40 Years Later," *The Nation,* December 27, 2009.

251 "We'll keep promoting peace in the way we do": Williams, "John & Yoko."

251 "Laurel and Hardy, that's John and Yoko": Norman, *John Lennon,* 627.

251 "all the serious people like Martin Luther King and Kennedy and Gandhi get shot": Wiener, "'War Is Over!'"

251   "Cold Turkey slipping down the charts": John Lennon, *The John Lennon Letters,* edited by Hunter Davies (New York: Little, Brown, 2012), 168.

251   "Really shouldn't have taken it": Gloria Emerson, "John Lennon Returns Award as a Protest," *New York Times,* November 26, 1969.

251   "War is over! If you want it": Wiener, " 'War Is Over!' "

252   "You've got to turn on and drop *in*. Or they're going to drop all over you": Wiener, " 'War Is Over!' "

252   Clown of the Year: Ray Connolly, *Being John Lennon: A Restless Life* (New York: Pegasus Books, 2018), 318.

252   Man of the Decade: Norman, *John Lennon,* 630.

252   "Not many people are noticing all the *good* that came out of the last ten years": John Lennon, interview with Desmond Morris, *Man of the Decade*, ATV, December 2, 1969, BeastlesInterviews.org.

252   "The sixties was just waking up in the morning, and we haven't even got to dinnertime yet": Lennon, interview with Desmond Morris, *Man of the Decade.*

CHAPTER 41

253   "John just wrote a great song and he wants to cut it as a single": David Browne, "Flashback: John Lennon Writes and Records 'Instant Karma!' in One Day," *Rolling Stone,* January 27, 2019.

253   "I'm going to record it tonight and have it pressed up and out tomorrow": Nick DeRiso, "Why John Lennon Recorded 'Instant Karma' So Quickly," UltimateClassicRock.com, February 6, 2016.

254   "there really is a reaction to what you do now": De-Riso, "Why John Lennon Recorded 'Instant Karma' So Quickly."

254 "Alan, whatever you're doing, keep doing it": DeRiso, "Why John Lennon Recorded 'Instant Karma' So Quickly."

254 "Uh, could you put the cymbals down?": Browne, "Flashback."

254 wants no input from Apple engineers: Geoff Emerick and Howard Massey, *Here, There and Everywhere: My Life Recording the Music of the Beatles* (New York: Gotham Books, 2006), 316–17.

254 "You're making Phil a bit uncomfortable": Emerick and Massey, *Here, There and Everywhere,* 317.

254 "How do you want it?": Browne, "Flashback."

254 "It sounded like there was fifty people playing": DeRiso, "Why John Lennon Recorded 'Instant Karma' So Quickly."

254 "I wrote it for breakfast": Rob Sheffield, "And in the End," *Rolling Stone,* August 17, 2020.

255 ten days after John first conceived of the song: Barry Miles, *The Beatles Diary Volume 1: The Beatles Years* (London: Omnibus Press, 2001), 368.

255 "That Would Be Something": Miles, *The Beatles Diary,* 369.

255 the solo work lifts his spirits: Barry Miles, *Paul McCartney: Many Years from Now* (New York: Henry Holt, 1997), 571.

255 *Top of the Pops*: Sheffield, "And in the End."

255 thirteen songs to fill a homemade eponymous album: Miles, *Paul McCartney,* 572.

256 All four Beatles have approval over who will polish the songs: Jim Irvin, "Get It Better: The Story of *Let It Be…Naked*," *MOJO,* 2003.

256 "harps, horns, an orchestra, and women's choir": Miles, *Paul McCartney,* 575.

256 "I would *never* have female voices on a Beatles record": Ray Connolly, *Being John Lennon: A Restless Life* (New York: Pegasus Books, 2018), 323.

256 "We're sorry it turned out like this—it's nothing personal":

Philip Norman, *Paul McCartney: The Life* (New York: Little, Brown, 2016), 413.

257 "The Beatles are alive and well and the Beat goes on": Miles, *The Beatles Diary,* 374.

257 start of a solo career or a break with the Beatles: Norman, *Paul McCartney,* 418.

257 PAUL QUITS BEATLES: Kitty Empire, "Paul McCartney Leaves the Beatles," *The Guardian,* June 11, 2011.

257 "I only had me to ask for a decision, and I agreed with me": "What Paul Said," *Record Mirror,* April 18, 1970.

258 "He gets all the credit for it!": Bob Spitz, *The Beatles: The Biography* (New York: Back Bay, 2006), 854.

258 "cardboard tombstone": Alan Smith, "New LP Shows They Couldn't Care Less: Have Beatles Sold Out?" *New Musical Express,* May 9, 1970.

258 "Musically, boys, you passed the audition": John Mendelsohn, "The Beatles: *Let It Be,*" *Rolling Stone,* June 11, 1970.

258 "no one wanted to be the one to say the party's over": Norman, *Paul McCartney,* 419.

259 "He's crying, she's crying, and we're just trying to hold on to ourselves": Joe Hagan, "Jann Wenner, John Lennon, and the Greatest *Rolling Stone* Cover Ever," *Vanity Fair,* November 2017.

259 "This music is bringing on the revolution, the unorganized overthrow of the establishment": David Felton and David Dalton, "Charles Manson: The Incredible Story of the Most Dangerous Man Alive," *Rolling Stone,* June 1970.

259 "It's not my conspiracy. It is not my music": "Helter Skelter," BeatlesBible.com.

260 "What's 'Helter Skelter' got to do with knifing somebody?": Miles, *The Beatles Diary,* 319.

CHAPTER 42

261   drink Dr Pepper while they play on a Mellotron: Jude Rogers, "Not the Only One: How Yoko Ono Helped Create John Lennon's Imagine," *The Guardian,* September 6, 2018.

261   "It was like a house of fun": *Event* magazine, "John and Yoko Unseen: Playing Pool at His White Mansion, Boating with His Son... Rare and Intimate Photos of Lennon's Last Idyllic Summer in Britain," *Daily Mail,* September 29, 2018.

261   "If you die, will I ever see you again?": Debra Wallace, "Julian Lennon on His Father's Legacy, White Feathers, and His New Book *Love the Earth,*" *Parade,* April 30, 2019.

262   a loss of $8 million: Barney Hoskyns, *75 Years of Capitol Records* (Cologne: Taschen, 2016).

262   "I should have been born in New York, I should have been born in the Village": Jann S. Wenner, "Lennon Remembers, Part Two," *Rolling Stone,* February 4, 1971.

262   *Grapefruit,* Yoko's book of poetry: Nell Beram, "The Book That Inspired 'Imagine,'" *Slate,* July 4, 2014.

263   "For Yoko, Happy Birthday, love John": "John Lennon Wrote 'Imagine' on His White Steinway. What Would You Write on Yours?" *Daily Mail,* July 23, 2011.

263   "I quickly jumped into a white Rolls-Royce with Nicky Hopkins": Alan di Perna, "'Imagine' This: How John Lennon and George Harrison Teamed Up to Record a Classic Album in 1971," *Guitar World,* May 2019.

263   "It's a piece of wood with strings on it. You just play it, OK?": di Perna, "'Imagine' This."

264   "I'm just a guy who writes songs": Alastair McKay, "Weekend's Best TV: Imagine All the People Who Adored John Lennon... Then Spare a Thought for David Cassidy," *Evening Standard,* November 23, 2018.

264 "always felt responsible for these people because they were the result of his songs": Rogers, "Not the Only One."

264 booked the Record Plant: Keith Badman, *The Beatles Diary Volume 2: After the Break-Up, 1970–2001* (London: Omnibus Press, 2001), 38.

264 "the air of a luxurious space capsule": Hendrik Hertzberg, "Poetic Larks Bid Bald Eagle Welcome Swan of Liverpool," *The New Yorker*, December 2, 1972.

265 "Harrison's guitar playing was more classically beautiful": di Perna, "'Imagine' This."

265 Only Ringo accepts: "The George Harrison Bangla Desh Benefit," *Rolling Stone*, September 2, 1971.

266 "wants to go onstage at George's Bangladesh thing. I'm not gonna do it": Dan Richter, "What John and Yoko's Butler Saw: A Surreal Account of the Lennons' Live-In Assistant During the Last Dark Days of the Beatles," *Daily Mail*, August 4, 2012.

266 "We are not trying to make any politics": Geoffrey Cannon, "George Harrison & Friends: *The Concert for Bangladesh*," *The Guardian*, January 4, 1972.

266 "What Woodstock was *said* to be": Cannon, "George Harrison & Friends."

267 "much easier for me to say I'm not taking *anything*, so I don't have to answer any questions": "The George Harrison Bangla Desh Benefit."

267 eventually embroiled in several lawsuits: Pierre Perrone, "Allen Klein: Notorious Business Manager for the Beatles and the Rolling Stones," *The Independent*, July 6, 2009.

CHAPTER 43

268 "You could say I fell in love with New York on a street corner": Philip Norman, *John Lennon: The Life* (New York: Ecco, 2008), 683.

268   six-month B-2 tourist visas: Jon Wiener, *Gimme Some Truth: The John Lennon FBI Files* (Berkeley and Los Angeles: University of California Press, 1999), 213.

268   "Mr. and Mrs. John W. Lennon": Hendrik Hertzberg, "Poetic Larks Bid Bald Eagle Welcome Swan of Liverpool," *The New Yorker,* December 2, 1972.

268   "cheaper and more functional to actually live here": Keith Badman, *The Beatles Diary Volume 2: After the Break-Up, 1970–2001* (London: Omnibus Press, 2001), 47.

269   "'You can have my wife, but you can't have my child'": David Sheff, "*Playboy* Interview with John Lennon and Yoko Ono," *Playboy,* January 1981.

269   "We love it, and it's the center of our world": Hendrik Hertzberg, "Everywhere's Somewhere," *The New Yorker,* January 1, 1972.

269   "America is the Roman Empire and New York is Rome itself": Ray Connolly, *Being John Lennon: A Restless Life* (New York: Pegasus Books, 2018), 347.

269   "They're like me...they don't believe in wasting time": Norman, *John Lennon,* 683.

269   "John has a New York temperament in his work": Hertzberg, "Everywhere's Somewhere."

269   "walk around the streets and parks and squares": Norman, *John Lennon,* 683.

269   "unbelievably creative atmosphere": Hertzberg, "Everywhere's Somewhere."

270   "Everywhere's somewhere, and everywhere's the same, really, and wherever you are is where it's at": Hertzberg, "Everywhere's Somewhere."

270   "I'm proud to be a New York hippie!": Hertzberg, "Poetic Larks Bid Bald Eagle Welcome Swan of Liverpool."

270   "we got moved on by the police, and it was all very

NOTES

wonderful": Steve Marinucci, "Anti-Establishment Icon David Peel Dies at 73," *Billboard,* April 6, 2017.

270　"Picasso spent 40 years trying to get as simple as that": Daniel Kreps, "David Peel, Folk Singer and Counterculture Figure, Dead at 73," *Rolling Stone,* April 7, 2017.

270　"We loved his music, his spirit, and his philosophy of the street": William Grimes, "David Peel, Downtown Singer and Marijuana Evangelist, Dies at 74," *New York Times,* April 9, 2017.

271　*The Pope Smokes Dope* by David Peel and the Lower East Side: Marinucci, "Anti-Establishment Icon David Peel Dies at 73."

271　"He was deadly serious, but he knew how to have fun": Dave Thompson, "Remembering David Peel," *Goldmine,* April 6, 2017.

271　"New York City is your friend": Hertzberg, "Everywhere's Somewhere."

271　"everybody seems to know everybody": Hertzberg, "Everywhere's Somewhere."

271　three hotel rooms: Badman, *The Beatles Diary,* 47.

272　"I can do the scene better": Badman, *The Beatles Diary,* 47.

272　"The close friendship between Jerry Rubin and John Lennon (and Yoko)": Ron Hart, "Yoko and the Yippies," *Rock & Roll Globe,* December 17, 2018.

272　"Yoko Ono told me and Abbie that they considered us to be great artists": Mitch Myers, "Activist Jerry Rubin's 1970 Protest Boogie with Bob Dylan, John and Yoko Chronicled in New Biography (Excerpt)," *Variety,* August 22, 2017.

272　the same building: Hertzberg, "Everywhere's Somewhere."

273　"imagine the body": Grace Glueck, "Art by Yoko Ono Shown at Museum in Syracuse," *New York Times,* October 11, 1971.

273 "She thinks up beautiful pure concept things, and I come up with a gimmicky reaction": Glueck, "Art by Yoko Ono Shown at Museum in Syracuse."

273 "There was going to be a secret Beatles reunion concert": Sean Kirst, "Imagine: John Lennon, and an Almost-Beatles-Reunion, in Syracuse," Syracuse.com, December 8, 2005.

274 "a black velvet hotpants suit": Glueck, "Art by Yoko Ono Shown at Museum in Syracuse."

274 a raucous semiprivate performance: Onondaga Historical Association, "John Lennon and Yoko Ono Make Art in Syracuse," CNYHistory.org, October 2015.

274 "*the* single of the year": Geoffrey Cannon, "George Harrison & Friends: *The Concert for Bangladesh,*" *The Guardian,* January 4, 1972.

276 "Lennon's won, hands down": Roy Hollingworth, "All We Need Is Lennon," *Melody Maker,* October 9, 1971.

276 "McCartney ballads, and McCartney rockers, the way McCartney should be doing them": Alan Smith, "John Sings Long Track About Paul," *New Musical Express,* September 11, 1971.

276 "the spokesman for the politically conscious avant-garde": John Mendelsohn, "Wild Life [US Bonus Tracks]," *Rolling Stone,* January 20, 1972.

278 Leslie Nielsen: "A Look Back at Mark David Chapman in His Own Words," *Larry King Live,* CNN.com, September 30, 2000.

278 Robert Goulet: Keith Elliot Greenberg, *December 8, 1980: The Day John Lennon Died* (Montclair, NJ: Backbeat Books, 2010), 23.

279 "quick picture": "A Look Back at Mark David Chapman in His Own Words."

279 *The Wizard of Oz*: James R. Gaines, "In the Shadows a Killer Waited," *People,* March 2, 1987.

280 *Playboy* magazine: Robert Rosen, *Nowhere Man: The Final Days of John Lennon* (New York: Soft Skull Press, 2000), 180.

280 *They're coming together*: Jack Jones, *Let Me Take You Down: Inside the Mind of Mark David Chapman, the Man Who Killed John Lennon* (New York: Villard Books, 1992), 18.

CHAPTER 44

281 "I wanna come home": Dave Marsh, "John Sinclair: Free John and Yoko," *Creem,* March 1972.

282 years behind bars: Agis Salpukas, "15,000 Attend Michigan U. Rally to Protest Jailing of Radical Poet," *New York Times,* December 12, 1971.

282 "High Priest of Heavy": Marsh, "John Sinclair."

282 "matching black leather jackets, unzipped to reveal 'Free John Now' T-shirts": Jon Wiener, *Gimme Some Truth: The John Lennon FBI Files* (Berkeley and Los Angeles: University of California Press, 1999), 121.

282 Sinclair is known as a poet and a music reviewer: Sean O'Hagan, "John Sinclair: 'We Wanted to Kick Ass—and Raise Consciousness,'" *The Guardian,* March 3, 2014.

282 "old, retired, and forgotten by the time they're thirty": Mike Gormley, "New Political Rock Group: The Up Begins Where MC5 Left Off," *Detroit Free Press,* July 3, 1970.

283 "Apathy won't get us anywhere": Marsh, "John Sinclair."

283 "It became journalism and not poetry": Anthony Fawcett, *John Lennon: One Day at a Time* (New York: Grove Press, 1976), 124.

283 "they were awful. The music was boring. And it was four a.m.": Marsh, "John Sinclair."

283 FBI agents compile reports based on informants' findings: Wiener, *Gimme Some Truth,* 113.

284 "an interesting piece, but lacking Lennon's usual standards": Wiener, *Gimme Some Truth,* 121.

284 "composed by Lennon especially for this event": Wiener, *Gimme Some Truth,* 113.

284 "Lennon had to read the lyrics from a music stand as he sang": Wiener, *Gimme Some Truth,* 121.

284 "I wrote a ditty about John Sinclair": Alan Glenn, "The Day a Beatle Came to Town," the *Ann Arbor Chronicle,* December 27, 2009.

284 "It was a beautiful thing to do": O'Hagan, "John Sinclair."

284 "two and a half years of agitating and organizing": Karen Dalton-Beninato, "John Sinclair Recalls the Song John Lennon Wrote to Free Him," *HuffPost,* December 6, 2017.

286 green dress: Jack Jones, *Let Me Take You Down: Inside the Mind of Mark David Chapman, the Man Who Killed John Lennon* (New York: Villard Books, 1992), 16.

287 "A real man doesn't have to take from a woman. He can give": James R. Gaines, "In the Shadows, A Killer Waited," *People,* March 2, 1987.

287 a world he doesn't understand: Jones, *Let Me Take You Down,* 16–17.

288 questioned something he did: Gaines, "In the Shadows, A Killer Waited."

CHAPTER 45

290 "use the available political machinery to screw our political enemies": Jon Wiener, *Come Together: John Lennon in His Time* (New York: Random House, 1984), 226.

291   "I think it would be well for it to be considered at the highest level": Elizabeth Mitchell, "New York Stories: How This Hastily Shot Image of John Lennon Became an Enduring Symbol of Freedom," *Daily News* (New York), June 11, 2016.

291   "strong advocates of the program to 'dump Nixon'": Robert A. Martin, "Thurmond Led Move to Deport Lennon," UPI, June 29, 1984.

291   "If Lennon's visa is terminated, it would be a strategy countermeasure": Martin, "Thurmond Led Move to Deport Lennon."

291   hasn't been able to reunite with her daughter: Keith Badman, *The Beatles Diary Volume 2: After the Break-Up, 1970–2001* (London: Omnibus Press, 2001), 68.

291   "It was a kidnapping and a very difficult situation": Chrissy Iley, "Yoko Ono: 'John's Affair Wasn't Hurtful to Me. I Needed a Rest. I Needed Space,'" *The Telegraph,* March 27, 2012.

291   "the Immigration and Naturalization Service has served notice on him": Jon Wiener, *Gimme Some Truth: The John Lennon FBI Files* (Berkeley and Los Angeles: University of California Press, 1999), 5.

292   "never heard of John Lennon, much less Yoko Ono": Hendrik Hertzberg, "Poetic Larks Bid Bald Eagle Welcome Swan of Liverpool," *The New Yorker,* December 2, 1972.

292   "out to get John and Yoko from the first moment I got into the case": Steve Marinucci, "The Story of the Man Who Saved John Lennon & Yoko Ono from Being Deported," *Billboard,* August 4, 2016.

292   "All extremists should be considered dangerous": Wiener, *Gimme Some Truth,* 129.

292   "Lennon and his wife are passé about United States politics": Wiener, *Gimme Some Truth,* 178.

293 "I suggest you tell them to get the hell out": Marinucci, "The Story of the Man Who Saved John Lennon & Yoko Ono from Being Deported."

293 FBI report mangled their home address: Wiener, *Gimme Some Truth*, 150.

293 "an agent behind every mail box": Patrick Cockburn, "FBI Admits Men in Dark Glasses Did Harass Lennon," *The Independent*, September 9, 1994.

293 "I thought he was being paranoid": Ray Connolly, *Being John Lennon: A Restless Life* (New York: Pegasus Books, 2018), 353.

293 "two guys interminably fixing a bike": Marinucci, "The Story of the Man Who Saved John Lennon & Yoko Ono from Being Deported."

293 "I felt followed everywhere by government agents": Connolly, *Being John Lennon*, 353–54.

294 "what was being done to him was wrong": Dave Swanson, "When John Lennon Was Ordered to Leave U.S. by Immigration Authorities," UltimateClassicRock.com, March 23, 2016.

294 "the Nixon administration [making] life intolerable": "Richard Nixon's Secret Battle to Deport John Lennon: President Feared the Beatle's Anti-Vietnam Campaigning Would Swing the 1972 Election," *Daily Mail*, September 4, 2016.

294 "so determined to remove anyone from the United States": "Richard Nixon's Secret Battle to Deport John Lennon."

294 "New York is the center of the earth and also because we want to find Yoko's daughter": Badman, *The Beatles Diary*, 69.

294 "But we love to be here": Badman, *The Beatles Diary*, 71.

295 Willowbrook parents filed a class-action lawsuit: Kristin F. Dalton, "The Horrors of Willowbrook State School," SILive.com, January 19, 2017.

295   "the work I was doing on behalf of the developmentally disabled": Geraldo Rivera, interview by the authors, 2019.

295   JOHN & YOKO WAIT & WAIT: Wiener, *Gimme Some Truth*, 266.

295   fruitlessly scour San Francisco: Badman, *The Beatles Diary*, 79–80.

295   "I know the whereabouts of Kyoko Cox": Wiener, *Gimme Some Truth*, 278.

296   "very distressed by what was happening to them": Geraldo Rivera, interview by the authors, 2019.

296   treatment from a Chinese acupuncturist: "Postscript," *New York Times*, October 7, 2010.

296   kept secret by referring to John "as J. L.": Scott James, "Family Opened Up the Door to John and Yoko," *New York Times*, October 7, 2010.

296   the One to One concert: Badman, *The Beatles Diary*, 81.

296   two Madison Square Garden performances, a movie, and a record: Don Heckman, "Lennon Concert Slated Aug. 30 in All-Day Fete to Aid Retarded," *New York Times*, August 17, 1972.

296   "We raised about a quarter of a million dollars": Philip Recchia and Lindsay Powers, "Looking Back on John Lennon's NYC Love Affair 35 Years After His Death," *New York Post*, December 8, 2005.

297   "Now more than ever, baby, Nixon now!": Michael Beschloss, "If Party Conventions Seem More Like Infomercials, Blame Nixon," *New York Times*, July 1, 2016.

297   "Hate to get personal about it": Tim Findley, "Outside the Convention: Cops and Confusion," *Rolling Stone*, September 28, 1972.

297   "I don't think the youth vote is in anybody's pocket": Beschloss, "If Party Conventions Seem More Like Infomercials, Blame Nixon."

297   "zippies, Yippies, hippies, crazies": Findley, "Outside the Convention."

297 "People who want to have bloody hands go over to the tent": Findley, "Outside the Convention."

298 "a member of the former musical group known as 'The Beatles'": Wiener, *Gimme Some Truth,* 4.

298 a publicity still of David Peel: William Grimes, "David Peel, Downtown Singer and Marijuana Evangelist, Dies at 74," *New York Times,* April 9, 2017.

298 "rock's greatest flattery": Paul DeRienzo, "David Peel, 74, the King of Pot, Punk and Protest," AMNY.com, April 13, 2017.

298 "I just really trust him, you know?": Findley, "Outside the Convention."

299 "captioned case is being closed in the NY Division": Wiener, *Gimme Some Truth,* 304.

CHAPTER 46

300 "something weird at the door": Francis Schoenberger, "He Said, She Said: An Interview with John Lennon," *Spin,* October 9, 2019 (reprint of 1975 interview).

300 "As he didn't lead the revolution, I decided to quit answering the phone": Schoenberger, "He Said, She Said."

301 "I can't believe this is fuckin' IT": Jon Wiener, "John Lennon and George McGovern: Another Side of the 1972 Campaign," *The Nation,* October 22, 2012.

301 "out of his head with drugs and pills and drink": Philip Norman, *John Lennon: The Life* (New York: Ecco, 2008), 704.

301 "She didn't come on to him at all": Norman, *John Lennon,* 704.

302 "coats in the next room, where John and this girl are making out, so nobody can go home": Norman, *John Lennon,* 705.

302 "It was very embarrassing": Ray Connolly, *Being John Lennon: A Restless Life* (New York: Pegasus Books, 2018), 356.

302 the Dakota: Carrie Hojnicki, "Inside New York's Most Famous Apartment Building," *Architectural Digest,* April 24, 2017.

302 twelve rooms and sweeping views of Central Park: Keith Badman, *The Beatles Diary Volume 2: After the Break-Up, 1970–2001* (London: Omnibus Press, 2001), 94.

302 "chockablock full of famous people": Christine Haughney, "Sharing the Dakota with John Lennon," *New York Times,* December 6, 2010.

302 "It is a big apartment, and it's beautiful, but it doesn't have grounds": Schoenberger, "He Said, She Said."

303 "That situation really woke me up": Norman, *John Lennon,* 705.

303 "John and I are not getting along. We've been arguing. We're growing apart": Albert Goldman, "John and Yoko's Troubled Road Part II," *People,* August 22, 1988.

303 "They had a loving relationship and it broke down because of all that pressure": Steve Marinucci, "The Story of the Man Who Saved John Lennon & Yoko Ono from Being Deported," *Billboard,* August 4, 2016.

304 travel together to Washington, DC, to witness testimony: Daniel Bush, "The Complete Watergate Timeline (It Took Longer Than You Realize)," *PBS NewsHour,* May 30, 2017.

304 Elvin Bell, an adviser to Nixon: Elvin C. Bell, "A Chance Meeting with John Dean, John Lennon and Yoko Ono," *Fresno Bee,* September 14, 2018.

CHAPTER 47

306 "I needed a rest. I needed space": Chrissy Iley, "Yoko Ono: 'John's Affair Wasn't Hurtful to Me. I Needed a Rest. I Needed Space,'" *The Telegraph,* March 27, 2012.

306 "I was hated and John was hated because of me": Iley, "Yoko Ono."

306 "I started to notice that he became a little restless": Iley, "Yoko Ono."

307 "So then I suggested L.A., and he just lit up": Philip Norman, *John Lennon: The Life* (New York: Ecco, 2008), 712.

307 "May Pang was a very intelligent, attractive woman and extremely efficient": Iley, "Yoko Ono."

307 "John will probably start going out with other people": Ray Connolly, *Being John Lennon: A Restless Life* (New York: Pegasus Books, 2018), 358.

307 May Pang—a young Chinese American woman, a Catholic, from Spanish Harlem: Albert Goldman, "John and Yoko's Troubled Road Part II," *People,* August 22, 1988.

307 "I just looked at her and said, 'Not me. I'm not interested'": Steve Marinucci, "The Abbeyrd Interview with May Pang," Abbeyrd.net, March 28, 2008.

307 "I had hoped her idea would pass": Marinucci, "The Abbeyrd Interview With May Pang."

308 Capitol Records fronts the expense of the trip: Norman, *John Lennon,* 714.

308 "not about me or them but the state of the world": Steve Marinucci, "Life with the Lennons: 'Imagine' Reissues Bring Back John and Yoko Memories for Elliot Mintz," *Variety,* October 8, 2018.

308 "when or even if they'd be getting back together": Norman, *John Lennon,* 714.

308 his signature French cigarettes: Harry Cockburn, "France Considers Banning Gitanes and Gauloises Cigarettes for Being 'Too Cool,'" *The Independent,* July 21, 2016.

309 "to sit on Capitol, to do the artwork and to see to things like radio promotion": Chris Charlesworth, "John Lennon: Lennon Today," *Melody Maker,* November 3, 1973.

309 "It was a big blow when they [the Beatles] split up, of

course": Barney Hoskyns, *75 Years of Capitol Records* (Cologne: Taschen, 2016).

309   "Someone told me it was like *Imagine* with balls, which I like a lot": Charlesworth, "John Lennon."

309   "He reached artistic heights and healed a lot of his personal relationships": Minnie Wright, "John Lennon: May Pang Sets Record Straight on Her AFFAIR with the Beatles Star," *Express,* January 18, 2020.

309   "he wasn't miserable for 18 months": Wright, "John Lennon."

310   "happiest times of my life": May Pang, *Instamatic Karma: Photographs of John Lennon* (New York: St. Martin's Press, 2008), xi.

310   "It wasn't by any means a lost weekend": Norman, *John Lennon,* 713.

310   "I've got to be honest, I never saw that in him at all": Elton John, *Me* (New York: Henry Holt, 2019), 115.

310   "a short tier below the BeatleStones on the mass pop scale": Wayne Robins, "Elton John: *Goodbye Yellow Brick Road,*" *Creem,* January 1974.

310   "Elton's notorious for being a very fast writer": Mark Savage, "Elton John on the Yellow Brick Road," *BBC News,* March 24, 2014.

311   "I took to him straightaway": John, *Me,* 115.

311   "dancing around with a man dragged up as the Queen, for fuck's sake": John, *Me,* 115.

311   "Fred Astaire and Ginger Beer": Norman, *John Lennon,* 718.

311   "You can't choose your drag name": Alexis Petridis, " 'This Is a Very Good Question, Bob Dylan': Elton John, Interviewed by Famous Fans," *The Guardian,* October 12, 2019.

312   "It was thanks to my mum that we started having conversations again": Joshua David Stein, " 'He Didn't Even Pretend to Let Us Win' ... Growing Up with the World's

Biggest Stars, by Their Children," *The Guardian,* March 29, 2020.

312 making its final crossing from Southampton to New York: John, *Me,* 117.

313 Elton John and Tony King will be aboard for the same voyage: John, *Me,* 117.

313 ten-year-old Julian immediately embraces his father: Norman, *John Lennon,* 722.

313 "charming, funny, and warm": Stein, "'He Didn't Even Pretend to Let Us Win.'"

313 "shocked to see 'a little man' and not the small child he remembered": Pang, *Instamatic Karma,* xv.

313 "a lot of time getting reacquainted as father and son": Pang, *Instamatic Karma,* xv.

313 "if he had his time over, he'd be different to Julian": Norman, *John Lennon,* 724.

313 "May was wonderful, even though she was young and inexperienced": Pang, *Instamatic Karma,* back cover.

CHAPTER 48

315 cedes total control to Spector: Ray Connolly, *Being John Lennon: A Restless Life* (New York: Pegasus Books, 2018), 360.

316 "The guys were all drinking—and John was being one of the guys": Frank Mastropolo, "John Lennon's Infamous 'Lost Weekend' Revisited," UltimateClassicRock.com, April 2, 2014.

316 "somebody had to be, you know, sane": Mastropolo, "John Lennon's Infamous 'Lost Weekend' Revisited."

316 "the Vampire": Connolly, *Being John Lennon,* 360.

316 "Spector pulled out a large gun and started chasing John through the hallways": Larry Kane, "The John Lennon We Did Not Know," Today.com, June 27, 2007.

316   "Listen, Phil, if you're gonna kill me, kill me": Philip Norman, *John Lennon: The Life* (New York: Ecco, 2008), 721.

317   "The original Hollywood Vampires was a drinking club": Barry Nicolson, "Inside John Lennon, Keith Moon and Alice Cooper's Legendary Hollywood Drinking Club," NME.com, September 8, 2015.

317   "drinking the blood of the vine": Nicolson, "Inside John Lennon, Keith Moon and Alice Cooper's Legendary Hollywood Drinking Club."

317   Hollywood rockers such as Cooper: Kory Grow, "Alice Cooper and Joe Perry on Hollywood Vampires' Drunk History," *Rolling Stone,* September 3, 2015.

317   covered the Beatles' "A Hard Day's Night": "Billion Dollar Babies Tour 1973," AliceCoopereChive.com.

318   "religion and everything else that causes fights": Grow, "Alice Cooper and Joe Perry on Hollywood Vampires' Drunk History."

318   "It was funny because neither one was a fighter": Nicolson, "Inside John Lennon, Keith Moon and Alice Cooper's Legendary Drinking Club."

318   "The difference between the two was that Harry loved to drink and was good at it": Norman, *John Lennon,* 727–28.

318   John and Harry show up at the Troubadour: Keith Badman, *The Beatles Diary Volume 2: After the Break-Up, 1970–2001* (London: Omnibus Press, 2001), 120.

319   "They taste like milk shakes": Kane, "The John Lennon We Did Not Know."

319   "Harry would keep feeding John drinks until it was too late": Kane, "The John Lennon We Did Not Know."

319   "I think we almost screwed up the act": Kane, "The John Lennon We Did Not Know."

319   "It was horrendous": Mastropolo, "John Lennon's Infamous 'Lost Weekend' Revisited."

320   "I'm Ed Sullivan!": Badman, *The Beatles Diary,* 120.

320   "With Love & Tears!": Badman, *The Beatles Diary,* 120.

320   "No comment!": Badman, *The Beatles Diary,* 120.

320   the district attorney investigates the events: Kane, "The John Lennon We Did Not Know."

320   "I had to pay her off": Badman, *The Beatles Diary,* 120.

320   "doing a lot of screaming the night before": Norman, *John Lennon,* 731.

321   "Where is all that yooooooo-deeeee-dooooo-dahh stuff?" Badman, *The Beatles Diary,* 121.

321   escape his own marital troubles: Chris O'Dell with Katherine Ketcham, *Miss O'Dell: My Hard Days and Long Nights with the Beatles, the Stones, Bob Dylan, Eric Clapton, and the Women They Loved* (New York: Touchstone, 2009), 263.

321   " 'So, this is where they did it' ": May Pang, *Instamatic Karma: Photographs of John Lennon* (New York: St. Martin's Press, 2008), 12.

322   "We were all sort of spooked by the legend of Marilyn, especially John": O'Dell and Ketcham, *Miss O'Dell,* 274.

322   "an official portrait of President Kennedy on the wall": Pang, *Instamatic Karma,* 12.

322   "This is my brilliant idea, to have us all live together and work together": Francis Schoenberger, "He Said, She Said: An Interview with John Lennon," *Spin,* October 9, 2019 (reprint of 1975 interview).

323   *"I'm the producer, man! I'd better straighten out.* So I straightened out": Schoenberger, "He Said, She Said."

323   Paul's own arrests for cannabis possession: Norman, *John Lennon,* 730.

323   Paul's in town for the forty-sixth Academy Awards: Badman, *The Beatles Diary,* 120.

323   sits behind the drum kit: Nick DeRiso, "Why John

Lennon and Paul McCartney's Final Session Was a Bust," UltimateClassicRock.com, March 28, 2016.

323   "Midnight Special": Badman, *The Beatles Diary,* 121.

323   "Don't get too serious, we're not getting paid": Badman, *The Beatles Diary,* 122.

324   "they made joyous music together that night": DeRiso, "Why John Lennon and Paul McCartney's Final Session Was a Bust."

324   "just watching me and Paul": Badman, *The Beatles Diary,* 122.

CHAPTER 49

325   "The affair was something that was not hurtful to me": Chrissy Iley, "Yoko Ono: 'John's Affair Wasn't Hurtful to Me. I Needed a Rest. I Needed Space,'" *The Telegraph,* March 27, 2012.

325   "I was prepared to lose him, but it was better he came back": Iley, "Yoko Ono."

325   "First they were directives to keep our relationship quiet": Minnie Wright, "John Lennon: May Pang Sets Record Straight on Her AFFAIR with the Beatles Star," *Express,* January 18, 2020.

326   "She'd call every day to remind us what to say": Wright, "John Lennon."

326   "Some days he would call me three or four times": Iley, "Yoko Ono."

326   "'What do I have to do to get out of here and back to her?'": Philip Norman, *John Lennon: The Life* (New York: Ecco, 2008), 716.

326   her tarot card reader, John Green: Albert Goldman, "John and Yoko's Troubled Road Part II," *People,* August 22, 1988.

326 multiple readings a day on any subject of her choice: Susan Reed and Fred Bernstein, " 'Friends' Cash In on John Lennon's Memory, and Yoko May Pay a Price," *People*, July 4, 1983.

326 "Yoko came to our house in England and asked if I would do her a favor": Paul McCartney, interview by the authors, 2019.

327 the Pierre hotel, on Fifth Avenue, in a suite right above Elton John's: Elton John, *Me* (New York: Henry Holt, 2019), 118.

328 "I'm out of favor at the moment": "Whatever Gets You Thru the Night," BeatlesBible.com.

328 Reverend Ike: Christopher Lehmann-Haupt, "Reverend Ike, Who Preached Riches, Dies at 74," *New York Times,* July 29, 2009.

328 "Let me tell you guys, it doesn't matter": Richard Buskin, "John Lennon 'Whatever Gets You Thru the Night,'" *Sound on Sound*, June 2009.

328 "fiddling about": Frances Katz, "When Elton John Met John Lennon," CultureSonar.com, June 27, 2019.

328 "he got bored easily, which was right up my street": John, *Me,* 119.

328 "Say, can I put a bit of piano on that?": Katz, "When Elton John Met John Lennon."

329 "He zapped in. I was amazed at his ability": Katz, "When Elton John Met John Lennon."

329 adds piano and harmony to "Surprise, Surprise (Sweet Bird of Paradox)": Nick DeRiso, "Revisiting John Lennon's Last Concert Appearance," UltimateClassicRock.com, November 28, 2015.

329 a steep wager as to just how high it will chart: John, *Me,* 119.

329 "So, I sort of halfheartedly promised": DeRiso, "Revisiting John Lennon's Last Concert Appearance."

329   "Elton John—*Elton John?????*—on keyboards and back-up vocals": Charles Shaar Murray, "John Lennon: *Walls and Bridges*," *New Musical Express,* October 5, 1974.

329   "the ice cream that follows a tonsillectomy": Ben Gerson, "Walls and Bridges," *Rolling Stone,* November 21, 1974.

330   *Walls and Bridges* is certified gold on October 22: Keith Badman, *The Beatles Diary Volume 2: After the Break-Up, 1970–2001* (London: Omnibus Press, 2001), 136.

330   "Remember when you promised..." DeRiso, "Revisiting John Lennon's Last Concert Appearance."

330   John will be working on Thanksgiving: John, *Me,* 119.

330   gardenias, her favorite flower: Tim Riley, *Lennon: The Man, the Myth, the Music—The Definitive Life* (New York: Hyperion, 2011), 660.

330   "the emotional thing was me and Elton together": DeRiso, "Revisiting John Lennon's Last Concert Appearance."

330   Dr. Winston O'Boogie: Richard Havers, "Elton John and John Lennon's Surprise Collaboration," UDiscoverMusic.com, November 16, 2015.

330   "an old estranged fiancé of mine called Paul": Jen Carlson, "38 Years Ago Today, John Lennon Performed at His Last Concert," Gothamist.com, November 28, 2012.

331   "it's an old Beatle number, and we just about know it": Carlson, "38 Years Ago Today."

332   "It was either that or [let] Klein have the whole thing": Barry Miles, *Paul McCartney: Many Years from Now* (New York: Henry Holt, 1997), 576.

332   "I didn't sign it because my astrologer told me it wasn't the right day": Ray Connolly, *Being John Lennon: A Restless Life* (New York: Pegasus Books, 2018), 371.

332   "the first anyone had ever heard of him having an astrologer": Connolly, *Being John Lennon,* 371.

332   he's no longer wanted onstage tonight: Allan Kozinn, "A

Fond Look at Lennon's 'Lost Weekend,'" *New York Times,* March 12, 2008.

333 Paul, the peacemaker, comes over to John and May's apartment: Kozinn, "A Fond Look at Lennon's 'Lost Weekend.'"

333 "The friendship was still there. They were brothers. There was no animosity": Kozinn, "A Fond Look at Lennon's 'Lost Weekend.'"

333 "give Julian a good time for his Christmas holiday, somewhere warm": Joe Capozzi, "John Lennon's Last Years in Palm Beach," *Palm Beach Post,* November 1, 2018.

333 "A few days in Palm Beach, a day or two at Disney World": Capozzi, "John Lennon's Last Years in Palm Beach."

334 "I don't like being famous": Capozzi, "John Lennon's Last Years in Palm Beach."

334 the Polynesian Village Resort at Disney World: May Pang, *Instamatic Karma: Photographs of John Lennon* (New York: St. Martin's Press, 2008), 101.

334 "Take out your camera": Pang, *Instamatic Karma,* 98.

334 "replaying the entire Beatles experience in his mind": Kozinn, "A Fond Look at Lennon's 'Lost Weekend.'"

334 "As he had started the group, he was the one to end it": Kozinn, "A Fond Look at Lennon's 'Lost Weekend.'"

CHAPTER 50

335 the twenty-first birthday party Dean Martin threw for his son Ricci: Ricci Martin with Christopher Smith, *That's Amore: A Son Remembers Dean Martin* (Lanham, MD: Taylor Trade Publishing, 2002), 141.

335 Other guests included Ringo, Elton John, Elizabeth Taylor: Martin and Smith, *That's Amore,* 141.

335 "He loved the old-time Hollywood stars": Roger Friedman, "David Bowie Was Introduced to John Lennon by

the Greatest Hollywood Icon," Showbiz411.com, January 11, 2016.

336   "Miss Taylor had been trying to get me to make a movie with her": "David Bowie Tells a Story About John Lennon," BeatlesArchive.net.

336   "I mean she was a nice woman and all": Cameron Crowe, "David Bowie: Ground Control to Davy Jones," *Rolling Stone,* February 12, 1976.

336   "'Don't mention the Beatles, you'll look really stupid'": "David Bowie Tells a Story About John Lennon."

336   "most uncool to actually say you liked the Beatles in any way, shape, or form": Jenny Desborough, "David Bowie John Lennon: Bowie Reveals Lennon's 'SPITEFUL Sense of Humour,'" *Express,* April 11, 2020.

336   "he defined for me, at any rate, how one could twist and turn the fabric of pop": "David Bowie Tells a Story About John Lennon."

337   "one of the brightest, quickest witted, earnestly socialist men I've ever met": Desborough, "David Bowie John Lennon."

337   "a really spiteful sense of humour which of course, being English, I adored": Desborough, "David Bowie John Lennon."

337   the elaborate sets for his Diamond Dogs Tour: Mick Brown, "David Bowie: 'I Have Done Just About Everything That It's Possible to Do,'" *Daily Telegraph,* December 14, 1996.

337   "today looked on with as much awe as a release by the Beatles in the sixties": Chris Charlesworth, "David Bowie: *Diamond Dogs,*" *Melody Maker,* May 11, 1974.

337   *The Rise and Fall of Ziggy Stardust and the Spiders from Mars*: Susan E. Booth, "'The Rise and Fall of Ziggy Stardust and the Spiders from Mars'—David Bowie (1972)," National Registry, Library of Congress, 2016.

338 "It's just fooking rock and roll with lipstick": Brown, "David Bowie."

338 Electric Lady Studios: Liesl Schillinger, "Jimi Hendrix's Electric Lady Studios Turns 45," *Wall Street Journal Magazine,* August 12, 2015.

338 add a cover of "Across the Universe": Jeff Giles, "Revisiting David Bowie's R&B Move, 'Young Americans,'" UltimateClassicRock.com, March 7, 2016.

338 "It's not a matter of craftsmanship; it wrote itself": David Sheff, *All We Are Saying: The Last Major Interview with John Lennon and Yoko Ono* (New York: St. Martin's Griffin, 2000), quoted in "Across the Universe," BeatlesBible.com.

339 eliminating the Sanskrit mantra "Jai guru deva om": Nicholas Pegg, *The Complete David Bowie,* 6th ed. (London: Titan Books, 2016), 5.

339 "It's one of my favorite songs, but I didn't like my version of it": Pegg, *The Complete David Bowie,* 4.

339 "'I don't want to do these interviews! I don't want to have these photographs taken!'": Giles, "Revisiting David Bowie's R&B Move."

339 "What was that riff you had?": Jack Whatley, "The Story Behind the Song: David Bowie and John Lennon's Middle Finger to 'Fame,'" *Far Out,* December 5, 2019.

339 "I play any guitar that pays": Kory Grow, "David Bowie Guitarist Carlos Alomar: 'He Was So Damn Curious,'" *Rolling Stone,* January 11, 2016.

339 "He goes in with about four words and a few guys": John Lennon and Yoko Ono, Interview by Andy Peebles, BBC Radio 1, December 6, 1980.

340 "God, that session was fast": Giles, "Revisiting David Bowie's R&B Move."

340 "John and I wrote a song together and we recorded and mixed it": Giles, "Revisiting David Bowie's R&B Move."

340 "I wouldn't know how to pick a single if it hit me in the face": "Today in Music History: David Bowie's 'Fame' Went No. 1," *The Current Morning Show,* Minnesota Public Radio, September 20, 2019.

340 "And we made a record out of it": John Lennon and Yoko Ono, Interview by Andy Peebles, BBC Radio 1, December 6, 1980.

340 Paul suggests that John come down to record with him in New Orleans: Ray Connolly, *Being John Lennon: A Restless Life* (New York: Pegasus Books, 2018), 372.

CHAPTER 51

342 "I had to concentrate on being pregnant for a whole nine months": Chrissy Iley, "Yoko Ono: 'John's Affair Wasn't Hurtful to Me. I Needed a Rest. I Needed Space,'" *The Telegraph,* March 27, 2012.

342 "having a baby was important to us and that anything else was subsidiary to that": David Sheff, "*Playboy* Interview with John Lennon and Yoko Ono," *Playboy,* January 1981.

343 John books a country house: Anthony Fawcett, *John Lennon: One Day at a Time* (New York: Grove Press, 1976), 119.

343 "Stay alive in '75. That's my motto": Francis Schoenberger, "He Said, She Said: An Interview with John Lennon," *Spin,* October 9, 2019 (reprint of 1975 interview).

343 chronicling all the highs and lows of his separation from her: Philip Norman, *John Lennon: The Life* (New York: Ecco, 2008), 743.

344 Simon and Garfunkel, who split in 1970: Will Levith, "Paul Simon Opens Up About Simon & Garfunkel Breakup," *InsideHook,* August 25, 2016.

344 "Hello, I'm John. I used to play with my partner, Paul": "17th GRAMMYs: Paul Simon and John Lennon Co-Presenting the GRAMMY for Record of the Year," Genius.com.

344 "Are *you guys* getting back together again?": "Paul Simon and John Lennon at the Grammy Awards Were Total Hilarity," SocietyOfRock.com.

344 "Thank you, Mother": Jörg Pieper with Ian MacCarthy, *The Solo Beatles Film and TV Chronicle 1971–1980* (self-pub., 2019), Lulu.com, 154.

344 "I was glad it was big, and it was quick, so we got maximum effect": Fawcett, *John Lennon,* 143.

345 That man is John Mitchell: "John N. Mitchell Dies at 75; Major Figure in Watergate," *New York Times,* November 10, 1988.

345 "the subject of illegal surveillance activities on the part of the government": Fawcett, *John Lennon,* 145.

346 grant a stay on the humanitarian grounds: Geoffrey Giuliano, *Lennon in America: 1971–1980, Based in Part on the Lost Lennon Diaries* (New York: Cooper Square Press, 2000), 238.

346 "It would have been unconscionable to deport him now": "A Truce Is Called in Lennon's Deportation Fight So He Can Comfort the Pregnant Yoko," *People,* October 13, 1975.

263 "governmental action was based principally on a desire to silence political opposition": Arnold H. Lubasch, "Deportation of Lennon Barred by Court of Appeals," *New York Times,* October 8, 1975.

346 Chief Judge Irving Kaufman: Marilyn Berger, "Judge Irving Kaufman, of Rosenberg Spy Trial and Free-Press Rulings, Dies at 81," *New York Times,* February 3, 1992.

346 "will not condone selective deportation based on secret political grounds": Lubasch, "Deportation of Lennon Barred by Court of Appeals."

347 "It's a great birthday gift from America for me, Yoko, and the baby": Lubasch, "Deportation of Lennon Barred by Court of Appeals."

347 "I feel higher than the Empire State Building!": Fawcett, *John Lennon,* 146.

347   "John and Yoko and Sean (three virgins)": Andy Greene, "50th Anniversary Flashback: Inside John Lennon's Long History with Rolling Stone," *Rolling Stone,* July 14, 2017.

——

348   "You wouldn't happen to know whether John Lennon might be planning on coming out today, would you?": Jack Jones, *Let Me Take You Down: Inside the Mind of Mark David Chapman, the Man Who Killed John Lennon* (New York: Villard Books, 1992), 25.

349   T-shirt promoting Todd Rundgren's 1978 solo album: James McMahon, "The Shooting of John Lennon: Will Mark David Chapman Ever Be Released?," *The Independent,* March 2, 2020.

349   brand-new Bic pen: Jones, *Let Me Take You Down,* 36.

349   *This is my statement*: "A Look Back at Mark David Chapman in His Own Words," *Larry King Live,* CNN.com, September 30, 2000.

349   *History and time*: Jones, *Let Me Take You Down,* 22.

350   personal items: Jones, *Let Me Take You Down,* 19.

350   "Did you see him?" Jones, *Let Me Take You Down,* 18.

351   "I came all the way across the ocean from Hawaii, and I'm honored to meet you": Jones, *Let Me Take You Down,* 31.

351   "You'd better take care of that runny nose": Jones, *Let Me Take You Down,* 31.

351   "beautiful boy": *CNN Special Report: Killing John Lennon,* CNN.com, December 8, 2015.

CHAPTER 52

352   "You're all pizza and fairy tales": Kurt Loder, "Paul McCartney: The *Rolling Stone* Interview," *Rolling Stone,* September 11, 1986.

352 "the best insult I could think of was to say, 'Oh, fuck off, Kojak'": Loder, "Paul McCartney."

353 "obvious to me that the two of them had run out of things to say": Tim Riley, *Lennon: The Man, the Myth, the Music—The Definitive Life* (New York: Hyperion, 2011), 641–42.

353 "John was wearing a long black tuxedo with tails": "John Lennon & Yoko Ono," *People*, February 12, 1996.

353 "Paul McCartney had made $25 million": Philip Norman, "Lennon Has Been Painted a Crazed Recluse. But the Truth Is Very Different—and Deeply Touching...," *Daily Mail*, October 6, 2008.

353 "it's going to take me at least two years": Norman, "Lennon Has Been Painted a Crazed Recluse."

353 "I wanted to be with Sean the first five years": Norman, "Lennon Has Been Painted a Crazed Recluse."

353 "I took a Polaroid of my first loaf. It was like an album coming out of the oven": "Picks and Pans Review: The Playboy Interviews with John Lennon and Yoko Ono," *People*, February 15, 1982.

354 "She's the world's most famous unknown artist": Charlotte Higgins, "The Guardian Profile: Yoko Ono," *The Guardian*, June 8, 2012.

354 amass five apartments: Robert Lasson, "A Luxury Building," *New York Times*, September 16, 1979.

354 the words *helter skelter* written in large letters across a wall of the studio: Stephen Birmingham, *Life at the Dakota: New York's Most Unusual Address* (New York: Random House, 1979), Kindle.

354 "John and Yoko were as bad as me when it came to shopping": Elton John, *Me* (New York: Henry Holt, 2019), 138.

354 "Imagine six apartments, it isn't hard to do, one is full of fur coats, another's full of shoes": John, *Me*, 138.

354 "My insecurity is having too many clothes": David Sheff,

All We Are Saying: The Last Major Interview with John Lennon and Yoko Ono (New York: St. Martin's Griffin, 2000), 99.

354 "Most artists like myself tend to keep to themselves": Christine Haughney, "Sharing the Dakota with John Lennon," *New York Times,* December 6, 2010.

355 Paul and John tune in to *Saturday Night Live*: "John Lennon & Yoko Ono."

355 turned down $230 million from Sid Bernstein: Philip Recchia, "Paul: We Can Work It Out; '79 Deal OK'd Beatles Reunion Any Time at All," *New York Post,* December 5, 2005.

355 "all you have to do is sing three Beatles songs": "April 24, 1976: John and Paul Almost Go on *SNL*," BestClassicBands.com, April 24, 2017.

356 watch for any Beatles entering the lobby: Phil Dyess-Nugent, "*Saturday Night Live (Classic)*: 'Raquel Welch,'" AVClub.com, September 29, 2013.

356 "Wouldn't it be funny if we went down": Riley, *Lennon,* 645.

356 "we decided it was too much like work": Paul McCartney, interview by the authors, 2019.

356 studio audience refuses to sing along: Dyess-Nugent, "*Saturday Night Live (Classic)*."

356 "It's not 1956 and turning up at the door isn't the same anymore": David Sheff, "*Playboy* Interview with John Lennon and Yoko Ono," *Playboy*, January, 1981.

357 a diagnosis of terminal stomach cancer: Ray Connolly, *Being John Lennon: A Restless Life* (New York: Pegasus Books, 2018), 384.

357 "I'm sorry I treated you the way I did, Dad": Riley, *Lennon,* 644.

357 "It's just bloody marvelous to talk to you again": Riley, *Lennon,* 644.

357 "They'd go to Central Park for picnics": "John Lennon & Yoko Ono."

358 United States should finally issue him a green card: Leslie Maitland, "John Lennon Wins His Residency in U.S.," *New York Times,* July 28, 1976.

358 "I wish to continue to live here with my family and continue making music": Chris Charlesworth, "John Lennon Gets His Ticket to Ride," *Melody Maker,* August 7, 1976.

358 "Justice for John & Yoko!": Hendrik Hertzberg, "Songs of the Poetic Larks," *The New Yorker,* October 10, 2010.

358 "prove that John was an important figure to the well-being of American society": Geraldo Rivera, interview by the authors, 2019.

359 "the Lennons will help do something about it": Charlesworth, "John Lennon Gets His Ticket to Ride."

359 "one of the great artists of the Western world": Charlesworth, "John Lennon Gets His Ticket to Ride."

359 "It's great to be legal again!": Maitland, "John Lennon Wins His Residency in U.S."

359 "See, I thought you would understand": Damian Fanelli, "George Harrison and Paul Simon Play 'Here Comes the Sun,'" *Guitar Player,* October 13, 2017.

360 George plays the opening chords to "Here Comes the Sun": Robert Rodriguez, *Fab Four FAQ 2.0: The Beatles Solo Years, 1970–1980* (New York: Backbeat Books, 2010), 65.

360 "God, it'd be cool to do something like that": Chris Handyside, *Fell in Love with a Band: The Story of the White Stripes* (New York: St. Martin's Griffin, 2004), 212.

CHAPTER 53

361 Linda Ronstadt sings onstage at the Kennedy Center: Emily Heil, "From Jimmy Carter to Barack Obama, Aretha Franklin Was the Soundtrack for Presidents," *Washington Post,* August 16, 2018.

361   a $175 suit he brought with him: Sarah Pruitt, "10 Un-expected Moments in Presidential Inauguration History," History.com, August 22, 2018.

361   "I used to be a Beatle": "The Famed Dakota: The Lennon Residence (1973–1980)," BeatlesHistorian.com.

362   the armed guard, nearly ten thousand strong, that Nixon marshaled in 1969: Pruitt, "10 Unexpected Moments in Presidential Inauguration History."

362   "We're living in a more tranquil period of society": Steve Ditlea, "The Bullish Boom in the Record World," *New York Times,* June 5, 1977.

362   "talking to guys and gals that have been through what we went through, together": Dave Sholin and Laurie Kaye, "John Lennon's Last Interview, December 8, 1980," BeatlesArchive.net.

362   the little boy sings: "Listen to a Home Recording of John Lennon Singing the Beatles with His Son Sean," *Far Out,* February 28, 2020.

363   "Anything you ever see on a commercial is a lie": David Fricke, "Sean Lennon on His Father, Yoko Ono, and His Own Musical Career," *Rolling Stone,* June 11, 1998.

363   a nighttime ritual for the two of them: Fricke, "Sean Lennon on His Father."

363   WE ARE THE TERRORISTS [FROM] THE FALN PUERTO RICAN INDEPENDENCE MOVEMENT: Jack Cloherty, Pierre Thomas, and Jason Ryan, "Beatle John Lennon Threatened in Extortion Plot, Says FBI," ABC News, December 1, 2011.

364    $100,000 in a "strong package": Cloherty, Thomas, and Ryan, "Beatle John Lennon Threatened in Extortion Plot."

364   "we are good preparedly for it": Cloherty, Thomas, and Ryan, "Beatle John Lennon Threatened in Extortion Plot."

364   "on this you can have our trust": Cloherty, Thomas, and Ryan, "Beatle John Lennon Threatened in Extortion Plot."

365   a thousand acres of land in Delaware County: "John Lennon's Travels in Ulster County, New York," *New York Almanack,* August 6, 2012; David Kamp, "Lennon at 70!," *Vanity Fair,* September 24, 2010.

365   a herd of registered Holstein cattle: Jay Cocks, "The Last Day in the Life," *Time,* December 22, 1980.

365   "sell a cow for $250,000": Cocks, "The Last Day in the Life."

365   bulletproof vests: Philip Norman, *John Lennon: The Life* (New York: Ecco, 2008), 783.

365   "I really don't want to leave Palm Beach": Joe Capozzi, "John Lennon's Last Years in Palm Beach," *Palm Beach Post,* November 1, 2018.

365   toured and rented under the pseudonym Mrs. Green: Capozzi, "John Lennon's Last Years in Palm Beach."

365   El Solano: Capozzi, "John Lennon's Last Years in Palm Beach."

365   Julian meets his half brother, Sean, for the first time: Capozzi, "John Lennon's Last Years in Palm Beach."

365   sixteenth birthday, April 8, 1979, with a family party on a chartered yacht: Capozzi, "John Lennon's Last Years in Palm Beach."

366   "Sunrises rejuvenate you. It recharges the batteries!": Capozzi, "John Lennon's Last Years in Palm Beach."

366   Cannon Hill: Christopher Twarowski, "Imagine: John Lennon on Long Island," *Long Island Press,* October 5, 2013.

366   "a gorgeous place": Twarowski, "Imagine."

366   "So different than waking up in New York": Twarowski, "Imagine."

366   "she's a workaholic": Sholin and Kaye, "John Lennon's Last Interview."

366 "It's better here than real life": Robert F. Worth, "Yoko Ono Says Ex-Aide Stole Tapes," *New York Times,* September 25, 2002.

CHAPTER 54

367 "send stuff, fan mail, to the house on Long Island for storage": Tyler Coneys, interview by the authors, 2019.

367 "a mocked-up album cover": Tyler Coneys, interview by the authors, 2019.

368 "All my life I've been dreaming of having my own boat": Brian R. San Souci, "There's No Place Like Nowhere," *Rhode Island Monthly,* May 10, 2010.

368 Billy Joel's home on Cooper's Bluff: Nick Paumgarten, "Thirty-Three-Hit Wonder," *The New Yorker,* October 20, 2014.

368 "Billy, I have all your records!": Philip Norman, *John Lennon: The Life* (New York: Ecco, 2008), 780.

368 "I'd like to go say hi to Billy Joel but I don't want to bother him": "Hear Billy Joel Pay Homage to John Lennon on His Birthday," *Hear & Now,* SiriusXM.com, October 9, 2016.

368 "We both respected each other's privacy": "Hear Billy Joel Pay Homage to John Lennon on His Birthday."

368 Paul Goresh: Anthony G. Attrino, "N.J. Man Who Took Last Photo of John Lennon Recalls Tragedy," NJ.com, December 07, 2015.

369 "casting a shadow over his life and creativity": San Souci, "There's No Place Like Nowhere."

369 *Megan Jaye,* a forty-three-foot Hinckley sloop: "John Lennon's Newport to Bermuda Sailing Voyage," *Newport Buzz,* December 8, 2019.

369 Hank Halsted: San Souci, "There's No Place Like Nowhere."

370 "John, since you're the least experienced sailor on board, I'm

appointing you ship's cook": San Souci, "There's No Place Like Nowhere."

370   "You just affected 50 million people there to the positive, big boy": Norman, *John Lennon,* 790.

370   "I'm going to raise my son": San Souci, "There's No Place Like Nowhere."

371   "I'm gonna need some help here, big boy": Norman, *John Lennon,* 791.

371   "He was thin, but very wiry and strong": Tyler Coneys, interview by the authors, 2019.

371   *It's like being onstage; once you're on there's no gettin' off*: David Sheff, "*Playboy* Interview with John Lennon and Yoko Ono," *Playboy,* January 1981.

372   "I feel like a Viking!": Keith Badman, *The Beatles Diary Volume 2: After the Break-Up, 1970–2001* (London: Omnibus Press, 2001), 252.

372   his dead sailor father: Norman, *John Lennon,* 792.

372   "a man who was just enraptured": Norman, *John Lennon,* 792.

372   *I was screaming sea chanteys and shoutin' at the gods!*: Ray Connolly, *Being John Lennon: A Restless Life* (New York: Pegasus Books, 2018), 392.

372   requests a guitar: San Souci, "There's No Place Like Nowhere."

CHAPTER 55

373   Undercliff, a house two miles from Bermuda's capital, Hamilton: John McCarthy, "How John Lennon Rediscovered His Music in Bermuda," *Daily Beast,* July 11, 2017.

373   his Ovation acoustic guitar: Ken Sharp, "Lennon's Last Session: The Making of *Double Fantasy,*" *Record Collector,* n.d.

373   two Panasonic boom boxes: Sharp, "Lennon's Last Session."

373   "This one's for Mister Starkey": Sharp, "Lennon's Last Session."

374   *That song's not good enough*: Robert Hilburn, "In My Life: Robert Hilburn's 'Corn Flakes with John Lennon,'" *Los Angeles Times,* October 11, 2009.

374   "I'm getting all this stuff": Dave Sholin and Laurie Kaye, "John Lennon's Last Interview, December 8, 1980," BeatlesArchive.net.

374   "Incredible song": Ken Sharp, *Starting Over: The Making of John Lennon and Yoko Ono's Double Fantasy* (New York: Gallery Books, 2010), 154.

374   Yoko has written a companion song: Sharp, *Starting Over,* 154.

374   "I like it to be inspirational—from the spirit": Sholin and Kaye, "John Lennon's Last Interview."

374   "for the first time since 1967": Sholin and Kaye, "John Lennon's Last Interview."

375   "It sounds just like Yoko's music": Travis M. Andrews, "Forty Years Ago, 'Rock Lobster' Launched the Career of the B-52s—and Revived John Lennon's," *Washington Post,* April 6, 2018.

375   *They've finally caught up to where we were*: Sholin and Kaye, "John Lennon's Last Interview."

375   "tribute to Yoko": Andrews, "Forty Years Ago."

375   *Double Fantasy—that's a great title*: Sholin and Kaye, "John Lennon's Last Interview."

375   "a dream that we have—which we share": Sholin and Kaye, "John Lennon's Last Interview."

CHAPTER 56

376   "I'm interested in doing something extra special": Ben Yakas, "Producer Jack Douglas Talks About His Last Night with John Lennon: 'Some A-Hole Shot Him When He Got Home,'" Gothamist.com, July 19, 2016.

376   "John wants to do a record; he wants you to produce it":

Yakas, "Producer Jack Douglas Talks About His Last Night with John Lennon."

377 "What I want to make here is a record about a middle-aged man": Yakas, "Producer Jack Douglas Talks About His Last Night with John Lennon."

377 "I'm facing middle age, I'm looking at forty": Yakas, "Producer Jack Douglas Talks About His Last Night with John Lennon."

377 "a househusband for the last five years and I want to get back to the music": Ken Sharp, "Lennon's Last Session: the Making of *Double Fantasy*," *Record Collector*, n.d.

377 "They tell me you're good, just don't play too many notes": Sharp, "Lennon's Last Session."

378 "John Lennon had more of a clear vision of what he wanted from the bass than anybody": David Fricke, "Sean Lennon on His Father, Yoko Ono, and His Own Musical Career," *Rolling Stone*, June 11, 1998.

378 "pretend it's Christmas": "Happy Xmas (War Is Over) by John Lennon," Songfacts.com.

378 "I like that a lot, don't forget it": Sharp, "Lennon's Last Session."

378 "Wait, I just wrote it": Yakas, "Producer Jack Douglas Talks About His Last Night with John Lennon."

378 "I think it's a smash": Sharp, "Lennon's Last Session."

378 Photographers compete for position outside the Hit Factory: Keith Badman, *The Beatles Diary Volume 2: After the Break-Up, 1970–2001* (London: Omnibus Press, 2001), 256.

379 "the first photographer authorized to photograph John Lennon in five years": Ray Kelly, "Boston Photographer Recalls Final John Lennon Recording Sessions," MassLive.com, January 7, 2015.

379 "He looked every bit a rock star": Kelly, "Boston Photographer Recalls Final John Lennon Recording Sessions."

379   Kishin Shinoyama: Carolyn Kellogg, "Video: An Intimate Look at John Lennon and Yoko Ono," *Los Angeles Times,* April 2, 2015.

379   Jay Dubin: Ken Sharp, *Starting Over: The Making of John Lennon and Yoko Ono's Double Fantasy* (New York: Gallery Books, 2010), quoted in interview with Amanda Flinner, "80s Video Director Jay Dubin," Songfacts.com, December 17, 2014.

379   "Okay, let me sing a little bit of a song for you": Sharp, *Starting Over,* Flinner, "80s Video Director Jay Dubin."

CHAPTER 57

380   John and Yoko announce their new project: Keith Badman, *The Beatles Diary Volume 2: After the Break-Up, 1970–2001* (London: Omnibus Press, 2001), 257.

380   "as if it were a play and we were two characters in it": Dave Sholin and Laurie Kaye, "John Lennon's Last Interview, December 8, 1980," BeatlesArchive.net.

380   Paul even negotiated a secret (until 2005) clause: George Lang, "Sir Paul Was Thinking Ahead in '79: In a Contract, the Ex-Beatle Had a Clause That Allowed Reunions," *The Oklahoman,* December 9, 2015.

380   Ringo has also signed with the label: Ken Sharp, "Lennon's Last Session: the Making of *Double Fantasy,*" *Record Collector,* n.d.

381   "Whatever John wants for this record, we'll give it to him!": Badman, *The Beatles Diary,* 257.

381   arrives dressed all in white: "Timeline: Year by Year, How David Geffen Invented Himself," *American Masters,* PBS.org, November 1, 2012.

381   "good numbers": "Timeline: Year by Year, How David Geffen Invented Himself."

381 "Listen! She's doing Elvis!": Robert Hilburn, "In My Life: Robert Hilburn's 'Corn Flakes with John Lennon,'" *Los Angeles Times,* October 11, 2009.

381 Geffen agrees to Yoko's terms: "Timeline: Year by Year, How David Geffen Invented Himself."

382 "You can do it anywhere in the world except for the Record Plant": Sharp, "Lennon's Last Session."

382 keyed private elevators for security: "Timeline: Year by Year, How David Geffen Invented Himself."

382 "It's a very magical environment for a kid": David Fricke, "Sean Lennon on His Father, Yoko Ono, and His Own Musical Career," *Rolling Stone,* June 11, 1998.

382 "He was looking at me all the time": Sholin and Kaye, "John Lennon's Last Interview."

382 "Good night, Sean, see you in the morning": Nick DeRiso, "Revisiting John Lennon's Comeback Album 'Double Fantasy,'" UltimateClassicRock.com, November 17, 2015.

382 "ask questions with answers that no one will hear": David Sheff, *All We Are Saying: The Last Major Interview with John Lennon and Yoko Ono* (New York: St. Martin's Griffin, 2000), viii.

383 a conversation that will run three weeks: Sheff, *All We Are Saying,* xiii–xiv.

383 "This will be *the* reference book!": Badman, *The Beatles Diary,* 262.

383 "It's been a long time since we've done this kind of thing": Sheff, *All We Are Saying,* xv.

383 granted sit-downs with the BBC, *Newsweek,* and other media outlets: Badman, *The Beatles Diary,* 263.

383 A parallel concern for MacDougall is the surge in the number of fans: Badman, *The Beatles Diary,* 263.

CHAPTER 58

384   "only two artists I've ever worked with for more than a one night's stand, as it were": Dave Sholin and Laurie Kaye, "John Lennon's Last Interview, December 8, 1980," BeatlesArchive.net.

385   "I was into making my own bread": Paul McCartney, interview by the authors, 2019.

385   strictly macrobiotic—sugar-free and dairy-free: David Fricke, "Sean Lennon on His Father, Yoko Ono, and His Own Musical Career," *Rolling Stone,* June 11, 1998.

385   "John and Yoko will be touring Japan, USA, and Europe": Keith Badman, *The Beatles Diary Volume 2: After the Break-Up, 1970–2001* (London: Omnibus Press, 2001), 265.

385   Wayne Mansfield: Scott Armstrong, "Skywriting; The Making of a Miles-High Billboard," *Christian Science Monitor,* April 16, 1981.

385   HAPPY BIRTHDAY JOHN AND SEAN—LOVE YOKO: Badman, *The Beatles Diary,* 265.

385   "We're almost like twins": Sholin and Kaye, "John Lennon's Last Interview."

386   "I couldn't have been happier to see them and how happy and lighthearted they were": Geraldo Rivera, interview by the authors, 2019.

386   "one of the most famous people in the world walking around New York City without security": Charles Shaar Murray, "John Lennon & Yoko Ono: *Double Fantasy,*" *New Musical Express,* November 22, 1980.

386   "This one's for Gene, and Eddie, and Elvis": Mike Joseph, "Revisiting John Lennon's Last No. 1: '(Just Like) Starting Over,'" UltimateClassicRock.com, December 27, 2015.

387   "It's a fifties song made with an eighties approach": Sholin and Kaye, "John Lennon's Last Interview."

387   "the same kind of period-sound as 'Starting Over'": Sholin and Kaye, "John Lennon's Last Interview."

387   "Please get me some pictures without Yoko": "Final Portrait of John and Yoko Appears on the Cover of 'Rolling Stone,'" History.com, November 16, 2009.

387   "They like the album too much": John Swenson, "Cry for a Shadow," *Creem,* March 1981.

CHAPTER 59

388   "I'm happy to be forty years old": Albert Goldman, "John and Yoko's Troubled Road Part II," *People,* August 22, 1988.

388   "The old bugger still has a wonderful voice by the way": Charles Shaar Murray, "John Lennon & Yoko Ono: *Double Fantasy,*" *New Musical Express,* November 22, 1980.

388   John and Yoko pose for the photographer in front of the Dakota: Keith Badman, *The Beatles Diary Volume 2: After the Break-Up, 1970–2001* (London: Omnibus Press, 2001), 268.

389   "Go on, Mimi, spoil yourself": Badman, *The Beatles Diary,* 268.

391   "Where are you staying in New York?": Jack Jones, *Let Me Take You Down: Inside the Mind of Mark David Chapman, the Man Who Killed John Lennon* (New York: Villard Books, 1992), 29.

391   "Why the hell did you ask me that question?": Jones, *Let Me Take You Down,* 30.

391   the coat holds the gun: Jones, *Let Me Take You Down,* 30.

391   two beers and a hamburger: Jones, *Let Me Take You Down,* 30.

392   visit Hawaii: Vicki Sheff, "The Betrayal of John Lennon," *Playboy,* March 1984.

392   set your mind: Sheff, "The Betrayal of John Lennon."

CHAPTER 60

393   the Teddy Boy look: Philip Norman, *John Lennon: The Life* (New York: Ecco, 2008), 805.

393   "Just a daddy": Dave Sholin and Laurie Kaye, "John Lennon's Last Interview, December 8, 1980," BeatlesArchive.net.

394   first worked together in 1970: Andy Greene, "50th Anniversary Flashback: Inside John Lennon's Long History with Rolling Stone," July 14, 2017.

394   "I really want Yoko to be on the cover with me": Billy Heller and Michael Kane, "We Were There on the Awful Night John Lennon Was Shot," *New York Post,* December 4, 2005.

394   "'I want to be with *her*'": "Final Portrait of John and Yoko Appears on the Cover of 'Rolling Stone,'" History.com, November 16, 2009.

394   the nude *Two Virgins* shot: Carl M. Cannon, "John and Yoko and Annie: An Enduring Image of Love," RealClearPolitics.com, January 22, 2016.

395   "This is our relationship": Greene, "50th Anniversary Flashback."

395   "Ooh, can I have one with the jacket?": Sholin and Kaye, "John Lennon's Last Interview."

396   "I hope to God that I die before Yoko": *CNN Special Report: Killing John Lennon,* CNN.com, December 8, 2015.

396   "just bubbling over with enthusiasm with everything in his life": Heller and Kane, "We Were There on the Awful Night John Lennon Was Shot."

396   "I'm ready to start all over again and get this thing going": Heller and Kane, "We Were There on the Awful Night John Lennon Was Shot."

—

398   "your car hasn't shown up yet": Keith Badman, *The Beatles Diary Volume 2: After the Break-Up, 1970–2001* (London: Omnibus Press, 2001), 272.

398   "hitch a ride with us": Badman, *The Beatles Diary,* 272.

399   pen won't write: Daniel B. Schneider, "F.Y.I.," *New York Times,* August 13, 2000.

399   "John Lennon, 1980": Schneider, "F.Y.I."

399   "a dream he's had several times": Bill Hoffman, "Lennon Killer's Wild Dreams About Yoko," *New York Post,* September 27, 2000.

399   "Do you want anything else?": "A Look Back at Mark David Chapman in His Own Words," *Larry King Live,* CNN.com, September 30, 2000.

CHAPTER 61

400   "*Double Fantasy* has just gone gold!": Keith Badman, *The Beatles Diary Volume 2: After the Break-Up, 1970–2001* (London: Omnibus Press, 2001), 272.

401   "John, are you all right?" *CNN Special Report: Killing John Lennon,* CNN.com, December 8, 2015.

401   "I think you just cut your first number one!" "Walking on Thin Ice by Yoko Ono," Songfacts.com.

401   "Should we stop at Wolf's for a hamburger?": Billy Heller and Michael Kane, "We Were There on the Awful Night John Lennon Was Shot," *New York Post,* December 4, 2005.

401   "I want to go home and kiss Sean good night": Badman, *The Beatles Diary,* 272.

402   security guard's name is Jose Perdomo: Jack Jones, *Let Me Take You Down: Inside the Mind of Mark David Chapman, the Man Who Killed John Lennon* (New York: Villard Books, 1992), 46.

402   Jose, a Cuban refugee: Amy Andrews, "CIA Link to John Lennon Death Possible Says New Documentary," IrishCentral.com, December 4, 2010.

403   Dakota residents like Lauren Bacall and Leonard Bernstein: Michael W. Freeman, "Book Relates Interesting History of the Dakota in N.Y.," *The Ledger* (Florida), January 3, 2008.

404   The *Wizard of Oz* photograph he left behind on the hotel-room dresser: James R. Gaines, "Mark Chapman: The Man Who Shot John Lennon," *People,* February 23, 1987.

404   in a combat stance: Patrick Doyle, Robert Lane, and Hugh Bracken, "Legendary Beatles Singer Shot Dead by Mark David Chapman," *Daily News* (New York), December 9, 1980.

404   At close range, Mark fires: Doyle, Lane, and Bracken, "Legendary Beatles Singer Shot Dead by Mark David Chapman."

404   "Help him, help him": Doyle, Lane, and Bracken, "Legendary Beatles Singer Shot Dead by Mark David Chapman."

405   "He's been shot, he's been shot": Keith Badman, *The Beatles Diary Volume 2: After the Break-Up, 1970–2001* (London: Omnibus Press, 2001), 272.

405   grabs his arm—the one holding the gun: Gaines, "Mark Chapman."

405   kicks it away: Gaines, "Mark Chapman."

405   get outta here: Gaines, "Mark Chapman."

406   pulls out his paperback copy of *The Catcher in the Rye*: Dave

Rosenthal, "Mark David Chapman—Lennon's Killer and 'Catcher in the Rye,' Up for Parole," *Baltimore Sun*, July 28, 2010.

CHAPTER 62

407   "Shots fired, 1 West 72nd Street": Billy Heller and Michael Kane, "We Were There on the Awful Night John Lennon Was Shot," *New York Post*, December 4, 2005.

407   "I heard the gunshots, the first I'd ever heard": "Where We Were When John Lennon Was Killed," *New York Times*, December 8, 2010.

408   James Taylor hears gunfire: James Lachno, "James Taylor: Five Things You Never Knew," *The Telegraph*, June 8, 2011.

408   "He shot John Lennon!": Heller and Kane, "We Were There on the Awful Night John Lennon Was Shot."

408   "Don't hurt me": Jack Jones, *Let Me Take You Down: Inside the Mind of Mark David Chapman, the Man Who Killed John Lennon* (New York: Villard Books, 1992), 47.

409   Porter Jay Hastings is ready to apply a tourniquet to John's wounds: Philip Norman, *John Lennon: The Life* (New York: Ecco, 2008), 806.

409   "It's okay, John, you'll be all right": Keith Badman, *The Beatles Diary Volume 2: After the Break-Up, 1970–2001* (London: Omnibus Press, 2001), 272.

409   "Cuff him, Steve": Badman, *The Beatles Diary*, 272.

409   "I acted alone": Jones, *Let Me Take You Down*, 47.

409   he's met the wounded man once before: Larry McShane, "The Day 'Love' Died: December 8th Marks 35th Grim Anniversary of John Lennon's Murder," *Daily News* (New York), December 5, 2015.

409   "Like weightlifters": McShane, "The Day 'Love' Died."

———

410   The police officers' names are Spiro and Cullen: Associated Press, "Lennon's Death Lingers for Those Who Were There," Today.com, December 5, 2005.

410   "Nobody's gonna hurt you": Keith Badman, *The Beatles Diary Volume 2: After the Break-Up, 1970–2001* (London: Omnibus Press, 2001), 272.

410   Cullen reaches down and grabs *The Catcher in the Rye* from the pavement: Associated Press, "Lennon's Death Lingers for Those Who Were There."

411   She stares at him through the glass: Jack Jones, *Let Me Take You Down: Inside the Mind of Mark David Chapman, the Man Who Killed John Lennon* (New York: Villard Books, 1992), 48.

CHAPTER 63

412   across the back seat: Vicki Sheff, "The Day the Music Died," *People,* December 10, 1990.

412   "Are you John Lennon?": Jimmy Breslin, "The Day John Lennon Died: Jimmy Breslin Writes Iconic Tale of NYPD Cops Who Drove the Dying Beatles Star to the Hospital," *Daily News* (New York), originally published December 9, 1980.

413   "expecting to see an ambulance pulling in": Dr. David Halleran, interview by the authors, 2019.

413   room 115: Alex Dunbar, "Doctor's Story of Night He Tried to Save John Lennon Inspires Movie," CNYCentral.com, November 19, 2015.

413   "Then we cut the clothes off and opened his chest": Dunbar, "Doctor's Story of Night He Tried to Save John Lennon Inspires Movie."

413 "Four entry wounds over his left chest, three exit wounds": Dunbar, "Doctor's Story of Night He Tried to Save John Lennon Inspires Movie."

413 "The patient didn't come in dead; he came in mortally wounded": Dr. David Halleran, interview by the authors, 2019.

414 "It can't be": Dunbar, "Doctor's Story of Night He Tried to Save John Lennon Inspires Movie."

CHAPTER 64

415 TV producer Alan Weiss: Billy Heller and Michael Kane, "We Were There on the Awful Night John Lennon Was Shot," *New York Post,* December 4, 2005.

415 "My ears are still ringing from the impact": "Enterprise Journalism Release—December 2, 2010," ESPN Press Room, December 2, 2010.

415 "At first, I didn't believe it": Alan Weiss, interview by the authors, 2019.

415 *my favorite Beatle:* "The Murder of John Lennon," *Crimes of the Century,* CNN.com, January 25, 2014.

416 "Here's my press card": Heller and Kane, "We Were There on the Awful Night John Lennon Was Shot," *New York Post,* December 4, 2005.

416 "Yoko Ono in a full-length fur coat on the arm of a police officer": Associated Press, "Lennon's Death Lingers for Those Who Were There," Today.com, December 5, 2005.

417 "Neil, I think John Lennon's been shot": Heller and Kane, "We Were There on the Awful Night John Lennon Was Shot."

417 "All My Loving" plays over the hospital sound system: Daniel Bates, "John Lennon's Killer Mark Chapman Told Cops: 'Sorry for Inconveniencing You' When They Arrived at the Scene," *Daily Mail,* December 6, 2015.

417 "totally ineffective": Heller and Kane, "We Were There on the Awful Night John Lennon Was Shot."

417 "I couldn't shake the feeling that we had failed this great man": Dr. David Halleran, interview by the authors, 2019.

417 "all of the major blood vessels leaving the heart were simply destroyed": Heller and Kane, "We Were There on the Awful Night John Lennon Was Shot."

418 "He can't be dead, he was just alive": Heller and Kane, "We Were There on the Awful Night John Lennon Was Shot."

418 "how much John Lennon affected the rest of the world": Tracy Connor, "How They Got Involved on a Fateful Night," *New York Post,* December 3, 2000.

CHAPTER 65

419 "John Lennon has been shot in front of his apartment building": "Enterprise Journalism Release—December 2, 2010," ESPN Press Room, December 2, 2010.

420 "makes rock concerts look like tea parties": Amy Davidson Sorkin, "John Lennon: 'It Makes Rock Concerts Look Like Tea Parties,'" *The New Yorker,* December 8. 2010.

420 "Remember this is just a football game, no matter who wins or loses": Sorkin, "John Lennon."

420 "There was a lot of crime in that area back in those days, and gunfire wasn't uncommon": Geraldo Rivera, interview by the authors, 2019.

421 "The most tragic aspect of this terrible thing is the ironic thing": Ray Rossi, "Watch: Do You Remember Where You Were When John Lennon Died?," New Jersey 101.5, December 8, 2014.

421 "Attempting to put John's life into context in real time was very challenging and extremely emotional": Geraldo Rivera, interview by the authors, 2019.

422   Phillip Michael, a maintenance man: Daniel B. Schneider, "F.Y.I.," *New York Times*, August 13, 2000.

423   "It's the most valuable artifact in rock and roll history": Megan Cerullo, "'Double Fantasy' Album Signed by John Lennon for Mark Chapman Up for Sale for $1.5M," *Daily News* (New York), July 16, 2017.

423   "I was just with him": Ken Sharp, *Starting Over: The Making of John Lennon and Yoko Ono's Double Fantasy* (New York: Gallery, 2010), quoted in interview with Amanda Flinner, "80s Video Director Jay Dubin," Songfacts.com, December 17, 2014.

423   wipes clean the session tapes dated December 8: Keith Badman, *The Beatles Diary Volume 2: After the Break-Up, 1970–2001* (London: Omnibus Press, 2001), 273.

423   "The shock is too great!": Albert Goldman, "John and Yoko's Troubled Road Part II," *People*, August 22, 1988.

CHAPTER 66

425   banging her head: Daniel Bates, "John Lennon's Killer Mark Chapman Told Cops: 'Sorry for Inconveniencing You' When They Arrived at the Scene," *Daily Mail*, December 6, 2015.

425   "Do you realize what you just did?": Bates, "John Lennon's Killer Mark Chapman."

426   "Chapman shot John Lennon because he wanted his moment of glory in the sun": "The Murder of John Lennon," *Crimes of the Century*, CNN.com, January 25, 2014.

426   "another Jack Ruby": Paula Schwed, "Lennon Slain in New York," UPI.com, December 9, 1980.

426   "premeditated execution": Schwed, "Lennon Slain in New York."

426   "We felt he was criminally responsible": "The Murder of John Lennon."

426   "borrowed a substantial sum of money—of which $2,000 was found on him": Schwed, "Lennon Slain in New York."

427   "finish the job Chapman started. I'm going to get Yoko Ono": Keith Badman, *The Beatles Diary Volume 2: After the Break-Up, 1970–2001* (London: Omnibus Press, 2001), 274.

CHAPTER 67

428   "That was like a really big shock in most people's lives, a bit like Kennedy": Michael Rothman, "Paul McCartney Remembers How He Found Out John Lennon Had Died," ABC News, December 8, 2014.

429   "shattered and stunned": Lily Rothman, "How the World Reacted to John Lennon's Death 35 Years Ago," *Time,* December 8, 2015.

429   "to rob life is the ultimate robbery": Tim Riley, *Lennon: The Man, the Myth, the Music—The Definitive Life* (New York: Hyperion, 2011), 677.

429   "Something's happened to John": Tom Skinner, "Ringo Starr on Finding Out About John Lennon's Death: 'I Didn't Know What to Do,'" *NME,* October 30, 2019.

429   "Cyn, I'm so sorry, John's dead": Cynthia Lennon, *John: A Biography*, (New York: Three Rivers Press, 2005), 7.

429   Keep the news from Julian: Lennon, *John*, 8.

429   Spitting image of his father: Lennon, *John*, 268.

430   "Don't run from them, it will just make it more difficult": Riley, *Lennon,* 676.

430   "I want to do what I can to help": Riley, *Lennon,* 676.

430   "play with Sean": Skinner, "Ringo Starr on Finding Out About John Lennon's Death."

431   *Someone's dead*: Elton John, *Me* (New York: Henry Holt, 2019), 175.

431   "I couldn't believe it": John, *Me,* 175.

431   hundreds of mourners: Lennon, *John,* 269.

432   reads his copy of *The Catcher in the Rye*: Katharine Shaffer, Stuart Marques, and Don Singleton, "Mark David Chapman Is Sentenced to 20 Years to Life in Prison in 1981 for Killing John Lennon," *New York Daily News,* August 23, 2015.

432   still smells pleasantly of gunpowder: James R. Gaines, "Mark David Chapman Part III: The Killer Takes His Fall," *People,* March 9, 1987.

432   a bulletproof vest: James R. Gaines, "Mark Chapman: The Man Who Shot John Lennon," *People,* February 23, 1987.

433   a "loner" who "had a screw loose": Rick Hampson, "John Lennon Shot 35 Years Ago: Suspect Described as 'Screwball' with No Motive," Associated Press, December 8, 2015.

433   They put a jacket over his head and lead him outside: Hampson, "John Lennon Shot 35 Years Ago."

433   Everyone on the planet now knows who he is: *CNN Special Report: Killing John Lennon,* CNN.com, December 8, 2015.

433   soundproof pen: Gaines, "Mark David Chapman Part III."

433   His name is Herbert Adlerberg: Gaines, "Mark David Chapman Part III."

434   Assistant district attorney Kim Hogrefe: *CNN Special Report: Killing John Lennon.*

434   "He committed a deliberate, premeditated execution of John Lennon": E. R. Shipp, "Chapman, in a Closed Courtroom, Pleads Guilty to Killing of Lennon," *New York Times,* June 23, 1981.

434   Judge Martin Rettinger: Mike Sager and Joyce Wadler, "A Confused Person," *Washington Post,* December 11, 1980.

434 Mark is sent to Bellevue Hospital for psychological examination: Associated Press, "Lennon's Death," CBS News, December 11, 1980.

434 Dr. Naomi Goldstein: Gaines, "Mark David Chapman Part III."

435 Adlerberg has received many death threats: Art Harris, "Memories of Chapman," *Washington Post,* December 12, 1980.

435 Jonathan Marks: Gaines, "Mark Chapman."

435 lusts for the limelight: Gaines, "Mark Chapman."

435 The prison is worried about snipers: Gaines, "Mark Chapman."

CHAPTER 68

436 MacDougall has taken charge of John's remains: Albert Goldman, "John and Yoko's Troubled Road Part II," *People,* August 22, 1988.

436 "the greatest rock musician in the world": Goldman, "John and Yoko's Troubled Road Part II."

437 "Why's Julian here? Where's Dad?": Cynthia Lennon, *John: A Biography,* (New York: Three Rivers Press, 2005), 270.

437 "Your dad's dead": David Fricke, "Sean Lennon on His Father, Yoko Ono, and His Own Musical Career," *Rolling Stone,* June 11, 1998."

437 "There is no funeral for John": "Remember Love," University Staff Shared Governance, University of Wisconsin at Madison, ous.wisc.edu, December 8, 2017.

437 scatters his ashes in a spot in Central Park: Goldman, "John and Yoko's Troubled Road Part II."

437 "Maybe he is watching me from above": Lynn Van Matre, "Don't Ask Julian About Dad: It's All on the Video," *Chicago Tribune,* December 8, 1985.

438   one hundred thousand people stand with their heads bowed: Joyce Wadler, "A Farewell," *Washington Post,* December 15, 1980.

438   The hand-lettered sign pleads, WHY?: Jeff Giles, "The Day Thousands Honored John Lennon with a Silent Vigil," UltimateClassicRock.com, December 14, 2015.

438   "I guess when you die you become much more bigger because you're part of everything": Keith Badman, *The Beatles Diary Volume 2: After the Break-Up, 1970–2001* (London: Omnibus Press, 2001), 274.

        —

439   He has never slept better in his entire life: James R. Gaines, "Mark David Chapman Part III: The Killer Takes His Fall," *People,* March 9, 1987.

440   "If he was obsessed with anything, it was bringing attention to himself": "The Murder of John Lennon," *Crimes of the Century,* CNN.com, January 25, 2014.

440   an epiphany one night while sitting in a lounge at Rikers Island: Gaines, "Mark David Chapman Part III."

440   "And then it hit me, like a joyful thing, that I was called out for a special purpose": Gaines, "Mark David Chapman Part III."

440   "stimulate the reading of J. D. Salinger's *The Catcher in the Rye*": Paul L. Montgomery, "Lennon Murder Suspect Preparing Insanity Defense," *New York Times,* February 9, 1981.

441   He shares his promotional plans with Bantam, the publisher of the paperback edition: Gaines, "Mark David Chapman Part III."

441   "Everyone will read *The Catcher in the Rye*": Gaines, "Mark David Chapman Part III."

441   tears up his copy of *The Catcher in the Rye*: Gaines, "Mark David Chapman Part III."

442   he's possessed by a demon: Gaines, "Mark David Chapman Part III."

442   "picturing all these little kids playing some game in this big field of rye and all": Katharine Shaffer, Stuart Marques, and Don Singleton, "Mark David Chapman Is Sentenced to 20 Years to Life in Prison in 1981 for Killing John Lennon," *New York Daily News,* August 23, 2015.

443   speak out about phoniness and corruption: Gaines, "Mark David Chapman Part III."

443   lack his superior intelligence: Gaines, "Mark David Chapman Part III."

443   a minimum of twenty years: Shaffer, Marques, and Singleton, "Mark David Chapman Is Sentenced to 20 Years to Life in Prison for Killing John Lennon."